Whether one agrees or not with the l , it
will provide an intellectual challenge to
planning, development and globalizat io
questions the prevailing wisdom in ci is
privileging of class analysis provides t if
themes covered in the sixteen chapters. l :
thinking and alternatives for social tra ... comes at a
perfect time to contribute to the debates.

Lourdes Beneria, Cornell University and author of *Gender, Development, and*
Globalization: Economics as if All People Mattered

Pathbreaking in its originality and breathtaking in its coverage, the truly outstanding volume David Ruccio has delivered is indispensable in critiquing a variety of prevailing developmental paradigms. Rather than simplistically noting the "failures" of capitalism, this book reveals how neoliberal development policies can be considered successful in terms of promoting the emergence and strengthening of capitalist class processes and the appropriation of surplus-value in Latin America and beyond. It is obligatory reading for scholars and students seeking to construct Marxian class analyses and to formulate alternatives to the world economy today.

Adam David Morton, University of Nottingham and author of *Unravelling*
Gramsci: Hegemony and Passive Revolution in the Global Political Economy

Development and Globalization is antiessentialist social theory at its very best. Whether re-reading socialist planning debates, economic and social development struggles in the global South, or capitalist and alter-capitalist theories of globalization, David Ruccio engages the contemporary conjuncture in fresh and exciting ways, demonstrating throughout the successes of the rethinking Marxism project and the immense potential and range of contemporary Marxian analysis. What Maurice Dobb did for twentieth-century critiques of socialist planning, capitalist development, and imperialist expansion, Ruccio redoubles for a new age of post-Communist and globalized political economy.

John Pickles, Earl N. Phillips Distinguished Professor of International Studies
and Chair of the Department of Geography, University of North Carolina at
Chapel Hill, and author of *A History of Spaces: Cartographic Reason, Mapping,*
and the Geo-Coded World

David Ruccio is a central figure in the exciting and innovative "postmodern" school of Marxian thought. Through his own writing and his stewardship of the journal Rethinking Marxism he has contributed immensely to this tradition. In this collection, Ruccio draws together, sharpens, and extends central insights from that school of thought and applies them to debates over socialist planning, economic development, and globalization. The essays demonstrate the depth of Ruccio's intellect and the range of his expertise, to be sure, while also conveying the power of the postmodern Marxian tradition in helping us to overcome the malaise that now affects much contemporary left scholarship about prospects for radical reform in the Global South. In Ruccio's hands, Marxism emerges as a vibrant tradition that continues to generate new avenues of scholarship and practical politics in pursuit of a more just world.

George DeMartino, Josef Korbel School of International Studies, University of
Denver and author of *Global Economy, Global Justice: Theoretical and Policy*
Alternatives to Neoliberalism

Development and Globalization

Since the mid-1980s, David F. Ruccio has been developing a new framework of Marxian class analysis and applying it to various issues in socialist planning, Third World development, and capitalist globalization. The aim of this collection is to show, through a series of concrete examples, how Marxian class analysis can be used to challenge existing modes of thought and to produce new insights about the problems of capitalist development and the possibilities of imagining and creating noncapitalist economies.

The book consists of fifteen essays, plus an introductory chapter situating the author's work in a larger intellectual and political context, and a foreword by Stephen Resnick and Richard Wolff. The topics covered range from planning theory to the role of the state in the Nicaraguan Revolution, from radical theories of underdevelopment to the Third World debt crisis, and from a critical engagement with regulation theory to contemporary discussions of globalization and imperialism.

Ruccio demonstrates that, in the current crises of capitalism, a rethinking of Marxian theory serves both to challenge the existing terms of economic debate and to contribute to the project of fostering noncapitalist alternatives. As such, it makes an invaluable contribution to the literature in this field and will prove useful to both researchers and professionals alike.

David F. Ruccio is Professor of Economics at the University of Notre Dame, USA.

Economics as Social Theory
Series edited by Tony Lawson
University of Cambridge

Social Theory is experiencing something of a revival within economics. Critical analyses of the particular nature of the subject matter of social studies and of the types of method, categories, and modes of explanation that can legitimately be endorsed for the scientific study of social objects, are re-emerging. Economists are again addressing such issues as the relationship between agency and structure, between economy and the rest of society, and between the enquirer and the object of enquiry. There is a renewed interest in elaborating basic categories, such as causation, competition, culture, discrimination, evolution, money, need, order, organization, power, probability, process, rationality, technology, time, truth, uncertainty, value, etc.

The objective of this series is to further facilitate this revival. In contemporary economics, the label "theory" has been appropriated by a group that confines itself to largely asocial, ahistorical, mathematical "modelling." Economics as Social Theory thus reclaims the "Theory" label, offering a platform for alternative rigorous, but broader and more critical, conceptions of theorizing.

Other titles in this series include:

1. Economics and Language
Edited by Willie Henderson

2. Rationality, Institutions and Economic Methodology
Edited by Uskali Mäki, Bo Gustafsson, and Christian Knudsen

3. New Directions in Economic Methodology
Edited by Roger Backhouse

4. Who Pays for the Kids?
Nancy Folbre

5. Rules and Choice in Economics
Viktor Vanberg

6. Beyond Rhetoric and Realism in Economics
Thomas A. Boylan and Paschal F. O'Gorman

7. Feminism, Objectivity and Economics
Julie A. Nelson

8. Economic Evolution
Jack J. Vromen

Development and Globalization

A Marxian class analysis

David F. Ruccio

Routledge
Taylor & Francis Group

LONDON AND NEW YORK

First published 2011
by Routledge
2 Park Square, Milton Park, Abingdon, Oxon OX14 4RN

Simultaneously published in the USA and Canada
by Routledge
270 Madison Ave, New York, NY 10016

Routledge is an imprint of the Taylor & Francis Group, an informa business

© 2011 David F. Ruccio

Typeset in Palatino by
Book Now Ltd, London
Printed and bound in Great Britain by
CPI Antony Rowe Ltd, Chippenham, Wiltshire

British Library Cataloguing in Publication Data
A catalogue record for this book is available from the British Library

Library of Congress Cataloging in Publication Data
Ruccio, David F.
Development and globalization : a Marxian class analysis / by David F. Ruccio.
    p. cm.
1. Marxian economics. 2. Social conflict. 3. Capitalism. 4. Economic development.
5. Globalization—Economic aspects. I. Title.

HB97.5.R75 2010
335.4'12—dc22

ISBN13: 978–0–415–77225–9 (hbk)
ISBN13: 978–0–415–77226–6 (pbk)
ISBN13: 978–0–203–84318–5 (ebk)

In memory of
Chuck Craypo
&
Julie Graham

Contents

Illustrations

Tables

Figure

Foreword

Stephen Resnick and Richard Wolff

One of the singular rewards of teaching occurs when students develop to become their teachers' teachers and colleagues. In this book of important essays, David Ruccio documents just such an evolution in our relationship to him. Writing this foreword provides us with an opportunity to welcome his analytical achievements and simultaneously to celebrate their contributions to broadening and deepening a new kind of Marxian social theory.

He uses (and very helpfully cites) a large body of recent work in rethinking basic Marxian economic theory (to which he also has contributed) in order to develop it in new and original ways. He applies this particular rethinking of Marxism to a host of urgent issues in the world today: economic planning, economic development, and globalization. The originality of the essays gathered here has already taught us much and will continue to reward re-readers as well as those encountering these critical studies in political economy for the first time. The book's importance flows partly from its timeliness. As he writes in the first essay, the capitalist crisis now torturing the world has, "now as at earlier stages in its development . . . called forth its Marxian other." Yet, that chapter also wisely warns that Marxism's critique of capitalism applies not only in and to its crises, but also between them.

Ruccio interweaves his economic analyses, grounded in a sophisticated, reworked Marxist theoretical framework, with his critical responses to alternative understandings grounded in other theories (both inside and outside the Marxian tradition). That framework goes by several names: nondeterminist social theory, aleatory materialism, and postmodern Marxism are prominent among them. They reflect the multiple currents of thought contributing to that framework (yet another of Ruccio's contributions was his coediting of an important book of essays that examined key contributors to this framework: Ruccio and Callari [1996]). Having understood the profound transformations – both theoretical and political – inside Marxism over the last half century, Ruccio shows their results' stunning productivity when applied to today's debates and struggles. This book exemplifies a new kind of Marxist social analysis and the remarkably rich insights it yields.

The essays in this book focus systematically and cumulatively on that particular Marxian concept of class that defines it in terms of the production, appropriation, and distribution of surpluses. Ruccio thus immediately differentiates his approach (and conclusions) from those that deploy different concepts of class (e.g., as sub-groupings of people according to the property they do or do not own, power they do or do not wield, consciousness they do or do not hold, etc.) Thus, state economic planning is interrogated in a new way: in terms of how it affects the multiple, different arrangements (what Ruccio's approach designates as *class structures*) of producing, appropriating, and distributing surpluses that coexist inside all societies. True to his nondeterminist, non-unilinear framework, he likewise investigates how a society's class structures influence the existence and qualities of state economic planning. Ruccio's essays explode the limits of the old, yet endlessly repeated, debates about planning versus markets – as if this simplistic either/or exhausted all that was interesting about the topic. He shows that planning, like markets, can and does affect the different class structures in any society in multiple, different ways depending on the entire social context. If planning ignores its class (conceived as surplus labor) context and effects, focusing instead on, say, output maximization, its unrecognized effects on class may result in a higher rate of class exploitation. In other words, one theory's measure of success – higher output – is another's measure of failure – higher exploitation. Consequently, many socialist commitments to and practices of planning are recast in an altogether new, critical light by Ruccio's analyses. The policy implications of this work are nothing short of momentous.

When Ruccio trains his class-focused lens on the issues of economic development, his work again breaks the hidebound boundaries of other studies, which fix on the dichotomies and repeated actual oscillations between two alternative "development models." On one hand are the laissez-faire, neoliberal models, while on the other are the state-interventionist models of economic development. The advocates of the first model credit it with achieving "successful economic growth" and the other side's model with relatively less success or failure to do so. The advocates of the second model run the identical argument, but with the credits reversed. In his justly famous article for *World Development*, Ruccio raised the question of class and thus focused on how each model affected the reproduction and growth of capitalist class structures (in their relation to employing and exploiting labor and in their relation to the other, noncapitalist class structures in the society). In class terms, he showed that the very meanings of "success" and "failure" change as, likewise, do our assessments of, and policies for, economic development. His argument rejects any notion of an intrinsic, unambiguous standard of success (or failure) to which we all must adhere and with which we should all, alike, work. Rather, different theories provide their different explanations of and criteria for what constitutes successful development.

Exposing the blindness of alternative theories to these class dimensions of economic development enhances Ruccio's demonstration of how both development models (and the oscillations between them) have served capitalism's modern growth. Along the way, he was able to newly appreciate the pioneering work of Harold Wolpe, as well as underscore the unique and original contributions to economic development literature and practice/policy enabled by deploying a well-defined Marxian class analysis carefully and systematically.

When Ruccio's class analysis interrogates the major globalization debates over the past several decades – from the French regulation school to Harvey, Hardt, and Negri – his essays once again expose the limits of those debates and their resulting blindnesses. Yet these essays of the book's third section go further. The class analysis broadens to include attention to the rich diversity of subject positions, or subjectivities, that class analysis implies. Through his productive collaboration with Serap Kayatekin, the range of subjectivities is examined in relation to the political possibilities of alliances and coalitions that might include anticapitalist agendas.

In writing this foreword, we were reminded of a question often asked of us: "What difference does a class-based, antiessentialist approach make?" Ruccio's book offers an answer. He repeatedly shows readers the heavy social costs incurred by ignoring the connection of the inner workings of the economy to the level and rate of class exploitation. Consider the widespread disappointment, frustration, and even anger at the failures of economic development across so many countries, at planning carried out in so-called socialist countries and at the impact of globalization on national employment and growth. Ruccio's essays show how and why remaining blind to how class contributes to these failures, and needlessly restricts analyses, options, and freedom to choose corrective actions. If this were all that the book argued, it would be well worth reading: but there is more.

The causal link between class and other social processes – the various nonclass topics examined in the book include planned versus free markets, state revenues and expenditures, agricultural productivity, and complex and differing subjectivities – is drawn in a nondeterminist way. The argument is relentless in showing how class processes are both causes and effects of nonclass processes. To our way of thinking, this mutual interaction between the two is a proper and fitting extension of (and tribute to) the overdeterminist logic introduced by Althusser and applied here by Ruccio to economics. We are proud and enthusiastic to welcome the publication of this book.

Introduction

1 Rethinking planning, development, and globalization from a Marxian perspective

When it was first suggested to me that I edit a book of my own essays on planning, development, and international political economy, I was not all that enthusiastic. These were essays that I had written over the course of 20 years or so, since finishing my doctoral dissertation in 1984. I hadn't really gone back to look at them since they were written, and I wasn't convinced anyone else would want to either.

I will admit, I did like the idea of gathering in one place pieces that had been written for different occasions and published (most of them) in widely dispersed journals and books. I also thought of friends and colleagues, who knew about my work in one area – for example, on Marxian theory or postmodernism and economics – but not necessarily on these topics. As for me, I had always thought of my writings in these different areas as being inextricably related, each one drawing from and informing the others.

Most importantly, it was the new conjuncture that convinced me to take the time to assemble the essays in this book and to compose this introduction. The current crises of capitalism have certainly stimulated interest in Marxism and Marxian analyses of economic and social reality,[1] though perhaps not in the bastions of mainstream economics where, while the potential for a "crisis in economic thought" has certainly been noted, the discussion of theory and policy continues to take place within very narrow parameters. As the world now knows, neoclassical economists were, for the most part, caught unawares when the crises broke out (they certainly didn't predict them nor did they consider them a likely occurrence). And they didn't have much to offer after the crises did erupt and then expanded into other sectors and regions, threatening to bring down not only the US economy but also the world economic order. The idea that capitalism itself was once again beset by crises and needed to be criticized and replaced has been far from their view – far from their initial hand-wringing about the realism of existing macroeconomic models and, later, their confident pronouncements that, perhaps with a bit of tinkering (such as government bailouts of financial institutions that were "too big to fail" and a moderate program of deficit spending or, for the more conservative, tax cuts), markets would right themselves and capitalist growth would soon resume.

But elsewhere, in other disciplines and outside the academy, there is a much more palpable sense both that the latest crises are endemic to capitalism and that mainstream economic thought (as taught in the academy and as practiced in think tanks and policymaking circles) needs to be radically questioned. Not surprisingly, Marxian theory – the concepts and analyses originally presented in *Capital* as well as the ideas elaborated by contemporary Marxian economists and other social theorists – has received renewed attention.[2] A wide variety of mainstream periodicals, from the *Economist* to the *New York Times*, have used front-cover and front-page stories to highlight the radical questioning of capitalism, the fundamental problems with orthodox economics, and the resurgence of interest in Marxism. Marxist thinkers, especially those who have demonstrated the interest and ability to move beyond the classroom and the usual academic publications, such as Richard Wolff and David Harvey, have found themselves welcomed in new quarters and with unfamiliar enthusiasm.[3] Students, in my experience and in that of many of my academic colleagues, have expressed a new inquisitiveness about, and openness toward, both dimensions of the Marxian critique of political economy: the critique of mainstream economic thought and the critique of capitalism. And workshops and conferences devoted to Marxian theory and ideas related to Marxism (from capitalist crises to the ideas of the commune and communism) have generated unprecedented levels of participation in the United States and around the world. Clearly, now as at earlier stages in its development, capitalism has called forth its Marxian other.

The new appreciation of the relevance of Marxian theory means a shift in focus from the analysis and critique of one form of capitalism – often referred to as free-market capitalism or neoliberalism – to any and all forms of capitalism. In other words, it represents a recognition that, historically and today, in the United States and around the world, there are many different kinds of capitalism. Some are more private, and based on private property and free markets; others are more oriented around the state, involving extensive government regulation and public property. Once this capitalist diversity is recognized, the problem is no longer one of the presence or absence of regulation – in the sense that the crises engendered by neoliberal free markets can be solved or fixed by bringing the state back in and by creating new forms of government regulation of financial and other markets – but concerns capitalism itself, with capitalist ways of organizing the economy, politics, and culture. That's a major change in both analytical focus and political orientation.

Still, as I see it, this resurgence of interest in Marxism, while quite welcome, also presents a number of potential problems. Let me briefly mention three. First, Marx and latter-day Marxists are often credited, in stark contrast to their mainstream counterparts, with understanding the real possibility of capitalist crises – that the kinds of economic crises that exist now are not the product simply of mistakes and oversights (although, of course, there have been plenty) or exogenous events (usually, in the mainstream view, associated with unwarranted government intervention) but are systemic, part of the "normal" workings of capitalism. The danger, however, is forgetting about the other side of the Marxian critique of political economy, the critique of capitalism when it is working well. That is, the current crises have created new audiences for Marxian perspectives but Marxism involves both an analysis of how capitalism regularly enters into crisis and how, outside of periods of crisis, when financial institutions are solvent, employment is growing, and so on, capitalist development is both the condition and consequence of exploitation. Or, as I once explained to a gathering of students in the course of discussing the relevance of *Capital* to current economic events: "Marx's view was that capitalism is a problem, both when it is working well and when it is not." Only time will tell if that particular dimension of the Marxist critique of political economy will transcend the current crises.

The second dilemma to which I want to draw attention is that the current "return to Marx" often involves a return to some of the most traditional, deterministic forms of Marxian theory. Much rethinking of Marxism has taken place since the 1960s – when, as now, many students, activists, and scholars rediscovered Marx – but it is sometimes difficult to detect the antideterministic moments of that rethinking in the appeals to Marxian "crisis theory" and much else in the current conjuncture. What I am referring to as traditional (or modernist) Marxian theory is based on the idea that capitalism has a "logic" (often identified as a set of "laws of motion" or a "drive," e.g., to accumulate capital) that inevitably propels it toward crisis.[4] According to the alternative (postmodern) version of Marxian theory (about which much more below), capitalism has a conjunctural history but no necessary trajectory. Therefore, whether or not crises occur depends on a whole host of nondeterministic factors; there's no inevitability or inexorable working-out of a logic.[5] So, while the current crises create the conditions for a new generation to discover Marx, there is also a risk of falling back on the more scientistic, essentialist, and deterministic versions of Marxian theory and of losing sight of the rethinking of Marxism that has revitalized Marxian thought in recent decades.

The third issue I want to mention pertains to the application of Marxian theory. The campaign to bury Marx, especially in the discipline of economics, means that there is little familiarity with the concepts and methods of actually carrying out a Marxian critique of political economy. What does Marxian theory have to contribute to ongoing debates – in economics, development, and other areas and disciplines? What does it mean to conduct a Marxian analysis of economic and social reality? While Marx's texts and latter-day interpretations of some of the basic concepts of Marxian theory are now widely available – through books, journals, and the Internet – it is not at all easy for students and others to figure out what a Marxian analysis actually looks like.

I would never demean the work of Marxian scholars in elaborating and debating contrasting interpretations of the categories and methodologies appropriate to Marxian theory (indeed, I have participated in some of these debates). However, it is still the case that concrete analyses of the current conjuncture – of the current crises of capitalism, the new left-wing governments in Latin America, the problem of global warming, the conflicts in Africa, and so on – are neither well known nor readily available.

That, in the end, is what convinced me to assemble and publish the essays in this volume. They provide a series of concrete examples of how Marxian theory can be used to intervene in existing debates – concerning planning, development, and globalization – and how Marxian theory can be extended to a wide variety of other issues and topics, in economics and beyond. They represent, therefore, not a complete inventory but a starting point, some specific examples of how Marxian class analysis and the critique of essentialism can be used both to interpret and to change the world.

Asking questions

I want to use the rest of this introduction to look back over the essays collected here and provide an overview of what it means to introduce Marxian class analysis into these debates. My aim is to provide readers with some context – autobiographical as well as political and intellectual – and to discuss both what I consider to be the relevance of each essay and the kind of work that remains to be done.[6]

In each case – for each article, chapter, or presentation (many of which, to my surprise, even got published) – I found myself asking two key sets of questions:

1   What was the debate? What were the key terms of debate? What was the existing common sense? What were the dominant perspectives, both mainstream and radical?
2   What new and different elements could Marxism – Marxian class analysis – add to the discussion? In what ways did it depart from the mainstream and radical common senses, and what new light could it shed on the issue at hand?

In all these cases, my orientation was less about giving advice "there" and more about shifting the terms of discourse "here." I have never been involved in economic policymaking, and I never considered offering advice to government or nongovernmental movements, especially in Latin America where I have spent considerable time and have conducted a great deal of field research. I have been involved in many political activities and movements over the years, but I've always understood the work embodied in these essays as operating at the level of ideas. I set out to intervene in a set of intellectual debates – to identify and disrupt the existing terms of debate, from a Marxian perspective – and not to offer conventionally conceived policy advice.

However, as a Marxist, I also understand the materiality of ideas. Thoughts form an integral part of social life; they are both conditions and consequences of what happens in the rest of society. Louis Althusser once referred to philosophy as "class struggle in theory" (1971, 18). The same is true of any contest of ideas, perhaps especially in economics, where different economic discourses – inside and outside the academy – both shape and are shaped by the development of capitalism. So, yes, I admit that, directly and indirectly, intervening in intellectual debates cannot but have policy implications, in relation to the changing contours of the class struggle. Thus, Marxian ideas do lend themselves to policies, not just to find equilibrium exchange-rates or the appropriate level of wages, but to radically transform the way society is organized around and through existing forms of class exploitation.

The debates about planning, development, and globalization are what interest me in the ideas contained in this book. And, of course, during the 25 years or so over which these essays were originally composed, the debates and the terms of debate have certainly changed. Just to give three examples: when I entered graduate school, planning was a central topic; it was discussed and debated by mainstream and Marxian economists alike. Then, after the demise of the neoclassical synthesis (and the rise of new forms of neoclassical theory, such as rational expectations, and the resurgence of previous forms, such as Austrian economics) and the Fall of the Wall (at least in the Soviet Union and Eastern Europe), planning quickly faded from view. By the same token, development was one of the most vibrant areas of economic analysis; the place where the limits of mainstream economics were readily acknowledged and discussions were necessarily interdisciplinary. Now, development economics has mostly been folded back into the discipline, with the resurgence of stages of growth and incentive-based microeconomic experiments. Finally, globalization didn't even exist when I was starting out – or, more accurately, the idea of globalization as it became a central problematic of orthodox economists (such as Jagdish Bhagwati and Dani Rodrik), radical thinkers and activists (especially those involved in the World Social Forum), and mainstream pundits (the most famous of whom, of course, is Thomas Friedman). Some of us worked on topics of international political economy, which we self-consciously counterposed both to the traditional international economics of trade and finance and the combination of mainstream economics and politics that became a growth area in political science.

The context, of course, has changed since I left graduate school. But, even as the discipline of economics has become more orthodox and less open to alternative perspectives, the intellectual and political landscape has produced new problems and challenges that harken back to the issues I take up in these essays. The crises of capitalism – not just the current financial crisis but also the many others, such as those pertaining to the distribution of income and wealth, the environment, energy, and urban areas – have placed the issue of planning back on the agenda (not to mention the fact that multinational corporations conduct their own kind of planning on a global scale). Similarly, the demise of neoliberalism and the rise of left-wing governments across Latin America (beginning with Lula and the Workers Party in Brazil and extending through Venezuela, Uruguay, Bolivia, and Ecuador and beyond) have presented a range of alternatives to the theory and policies of mainstream development economics. And, of course, the original Gulf War, as well as the ongoing occupations of Iraq and Afghanistan, the rise of intranational military conflicts, and the antisweatshop movement have disrupted the idea of a homogeneous, seamless world order and placed issues like imperialism and unequal global transfers of value back on the agenda.

My point is not that, over the course of recent decades, there has been a return to previous issues or theoretical perspectives, but that ideas which appear to have been settled at one point in time become unsettled at another point. We are in the midst of one such unsettling right now, as mainstream ideas are being challenged and alternatives being imagined and enacted. The Marxian critique of political economy has played a key role in defining those challenges and alternatives, and the renewed attention to Marxian theory gives these essays a fresh relevance.

A bit of autobiography

Like many of my generation, I became involved in these debates at a relatively early age, in the context of the Vietnam War. That's when many of us "discovered" colonialism and imperialism – as a way of making sense of events "here" and "there," during that time as well as historically, and of contesting the terms of debate between prowar hawks and antiwar doves. The concepts provided us with a structural explanation, instead of seeing the war as a policy option, a misguided decision on the part of politicians and generals; we came to understand the war in the context of the history of US foreign policy and the growth of the military-industrial-academic complex. It made us anticapitalist instead of merely antiwar. That's how many of us got started in the 1960s. As fledgling members of the so-called New Left, we also discovered Marxian theory and socialism as viable alternatives to liberal economic and social thought and capitalist imperialism. North Vietnam, the Cuban Revolution, the Cultural Revolution in China – all had an impact on us in terms of imagining socialist ways of organizing the economy and society and, in particular, the possibility of a socialism different from the one that had been constructed in the Soviet Union.

For other generations, things are different, of course, although not completely unrelated. The immediately preceding generation (my professors in college and graduate school) had witnessed US involvement in the Korean War and been active in the civil rights and early student movements. The next generations (my students over the course of the past 27 years) have lived through the Gulf War, the current wars in Afghanistan and Iraq, and the alter-globalization movement. These events, and the attempt to make sense of them, serve as conditions of existence for becoming interested in and doing the kind of work contained in this volume.

In my case, the fact that I spent a year in Brazil as an exchange student (1970–71), during the worst year of the military dictatorship, and then a year each in Peru (while in college) and in Portugal (after college), had an enormous impact on my life and thinking. These overseas travels allowed me to see, experience, and attempt to make sense of what was going on in different parts of the world and to think about their connection to what was transpiring in my home country. So, for example, I began the process of analyzing the combination of political repression and economic inequality in Brazil, Peru, and pre-revolutionary Portugal in relation to the history of capitalism in those countries and the changing contours of capitalism in the United States and around the world. And, of course, I was assisted in this project by the books and journals I chanced upon at the time, since little of this was assigned in my courses (but, fortunately, they were available in bookstores and libraries): Herbert Marcuse's *Essay on Liberation*, the North American Congress on Latin America's *Latin America and Empire Report*, William Appleman Williams's *The Tragedy of American Diplomacy*, *Monthly Review*, *Science and Society*, volume 1 of *Capital*, Althusser and Balibar's *Reading Capital*, Barry Hindess and Paul Hirst's *Precapitalist Modes of Production*, and the *Review of Radical Political Economics*.[7] In fact, I went to my first Union of Radical Political Economists' (URPE) summer conference in 1976, after graduating from college. It became clear to me there that, within URPE, there was a great deal of interest in Marxism – along with considerable non-Marxist and even anti-Marxist sentiment. I quickly discovered that this tension has been persistent in radical thought, including radical political economy, especially in the United States. It is a tension based on both theoretical and methodological differences: for example, while some heterodox economics used radical or left-Keynesian theory, others turned to the Marxian tradition; a focus on unequal power stood in contrast to investigating the conditions and consequences of class exploitation; and, while some emphasized "economic analysis" as defined by the mainstream of the discipline, others adopted a more interdisciplinary orientation. Such differences persist today among heterodox economists.

Which leads me to my arrival at the University of Massachusetts in 1977. The reason I originally went there was to study Marxism, not to become a professor (since, among other things, as the first person in my family to go to college, I had little idea what an advanced degree really was). My thinking was that, after a few years, I'd have to leave my studies and get a paying job doing something else. (I really didn't know what that was but, unlike many of my students today, I didn't really worry about it. The world was different then.) A couple of years in, and having completed my coursework and passed my comprehensive examinations, I learned that my fellow doctoral students were actually getting teaching jobs. And there might even be the possibility of tenure! In other words, I went to UMass originally to study, not to receive training for any kind of job or career, and certainly not with the intention of becoming an economist, much less a member of the American Economic Association.

Rethinking Marxism

As it turns out, I arrived at UMass at a particularly exciting time. In the late 1970s, there was a general agreement, among both faculty and students, that the department was primarily concerned with extending the frontiers of radical political economy. There certainly was no unanimity, among either the students or the faculty, about the particular direction that radical political economy should take, about what the focus of expanding the boundaries would and could be. However, we did share the general idea that, in our different ways, our task was to use our time in the UMass program to push radical political economy in new directions.

I and many others were most excited about, and drawn to, the theoretical work in which Richard Wolff and Stephen Resnick were engaged, for at least three reasons. First, it was clear they took Marxism and the Marxian tradition seriously and were not interested in following others who were moving outside and away from that tradition. Second, while they expressed respect for some of the key thinkers and texts in that tradition, they had also begun the process of rethinking some of the key concepts and conceptual strategies of the received wisdom. Third, they emphasized Marxian theory, reading and working in an interdisciplinary fashion (taking up especially the ideas being forged within post-analytic philosophy), instead of adhering to the protocols of "doing economics."

At the time I arrived, Resnick and Wolff were working their way through recent books by Althusser, Hindess and Hirst, and others who were producing a new kind of Marxian approach to the analysis of social formations. They had collaborated with their new colleagues to create the premier department of radical political economy in the United States, and they were now engaged with graduate students (as well as teaching undergraduate students) in a collective project to revise and reinvigorate Marxian theory.

Over the course of the past 30 years, their work, as well as that of former students and colleagues who were drawn to the project, has grown and expanded to encompass a wide range of themes and concerns.[8] However, from the very beginning, three ideas were central to the goal of rethinking Marxism.[9]

First, the theory of knowledge appropriate for Marxian theory represented a radical break from both forms of traditional epistemology, empiricism and rationalism. Instead of relying on a notion of absolute truth, a Marxian approach was better characterized as a partisan relativism: relativism, in the sense that it involved a recognition that different truths were produced within different discourses, and there was no way of stepping outside the realm of knowledge to declare one or another theory to be the correct one; and partisan, because different knowledges had different social consequences, and arguing on behalf of one theory over others represented a stance in favor of one set of social consequences over others. Thus, for example, it became possible to argue both that Marxian and neoclassical economic theories produced different, relative truths and that Marxian theory was preferable to neoclassical theory because of their different implications for the economic and social world.

Second, Marxian theory was not based on an economic determinism. The focus on the economic dimensions of social formations such as capitalism was a contingent, conjunctural phenomenon, a result partly of the fact that our work was situated in and around the discipline of economics and partly because class was defined as an economic phenomenon. But no causal priority was attached to this focus. Indeed, extending the concept of overdetermination which Althusser had initially borrowed from Freud's interpretation of dreams, Resnick and Wolff's rethinking of Marxism eschewed any and all causal essences. Conducting a class analysis meant attributing discursive but not causal priority to class; it also involved analyzing the ways in which the existing class structure could be considered to be both cause and effect of all the other nonclass aspects of society.

Finally, Resnick and Wolff redefined what it meant to conduct a Marxian class analysis. In particular, they connected Marx's theorization of class across the three volumes of *Capital* and produced a notion of class processes: aspects of society in and through which surplus labor was performed, appropriated, distributed, and received. Thus, for example, under capitalism, surplus labor was performed by wage-laborers, appropriated (as a form of social theft) by capitalists, and distributed by them to still others (such as other capitalists, banks, the government, etc.). In addition, individuals might occupy more than one class position (thus complicating notions of the working class, the capitalist class, etc.) and societies might have more than one class structure (such as capitalism, feudalism, slavery, etc.). Thus, conducting a Marxian class analysis became a matter of analyzing the various forms that surplus labor took in any given society (like the United States or Brazil) or institution (such as an enterprise, household, or the state), how those class processes affected and were affected in a contradictory fashion by the nonclass processes in society and how, as a result, the class structure was changing over time.

Those were the three innovations that initially drew me to Resnick and Wolff's rethinking of Marxism, and which are reflected in the remaining essays in this volume. Later, as I began to think about a dissertation project, I became interested in two main areas: methodology (especially the whole panoply of issues surrounding the role of mathematical models in economic theory) and development (especially in Latin America). And that's what inspired my dissertation. The original idea was to investigate the role of planning in socialist Cuba (I had received permission from the Cubans to spend a year there but, alas, no funding from the Social Science Research Council). So, like many initial dissertation ideas, it became something else: a critical analysis of what was then called optimal planning theory, the use of static and dynamic optimizing models in planning a socialist economy. This required learning the mathematics (I had focused my studies elsewhere in college) and thinking critically, from a Marxian perspective, about the use of such mathematical models in building socialism.

That was my doctoral dissertation, and the basis of my first publications – after being hired in 1982 by one of the small number of other economics programs where, until now, students have been encouraged to study both mainstream and heterodox approaches, the Department of Economics at the University of Notre Dame.[10]

In lieu of a conclusion

I have included a short introduction at the beginning of each of the three sections into which the remainder of this book is divided. There, I explain the context for the essays contained in those sections and the questions I was attempting to address. Here, I want to identify some of the main themes that run through and across the chapters.

First and foremost, this work demonstrates that a Marxian class analysis leads to theoretical perspectives, empirical investigations, and policy proposals that represent a sharp break from mainstream economics, both liberal and conservative. Whether the focus is on individual decision making and the celebration of private property and free markets (which, until recently, was hegemonic in the discipline of economics) or on economic and social structures and a positive role for government intervention (the previous liberal orthodoxy, and the one that is now ascendant in the wake of the current crises), conventional economic discourse simply does not permit the perspectives and approaches that stem from the Marxian critique of political economy.

I also hope to have shown that Marxian theory is different from other heterodox approaches. In my view, it is not enough for radical economists to emphasize such problems as the growth of financial institutions, the power of multinational corporations, and the persistence of poverty or to seek solutions to these problems by promoting the accumulation of capital, regulating financial transactions, or encouraging higher levels of foreign aid. It is incumbent upon us to connect our explanations to the complex class dynamics of the societies we are analyzing. Marxian analysis not only allows us to pose different questions – for example, about the relationship between the class structure of national and global economies and such problems as "hot money," the internationalized structure of investment and production, and inequalities in the distribution of income and wealth – it also encourages us to place the transformation of class structures on the agenda of economic and social change.

By the same token, we cannot confine ourselves to a purely economic analysis. The issues of knowledge, causality, and subject formation are always implicated in the transdisciplinary orientation of Marxian theory. The Marxian critique of political economy comprises, among other things, a critique of the idea that the economy and economics are closed, self-contained entities. In addition, a Marxian approach (like all forms of economic analysis) is more than an attempt to understand what is going on "out there"; it is also always constructive of the social subjectivities and political imaginaries of economists and economic agents.

Finally, while I don't expect this kind of research to have direct policy implications, at least as understood in conventional policymaking circles, I do think it generates new understandings of what policy can be and broadens our sense of what policies are desirable. When class serves as the starting point of investigation – when the goal is to produce a Marxian class analysis, without invoking class as a causal essence – it becomes possible both to see how the existing class structure is a condition of economic and social problems and to imagine, in concrete ways, how a fundamental change in that class structure needs to, and can, take place.

My aim in this book is to present various examples of how one might apply Marxian class analysis to issues in planning, development, and globalization. These are certainly not the only options nor do they represent a complete list of possible topics. I consider them merely a starting point, for my own work and that of others. If they suggest to readers the power of Marxian class analysis in these and other areas – even when the approach I adopt is criticized or superseded – then I will consider it to be a success.

Acknowledgements

I have reproduced the appropriate acknowledgements at the end of each chapter. Here, I want to thank the following individuals: Routledge's Robert Langham, for encouraging me to bring this volume into print, and

Simon Holt, for careful editorial assistance; Snehashish Bhattacharya, for helping me produce electronic versions of the original essays; Nick Krafft and Sean Mallin, for reading over and offering helpful suggestions on this chapter; Mecamutanterio, for enthusiastically granting permission to use the cover illustration; my various coauthors, for stimulating collaborations and kind permission to use our joint work here; and Stephen Resnick and Richard Wolff, for agreeing to contribute a thoughtful foreword and for being such committed and generous teachers, comrades, and friends over more than three decades.

I also want to thank the following journals and publishers for permission to use my previously published material: *Research in the History of Economic Thought and Methodology*, *Research in Political Economy*, Allen & Unwin, *Latin American Perspectives*, Random House, Westview Press, *World Development*, Kluwer-Nijhoff, M. E. Sharpe, Duke University Press, *Review of Radical Political Economics*, *Economy and Society*, and *Rethinking Marxism*.

Notes

1   I use the plural "crises" deliberately, to indicate both that the problems that currently beset capitalism are many in number and that there is no single cause of those problems.

2   Marx is not the only "forgotten figure" who has resurfaced in current discussions. The ideas of other past critics of mainstream economics – especially John Maynard Keynes, Karl Polanyi, and Hyman Minsky – have also been rescued from the obscurity created by neoclassical economists' obsession with individual choice, private property, and free markets and fetishism of mathematical modeling.

3   Both Wolff and Harvey speak to audiences of students, scholars, and activists, on and off campus, on a regular basis. In addition, each has made Marxian theory accessible in other formats: Wolff, in a DVD and a new book, both titled *Capitalism Hits the Fan* (information available at www.rdwolff.com); while Harvey has produced 13 video lectures on *Capital* (available at http://david-harvey.org).

4   This idea of an economic logic driving the system is closely connected to the traditional base–superstructure interpretation of Marxian theory, in which the economic base determines – in the first or last instance – all other aspects or "levels" of society. Unfortunately, many who refer to Marx (both supportive and dismissive) continue to invoke such an economistic interpretation.

5   Both versions of Marxian theory – modernist and postmodern – are discussed at length in Chapter 6 of Ruccio and Amariglio (2003).

6   Additional details concerning the content and context for the work contained in this volume can be found in an interview conducted with members of the *disClosure* editorial board: Tina Mangieri, Matt McCourt, Natalia Ruiz-Junco, and Jeff West (2004).

7   The one exception was a remarkable opportunity, in my final semester, to co-teach a course on *Capital* with one of my undergraduate professors, David Vail, to whom I owe an enormous debt.

8   Early on, the project assumed an institutional form, first as the "journal group" (a monthly seminar in which the work being produced by Resnick, Wolff and

interested graduate students was discussed, with the goal of eventually starting a journal dedicated to the rethinking of Marxism) and then as the Association for Economic and Social Analysis, which has sponsored a series of local, national, and international conferences. Later, the group established *Rethinking Marxism: A Journal of Economics, Culture & Society*, which began publication in 1988. I have been a member of the editorial board from the very beginning and served as the editor from 1997 to 2009.

9 The original ideas are presented in Resnick and Wolff (1982 and 1983a) and then further elaborated in Resnick and Wolff (1987b).

10 In 2003, the university decided to divide the existing department into two: one, the Department of Economics and Econometrics, to focus exclusively on neoclassical economics; the other, the Department of Economics and Policy Studies, to continue the broader approach for which the department had become well–known both in the United States and around the world. As I was in the midst of writing this chapter, in January 2010, the university announced its intention to eliminate Economics and Policy Studies and, with it, the long tradition of theoretical pluralism and social justice in economics at Notre Dame.

Planning

Planning was in the air when I set out to write my first two essays on socialist planning. It was being theorized and debated by both mainstream and radical economists, as part of the unfortunate dichotomy associated with markets: the debate was cast as markets versus planning and the individual versus the state. The assumption was that mainstream economists preferred markets, while heterodox economists sided with one or another form of planning – more or less the same presumption as today, in the debate over the current crises of capitalism (with government intervention and regulation invoked in the place of planning). I consider the terms of the debate to be unfortunate for a number of reasons: markets and planning were taken to be alternative modes of allocating scarce resources, as if that goal was shared; each taken to be unitary, such that the market and planning were understood to be singular entities); each was presumed to correspond to a different approach to economics, in the sense that markets were presumed to be neoclassical while planning corresponded to Marxism.

In mainstream economics, planning was tied to a particular use of static and dynamic optimizing models, guided by the following question: can the state make decisions that mimic the results of individual self-interested actors who own private property and express their choices in decentralized markets? The answer was: in principle, yes, but the information requirements were simply too large for any single entity like the state to make the appropriate decisions.

In traditional Marxian theory, planning was tied to state ownership of the means of production. Thus, socialism was defined as a particular regime of property ownership, and state planning was portrayed as a mechanism for allocating scarce resources that was more efficient and stable than markets.

My first reaction was: that's it? That's what planning and socialism are reduced to, state decision making rather than private markets? And, since this was a debate carried out through the use of mathematical programming models, isn't there a problem with the presumption that mathematics is essentially a neutral instrument in both neoclassical economics and socialist planning models? The goal I set for myself was to look at socialist planning from the perspective of the theory with which it was associated – to conduct a Marxian class analysis of socialist planning.

One approach I adopted was to invoke the antiessentialist dimension of the rethinking of Marxism in which we were engaged, and to critically examine the essentialisms in and of socialist planning; that is, to identify and elaborate alternatives to methodological and epistemological essentialism. As I saw it, methodological essentialism existed when planning was reduced to a single, theoretical dimension governed by its goals as a teleology, while epistemological essentialism was present in either rationalist and empiricist (or both) conceptions of mathematical models as uniquely capturing reality or as neutral instruments for analyzing problems and communicating results.

The alternative was to move beyond both forms of essentialism and to conceive of socialist planning as a complex social activity – involving political, cultural, and economic (including class) processes – in which mathematical models are metaphors that change, and are changed by, the reality they are used to model. This allowed me to denaturalize planning, to posit the existence of different kinds of planning (and, by extension, different kinds of markets) and to challenge the fetishism of formal, mathematical models in theories of planning (and, by extension, economic theory generally).

The critique of essentialism, in turn, cleared the way for an investigation of the social – including class– consequences of planning: for example, maximizing income that leads to increased exploitation versus changing class structures in a more collective or communal direction.[1] In particular, I showed that focusing on technique instead of class transformation introduces an "aggregation error" (when, for example, industrial and agricultural sectors include two different class structures of production) that might undermine the ostensible goal of socialist planning. Thus, for instance, a plan designed to maximize domestic consumption of manufacturing goods and food might undermine some of the conditions of existence of the communist class process, leading to new struggles and alliances that might have the effect of promoting more ancient and capitalist exploitation. So, what would be considered an unambiguous success from the perspective of mainstream economics (an increase in national product) would be a disaster in terms of Marxian theory (an increase in exploitation and the decline of workers' ability to appropriate the surplus they created). This was also my way of thinking about what had happened in the Soviet Union and Eastern Europe, as well as contemporary events in China, Nicaragua, and elsewhere.

Generally, then, in applying Marxian class analysis to optimal planning, I was led to consider, not only the methodological and epistemological problems, but also the social consequences of thinking about and practicing socialist planning in the technical, nonclass terms of optimal planning theory.

While working on those essays, I was invited to travel to Nicaragua by Valpy Fitzgerald (a professor at the International Institute for Social Studies at The Hague and then economic advisor to the Sandinista government) who challenged me to look at a "real world" case of economic planning. Not unlike many scholars, students, and citizens (as I discovered when I gave off-campus talks about Nicaragua and found that many in the audience had been there, often more than once), I visited Nicaragua and made many return visits, lasting from a few weeks to a few months.[2] I never expected my work to directly "help" the Nicaraguan government but I certainly did want to challenge the terms of debate about Nicaragua and about the possibility of socialist transition that existed in the United States, in both mainstream and radical circles.

A couple of things surprised me when I initiated the project of investigating and trying to make sense of the role of planning and the state in the Sandinista Revolution. I was struck both by the paucity of Marxian analysis of a movement and a situation that were closely associated with Marxism (even among those sympathetic to the Revolution) and by how analysts (again, even among supporters) appeared to have little background in literatures of other socialist experiences, e.g., the Industrialization Debate in the Soviet Union. I found little in the way of class analyses of the Revolution and when, for example, I coined the term "war Sandinismo," no one appeared to understand the connection to the Soviet experience of war communism. My goal was therefore clear: to conduct a Marxian analysis of Nicaragua under the Sandinistas, focusing particular attention on the role of the state and planning.

And, with the help of Fitzgerald and friends I had made in Nicaragua, I was quite fortunate: I was given access to planning documents that have never been published, and I was able to bring to the table the concepts that had come out of our rethinking of Marxian theory. As it turns out, I encountered the same problem as in my prior work on planning theory: the terms of debate that defined transitional or socialist societies in terms of the state were bound up in the "markets versus planning" dichotomy. In my view, changes in property ownership were only one among many changes, including class changes, that were taking place in Nicaragua; and there was no single theory or approach to planning but many different approaches, both theoretical and practical, with different social consequences. In other words, I understood socialism to be a complex process of class transformation: that is what interested me in delving into the concrete details of the Sandinista Revolution.

First, I measured the increase in the size of the state in various sectors of the economy during the first 6 years of the Revolution and then detailed the initial steps in the direction of economic planning (from the setting up of the Ministry of Planning and the publication of Plan 80, to struggles within the state over who would control the planning and the various austerity plans through 1985). Then, I analyzed Sandinista attempts to make the state the "center of accumulation." The idea formulated by Fitzgerald and the Nicaraguan economic team was that the state would gain control of the surplus – directly and indirectly – and direct the use of that surplus by planning investment flows and thus govern the pace and form of economic growth. My own approach was different: I wanted to look at the sources of revenue to the state as a way of determining its ability to create a certain "relative autonomy" from the existing class structure in order to carry out a transitional project to a different class structure. In Nicaragua, the changing structure of the state led to a "fiscal crisis" of internal and external indebtedness, since neither state-sector savings nor the siphoning-off of profits from private capitalists could match increased expenditures. Thus, the contradictory results of "war Sandinismo" and an increasing role of the state in the Nicaraguan economy were, on one hand, a strengthening of capitalism and, on the other hand, other changes (such as cooperative production, literacy campaigns, an improvement in the status of women and minorities, and so on) that might lead, at some point in the future, to a radical change in the role of the state in providing the conditions of existence of capitalism. One consequence was that the state became the center of accumulation by default, as many capitalists either lowered their level of accumulation or disinvested (for example, engaging in capital flight), which in turn decreased their significance in the provision of state revenues.

I returned to these themes in articles originally published in *Development and Change* and *Latin American Perspective*. Basically, I examined the class structure of state finances, on both the revenue and expenditure sides, as a way of going beyond the mere increase in the size of the state documented by others (both opponents and supporters) to investigate its changing class nature. I discovered that there had been a qualitative change in the state, in terms of its class finances, as it created not only new sources of both appropriative and distributive class revenues (from new state capitalist enterprises and increased participation in marketing and credit activities) but also new tensions and struggles, for example, with state workers and nonstate enterprises. All of these changes were taking place in the context of negative "external" conditions, such as declining terms of trade, natural disasters, and foreign aggression. I therefore devised a new conception of the "transitional state" (in Nicaragua, Cuba, and elsewhere) in which those who occupy positions within the state attempt to create a political space that, at one and the same time, increases state involvement in creating the conditions of existence of capitalism (involved in both domestic production and, especially, export production) and spawns new activities that have as their goal the transition beyond capitalism.

My research on the Sandinista Revolution led, in turn, to the formulation of two key theoretical and political questions. First, how can the transitional socialist state eliminate its noncommunal distributive class positions and expand its new position in both receiving communal surplus and providing some of the conditions of existence of nonexploit-ative forms of production outside the state? Second, how can the state eliminate its position as a capitalist exploiter (for instance, in state capi-talist enterprises) and itself become a site of collective or communal class processes, in which the workers themselves are not excluded from appro-priating the surplus they produce? My goal was to place those questions on an agenda that had been straitjacketed, then as now, by the "state versus market" dichotomy.

The severe imbalances created by the foreign aggression and the Revolution itself not surprisingly wreaked havoc on the Nicaraguan macroeconomy. So, my next project was to introduce the rethinking of Marxian theory into the debate concerning stabilization and adjustment. That's the issue I turn to in the next section, on development . . .

Notes

1 Here's a true story, one I've often told to graduate students who have received negative comments about their work: in the months after my very first journal submission, to the *Journal of Comparative Economics Systems*, I waited anxiously for the editor's response. Finally, and unfortunately, it arrived. My article had been summarily rejected and, in the brief letter accompanying the bad news, I was informed that my attempt to inject class into the discussion of socialist planning made me responsible for the deaths of millions of peas-ants in Stalin's collectivization campaign. That was my first – but certainly not last – real taste of the punishments meted out by mainstream economists to maintain control over the discipline. I was consoled by one of my own mentors, who passed on the story that Paul Baran had to submit his most famous article, "The Political Economy of Backwardness," some 20 times before it was finally published.

2 Those talks – in churches, schools, and community centers – in the United States served as the basis of a speech I was invited to give to the students and faculty at the Central American University in Managua. I was asked to speak about the solidarity campaign in the United States. Clearly, they were expecting that I would argue that the robust campaign that had emerged back home would serve to protect their revolution. Much to the consternation of my hosts, I began my talk with the following contradiction: the solidarity campaign for Nicaragua was one of the largest and most enthusiastic in US history, and it had absolutely no impact on US foreign policy. I then proceeded to unravel that contradiction by explaining that the key mistake of the sincere and well-meaning campaign (which encompassed lonely vigils outside the offices of members of Congress and large demonstrations in major US cities) was to support a revolution "over there," and not to connect that support to the interests of US citizens. In other words, they (or, rather, we, since I was an active participant in the campaign) had never succeeded in explaining why North Americans should see it as being in their national interest to support a revolution in Central America. So, the campaign ultimately failed either to protect the Nicaraguan Revolution or to change the terms of debate within the United States.

2 Essentialism and socialist economic planning: A methodological critique of optimal planning theory

> Up to the present time all of these technical-economic problems have been solved more or less haphazardly by eye or by feel, and of course the solution obtained is only in rare cases the best ... The possibility now exists in a number of cases to obtain not an arbitrary solution but to find the optimum solution by a definite, scientifically based method.
>
> L. V. Kantorovich (1960, 387)

> The choice is not simply between the market and planning, but between different kinds of planning.
>
> Jacques Atali (1978, 56–57)

Optimal planning (OP) theory is typically viewed as the result of the application of modern economic and mathematical tools to the question of socialist economic planning. Such a judgment, shared for the most part by the optimal planners themselves, is based on a commitment to the notion of a singular international economic science, defined as the study of economic optimization under some initially endowed conditions.

According to the alternative view presented here, the optimal planners' identification of socialist planning with a problem of mathematical programming is conditioned by an "essentialist" (this term is defined in detail in later sections of this chapter) mode of reasoning. In particular, OP theory reductively defines the complex activity of socialist planning as a purely theoretical procedure, one that directly corresponds to the goals of socialism. Furthermore, the optimal planners employ a set of mathematical models which, they maintain, capture the essence of social reality. In the terms elaborated below, OP theory involves an essentialist, nonclass concept of socialist planning, including an essentialist notion of planning theory itself.

The criticism of those forms of essentialism leads to the development of a different concept of socialist planning – one that emphasizes the complex, contradictory nature of that activity – and of an alternative conception of the role of mathematical models in planning theory.

The critique-cum-reformulation that is proposed here is part of a larger project of elaborating a nonessentialist or nondeterministic interpretation of Marxist theory. It also recognizes the contrasting social consequences of different theories. In particular, socialist planning is not a self-evident object *given to theory* for which only a concrete methodology remains to be elaborated. Rather, socialist planning is itself an object of knowledge – i.e., an object *constructed in theory*. And how it is variously understood (by, among others, its practitioners) will influence how it is variously practiced.

Optimal planning theory

That which is known today as OP theory[1] has its origin in the early work of L. V. Kantorovich, first published in 1939.[2] That early form of OP theory was due to the generalization of the solution to a problem of production scheduling in the Plywood Trust and its application to various questions of efficient production scheduling and organization in the fields of manufacturing, construction, transportation, and agriculture. The author recognized

> two ways of increasing the efficiency of the work of a shop, an enterprise, or a whole branch of industry ... One way is by various improvements in technology ... The other way ... is improvement in the organization of planning and production.
>
> (1960, 367)

Kantorovich demonstrated the usefulness of following the second path. The immediate result was a numerical, iterative algorithm for determining the optimal variant of a production plan (e.g., to maximize output or minimize scrap) considering a number of limiting conditions (e.g., a given production mix and quantity of inputs). His particular framing of the constrained optimization problems and their solutions was quite similar to that which is studied today under the general theory of linear programming. The "best" variant of the enterprise plan, calculated according to his "resolving multiplier method," was capable of raising the use-value or technical efficiency of production by 4–5 percent over more conventionally chosen methods.

The publication of Kantorovich's *Best Use of Economic Resources* in 1959 signaled the end of a 20-year period of official silence on his earlier pioneering work.[3] More importantly, it marked the transformation of that work into the theoretical foundation of today's OP theory. The technical development that characterized enterprise planning calculations in 1939 assumed the form of a heuristic breakthrough with respect to the general problem of socialist planning. The new objective of OP methods was to achieve "a harmonious combination of general and local interests" by furnishing an optimal national plan, one that achieved maximum production with scarce resources. The "resolving multipliers," the numbers utilized in calculating the most efficient enterprise plan, were renamed "objectively determined valuations" and reinterpreted as the set of (shadow) prices with which the optimal physical plan could be implemented. The fundamental objective of socialist planning was reformulated as achieving optimality in the level and efficiency of production; that goal was to be achieved by research into the concepts and techniques of mathematical programming.

Two major points emerge from this interpretation of OP theory. On one hand, OP theory is a unifying term attributed to a set of conceptual strategies which, although still changing and developing, have undergone a singularly important historical transformation. Where once, in the earliest work of Kantorovich, OP theory designated one technique among others for raising the technical efficiency of production within the larger practice of planning the socialist economy, today it denotes the unique theory whereby socialist planning should be theorized and practiced. There are two moments in that conceptual transition that deserve emphasis. First, what was originally considered a *technique* was modified and transformed into the general *theory* of socialist planning. Second, *a* technique (i.e., one among others) was recast as *the* unique theory of socialist planning.

On the other hand, the discourse of the optimal planners hinges crucially on the concepts of optimality and duality which emerge from mathematical programming theory. Using the standard notation of linear programming, the planning problem is equivalent to the formulation and solution of the following corresponding primal and dual problems: variables x and p should be chosen so as to

Primal	*Dual*
max $(c'x)$	min $(p'b)$
x	p
subject to $Ax \leq b$	subject to $p'\, A \geq c'$
$x \geq 0$	$p' \geq 0'$

where, for example,

   c' = a $1 \times n$ vector of weights attached to the unknown sectoral output levels;
   x = an $n \times 1$ vector of sectoral output levels;
   A = an $n \times n$ matrix of technical coefficients;
   p' = a $1 \times n$ vector of shadow prices of given resources;
   b = an $n \times 1$ vector of given resource constraints.

According to the optimal planners, the solution to the global optimal plan (the solution to the primal problem, x^*) maximizes something called "national economic welfare"; that global optimality can be achieved through the solution to the series of suboptimization problems, e.g., on the part of individual enterprises, according to the "objectively determined valuations" (the solution to the corresponding dual problem, p^*). The result is the OP understanding of socialist planning as a problem of mathematical programming.

This brief summary should not be taken to imply that the optimal planners understand the problem of socialist planning merely as the formulation of and solution to an enormous linear program. The research program generated by the OP approach to socialist planning includes extensive work on problems of nonlinear (read: *not necessarily linear*) – integer, quadratic, and stochastic – programming. In addition, the optimal planners have devoted considerable attention to the study of a variety of multilevel, multistage planning schemes (including research into decomposition algorithms and optimal control models for long-term, perspective planning). However, such efforts are understood, not as a break from, but as further refinements and extensions of the central problematic specified above.

Nor have the optimal planners remained at the level of simply theorizing about the problem of socialist planning. The OP discourse also encompasses a set of policy directives: the Proposal for an Optimally Functioning Socialist Economy (POFSE). In general, the objective of the POFSE is to transform the socialist economy into one vast attempt at economic optimization. In particular, guided by the theorems of mathematical programming, the optimal planners have advocated such policies as the increased use of prices in planning (prices for labor, fixed capital, and natural resources), the calculation of such prices according to optimal pricing schemes and the use of accounting-profit maximization as the optimality criterion of socialist enterprises. The POFSE can be understood as a policy program that seeks to ensure the realization in the course of socialist planning of the concepts of optimality and duality, the cornerstones of OP theory.

Past commentators have frequently noted certain limitations of this theory of optimal socialist planning and the obstacles encountered in actually implementing something like the POFSE. For example, Swann (1975), following Ellman (1973), recognized that linear programming prices are not applicable in the context of significant nonlinearities (i.e., where there are increasing or decreasing returns to scale). As a result, OP theory is said to lack "universality in its ability to describe the real world" (1975, 52). Other problems enumerated by Swann include the difficulties involved in specifying a society-wide objective function and in encouraging economic administrators to make decisions on the basis of optimal criteria. Barden (1975) has noted additional problems in the work of the optimal planners. He has criticized OP theory for its focus on the development of the productive forces to the exclusion of the social relations of production and for not being able to adequately handle the eventual emergence of a non-stratified society. The incentive structure of optimal planning may be incapable, according to Barden, of motivating something called the "communist individual."

The most perceptive optimal planners, confronted with these criticisms and with the less-than-universal acceptance of OP theory in the USSR and elsewhere, have acknowledged the existence of many of these same problems. Their attention to the nonlinear "complexity of the real world" continues to provoke research into nonlinear programming models. Some, like Kornai (1970, 1975), have focused on the status of the objective function and have rejected the use of society-wide optimality criteria. The alternative problem faced by Kornai's planner is to produce a set of "alternative scenarios." Others appeal to the nonplanning political decision makers to give to the planners the objective function to be optimized. Finally, many of the optimal planners recognize that the methods and procedures of optimal planning have not reached the level of development that would sanction the wholesale replacement of the existing planning system. Because of its current limitations, OP theory requires further extensions, refinements, and modifications before it can eventually become the unique system of planning under communism.

The main elements, and some of the widely recognized limitations of OP theory, have been identified in this succinct exposition. However, even the most perceptive defenders and critics of OP theory have failed to address the methodological underpinnings of that theory. In this sense, the present criticism does not represent yet another plea to make OP theory more realistic or to include additional factors in the theory. Nor is my criticism based on the idea that the optimal planners introduce their subjective preferences or "values" into the activity of planning and that an alternative approach to socialist planning would escape the effects of such "values." I do not presume that there is such an "objective," non-value-laden form of socialist planning. According to the approach elaborated below, any activity of socialist planning, whether involving optimal planners or not, would be partly determined by the planners' particular conception of the planning problem (the planners' "values"). Rather, OP theory is criticized below for its particular essentialist and nonclass conception of socialist planning. Such a theory of planning, it is further argued, has social consequences that may actually undermine socialist goals. This alternative criticism of OP theory leads to a different, nonessentialist approach that explicitly incorporates a way of addressing the crucial class issues of socialist planning.

Essentialism in theory

It is necessary to start with a brief definition of unfamiliar terms.

Essentialism *in* theory, or *methodological* essentialism (cf. *epistemological* essentialism, discussed in the section below under Essentialism of theory), refers to the tendency to conceptualize social processes in terms of causal essences. Definitions of complex phenomena become one-dimensional and causation tends to run in one direction. On one hand, there is the essentialism that exists in the reductionist definition of a complex social activity or social site in terms of only one of its component social aspects or processes. An all too common example is the state. Whereas Marxist theory defines the state as a particular site in society, composed of myriad political, economic, and cultural processes, other approaches tend to focus exclusively on its political dimension.[4] On the other hand, methodological essentialism is present in attempts to explain the existence of an ensemble of social processes as the simple effect of one of those social processes. For example, neoclassical economic theory is at least partly defined by the role it attributes to individual utility as the essence of all other aspects of society. In both cases, an essentialist form of determination is posited to account for the interaction among social processes.[5]

Essentialism, then, refers to a wide variety of different attempts to interpret social reality in terms of causal or definitional essences. An essentialist analysis of social phenomena may involve "monocausation," the positing of a single factor as the essential determinant or defining characteristic of all other phenomena; it may also involve attributing causal or definitional priority to more than one essential factor, in the sense of multiple essences. The result in all such cases, however, is that some aspects of social reality are reduced, in either a causal or definitional sense, to some other aspect(s) of that reality.

These types of essentialism in theory can be counterposed to an alternative conception of the relations among social processes in terms of "overdetermination."[6] According to a nonessentialist, overdeterminationist approach, each social process is conceived to be influenced, conditioned, and otherwise constituted by the effects of all other social processes. In fact, overdetermination means that each social process is conceived to exist only insofar as all other political, economic, and cultural processes necessary for its existence combine in such a way that it can and does exist. Therefore, overdetermination is not equivalent to simple multiple causation. The analysis of social reality in terms of overdetermination emphasizes the participation of *all* aspects of that reality in the complex *constitution* of each and every other aspect of that reality. Thus, an approach based on overdetermination eschews any and all forms of essence-phenomenon causation among social processes; in addition, it focuses on the contradictions with which social processes are beset as a result of their complex constitution by the effects of all other social processes.

In identifying socialist planning with the formulation and solution of a mathematical programming problem, the work of the optimal planners is characterized both by the *definitional* essentialism and by the *causal* essentialism introduced above. On one hand, socialist planning is defined as the choice of the appropriate mathematical programming model and the rather formalistic manipulation of that model, i.e., as a purely theoretical procedure. This conception of socialist planning, that reduces it to a theoretical process, disregards the other, nontheoretical processes which, together with the theoretical process, comprise the social activity of planning. Complexity is thereby reduced to one-dimensionality.

On the other hand, socialist planning is conceived as a simple means to an end – as a noncontradictory activity that is determined by its goals. Socialist planning, in OP theory, occupies the same status as something called "socialist ownership of the means of production" as a necessary mechanism derived from the goal of achieving socialism. Thus, the goals occupy the position of the essential determinant of the activity of socialist planning, giving it a teleology of movement by defining its origin and its end. Socialist planning is merely an expression, a phenomenon of those essential goals, while also one of their ultimate guarantors. In this sense, contradiction is neglected in favor of the teleology of an essential subject.

Socialist planning, according to the alternative approach followed here, cannot be reduced to its theoretical process, nor can it be conceived as simply conforming to its stipulated goals, however formulated. Rather, as explained immediately below, that social process and those goals are themselves contradictory (since overdetermined) and are only some of the determinants of anything like socialist planning that is put forward as a means. It is necessary, then, to produce an alternative, nonessentialist concept of the activity of socialist planning.

For purposes of analytical convenience, socialist planning may be conceived initially as a complex, contradictory social practice or site within society, composed of cultural, political, and economic processes. It includes, of course, a process of theorizing – the production of the facts of planning and the theoretical working on those facts to produce the planning document. That theoretical process is itself multidimensional: the process of producing and changing concepts to generate statements about social reality involves such diverse moments as the technico-mathematical manipulation of variables; the construction of the variables to be so manipulated; and the theoretical determination of how to construct those variables and how to interpret their mathematical manipulation. Thus, no sharp dichotomy of the theoretical and technical is warranted; the conventionally conceived more technical operations are theoretical in nature, and vice versa. Moreover, the various theories of planning (including the planners' "values") are influenced and conditioned by the other theories and theoretical debates in the social formation in which planning is practiced.

The cultural processes include considerably more than the purely theoretical. The daily activity of the planning "laboratories" and the product of that activity – the plan – owe as much to patterns and norms of persuasion as to the particular language through which the various results are formed and communicated.[7] The "cycle of credibility" among the planners, along with the various levels and types of education that are brought by the planners into their work, must be included among the prominent features of that activity. The realm of informal conversation – among the "insiders" and between the planners and nonplanners – must not be forgotten. Nor can a lack of significance be attributed to the structure of the relations among the various programs of planning (e.g., gathering data, proposing models, performing calculations, and producing the written documents). In sum, there are many cultural processes that must be investigated to produce an adequate, fully social concept of socialist planning.

Nor can the analysis end there. The activity of planning comprises myriad political processes, including the legal status of the planning institutions and of the plan itself. The relationship among the planners also includes an administrative hierarchy in the form of patterns of supervision and direction. In fact, there exists what might be called a political division of labor in *plan formulation* (which questions pertain to which entities?) and in *plan implementation* (who receives what pieces of information and who makes the various different types of decisions?).

An investigation into the economic aspects of planning begins with the coordination of the various parts of the planning procedure. The planning "laboratory" may, in fact, be viewed as a workplace, which includes the instruments of labor and, more broadly, its productive forces (encompassing the organization of the activity itself). In addition, the planning activity itself may be financed by a direct transfer of surplus labor (and/or its products) that has been performed and appropriated elsewhere in the social formation. Thus, the planners may participate in what is described below as a subsumed class process.[8]

In this manner, through the elaboration of its component processes along the lines sketched here, the planning activity can be conceived as a complex, fully social site or activity. The final step in this investigation entails a recognition of the impact of the remaining social processes of the social formation – those that make up the other, nonplanning practices – on the processes involved in planning. Thus, each of the various social processes in which the planners participate is conceived as a unique point of convergence of the effects of the other social processes of the social formation. For example, the process whereby planners secure a particular distribution of surplus labor may be overdetermined by prevailing cultural conceptions of the social status of "specialists," by forms of administration in the enterprise and in the state and by the various modes of appropriating and distributing surplus labor elsewhere in the social formation. No process that figures in the planning relationship escapes from such a complex determination. In addition, it is expected that the overdetermination of the component social processes of planning would produce specific contradictions, and thus the movement and development of that social practice. For example, the encouragement of a conception of planning as a purely technical procedure, divorced from economic policy (as, for example, in the USSR under Stalin), might lead to a decline in the social status of the planning "specialists," while requiring an increase in subsumed class payments to the planners to maintain their allegiance to the project of planning and their silence on matters of economic policy.[9]

The general perspective, then, is that the complex social nature of the activity of planning and the social construction of plans exist at two different levels of analysis: at the level of the component social processes of planning and at the level of the complex determination of each of those processes by all other social processes of the social formation. The result is a conception of socialist planning as a complexly composed social site beset with contradictions, a practice whose component social processes are overdetermined by, and participate in, the overdetermination of the remaining social processes of the social formation in which that activity is located.

It has been demonstrated, then, that the optimal planners' tendency to define socialist planning in terms of only one of its aspects (the theoretical process) and to reduce planning to a single, noncontradictory determinant (given socialist goals) involves a double essentialism. That double methodological essentialism in OP theory raises the issue of the optimal planners' conception of theory itself. It is argued below that the conception of socialist planning produced by OP theory occurs together with a similarly essentialist epistemology. Indeed, those two types of essentialism – in and of theory – seem to condition the existence of one another.

Essentialism of theory

Again, an initial definition of new terms is necessary. The second type of essentialism that conditions the OP conception of socialist planning is epistemological, i.e., that which is referred to above as an essentialism of theory. The work of the optimal planners is informed by both forms of the classical Subject–Object theory of knowledge, empiricism and rationalism. To briefly elaborate, both empiricist and rationalist arguments attempt to close the process of production of knowledge by guaranteeing its absolute truth: they act as ultimate validity criteria. Thus, for example, empiricist modes of argument refer to some extradiscursive reality (e.g., the "facts" or "history," against which any and all theories can be compared and validated). Each theory is then declared to reflect, or not to reflect, the essential "facts" of the extradiscursive reality. Rationalism, on the other hand, reverses the terms of the empiricist proof and declares that the Truth of the theory is guaranteed by its ability to capture the essence of social reality. Once that identification of theory and reality is achieved, then – according to rationalist procedures – successive Truths are produced by more or less deductive elaborations of the theory.[10]

The optimal planners' approach to socialist planning relies crucially on a particular notion of theory, connected in turn to a particular conception of mathematical forms of discourse. Their use of mathematical relationships and models is justified by various arguments, of which the following are the most common:

1   Mathematics and mathematical relationships are conceptually neutral. They are devoid of content (i.e., merely formal, logical relationships) until they are used within a particular science.
2   Economico-mathematical models are objective, scientific models produced within an international economic science.
3   Mathematical programming models capture the "strategic relationships" of the phenomenon under study.
4   Mathematical programming models correspond to the essence of the socialist economy.
5   The Truth of the mathematical models of OP theory is guaranteed by their practical application, by their superiority to other models of planning.
6   Mathematical methods of planning constitute an "objective" means of planning, in contrast to so-called subjective methods of planning.

It can be shown that all of these arguments, and others, contain either empiricist, rationalist, or both modes of epistemological closure. The paradoxical result is that the optimal planners become obsessed with epistemology in the very denial of its importance within their discourse.

The argument can be summarized briefly as follows. Mathematical models serve, in OP theory, as representations of an "essential core" of the social phenomena under study. By virtue of their unique ability to capture the "strategic relationships" of that reality, those models are understood to comprise the singular (OP) theory which corresponds to the given socialist goals. Moreover, the rationalist manipulation of those modeled variables and relationships produces, via deduction, further Truths concerning the nature of that modeled reality. Thus, to return to the concepts elaborated above, the theoretical process is conceived to correspond to its object, which in turn is given to it independent of thought. The optimal planners come to view the theoretical process as operating through a unique theory, which corresponds to a uniquely defined, extra-discursive reality.

OP theory does include the possibility that the mathematical models may change; for example, stochastic programming models may be substituted for linear programming models, as a result of the relative inadequacy of previous models in representing the empirically given reality. However, the OP conception of that sequence of models is that it constitutes a path of successive approximations to the absolute truth of the modeled phenomena.

Drawing on recent work in the "philosophy of mathematics," the connection can be made between the OP conception of socialist planning through mathematical models and one of the contemporary "foundational" schools of thought in mathematics.[11] The "formalist" school, as it is known, conceives of mathematics as a purely logical structure, devoid of conceptual content. It is but a simple step from that theory to the OP conception of mathematics as being a "neutral" conceptual tool in some ultimate sense, and to the view that mathematical models constitute a universal scientific language.[12] The task is to explain how this conception of mathematics has the effect of mathematical models' becoming the *subjects* of reality in OP theory and how the existence of such subjects rules out the fundamental Marxist notion of *process*. The presence of epistemological essentialisms in OP theory, it can be shown, not only conditions the existence of its conception of mathematical models, but is also intimately related to the essentialist view of social processes at work in that theory.

The argument continues with the conclusions arrived at above. Thus, the OP conception of mathematical models as representing the Truth of reality means that the paths of social change are perforce conceived as the product of a structural necessity. The focus of OP theory is the "equilibrium state" or optimal solution, although process and movement may be used as metaphors for the attainment of that final state.

There are two senses in which this conception of the "state of optimality" violates the alternative notion of the overdetermination of social processes. First, because of the operation of a structural necessity, the achievement of the state is conceived to be guaranteed by the movement of social processes. Second, it is the state which is the focus of attention (i.e., what is important) and *not* the process of movement. Thus, to play on a phrase in Althusser (1976), mathematical models constitute a "subject without a process" in OP theory.

An alternative approach is to concentrate on process, on the social processes in continual movement and development and on contradiction. The mathematical models, and their associated equilibrium states and optimal solutions, might then be used as metaphors or heuristic devices designating parts of that contradictory movement. They would be used, where necessary, to consider in artificial isolation one aspect or another of that movement, to explain a moment in that process. This limited role must be further restricted to remain consistent with the concept of overdetermination. Because of the focus on process and contradiction, each mathematical relationship or model must be problematized (i.e., dismantled) immediately upon being specified. If, indeed, a set of mathematical relationships can serve to "model" social processes, then the movement and contradictions of those processes undermine the relationships of the model as soon as it is specified.

This conception of the relationship between mathematical models and planning theory does not constitute a flat rejection of the use of mathematical models in socialist planning. Rather, the objective is to redefine the status of those models, accepting a restricted use of mathematical relations as metaphors to illustrate and develop the concepts and statements of planning theory.

An additional implication of the epistemological essentialism in OP theory concerns the concepts of science and scientific community. The presence of rationalism in OP theory conditions the existence of its concept of a universal economic science (in the singular!). That science is characterized by the degree to which it can be expressed in mathematical terms and by its ability to transcend different "ideological" points of view and different social formations. The implication is that the members of the "scientific community" of planners share in that scientific Truth and enter into theoretical disputes on the basis of a common methodology and a (present in its absence) common epistemology.

This last argument can serve to account for the ability of optimal planners and neoclassical economists to meet and discuss "common" scientific questions in international conferences far more readily and harmoniously than can their counterparts in history, sociology, and other disciplines.

Social consequences

The preceding sections explored the various types of essentialism that inform the optimal planners' theory of socialist planning. At the same time, it was possible to elaborate an alternative conception of planning and of mathematical models in planning theory based on different, nonessentialist notions of social determination and of theory itself, summarized by the concept of overdetermination. The next task, then, to complement the discussion of the theoretical effects of essentialism, is to explain briefly the contrasting social consequences of essentialist and nonessentialist theories of socialist planning.

Such an analysis seeks to elaborate the following general argument: first, different conceptions of planning are understood to have different implications for the actual practice of planning. In other words, how planning is variously practiced is partly determined by the different theories in and through which its practitioners conduct and assess the consequences of their tasks. Second, those distinct planning practices are conceived to produce different, contradictory effects on the social processes of the social formation in general and on the class structure in particular. Thus, according to this argument, different (essentialist and nonessentialist) methodologies and epistemologies not only have determinate theoretical effects, they are also expected to have contrasting social implications vis-à-vis the movement or transition of the social formation as a whole.

More specifically, an essentialist theory of socialist planning such as OP theory, which operates with a noncontradictory notion of optimality, and devotes little attention to class, approaches the crucial questions of socialist planning in a manner quite distinct from one that emphasizes overdetermination and the centrality of the class process.[13] They provide very different answers to such questions as the following: What do planners look at in the course of planning? How do they investigate the consequences of planning? What are determined to be the relevant circumstances of such planning? And what interactions are important among the processes that are planned?

In the case of OP theory, the responses to such questions are generally taken as given – i.e., given from outside the planning activity itself in the form of the optimality criterion or objective function of the mathematical program. Once the optimality criterion is provided, the techniques of optimal planning can be applied to determine, under the appropriate set of constraints and simplifying assumptions, the unique point of optimality. For example, the correct set of gross output norms or level of investment can be calculated once the planners are provided with the criterion of maximizing consumption in the terminal year of the 5-year plan. Both the goals of planning and the movement toward those goals are conceived in a noncontradictory fashion. The result is a notion of a harmonious path of movement toward given goals through a set of given techniques. An alternative approach would be to conceive of both the goals and the attempted movement to reach those goals as being overdetermined and thus contradictory – the goals themselves being a product of the various struggles and compromises in the social formation in question.

It should be noted that the argument is not that certain goals of planning should not be specified nor that one or another optimality criterion (e.g., maximizing consumption, minimizing labor inputs or maximizing growth rates) is a more appropriate objective of socialist planning. The emphasis here is on the status of any optimality criterion, the way in which it is conceived and the social consequences of that conception.

Let us now consider a simple, more concrete example to illustrate the preceding argument. In any particular social formation in which a revolution has taken place and socialist planning has been instituted, it is expected that a complex class structure would be present. Allowing for the existence of both fundamental and subsumed classes,[14] even communism would exhibit its own complex class structure. Here we can assume a social formation in which both the communist fundamental class process (the communal appropriation of surplus labor) and the ancient fundamental class process (the appropriation of surplus labor by independent producers from themselves) coexist.[15] There is no need to indicate the relative predominance of one class process over another in this case; nor is there a presumption that this social formation must necessarily move in the direction of the social predominance of either one of the two fundamental class processes.

Each fundamental class process has its political, economic, and cultural conditions of existence. For brevity's sake they are not listed here, except to the extent that two conditions of existence are common to both fundamental class processes, namely, forms of commodity production and circulation and forms of planning. In other words, the direct producers in both class processes produce commodities and both "sectors" are included in the national plan.[16] One such example might be that manufactured items for domestic consumption are *communist commodities*, and that *ancient commodities* take the form of domestic foodstuffs, as well as export crops that generate foreign exchange for the purchase of noncompetitive imports for domestic (communist) manufacturing.

It is expected that, in such a situation, different conceptions of planning, and thus different planning practices, would produce contrasting economic, cultural, and political arenas of tension, struggle, and compromise between and among the specified fundamental classes and the subsumed class of planners.

For example, the essentialist conception of planning discussed above might result in the calculation of a new set of (optimal) relative prices with the objective of maximizing consumption. The new prices might induce ancient food producers to substitute the production of domestic foodstuffs for export crops. One result would be a rise in the level of domestic consumption (communist producers purchasing more of the previously scarce state-subsidized primary food products) which would give the desired effect.[17] However, an additional outcome might be either:

1   a decline in the level of purchases of imported inputs for communist manufacturing production, due to the shortage of foreign exchange; or
2   the acquisition of foreign loans to finance the existing level of imports.

In the former case, the lack of spare parts might cause a decline in the level of labor productivity. In turn, the lower level of productivity might create the conditions in which it is required that there be an increase in the rate of communal surplus labor appropriation to maintain the existing rate of communist accumulation. In the latter case, a class of foreign bankers might become subsumed to the communist class process, requiring an increase in the level of communally appropriated subsumed class (interest) payments. Thus, an additional result might be a new set of alliances between the ancient producers and the communist producers, and between the ancient producers and the subsumed class of planners. However, new tensions between the communist direct producers and the subsumed class of planners and/or foreign bankers might also emerge. Some of the resulting tensions might develop into struggles that have as their object the quantitative and qualitative dimensions of the appropriation and distribution of surplus labor. Similarly, nonclass struggles might also emerge, for example over concepts of national sovereignty and religious ideas.

In contrast, a conception of planning that begins with class and overde-termination would seek to analyze the contradictory social implications of any attempt to maximize the level of domestic consumption and to imple-ment such a price reform. There is no necessary reason to assume that such a different conception would produce a "correct" set of alliances and conflicts. The effects of the social processes of planning are only some of the constitutive elements in the movement of the social processes of the social formation as a whole. However, a conception of planning that is based on essentialism and that "forgets" about classes and the contradic-tory consequences of the objectives and procedures of planning may promote the conditions of existence of the conflicts and alliances sketched above. Furthermore, the emergence of such tensions and compromises may undermine the social existence of the communist class process itself. Thus, an essentialist conception of planning may make possible the transi-tion to a social formation in which the communist fundamental class process is even further from becoming socially dominant.

An alternative approach

This criticism of the presence and likely social effects of the various forms of essentialism and the general absence of class in OP theory does not entail a general rejection of socialist planning. It does, however, presup-pose a Marxist reconceptualization of the practice of socialist planning. Planning in a socialist society is a complexly constituted social site with contradictory class and nonclass social consequences. In addition, this critique-cum-reformulation serves as the basis of a method of socialist planning that contrasts sharply with that of the optimal planners. In this sense, the present criticism of the work of the optimal planners leads to a different way of doing planning and thus to a different set of probable social consequences. This means that Marxist theory has something more and different to offer the practice of socialist planning than just the distinc-tion between two groups of productive and unproductive expenditures in socialist national income accounts.[18]

The alternative method of planning indicated here presumes the Marxist conception of planning and the nonessentialist understanding of mathematical models developed above. This non-OP method includes a different set of concepts for planning. In particular, the concepts intro-duced below focus on issues of class. This concern with a particularly class-theoretic method of planning is, in part, provoked by the general absence of class concepts in OP theory. It is also consistent with a variety of Marxist notions of socialism which, however much they may differ, at least acknowledge the importance of dealing with class issues.

This alternative approach to planning can be illustrated by reference to the specific case of the distribution of income. Income distribution is not, in general, a central concern in OP theory. Most optimal planning problems follow the work of Kantorovich in which "consumption was considered independently of the character of utilization of labor, and it was assumed that the problems of distribution – wages and retail prices – were to be solved separately" (1976, 42). Even where the optimal pricing of labor is argued for, the actual payment to labor in the form of wages is not considered equal to its optimal valuation. In other words, the optimal planners do not theorize or advocate flows of income in terms of the shadow prices of factors of production. Income distribution is determined more or less independently from the optimal plan, for example, by national wage scales, enterprise incentive funds, and/or state redistribution through taxation and public consumption goods (Mudretsov and Shargunov, 1976).

However, the question of what is distributed in the form of income, if not the actual mechanism of that distribution, is generally theorized in nonclass terms in OP theory. Scarce "factors of production" make their respective contributions to total output. The optimal combination of these factors results in an optimal national product. This total product is then distributed in the form of income: "wages and salaries," public consumption, state revenues, and so on. Therefore, the optimal planners operate with the notion of a relatively harmonious distribution of the national product among the individuals in society.

There are two elements that figure prominently in this OP conception of income distribution. First, socialist production is reductively defined as the optimal production of use-values – that is, products whose social usefulness is designated by a society-wide optimality criterion. Second, the income receipts of individuals and individual organizations (such as enterprises, regions, the state) are theorized in terms of the distribution of these use-value outputs. The result of this common approach is that the concepts of income distribution that are used in optimal planning succeed in abstracting from class.

These nonclass notions of income may serve, in turn, as the basis for attempts to equalize the distribution of "wages and salaries." However, movements in the direction of such equalization may well mask important offsetting changes in the class distribution of income.

The method of planning proposed here is informed by a different, Marxist notion of income distribution, one that begins with class. It draws on recent work by Resnick and Wolff (1983c) in reconceptualizing income in specifically class-theoretic terms. This approach is distinguished by three major considerations for the purposes of socialist planning.[19] First, receipts of income can occur within class and nonclass processes. They are designated as class and nonclass incomes, respectively. Second, class incomes comprise both fundamental and subsumed class incomes. Third, it is expected that there is a variety of fundamental and subsumed class incomes that depends on the multiplicity of fundamental and subsumed class processes in a particular social formation. Each concept is introduced below in terms of a single class process – the capitalist fundamental class process – and then generalized to the case of multiple class processes. The result is a class-theoretic notion of the distribution of income that allows us to reconceptualize, and plan, the income receipts of an individual or a socialist organization within a complex class structure.

Fundamental class incomes are received by individuals who occupy positions in fundamental class processes. Each fundamental class process is defined as the performance of necessary and surplus labor and the appropriation of that surplus labor. Under the assumptions of this discussion, then, occupants of fundamental class positions receive incomes that are equal to the value of necessary and surplus labor. In the case of capitalism there are two class positions – productive laborers and capitalists – and two fundamental class incomes – v and s – that are received by the occupants of those two positions. Selling the commodity labor power involves an equivalent exchange, a receipt of v by the productive laborer equal to the value of labor power, the capitalist form of necessary labor, nl. The capitalist receives s (surplus-value), the capitalist form of appropriated surplus labor, by virtue of exploitation, that is for doing nothing. In an analogous fashion, the occupants of positions in other, noncapitalist fundamental class processes receive income designated as nl^k and sl^k (where k represents the particular feudal, ancient, etc. fundamental class process).

An interesting case is presented by communism. The communist fundamental class process was defined above as the communal appropriation of surplus labor. Thus, the performers of necessary and surplus labor also occupy the position of the communal appropriators of surplus labor. For purposes of this discussion, communist producers are understood to receive both fundamental class incomes: $nl^{Com} + sl^{Com}$.

Incomes are also received by occupants of subsumed class positions. By virtue of their participation in subsumed class processes, they receive distributed shares of appropriated surplus labor for providing some of the conditions of existence of the fundamental class processes. For example, the capitalist fundamental class process has, subsumed to it, a class process in and through which direct transfers of surplus-value are made in the form of subsumed class income. Some examples of capitalist subsumed class income receipts are interest payments to moneylenders, dividends to holders of preferred stock, rent to landowners, and taxes to the state. Class processes subsumed to the other fundamental class processes are expected to generate analogous subsumed class incomes. Given the diversity of such flows of value as subsumed class incomes, they are designated as Σssc^k (thus, for example, Σssc^c represents capitalist subsumed class incomes).

Finally, it is recognized that incomes may be generated within certain nonclass processes, Σnc. That is, it is probable that there is a variety of flows of income to occupants of positions other than fundamental and subsumed class positions in any particular social formation. For example, in the case of capitalism, not all sales of labor power include a corresponding receipt of v: the commodity labor power may be sold to non-capitalists and involve, in turn, a nonclass income.

In a similar vein, there is no fixed set of such nonclass processes and nonclass incomes. What is a nonclass income-generating process in one social situation may become a class process, involving a class income, under other social conditions. Consider the payment of housing rent by a worker to a landlord. If that worker is a productive laborer within the capitalist fundamental class process, then the rent payment is a nonclass flow of value to the landlord. According to the preceding discussion, the landlord occupies neither a fundamental nor a subsumed class position in obtaining this income. However, if the rent is paid by a communist producer, the landlord (e.g., the state) may occupy a position subsumed to the communist fundamental class process and hence receive a transfer of communally appropriated surplus labor in the form of a subsumed class income. The particular (fundamental and subsumed) class and nonclass nature of income receipts is, according to this approach, always constituted by the totality of social conditions within which the income-generating social process occurs.

Drawing together these various components, the following general expression has been proposed for the income receipts of an individual in the context of capitalism: $Y_i = v_i + s_i + \Sigma ssc_i + \Sigma nc_i$ (Resnick and Wolff, 1983c). This equation may be generalized to include the present discussion's focus on the possibility of multiple class processes within socialism as

$$Y_i = \sum_k nl_i^k + \sum_k sl_i^k + \sum_k \Sigma ssc_i^k + \Sigma nc \qquad (2.1)$$

Thus, each individual recipient of income may occupy a variety of fundamental, subsumed and nonclass positions within a socialist society. According to the example of the previous section, equation (2.1) would be specified in the following manner:

$$Y_i = nl_i^A + nl_i^{Com} + sl_i^A + sl_i^{Com} + \Sigma ssc_i^A + \Sigma ssc_i^{Com} + \Sigma nc_i$$

where A refers to the ancient fundamental class process and Com to the communist fundamental class process.

Depending on the specific configuration of class and nonclass processes in a social formation, this approach may be used to theorize the class and nonclass distribution of income for an individual person or within a social site (an enterprise, planning agency, or family) or geographic entity (a region or nation). In all of these cases, it is possible to take into account the variety of existent class and nonclass processes in a social formation, the multiple class and nonclass positions occupied by any individual in that social formation and the complex class and nonclass structure of the diverse social institutions or sites within the social formation. In particular, it becomes possible to use this new information in the course of socialist planning and to intervene to change the class and nonclass distribution of income in the desired direction.

In contrast, the optimal planners' theorization of income aggregates and, thus, abstracts from the differences introduced in the preceding discussion. The receipt of income, in OP theory, is understood as obtaining a portion of the undifferentiated (with respect to class) total quantity of produced use-values. Thus, the focus of the optimal planners is on changes in such magnitudes as "wages and salaries" or "national income," whereas significant class changes may occur within these magnitudes. Income may shift from one fundamental class form to another, from a fundamental class form to a subsumed class form, or from either of the class forms to a nonclass form. Such changes may represent a particular class dynamic occurring within the social formation and may, in turn, lead to further movement. These developments would, literally, not be seen by the optimal planners.

The differences between the two approaches can be further illustrated with a specific example concerning "regional income."[20] Within OP theory, the income of a region is conceptualized as the sum of incomes, Y, of the individuals within that region. This means, according to the alternative approach presented here, that the aggregate income of a region is composed of a variety of fundamental class, subsumed class, and nonclass incomes, or

$$Y = \sum_k nl^k + \sum_k sl^k + \sum_k \sum ssc^k + \sum nc \qquad (2.2)$$

(where the subscript i has been dropped to represent the summation over individuals). Thus, for example, the income of a particular region that comprises the communist and ancient fundamental class processes, their respective subsumed class processes, and diverse nonclass processes can be represented by the following equation:

$$Y = nl^{Com} + nl^A + sl^{Com} + sl^A + \sum ssc^{Com} + \sum ssc^A + \sum nc$$

It may be possible, then, for the optimal planners to maximize total income in this region but fail to take account of shifts within that total. Significant aspects of the class development of this region would be excluded from consideration. For example, the rate of appropriation of communal surplus labor (sl^{Com}/nl^{Com}) might rise or the generation of income may be shifted from the communist to the ancient class process (measured by an increase in $[nl^{Com} + sl^{Com} + \sum ssc^{Com}]/[nl^A + sl^A + \sum ssc^A]$) at the same time that the optimal objective of maximizing regional income is achieved.

One of the implications of this analysis is that transforming the class distribution of income may be more important with respect to the goal of achieving socialism than such objectives as maximizing the level of "income" or promoting increased equality in the nonclass "distribution of income" (as defined in OP theory). The alternative method of planning proposed here explicitly includes a class-theoretic notion of income to this end. Therefore, in sharp contrast to the consequences of the methods and procedures of optimal planning, the planners using this alternative approach can produce a class knowledge of the social formation and directly intervene to transform the class structure of socialism in a manner consistent with socialist goals.

(original version published in 1986)

Acknowledgements

This paper presents some of the principal arguments of my unpublished PhD dissertation, "Optimal Planning Theory and Theories of Socialist Planning" (University of Massachusetts-Amherst, 1984). I gratefully acknowledge the assistance of the members of my dissertation committee – Stephen Resnick, Richard Wolff, Donald Katzner, and Johnnetta Cole – and the comments of Warren Samuels, John Davis, and several anonymous referees on an earlier draft of this paper.

Notes

1   Swann (1975) is a useful, short introduction to OP theory. A more extensive summary of the various aspects of OP theory can be found in Ellman (1973) and Zauberman (1976). Samuels (1979) confronts OP theory with an important set of questions and concerns.

2   Translated and published in English, with an introductory note by Tjalling C. Koopmans, as Kantorovich (1960).

3   Translated and published in English as Kantorovich (1965). That same year (1959) saw the publication of a related volume, *The Use of Mathematics in Economics* (Nemchinov 1965), which included contributions by Kantorovich, Oscar Lange, A. A. Lur'e, and V. V. Novozhilov.

4   Both views of the state are discussed by Resnick and Wolff (1983b).

5   For a discussion of different views of economic theories in general, see Wolff *et al.* (1982). See Resnick and Wolff (1979, 1983a) for a more complete discussion and criticism of the various forms of essentialism in theory.

6   The concept of overdetermination represents the strong antiessentialism of Marxist theory. Originally borrowed from Sigmund Freud, and subsequently transformed and extended, overdetermination orients the causal explanation of social phenomena in terms of the notions of mutual constitutivity and relative autonomy. On one hand, the overdetermination of social processes means that they are mutually constitutive – that each social process participates in the formation of all other processes. On the other hand, overdetermination implies that each process is conceived as a relatively autonomous nodal point, a nexus of determinations with its own position in the constellation of causal relations. Thus, each process is understood to be constituted only by the effects

emanating from all the other social processes and, as a relatively autonomous process, to participate in its own right in that complex web of mutual determinations. This understanding of overdetermination is counterposed to notions of simple multiple causation, of simple reciprocal causality, and of relations between processes as separate things linked externally by a causal effect. It is also unrelated to the mathematical concept bearing the same name, which designates a simultaneous equation system in which there are more equations than unknowns.

7 This discussion of the cultural processes of planning was inspired by the analysis of a different group of "scientists" by Latour and Woolgar (1979).

8 See note 16, below.

9 Cf. Lecourt (1977).

10 The most thorough contemporary critique of classical epistemology, albeit from a non-Marxist position, is that of Rorty (1979). The definition and criticism of empiricism and rationalism as they appear here are more fully elaborated in Resnick and Wolff (1983a).

11 An explanation and criticism of the contemporary foundational debates in mathematics can be found in two recent volumes: Davis and Hersh (1980) and Kline (1980). See also my review essay (Ruccio 1984b). Georgescu-Roegen (1971), especially Chap. 2, "Science, Arithmomorphism, and Dialectics," provides an important critical discussion of the use of mathematical models in economic theory. However, our approaches differ in crucial respects. Other important sources for the present discussion of mathematical models in social theory include Hindess (1971), Raymond (1978), Badiou (1970), and Cavaillès (1962).

12 For a penetrating criticism of the conception of mathematics as a neutral language, see Bachelard (1949) and Lecourt (1972).

13 A brief explanation is in order. The antiessentialism that guides the present effort – a disputation of all *causal* priorities in the explanation of social phenomena – does not preclude *discursive* priority being attached to one among the myriad social and natural processes. The notion of the "centrality of the class process" indicates the use of the concept of class process as the entry point and goal of the Marxist analysis of social formations. This discursive priority (centrality) of the class process refers to the object of Marxist theory, oriented by such questions as the following: What are the existent class processes? How are they constituted? How are they changing? It is expressly *not* a matter of designating the class process as the most important determinant of social life nor of conferring on that concept an elevated status from which all others are deduced.

14 The fundamental class process is one among the myriad economic processes that indicates the particular process of the performance and direct appropriation of surplus labor. Surplus labor is that labor performed by the class of direct producers which is the part of total labor in addition to necessary labor. Necessary labor, in turn, is defined as that amount of total labor which is performed by the direct producers equivalent to the reproduction of the social (*not* merely biological or minimum) conditions of their existence as a class. The different modes of surplus labor appropriation designate the various types of the fundamental class process (e.g., the capitalist, slave, feudal, ancient, and communal class processes). The subsumed class process, in turn, is defined as the process of the initial distribution of previously appropriated surplus labor. It is a transfer that is made for the performance, by the corresponding subsumed class(es), of one or another condition of existence of the fundamental class process. For example, in Volumes 2 and (especially) 3 of *Capital*, Marx (1967) discusses several different classes subsumed to the capitalist

fundamental class process. In particular, he analyzes the subsumed class activities of merchants, moneylenders, and landlords, and transfers of surplus-value to them. For a more extended discussion of the concept of (fundamental and subsumed) classes as it is used here, see Resnick and Wolff (1982) as well as Feiner (1982) and Jensen (1982).

15   For a more complete definition of the ancient class process, see Weiss (1982) and Hindess and Hirst (1975, 82–90).

16   Although confusion continues to exist in the Marxist literature on economic development and socialist planning concerning the relationship between commodity production and capitalism, Marx's analysis is quite clear on this point: he noted numerous forms of noncapitalist commodity production (e.g., 1967, Vol. 2, 110). Here, his specific references are extended to include commodity production as a condition of existence of the communist fundamental class process.

17   The relevant assumption is that the relative, net-of-taxes purchase price to the ancient producers has risen, while the retail price to the consumers has remained constant, thus allowing for an increase in purchases by communist producers. An analysis of the flows of surplus labor necessary to finance the increased state subsidies of domestic foodstuffs (the difference between the producer and consumer prices) might identify additional arenas of tension and compromise. However, that analysis is not conducted here.

18   I put the following question to an economist in the Cuban central planning agency (JUCEPLAN): "What contribution does Marxist theory make to the planning of a socialist economy?" To which the reply was, "The distinction between the productive and unproductive spheres of the national economy."

19   The subsequent discussion in the text theorizes all incomes as flows of value. Therefore, it assumes that the circulation of commodities is a condition of existence of all fundamental class processes and that all of the class-specific income flows are commensurable on the basis of Marx's notion of abstract labor (see Marx, 1967, Vol. 1, 37–46 and passim). In other words, incorporating various class incomes into a single equation involves a particular abstraction from the specific class nature of those incomes. The theoretical condition of existence of this abstraction is that each income is assumed to be the equivalent of a particular quantity of abstract labor.

20   Baranov *et al.* (1981) use a notion of regional income as one of the objective functions to be maximized in a multistage system of optimal planning.

3 Planning and class in transitional societies

Socialist planners currently face a bewildering assortment of planning theories from which to choose. General models (material balances, input–output, optimal planning, etc.) and specific techniques (iterative aggregation, dynamic input–output, stochastic programming, etc.) proliferate, both in the literature and in practice. However, the discussion of the appropriate criteria for choosing between alternative approaches has been largely silent on one crucial dimension: the likely social implications of these various approaches for transitional societies.

This paper attempts to deal with the too-often neglected issue that different theories of planning have significantly different consequences for the societies in which planning takes place. In particular, it is demonstrated below that a theory of socialist planning such as optimal planning (OP) theory, with its emphasis on technique and output maximization, approaches the crucial issues of planning in transitional societies in a manner quite distinct from one that begins with class and focuses on the class transformation of socialism. In addition, this analysis suggests the rather important result that a supposed socialist objective of fostering a transition to communism may be undermined by a kind of socialist planning ostensibly dedicated to that transition. The conclusions may well be relevant in evaluating the historical planning experiences of the USSR in the 1920s, Cuba in the 1970s, and China, Poland, and Nicaragua in the 1980s.

The first section of this paper details the logical inconsistency inherent in OP theory, which focuses on technique to the general exclusion of the class aspects of transitional societies. It is then demonstrated that this inconsistency introduces a serious measurement error into socialist planning. A further section analyzes some of the probable social consequences of the optimal planners' "technicist" approach to planning in transitional societies and a short concluding section presents some of the general implications of alternative approaches to socialist planning.

Output maximization vs class transformation

The theoretical origins of OP theory in the work of Kantorovich (1965) and the procedures and results of the later optimal planners in the USSR and elsewhere have been extensively documented.[1] Some of the specific limitations of OP theory have also been duly noted. For example, the more perceptive commentators have observed the tendency of the optimal planners to equate socialist planning with the appropriate calculating procedure – in particular, with a problem of mathematical programming – and thus to "forget about" the other dimensions of planning. Nove has remarked that "[i]t is important to emphasize that the planners, or the State cannot be treated as a single unit with uniform goals and identical interests" (1968, 286). In a similar vein, Ames has noted the bias toward seeing the Central Planning Board – the center – as an "indivisible atom" (1971, 437). Ellman has summarized his own extensive analysis of OP theory in the following manner: "Experience has shown that the process of plan implementation is not a harmonious socially rational process for the attainment of pre-determined goals" (1979, 79).

From among the ranks of the optimal planners themselves, Kornai has criticized the one-dimensional conception of planning associated with OP theory. In contrast, he has gestured toward an alternative conception based on the notion that "[i]n planning interests conflict and compromises are born according to the prevailing political power relations" (1975, 427).

All of these comments display a marked critical sensitivity to the tendency of the optimal planners to make socialist planning a neutral technique. In this sense, they leave open the option of assessing the contrasting social consequences of different approaches to planning. However, they are ultimately unsuccessful in analyzing the effects of, and formulating an alternative to, the optimal planners' choice of technique as the "entry point" of OP theory. They fail to see that technique becomes the central organizing concept of OP theory, the key concept in and through which the optimal planners theorize the various processes and consequences of socialist planning. Technique, however, turns out to be only one of a wide variety of possible entry points into planning. In particular, for the purposes of socialist planning, the implications of this choice of technique for the logical consistency and social consequences of socialist planning can be demonstrated by counterposing to it the use of class as the entry point in an alternative approach.

To say that the optimal planners enter their analysis of socialist planning through the concept technique is to make a statement that summarizes various aspects of OP theory. It emphasizes the optimal planners' definition of socialist planning as a purely technical problem: one that lends itself to a purely technical solution. It serves to point out that the optimal planners understand optimal socialist planning as the correct technical answer to a technically posed question. The end result is that socialist planning, in OP theory, is understood to be governed by the application of a technique – mathematical programming – to a given, technically defined problem: the maximization of output.[2]

This "technicist" conception of planning deliberately suggests the importance of a particular interpretation of technology in the analysis of social reality. A conventional understanding of technology is that it is an extrasocial phenomenon, a set of mechanisms that intercedes *between* society and nature while remaining external to both. It is conceived as a means of transforming nature for the benefit of society. In that sense, it may have a purpose that is socially defined but its particular form is understood to be determined by the natural laws that govern the transformation of the natural object into a socially useful object. Technology is the sole domain of the engineer, who intervenes in the realm of nature by applying knowledge of the natural sciences. Thus, technology is understood to operate in a space which is defined by the purely technical prerequisites of given, extrasocial elements.

To say that OP theory is characterized by a technicist conception of socialist planning means that planning is conceived as a technology in the above sense. The practice of planning is theorized as a formal mechanism – a methodology or routine – for achieving a given goal. It occupies the space between the socially defined goal and the given object – the elements of the system to be planned. The application of the planning technology serves as the means to achieve *in actu* the goal that the "collective ownership of the means of production" achieves *in potentia*. Hence, the optimal planners tend to emphasize a methodology of optimization or the technical procedures of optimal calculations.

The result of such an approach is that priority is given to the concept of technique. The point is not that OP theory was not originally a possible solution to a limited set of technically defined problems of production scheduling. Nor is it that planning theory should not concern itself with the use and further elaboration of quantitative techniques and mathematical models. Rather, in utilizing the concept of technique as its entry point, OP theory "sees" the problem of planning as a particular technical problem which requires, for its solution, the application of the correct technique.

The role of the concept technique as the entry point of OP theory naturally has effects at the level of its operational concepts – the concepts in and through which optimal plans are formulated and calculated. To turn to the traditional canonical representation as a linear program, the coefficients of that problem are generally taken to be the direct representation of technological data and linkages.

Consider the following typical problem: variables x^t and y^t should be chosen so as to

Primal	*Dual*
Max $c^t x^t$	Min $y^t b^t$
subject to $A^t x^t \leq b^t$	subject to $y^t A^t \geq c^t$
$x^t \geq 0$	$y^t \geq 0$

With the possible exception of the coefficients of the primal objective function (c^t), the elements of the remaining vector and matrix (b^t and A^t) are considered to be given to the planners by the technical conditions of the problem at hand. It is not surprising, then, that the manipulation of those data is considered to be a purely technical solution in the form of plan indicators, which correspond to the given planning problem. The methods and procedures of optimal planning acquire the omnipotence of technology in the face of the technical problem of planning. In this sense, technology and technique become too much like religious symbols of the planners.

An alternative interpretation is to consider such coefficients as theoretical objects. What does this mean? Viewed as concepts, rather than as immediately given "facts" or direct representations of technical relationships as in OP theory, the coefficients of linear programming and other planning models can be seen as the products of particular models of theorizing. The relevant coefficients, then, would presumably vary across different theoretical frameworks. For example, coefficients that appear in one planning model, produced in and through one framework of analysis, might not appear in other models. Similarly, the elements of the various matrices and vectors of the linear programs would contain different numbers as a result of being measured according to different conceptual frameworks. Those coefficients would be transformed – indeed, they would only exist – according to the concepts and conceptual frameworks through which such measurements are carried out. They would depend, in particular, on the entry point of the theory in which they are produced and manipulated. According to this alternative view, the coefficients of any and all planning models are subject to different, inherently theoretical determinations.

One of the possible results of the optimal planners' tendency to conceive of socialist planning in technical terms is an inclination to import what are considered to be similarly technical notions and procedures from other, essentially capitalist, societies. This tendency to introduce "neutral," "universal" technologies into transitional societies may occur in economic planning, as well as in such diverse areas as medicine, the natural sciences, police control, warfare, the organization of the labor process, and the administration of enterprises. Instead of examining the implicit social effects of these "technologies" and transforming them so that they are more consistent with the social conditions and goals of socialism, a technicist conception of socialist planning, and of socialism in general, may prove to be an obstacle to the emergence and development of the social conditions of communism.

Aggregation and class

An additional effect of this focus on technique is that a logical inconsistency is introduced into socialist planning theory. Although there are certainly many parts to its definition, building socialism presumably includes, at a minimum, a particular way of addressing class issues and of promoting the transition to a different, communist class structure. However, the use of technique as the entry point of the OP theory of socialist planning displaces class as an object of analysis. The optimal planners do not begin with class; hence, they do not seek to elaborate a class knowledge of planning or of the class effects of that activity on the society in which socialist planning takes place. In addition, the class aspects of transitional societies tend to be neglected, even as OP theory focuses on the maximization of the production of use-values or output. Class is neither a starting point nor a secondary concern in OP theory. The concept of class is generally absent in the work of the optimal planners.[3]

Let us now consider an example that will illustrate the problems associated with the use of technique as entry point and the absence of class in the operational concepts of approaches to socialist planning such as OP theory. The procedure employed will be to show that this exclusion of class and the focus on technique are tantamount to introducing a serious measurement error.

The basic problem facing the optimal planners is to determine the (non-negative) vector of optimal activity levels that maximizes national product, subject to the given resource constraints. The primal problem is as stated above (but the time superscripts have been dropped for convenience):

Max cx

subject to $Ax \leq b$

$x \geq 0$

Let us assume that the economy is divided into two sectors (or industries), food (F) and manufacturing (M). Let the matrix of input–output coefficients A^{OP} have two columns and three rows, representing the flows of the three given resources (including labor, L) per unit output of the two sectors:

$$A^{OP} = \begin{bmatrix} a_{LM} & a_{LF} \\ a_{MM} & a_{MF} \\ a_{FM} & a_{FF} \end{bmatrix}$$

The other elements of the program are defined in a corresponding fashion: c, the row vector of weights or prices attached to the output of the two sectors; x, the column vector of activity levels of the two sectors; and b, the column vector of given quantities of food, manufactures, and labor available as inputs.[4] There are therefore two decision variables – the sectoral activity levels x_M and x_F. The solution vector $x^* = (x_M^*, x_F^*)$ is the optimal plan, in the sense that it maximizes the national product (the objective function cx) subject to the requirement that, for each single resource, no more of it can be used than the existing quantity. As is well-known, the solution to the dual problem gives the shadow prices of the constraints; it indicates the degree to which the elements of the resource vector "bind" the optimal solution.

The basic model of the optimal planners appears to be straightforward. Yet, as is fairly obvious, the solution is only optimal relative to the coefficients and parameters of the problem as specified. For example, so-called measurement errors will lead to a mis-specified system of equations and, hence, to less than optimal solutions. One of the major problems of the OP model is its sensitivity to such errors, introduced through aggregation procedures. What I demonstrate is that the model with which the optimal planners work tends to be subject to such errors because it may aggregate the different class-specific activities we assume to exist within the various economic sectors. In other words, in a society characterized by different class structures – a given to all socialists – the neglect of such class information by planners leads to a less-than-optimal solution.

To see this, consider the following specification of the model which is assumed to underlie the above OP problem. The economy remains divided into the two sectors: food and manufacturing. Each sector, however, comprises two different production activities, designated here by their distinct component class processes. That is, the production of use-values is seen to include different processes of surplus-labor appropriation. Suppose, by way of illustration, that each sector involves both the appropriation of surplus-value by capitalists from productive laborers and the appropriation of surplus labor by independent producers from themselves. Following the Marxian tradition, let us call the former *capitalist* and the latter *ancient*.[5] Such activities can be translated into the linear programming framework of the preceding discussion by adjoining the coefficient vectors representing the class-specific methods of production in each sector. A (5×4) matrix of input–output coefficients A^C is obtained where

$$A^C = \{a_{ij}\} \quad i = 0, 1, \ldots, 4; j = 1, 2, \ldots, 4;$$

and $0 = $ labor;

$1 = $ C/M, capitalist manufacturing;

$2 = $ A/M, ancient manufacturing;

$3 = $ C/F, capitalist food production;

$4 = $ A/F, ancient food production.

Each coefficient in A^C represents the flows of the given resources, now five (including L), per unit output of the class-specific activities. For example, the element $a_{A/M,C/F}$ measures the requirements of manufactured goods from the ancient activity by capitalist food production. Another coefficient, $a_{C/M,A/F}$, represents the flows of capitalist manufactures to ancient food production.

If the linear programming problem were reformulated to include A^C, the remaining vectors would be redefined in a corresponding manner: c would become a row vector of four class-specific coefficients of the objective function; x, a column vector of four class-defined activity levels; and b, a column vector including L and four other resources, one from each sectoral activity. There would also be four decision variables ($x_{C/M}$, $x_{A/M}$, $x_{C/F}$, $x_{A/F}$), one for each class-specific sectoral activity. Therefore, the optimal plan, $x^* = (x^*_{C/M}, x^*_{A/M}, x^*_{C/F}, x^*_{A/F})$, would itself be redefined in the class-theoretic terms of the four activities. The new optimal plan would give the planners information concerning the class structure of the social formation and allow them to intervene explicitly to move that class structure in the desired direction.

Given the assumed existence of this underlying class-theoretic model, the first OP problem cannot be interpreted as merely a less detailed formulation. Indeed, the basic model of the optimal planners abstracts from the class-specific activities in each sector and also falls victim to all of the pitfalls of aggregating them. What allows – perhaps even compels – the optimal planners to aggregate the class-specific planning problem of A^C into the classless problem of A^{OP} is their use of technique as entry point.

According to the alternative conception of socialist planning proposed here, the (5×4) matrix of coefficients A^C can *never* be collapsed into the (3×2) matrix A^{OP}. To do so is to forfeit crucial information concerning the class nature of the transitional society. More importantly, abstracting from class will run the risk of undermining the socialist goal of transforming the class structure of that socialist society.

It is possible, of course, to consolidate A^C into A^{OP} by the appropriate rules of aggregation.[6] However, that technical procedure is beset by three major types of problems: proportionality and weighting considerations, the loss of information, and planning policy.

First, such aggregation requires both the proportionality of the columns and rows of the relevant blocks of the underlying matrix and knowledge of the weights attached to the class processes in each sector. For example, one possible formula for calculating the input–output coefficient of manufacturing goods to agriculture is

$$a_{MF} = w_3(a_{C/M,C/F} + a_{A/M,C/F}) + w_4(a_{C/M,A/F} + a_{A/M,A/F})$$

where $w_3 = x_{C/F}/x_F$ (the share of the capitalist activity in total food production) and $w_4 = x_{A/F}/x_F$ (the share of the ancient activity in total food production). The coefficient $a_{M/F}$ is valid only on condition that:

1   the separate coefficients of which it is a weighted average are nearly
    equal in value; and
2   the weights $(w_1, \ldots, w_4)$ themselves are relatively constant (or, failing
    this, at least not correlated with the class coefficients).

In other words, it must be assumed both that each class structural activity
has similar input needs and that the output of each of these activities is
required in the same proportion by the other activities.

However, the production of agricultural goods within activities that
include capitalist and ancient class processes cannot be expected to "look"
the same (i.e., to be represented by similar vectors of input–output coefficients). Each production activity includes a specific class process. Each one
of these class processes is, in turn, influenced and conditioned by all of the
remaining class and nonclass (economic, political, and cultural) aspects of
the society in question. Each class-specific coefficient of the planning
problem represents the different aspects of the range of government decisions and institutions in the wider society. Thus, although these activities
may be said to produce similar use-values, their class-specific inputs and
outputs are fundamentally distinct. They are produced under different
social conditions, and their production has similarly different social
effects. Because of this, their coefficients are not merely numbers that can
be mathematically manipulated by abstracting from the class-specific
nature of the activities. Similarly, the use of the intrasectoral weights
$(w_1, \ldots, w_4)$ to form A^{OP} presupposes exactly what the underlying problem
seeks to determine – namely, the level of participation of the two different
production activities in the gross output of each of the two sectors. Thus,
even if the underlying class coefficients remain unchanged, the nonclass
matrix A^{OP} would vary, based on the results from the optimization of the
unaggregated class-theoretic problem. In general, then, the de facto aggre-
gation of A^{C} into A^{OP} by the optimal planners cannot be said to conform to
the necessary conditions. Because of the resulting mis-specification, the
use of A^{OP} is likely to lead to solutions which are quite different from those
of the class-theoretic model.

Second, the use of A^{OP} represents a loss of crucial data for the purposes
of socialist planning. Class-theoretic information cannot be used directly
as an input into the model, nor is such information forthcoming from the
model, either to be incorporated into the plan or as input into other deci-
sion-making activities. In contrast, the use of a model based on A^{C} allows
for the use of class-specific coefficients in the objective function and class-
specific constraints. For example, the respective coefficients of the activities in the objective function can be specified with the goal of changing the
existing social weights attached to the outputs of the class-specific production activities. It is possible to use the constraints to either fix the capacity
limit or to shift additional resources to one or another of the class-defined
activities. It may even be beneficial in a particular situation to lower the

value of the objective function by constraining one of those activities. In other words, it becomes possible to explicitly incorporate various objectives concerning the transformation of the class structure of the society into the planning problem.

The solution to the primal problem of the model based on A^C gives the optimal level of each one of the class-specific activities, while the solution to the dual problem represents the shadow prices of each of the class-specific constraints. The latter variables provide the necessary information for a class-theoretic sensitivity analysis (i.e., an analysis of the effects on the optimal solution of changes in the coefficients and constraints of the problem). In addition, then, the disappearance of classes from the OP model suggests that the optimal planners work with a severely reduced, classless body of information.

Third, and most importantly, the optimal policy associated with the results of calculating the optimal plan on the basis of A^{OP} instead of A^C may have effects that undermine the goals of that planning. Although the OP model is silent about class – and thus no class-defined activity will be specifically included or excluded from the plan – the optimal *policy* based on that plan must, in fact, discriminate against one class process in favor of another. For example, the utilization of the shadow prices calculated from the dual program of the OP model may undermine the conditions of existence of capitalist agriculture in favor of ancient food production. The combined effect of the various elements of the optimal plan would be likely to provide varying degrees of subvention and restriction of the class processes of the society in question. The result would be to change the social existence of those class processes by applying a nominally classless policy. Indeed, one consequence of the nonclass optimal plan may be to undermine the goal of achieving socialism by creating the conditions leading to the demise of the very class process with which that goal is associated.

The model of output maximization used by the optimal planners, then, may be the aggregated form of an underlying class problem. The argument here is not, however, that the optimal planners "see" classes and then eliminate them from their model. This is the point: *their mathematics allows them to disregard class from the outset*. OP theory produces its account of the planned socialist economy by constructing a model in which classes disappear. The very theoretical condition of existence of that aggregation is, in fact, the nonclass entry point of technique that characterizes the work of the optimal planners.

Social consequences[7]

Let us consider an extension of our previous example to illustrate some of the social consequences that may result from a "technicist" approach, such as that of the optimal planners.

As before, in any specific society in which such planning takes place, different class processes may be present. The society would then comprise different class structures. Consider, for example, a socialist society in which some production activities are carried out on the basis of the appropriation of surplus labor by independent producers from themselves, and some on the basis of the communal appropriation of surplus labor. Let us call the former, as before, "ancient"; the latter is given the name "communist" in the Marxian tradition. This communist class process is one in which the collectivity of performers of surplus labor also always forms part of the collectivity of appropriators of that surplus labor.[8]

For brevity's sake, the diverse economic, political, and cultural processes that combine to influence, and otherwise complexly determine, the existence of these two class processes are not specified. However, two of these conditions of existence that are common to the communist and ancient class processes (namely, forms of commodity production and planning) deserve some discussion. Communist and ancient commodities are, of course, different since they are produced within different class-structural activities.[9] Direct producers in the two class processes produce these different commodities, which, in turn, are assumed to be exchanged through a state distribution agency according to prices stipulated in the national plan.[10]

An additional simplifying assumption is that this society is characterized by a particular, historically determined social division of labor in which the communist class process produces only or mainly manufactured goods, while the ancient class process is located primarily in agriculture. One such example is where manufactured items for domestic use are communist commodities and ancient commodities take the form of domestic foodstuffs and export crops (which require foreign exchange for the required purchase of noncompetitive imports for communist manufacturing).[11] Although there is no need to indicate the relative predominance of one class process over another in this case, one index of the complex relationship between the communist and ancient class processes under the present assumption is given by the internal terms of trade between communist manufacturing and ancient agriculture, $P = P_M/P_F^D$ (where P_M represents the price of manufactures; P_F^D, the price of domestic foodstuffs). These terms of trade indicate the extent to which one of the conditions of existence of both the communist and ancient modes of surplus labor appropriation – the realization of exchange-value through commodity circulation – is being, or is failing to be, favorably secured. Therefore, P is one of the indices of the numerous factors influencing the reproduction over time of the two class processes in the present example.

Both fundamental classes of ancient and communist producers must, in addition, distribute shares of their appropriated surplus labor to secure their various conditions of existence provided by, what have been called elsewhere, their respective "subsumed classes."[12] Planners, state merchants and bankers, and political party officials, among others, receive such transfers of surplus labor for providing some of the specific economic, political, and cultural conditions of existence of the ancient and communist modes of surplus labor appropriation. They therefore occupy ancient and/or communist subsumed class positions, depending on whether their received share of surplus labor is from the ancient and/or communist class processes.

Assume now that the optimal planners formulate an optimization problem (which does *not* include class variables in its framework) in which the objective function is to maximize domestic consumption of both food and manufactures. Suppose that a price reform is decided in this plan. In particular, a new set of relative (shadow) prices occurs, in which the internal terms of trade, P, fall. Since this country is also assumed to be a relatively small exporter of agricultural goods, the price of its exports remains approximately equal to the unchanged world price. The new state-enforced domestic terms of trade might then lead ancient food producers to substitute the production of more profitable domestic food-stuffs for export crops.

One result of maximizing consumption and implementing the new prices would be a rise in the level of consumption, as communist producers purchase more of the previously scarce state-subsidized food products, which would give the desired effect.[13] However, an additional and unexpected outcome might be either:

1   a decline in the level of purchases of imported inputs for communist manufacturing production, due to the new shortage of foreign exchange created by the movement of ancient producers out of export production, or
2   the acquisition of foreign loans to finance the existing level of required imports.

The implications of these unplanned effects vis-à-vis the class and nonclass processes of the society in question need to be further investigated.

In the former case, the created lack of imported spare parts might produce a decline in the level of labor productivity in manufacturing. In turn, the lower level of productivity might generate the conditions in which there is an increase in the rate of communal surplus labor appropriation to maintain the existing rate of, say, communist accumulation. In this case, Taylorism and other forms of "scientific management" might be borrowed from other societies and introduced by the subsumed class of enterprise managers to boost the productivity of communist producers. Alternatively, the distribution of surplus labor to other subsumed classes could be reduced to maintain the rate of accumulation in communist manufacturing. If, instead, external loans are contracted, a class of foreign bankers might become subsumed to the communist class process, requiring subsumed class interest payments of communal surplus labor to them.

As a result, new sets of alliances among communist workers, ancient producers, and the subsumed class of planners might arise. For example, the direct producers in the communist and ancient class processes might form an alliance because the level of consumption of the communist workers has been favorably affected by the price-induced decision of ancient producers to switch to domestic food production. At the same time, the improvement in the conditions of ancient commodity production through the price reform would perhaps serve as the basis for an alliance between ancient producers and optimal planners.

However, new tensions between the communist workers and the subsumed classes of planners, bankers, and/or enterprise managers might also emerge. The focus of these tensions would be the perceived relationship between, on one hand, the planned price reform and the new subsumed class interest payments to bankers and, on the other hand, changes in the labor process and expectations of a decline in future, as opposed to present, consumption. Communist producers might form an alliance among themselves and with other social classes to seek improvements at the expense of subsumed class payments to planners, bankers, and managers. An alternative possibility would be a coalition among a subset of these four classes, with the aim of maintaining the existing rate of communist accumulation and reducing subsumed class payments to other claimants on communally appropriated surplus labor.

Some of these tensions might develop into complex class struggles over the quantitative and qualitative dimensions of the appropriation and distribution of both types of surplus labor. Occupants of the different class positions could be found on various sides: some of the communist producers might combine with the ancient producers and the subsumed class of foreign hankers who, as a condition of granting new loans or rescheduling debt servicing, could demand that ancient commodity production be reinforced; an opposing alliance between the other communist producers and the planners might form around the proposal to extend the communist class process into agricultural production at the expense of the ancient class process. A different class struggle might ensue and different set of alliances be engendered over communist manufacturing: communist producers might be joined by the ancient producers, along with some of the planners, to resist increases in the rate of communal surplus labor appropriation. It is quite possible that the other planners, enterprise managers, and foreign bankers would support increases in the rate of communal surplus labor appropriation to maintain the existing rate of communist accumulation and to allow for subsumed class interest payments. An alternative is that these various fundamental and subsumed classes might form an alliance to struggle to decrease the distribution of communal surplus labor to subsumed classes other than planners, managers, and bankers – for instance, to members of a particular political party occupying positions in the state.

Similarly, nonclass struggles might also emerge over nonclass aspects of the transitional society, for example, over concepts of national sovereignty, property rights, and religious practices. State administrators and political party officials could be accused of sacrificing a "national interest" to the demands of foreign bankers, or a threat of foreign intervention could be used to enforce a compromise among the various contending classes. Ancient producers might demand economic and political guarantees for the maintenance of private property on land designated for agricultural production. Communist producers, from their position as subsumed class owners of the means of production, might challenge the authority of enterprise managers in directing the use of those means of production. Finally, religious ideas concerning human needs or forms of property ownership, along with the institutional position of the church in activities such as education, might become the nonclass objects of struggle of the various occupants of the different class positions.

The preceding analysis suggests the significant conclusion that the planning activity itself would be a changed site of the conflicting demands by, among others, the occupants of the fundamental class positions of communist and ancient producers and those who occupy the subsumed class positions of planners, bankers, and enterprise managers. The social activity of planning might be called upon to provide the effects that secure some of the economic and noneconomic conditions of existence of the communist and ancient modes of surplus labor appropriation. Suppose, for example, that the planned terms of trade (P) become the focus of the changed interaction among the classes of the transitional society. Ancient producers, along with their class allies, might demand further movement of the domestic terms of trade in their favor. The opposite demand might be made by some communist producers and enterprise managers subsumed to the communist class process.

Alternatively, the degree of centralization of planning decisions might be called into question. The degree of centralization is defined here as the extent to which the activity of planning has access to subsumed class revenues by virtue of its location within the state. Thus, decentralization proposals to promote, for example, the increased autonomy of both communist and ancient commodity-producing enterprises might threaten to transfer some processes that make up the planning activity from the state to other social sites within the society. Complicating such tensions might be the planners' own attempts to oppose any changes that threaten to decrease the flows of subsumed class income to them. In particular, the planners might resist the transition from participating in a subsumed class process in the state to occupying a nonclass position, still as planners, in the state or in a different social site. The activity of planning may he shifted to manufacturing enterprises or farms, or it may be done away with altogether.

Conclusions

In the preceding section, I discussed some of the probable social effects of the optimal planners' nonclass approach to planning. In contrast, a theory of planning that begins with class and focuses on the contradictory class (and nonclass) effects of planning would seek to analyze the class (and nonclass) implications of any attempt to maximize the level of domestic consumption and to implement such a price reform. The degree of complexity of such analysis is not the issue. My alternative theory is distinguished from that of the optimal planners, not on the basis of any intrinsic analytical complexity, but rather in terms of the specific concepts and conceptual strategies with which the analysis of planning is conducted. Most importantly, these two different theories of planning can be juxtaposed on the basis of their likely social consequences.

The alternative conception of planning proposed here begins where OP theory tends to leave off, with the issue of class. In a manner that is probably consistent with the stated objective of the optimal planners, the methods and outcomes of socialist planning are considered from the perspective of achieving at least one supposed socialist goal: the emergence and development of the conditions of existence of the communist class process. It follows, then, that socialist planning procedures would have to explicitly address the outcomes of the planning activity on the class structure of the transitional society in question. It is doubtful that an approach to planning that seeks merely to maximize output or consumption, given inputs, can affect the class structure and the general movement of the transition in the desired direction.

According to this alternative, class-analytic planning theory, the concrete measures stipulated in the plan are conceived from the outset to have contradictory effects vis-à-vis the conditions of existence of the fundamental and subsumed class processes. In particular, it is recognized that any planned policy must discriminate against one or another fundamental class process in favor of the others. Thus, each price reform, wage policy, or decision to construct a factory in a specific region can be analyzed in terms of its complex class effects. The task of the planners would be to investigate the differing degrees of support or constriction that the plan provides to the existing class processes, and any others that emerge or cease to exist as a result.

For example, the "decollectivization" campaign in China, in existence since 1978, which is intended to raise the growth of agricultural output and farmers' personal income, appears to have been accompanied by movement away from the communal appropriation of surplus labor and by the fostering of the conditions of existence of the ancient class process in the form of "companies" and "economic associations."[14] In a similar vein, planning within the Nicaraguan "mixed economy" has had the explicit objective of reaching and surpassing pre-insurrection levels of efficiency and production. While relatively successful according to those criteria, the concrete planning measures undertaken by the Sandinista government also appear to have had the effect of reinforcing, at least in the short run, the extraction of surplus-value from productive laborers in both the state and private sectors.[15]

The relevant questions are the following: what are the different class consequences of alternative approaches to socialist planning, and what effects do these class consequences of planning have on the socialist objective of producing a transition to communism? These class-analytic questions are barred from the outset in theories of planning such as OP theory.

There is no reason, of course, to assume that a different, class-theoretic approach to planning would necessarily generate the "correct" set of alliances or conflicts among the contending classes of the transitional society. It would, however, produce a particular class knowledge of the planned society – an analysis of the social conditions within which each of the fundamental and subsumed class processes changes and develops. Thus, it would provide the theoretical basis of the planners' interventions to promote one or another of those class processes.

The practitioners of OP theory and related planning theories operate with a different conception of planning, one that begins with technique and abstracts from classes and the contradictory class and nonclass consequences of the goals and procedures of planning. Such planning theories may, in turn, foster the conditions of the very conflicts, alliances, and struggles sketched above. Furthermore, and most importantly, the emergence of such tensions and conflicts may undermine the social existence of the communist class process itself. Indeed, a classless conception of socialist planning may make possible the transition to a society in which communism is even further from becoming socially predominant. This is a negation of the very objective of a socialist society and socialist planning.

(original version published 1986)

Acknowledgements

I am grateful to Stephen Resnick, Richard Wolff, and Frederic Curtis for comments on an earlier version of this paper. The responsibility for the final result is, of course, my own.

Notes

1   The historical development and present state of OP theory are discussed in Ruccio (1984a). Swann (1975) is a useful introduction to the work of the optimal planners; a more complete treatment can be found in Ellman (1973).

2 More accurately, the technical problem of socialist planning may be defined in the OP literature as the maximization of total output at a point in time or over time, of output per capita or total consumption, or any one of a wide variety of such objective functions. The point is that the goal of socialist planning is usually considered to be the technical production of use-values.

3 There is, however, one exception. The last published article by Nemchinov (1965) does reflect at least a minimal concern with a notion of class. Moreover, his treatment is instructive: it exemplifies the fundamentally different and relatively unimportant status of class in OP theory, compared to the alternative conception of socialist planning advanced below. Unfortunately, space limitations preclude an analysis of his model.

4 This basic model can obviously be generalized and otherwise expanded to include a large number of more detailed considerations. For example, final demand and capacity constraints could be introduced. Similarly, the number of sectors and resource constraints could be increased. However, as will become clear below, such modifications would not alter the basic argument presented in the text.

5 For a definition and more complete discussion of the "capitalist fundamental class process," see Resnick and Wolff (1982); for the "ancient fundamental class process," see Weiss (1982) and Hindess and Hirst (1975, 82–90).

6 For example, as discussed by Dorfman, Samuelson, and Solow (1958, 240–43).

7 This section is a considerably revised and expanded version of the example presented in Chapter 2.

8 This communist class process is expressly not construed here as merely the "collective ownership of the means of production." That form of ownership may well be part of the institutional setting of the communal appropriation of surplus labor. However, it may also condition the existence of other, noncommunist class processes, including the capitalist extraction of surplus-value. The existence of the political condition "collective ownership" does not guarantee the existence of the class process of communal surplus labor appropriation.

9 Although much of the Marxian literature on both socialist planning and economic development continues to conflate commodity production and capitalism, such that the existence of commodity production more or less automatically implies the existence of capitalism, Marx's analysis is quite clear on this point. He analyzes the production of commodities as one of the many conditions of existence of, rather than equivalent to, the capitalist class process. Indeed, he noted numerous forms of *noncapitalist* commodity production (e.g., *Capital*, Volume 2, 110). Here, his specific references are extended to include commodity production as a condition of existence of the communist class process. That is, commodity production may condition the existence of the communal appropriation of surplus labor.

10 An alternative would be the case in which ancient producers sell a portion of their total production at prices set by the planners and the remainder in "free peasant markets" at unregulated prices. However, to consider such an alternative here would not significantly alter the results and would complicate the analysis unnecessarily.

11 In a "peripheral transitional economy," such as Sandinista Nicaragua, it is more likely to be the case that the ancient class process is predominant in the production of domestic foodstuffs and export agriculture involves for the most part the capitalist extraction of surplus-value. Again, treating an additional class process for the purposes of this example would make the analysis unwieldy.

12 The subsumed class process refers to the initial *distribution and receipt* of surplus labor, to secure the conditions of existence of a fundamental class

process, as distinct from the prior *performance and appropriation* of that surplus labor, which is termed a fundamental class process. Thus, individuals who occupy positions in the process of distributing and receiving surplus labor occupy subsumed class positions, and those who participate in the performance or appropriation of surplus labor occupy fundamental class positions. The concepts of fundamental and subsumed class processes were developed by Resnick and Wolff (1982), based on Marx's analysis in *Capital*. For example, Marx clearly distinguished the fundamental class position of "industrial capitalist," involving the extraction of surplus-value through exploitation, from the subsumed class positions of "merchant capitalist" and "finance capitalist," who receive distributions of surplus-value once it has been extracted.

13 The relevant assumption is that the relative, net-of-taxes purchase price to the ancient producers has risen, while the retail price to the consumers has remained constant, thus allowing for an increase in purchases by communist producers. A class analysis of the flow of revenue necessary to finance the increased state subsidies (the difference between the producer and consumer prices) might identify areas of tension and compromise in addition to those discussed below. However, that analysis is not conducted here.

14 These are the changes in the Chinese class structure that can be derived from the analysis of the post-1978 policies by, for example, Nolan (1983).

15 Ruccio (1987). As Lenin argued in the case of the NEP (New Economic Policy) in the USSR, it may be necessary to strengthen capitalism in the short run to create some of the conditions for the transition to communism in the longer term.

4 The state and planning in Nicaragua

Most theories of transitional or socialist societies make the state the primary feature of such societies. This focus on the state usually means that something called "public" or "state ownership of the means of production" and "state economic planning" are made the defining characteristics of transitional economies. The fundamental theme of these approaches is the rather simple juxtaposition of market-oriented and planned economies.[1]

This emphasis on the essential role of the state is as true in the case of Nicaragua as elsewhere. For example, the transitional project of the Sandinista National Liberation Front (FSLN) is often summarized as the construction of a new state to guarantee the interests of the "majority." In addition, much of the literature on the Nicaraguan economy concentrates on changes in the relative quantitative weight of the state and private sectors since 1979. A standard question in this literature is whether or not the Nicaraguan "mixed economy" is inherently unstable and/or doomed to failure.[2]

The role of the state and planning in Nicaragua since 1979 is also the focus of the present chapter. However, the approach adopted here constitutes a departure from previous analyses by avoiding two major errors. First, the Nicaraguan transition is not reduced to the mere existence of enhanced state ownership of the means of production. The changes in property ownership since 1979 certainly mark a more or less sharp departure from the period of the Somoza regime; however, such changes constitute only some of the elements conditioning the existence of a transitional project in Nicaragua. Second, the sterile juxtaposition of the market and planning as alternative allocative mechanisms is rejected in favor of a perspective that emphasizes the existence of different kinds and theories of socialist planning and the contrasting social effects of different approaches to such planning.[3]

In sum, it cannot merely be assumed that a shift toward state property ownership and the existence of economic planning are equivalent to a socialist transition. Such changes may participate in creating some of the necessary transitional conditions; they may, however, have the opposite effect, reproducing the preexisting class structure and even undermining the transitional project. Therefore, the transfer of property ownership and the activity of state planning must be analyzed in terms of the contradictory effects they have on the emergence and strengthening of transitional elements in situations such as the Sandinista Revolution in Nicaragua.

The remainder of this chapter examines some of the ways in which the state and planning have participated in shaping the Nicaraguan transition during the 1979–85 period. The first section analyzes some of the major changes in the role of the state in Nicaraguan political economy under the Sandinistas. The second section focuses on the early attempts at planning in revolutionary Nicaragua. The third section lays out some of the contradictory effects of the Nicaraguan state conceived to be the "center of accumulation." A short concluding section analyzes the most recent planning efforts and presents the specific implications of my analysis of the state and planning in Nicaragua.

State and economy in Nicaragua

It would appear that any far-reaching set of social reforms, such as those called forth by the FSLN-led movement against the Somoza regime, requires an extensive restructuring of the state. No simple change of president or ministers is sufficient in that context. This restructuring is necessary because, on one hand, the state under Somoza was involved in important ways in providing some of the political, economic, and cultural conditions under which the prevailing class structure was reproduced over time. The National Guard was, of course, the most notorious institution. However, we would also have to include the effects of such diverse entities as the Supreme Court, the public education system, the Central Bank, and the Nicaraguan Coffee Institute. They, and the other institutions that comprised the state during the Somoza period, had played an important role in creating and maintaining the Nicaraguan class structure through 1979. On the other hand, the Sandinista project of reconstruction and transition implied a different set of social conditions. In this sense, it was necessary both to dismantle many of the economic, political, and cultural aspects or processes that made up the previous state and to create a different state based on a different set of such processes.[4]

In general, any such attempt to restructure the state will probably involve some combination of three different kinds of change:

1 the maintenance and expansion of some processes previously performed in the state;
2 the shifting of other social processes from nonstate "sites" or locations to the state itself; and
3 the transfer of still other social processes from the state to sites outside the state.

It also means that tensions and struggles may emerge among and between occupants of positions in the state and occupants of positions in other social sites over exactly what processes will be performed in and through the state. Both of these developments occurred from 1979 onward in the course of constructing the new Nicaraguan state.

The downfall of Somoza led to the maintenance and improvement of programs in certain areas in which the state had previously been involved. For example, public expenditures on health and education, although not unknown under the Somoza regime, expanded considerably under the Sandinistas, especially in the early years.[5] The social security system was also greatly widened, in terms of both its coverage and sponsored programs.[6] In a different vein, the National Guard was disbanded and a new army formed from the original Sandinista forces. Subsequent external aggression forced the current Nicaraguan state to increase defense spending; in 1985 this reached 40 percent of total government expenditures.[7]

One of the major themes underlying the early changes in the composition of the Nicaraguan state was, as is well known, its extension into areas previously restricted, in large measure, to private ownership. Prior to 1979, for example, the Nicaraguan state had only marginal direct participation in the production and distribution of commodities. The role of the so-called public sector was limited to a relatively low level of social services (especially health and education), utilities, internal security, specialized development banks, and the Central Bank. The total state sector (including central government and decentralized entities), in quantitative terms, directly controlled only about 15 percent of Nicaragua's GDP.

The role of the state changed considerably after the Sandinista victory (see Table 4.1). Among the first measures of the FSLN was the nationalization of most of the banking and insurance sector (excepting a few foreign banks) and the commercialization of exports. State corporations were established to administer the financial system (CORFIN, the Nicaraguan Finance Corporation, and INISER, the Nicaraguan Insurance and Reinsurance Institute), whereas the control of external trade became the responsibility of the Ministry of External Commerce (and some six exporting enterprises). The government also greatly expanded its participation in the area of construction and transportation. Therefore, within the first 6 months of taking power, the Sandinista state had extended its participation in the "service" sector far beyond the traditional public enterprises that functioned in that sector under Somoza.[8]

Apart from these government services, a number of new entities were formed in the natural resource, agriculture, and industrial sectors. For example, the state significantly increased its presence in the areas of forestry, gold and silver mining, and fishing.[9] In addition, the enterprises and other property directly owned by Somoza, and by close associates of

Table 4.1 State participation in domestic production, 1980–84 (percentage of total)

Activity/sector	1980		1981		1982		1983		1984[c]	
	APP^a	AP^b	APP^a	AP^b	APP^a	AP^b	APP^a	AP^b	APP^a	AP^b
Gross domestic product	36.2	63.8	37.1	62.9	44.2	55.8	41.2	58.8	42.7	57.3
Primary	16.7	83.3	20.3	79.7	22.2	77.8	22.0	78.0	24.4	75.6
Agriculture	17.9	82.1	20.0	80.0	21.9	78.1	20.2	79.8	24.0	76.0
Livestock	10.4	89.6	13.0	87.0	21.0	79.0	24.0	76.0	22.3	77.7
Forestry	48.6	51.4	74.4	25.6	34.9	65.1	45.8	54.2	32.9	67.1
Fishing	59.5	40.5	78.1	21.9	48.7	51.3	68.9	31.1	82.3	17.7
Secondary	38.7	61.3	39.4	60.6	42.3	57.7	43.8	56.2	43.4	56.6
Manufacturing	30.1	69.9	31.5	68.5	36.0	64.0	37.2	62.8	37.2	62.8
Construction	97.2	2.8	87.4	12.6	87.9	12.1	92.9	7.1	92.9	7.1
Mining	100.0	–	100.0	–	100.0	–	100.0	–	100.0	–
Tertiary	43.7	56.3	43.9	56.1	56.6	43.4	51.0	49.0	51.5	48.5
Commerce	30.0	70.0	30.0	70.0	45.7	64.3	32.0	68.0	32.0	68.0
General government	100.0	–	100.0	–	100.0	–	100.0	–	100.0	–
Transport and communication	12.1	87.9	14.6	85.4	66.5	43.5	58.8	41.2	58.8	41.2
Banking and insurance	100.0	–	100.0	–	100.0	–	100.0	–	100.0	–
Energy, electricity and water	100.0	–	100.0	–	100.0	–	100.0	–	100.0	–
Housing property	3.0	97.0	3.0	97.0	3.0	97.0	3.0	97.0	3.0	97.0
Other services	10.0	90.0	10.0	90.0	11.5	88.5	11.5	88.5	11.5	88.5

Source: unpublished data from the Nicaraguan Centro de Investigaciones y Estudios de la Reforma Agraria

Notes

a APP = Area of People's Property
b AP = private sector
c preliminary data

the Somoza regime who left the country after December 1977, became state property. Those holdings included some 168 factories (mainly plastics, timber, foodstuffs, building materials, paper, metal and machinery, and pharmaceuticals), making up 25 percent of the country's industrial plant, and two million acres of agricultural property that encompassed about half of the farms larger than 500 manzanas (one manzana is approximately 1.7 acres). These enterprises formed the basis of the Area of People's Property (APP). They were managed for the first 5 months by the National Reconstruction Trust Fund; they then came under the management of the People's Industrial Corporation (COIP) and the Nicaraguan Agrarian Reform Institute (INRA).

By the end of 1980, the state accounted for 18 percent of total agricultural production, 30 percent of manufacturing, 44 percent of services, and 100 percent of such sectors as mining, banking, and insurance. In all, a little more than one-third of the country's GDP in 1980 was generated within state entities. This level of participation of the state in the Nicaraguan economy has been relatively stable since then.

In addition, the past 6 years have seen the state become involved in a wide range of other activities. It has increased its participation in the storing, transport, and distribution of domestic products – through, for example, the Nicaraguan Enterprise for Basic Food Products (ENABAS). The emerging trade gap has led to strict state control over foreign exchange (with foreign exchange rationing and multiple exchange-rates) and import controls. Prices for six basic consumer items are controlled and some 50 other prices are "regulated." In the area of labor relations, the state has established (and enforced) new minimum wages and a scale for all other wages and salaries (through the Labor Ministry's National System of Ordering Work and Salaries, SNOTS), promoted labor unions and collective bargaining agreements, and, under the temporary emergency laws, prohibited strikes.[10]

This quantitative expansion of the scope of Nicaraguan state activities was accompanied by a qualitative transformation of the state. The new state comprises a different set of political, cultural, and economic processes from those of the state under Somoza. In particular, as far as the Nicaraguan class structure is concerned, the state has expanded its enactment of processes that secure the conditions (from marketing and credit to lawmaking and education) under which capitalists and others engage in production. In addition, the Nicaraguan state itself has come to occupy the position of capitalist commodity producer for both domestic and international markets.

The quantitative and qualitative restructuring of the Nicaraguan state also involves a new set of potential tensions and struggles over the range of social processes performed in and by the state. To take a noneconomic example, the cultural process of education involves not only who is taught but also what is taught. Education involves the training of potential workers as well as the dissemination of conceptions of life, work, politics, and so forth. Therefore, given the changed content of the Nicaraguan educational system since 1979, it is not surprising that capitalists and other occupants of positions in sites outside the state have struggled with occupants of positions within the state over the effects of state-sponsored education. Similar tensions and struggles have emerged over a wide range of other state initiatives, including property ownership, marketing, price setting, law enforcement, and defense.

An additional issue concerning this transformation of the Nicaraguan state (and one that is especially relevant for the question of transition) is the extent to which these social processes may lead to changes in the Nicaraguan class structure. In particular, because changes in property ownership and the expansion of state activities do not, of themselves, mean the elimination of capitalism, two further questions become relevant. Are the conditions being created whereby the state can eventually restrict and/or eliminate its own role in reproducing capitalism? Similarly, do the activities of the new state mean that the reproduction of the conditions of existence of capitalism will be restricted and/or eliminated in other, nonstate sites (private enterprises, churches, families, etc.) in Nicaraguan society?

Nicaraguan planning

Once the initial steps of restructuring the Nicaraguan state were taken, the stage was set for reactivating and transforming the Nicaraguan economy. The fact that the state had become a site where not only commodity production took place (in the APP) but also where such activities as the creation of money and money lending and the internal marketing and distribution of commodities were carried on, meant that no sector of the economy could ultimately escape its influence. The Nicaraguan economy was far from being a wholly state-run economy but the various activities that made up the new state would have far-reaching effects throughout Nicaragua; and, consciously or unconsciously, the intervention of the state must be governed or shaped by some broad view of ends to be pursued and of the effects of attempting to pursue those ends – in other words, by a general plan for the economy. State planning in Nicaragua was born out of this de facto situation.

To be clear, however, the existence of state planning does not mean that compulsory production and other targets are formulated in the planning ministry and carried out by lower-level state and nonstate entities. Economic planning in Nicaragua has never corresponded to the textbook description of the "centrally planned economy."[11] Rather, if by planning we mean the exercise of state authority to intervene in and partially regulate the economy, then a commitment to planning in official circles and concrete attempts at planning existed almost from the start.

The Ministry of Planning (MIPLAN) was one of the first ministries organized during the initial six months of Sandinista power. The conditions facing the new regime and its planners have been well-documented by FitzGerald, the World Bank, and ECLA.[12] The destruction and disruption caused by the insurrection, the inherited external debt, and the necessity of reorienting the existing model of development all called for immediate measures bound together by a global plan of action. The first meetings in MIPLAN to discuss this situation took place during July and August of 1979. Those meetings led to the first discussions concerning the "Sandinista model of development" and to studies of the various areas of the economy (the APP, the structure of agriculture, the possibility of an agrarian reform, etc.). The first general outlines of an economic program for 1980 were presented to the Junta of the Government of National Reconstruction (JGRN) and the National Directorate of the FSLN (DN-FSLN) and subsequently approved on 22 October 22 1979. After successive drafts of the more detailed program, and after the naming of Sandinista Comandante Henry Ruiz as Minister of Planning in the December 1979 reorganization of the government, the "Program of Economic Reactivation to Benefit the People" was finally approved in mid-January of 1980.[13]

Plan 80, as it came to be known, was widely disseminated throughout the country – in both its full form and in more popular versions. The general aim of Sandinista economic policy, as announced in the economic program, was the "defense, consolidation, and advance of the revolutionary process" to overcome the combination of conjunctural difficulties (for example, the financial crisis and the drop in agricultural production) and structural problems (primarily, what was considered to be the "dependent" nature of the Nicaraguan economy). The long-run objective was to "initiate the process of transition." The more specific objectives outlined in the program were fourfold:

1   to reactivate production and distribution with the aim of satisfying the "basic needs" of the population;
2   to build and maintain a level of "national unity" among various key social groups (specifically, as the program saw them, wage and salary workers, small producers and artisans, professionals and technicians and "patriotic entrepreneurs");
3   to construct the new Sandinista state (discussed in the preceding section); and
4   to establish and maintain macroeconomic and external sector balances.

The institutional context for carrying out the program would be a "mixed economy" (because of the continued existence of domestic and international markets) in which the state would be the "center" of reactivation and transition. Notwithstanding this emphasis on the role of the state, the program does make reference to the importance of production in nonstate enterprises. For example, of the total of 140,000 manzanas programmed to be devoted to coffee production, only 16 percent would be under the direct control of INRA.[14] At the same time, private investment was expected to be minimal: probable investment was expected to reach 2,700 million córdobas during 1980, with only 470 million of that total coming from capitalists and other producers in the private sphere.[15]

The full-scale reactivation of the economy was designed to be carried out over 2 years: 1978 levels of economic activity would be reached by the end of 1980, and 1981 would see the achievement of levels of the previous "normal year" – 1977. In practice, this would mean using existing excess capacity to reach an overall economic growth rate of 23 percent. In particular, services were programmed to rise to levels approximately 37 percent higher than in 1978, but "material production" would still be 9 percent less than in that year.[16]

The overall model of export-led growth was not to be fundamentally altered at this stage of development in the revolutionary process. The "differential rent" captured from the "comparative advantage" of Nicaraguan exports of agricultural goods would continue to serve as the basis of earning foreign exchange to purchase necessary imports. However, the overall balances of the program demonstrated that an "external gap" (consisting of the trade deficit, service payments, and an increase in international reserves) would remain and amount to some $370 million. This was exactly equal to the calculated need for external funds.

The final chapter of Plan 80 presented the planners' expectations of the "dynamic and tensions of reactivation." Fundamentally, it was argued that increasing incomes (especially of the poorest sections of the population) and using existing excess capacity would run up against constraints imposed by supply inelasticities in agriculture, the shortage of foreign exchange, and the fact that modifications in the composition of demand generated by a changed distribution of income would not find the corresponding supply, at least in the short term. In addition, it was acknowledged that private producers, given the wide range of political and other changes taking place, might not achieve the levels of production programmed for them.

Plan 80, then, was a document that attempted to lend coherence to the variety of state initiatives during the first full year of the Sandinista government. It was not, as argued above, a set of obligatory goals that were (or could have been) imposed on the various state and nonstate entities involved in the economic reactivation. Rather, the program outlined in Plan 80 was the product of the joint effort of hundreds of state officials, in conjunction with some representatives of mass organizations and large private capitalists, with the aim of providing an overall framework for specific policies and for analyzing the expected effects of those policies.

The implementation of the program was, of course, delayed by its late publication. Additional disruptions were caused by difficulties inside the JGRN (Junta member Alfonso Robelo finally resigned on 12 April 1980),[17] the lack of any centralized direction, and the fact that the nine proposed Coordinating Program Commissions (CPCs) never quite got off the ground. MIPLAN held its first public seminar on planning in Nicaragua in May of 1980, to take stock of this first Sandinista experience with planning and to begin the preparations for pulling together an economic program for 1981. Not surprisingly, at least from MIPLAN's perspective, the lessons drawn from the 1980 seminar (and basically repeated in its 1981 counterpart) were that ministerial "feudalism" and the lack of state discipline were at the root of the problems encountered in putting into effect the economic program for 1980.[18] These conclusions expressed MIPLAN's concern that, although entirely devoted to economic planning, it was just one among 20 other ministries and that Plan 80 was not binding on the other state entities.

Therefore, MIPLAN, although the official center for the elaboration of economic programs and other planning documents, has never enjoyed anything like a complete monopoly over planning activities, short-term or annual. This is not unlike other experiences of socialist planning.[19] MIPLAN initiated its activity of formulating plans for the year ahead in 1979, but economic policy was made throughout the year by the interministerial "economic council." Emergency economic programs, negotiations with individual capitalist enterprises, and the continual search for foreign markets and sources of external credits and loans tended to supersede the best-laid plans of prior months. In addition, independent decisions by other ministries, especially one with the weight of Agricultural Development and Agrarian Reform (MIDINRA), would change the parameters according to which the original program was drawn up.

Finally, it must be kept in mind that economic planning has never obeyed the relatively simple conception of a one-to-one correspondence between acts stipulated in the plan and the broad economic and social consequences they are so often said, at least in principle, to bring about. Economic plans, whether obligatory or not, represent only one set of proposed interventions in the economy and wider society at any point in time. The complex effects of those planned initiatives are always modified and transformed by the effects of changes in other parts of the state and in other, nonstate sites to produce the various paths of movement registered in the remainder of the economy and society. Moreover, the activity of state economic planning is, in turn, affected by those other changes.

To fully appreciate this conception, consider the following example. The attempt to centralize the activity of economic planning in one ministry and to impose the results of that activity on other state entities may lead to tensions and struggles with those other entities over the nature and scope of that particular approach to state economic planning.[20] At the same time, planned limits on wage increases may lead to a shortage of labor in the "formal" economy. Employers might respond by attempting to pay wages (in the form of money or in kind) above the official rates. These unplanned wage payments might, on one hand, upset the planned macroeconomic balances; on the other hand, the low official wages might induce the movement of labor out of the formal sector into the "informal" economy. The latter set of activities is even less amenable to state economic planning. The result of these and other factors that change and modify planned initiatives may be that the activity of planning in the state is itself reorganized. State planning may even be dismantled altogether.

In the case of Nicaragua, the tensions and struggles over economic planning within the state do not appear to have been over whether or not there would be some form of economic planning; rather, they seem to have involved the issue of who would hold the power over economic planning within the state. Thus, the activity of state economic planning did not disappear. Instead, MIPLAN was eventually replaced (in early 1985) by a Secretariat of Planning and the Budget (SPP). In formal organizational terms, the SPP is no longer a separate ministry charged with the responsibility of drafting annual plans and attempting to induce other ministries and state entities to make decisions consistent with the plans. The SPP is now considered to be a cabinet office – a technical office without ministerial rank – attached to the National Planning Board (CNP). The CNP, in turn, replaced the "economic council" and is made up of the heads of the relevant ministries organized into five basic economic areas: foreign aid, agriculture and marketing, finance, industry, and infrastructure.

The evaluation of the outcomes of the first economic program brought to the fore the difficulties experienced and the wide-ranging nature of the changes that had taken place in the first year and a half under the new Sandinista government. Not surprisingly, fulfillment of the quantitative targets stipulated in Plan 80 was uneven. The overall rate of growth of GDP, although not of the magnitude projected in the program, did reach 10 percent. Exports were lower than expected (down 24.7 percent with respect to the 1979 level) and imports rose more rapidly than projected (by some 75.8 percent over 1979), leading to a widening trade gap (24 percent of GDP) at the end of 1980. Agricultural production in 1980 was based on the area planted in 1979; thus, the disrupted 1979–80 agricultural cycle meant that production levels fell by 11.6 percent in that year. However, the area planted in 1980 for the 1980–81 cycle surpassed the programmed area. Industrial production reached 90 percent of the planned level, growing at a rate of 7.3 percent during 1980. In terms of traditional national income accounting, the results of 1980 demonstrated that economic reactivation had, in fact, taken place. However, it was also the case that this reactivation had generated widening internal and external "gaps": domestic inflation reached 27 percent (down from 1979 but far above historical rates of inflation), and foreign debt and the trade deficit were growing at alarming rates.

An overall assessment of 1980 by MIPLAN was presented in the economic program for 1981:

> Even if the economic reactivation was very dynamic, it was also uneven. In effect, it was more notable in production for domestic consumption than in export production. Similarly, it was more substantial in the countryside than in the city, and more dynamic in the APP and small-scale production than in the capitalist sector.[21]

The evaluation of the first year of the Nicaraguan "planned economy" also revealed that other changes and difficulties, not captured in the national income accounts, characterized the situation through the end of 1980. New forms of property and organization had emerged, especially in agricultural production: state capitalist farms (UPE) had been organized on INRA land, while production and credit and service cooperatives had begun to form among relatively small-scale capitalist and noncapitalist producers in the countryside.[22] These new enterprises existed side by side with traditional large-scale private capitalist farms and agroindustrial complexes. It was also noted that the process of "social differentiation" had accelerated among the other agricultural producers. That is, the smallholding "peasantry" was becoming increasingly polarized: at one pole, producers who employed wage-labor and had access to additional land by buying or renting land from others, and, at the other pole, producers who were forced to sell their labor power and rent and/or sell their land to that first group. Finally, in terms of the organization of production, "labor productivity" (defined and measured as the total value of production divided by total employees) had dropped precipitously within the APP during the course of the year, but had remained virtually constant in private enterprises.

Income distribution had also been modified in important ways during the course of 1980. Such measures as the creation of new jobs (112,300 new jobs were generated, bringing down the official unemployment rate to 17.5 percent), the lowering of rents on agricultural lands, an increase in agricultural producer prices, the extension of credit, an increase in minimum wages (but a decline in average real wages), and state control and subsidies of basic consumer goods all contributed to changing the existing distribution of income. This same modification of key prices also had the effect of widening the town–country price "scissors" that had originally emerged in 1978: the prices offered to the producers of domestic foodstuffs continued to *fall*, through the end of 1980, with respect to the prices at which they purchased manufactured goods. At the same time, the prices paid to the producers of agricultural exports rose in comparison to industrial prices. Therefore, although the overall price scissors widened during the course of 1980, the effects on relatively small-scale independent agricultural producers (located primarily in domestic food production) and larger scale capitalist producers (with a high percentage of export production) were uneven.

The experience gained from drawing up and attempting to carry out Plan 80 formed the basis of the second Sandinista economic program, the *Economic Program of Austerity and Efficiency*.[23] Formal preparations for this Plan 81 began during the month of June with the drafting of the qualitative aims and quantitative sectoral "control figures" for the year ahead. In conjunction with the DN-FSLN and the JGRN, the strategic objectives of the economic program were worked out during September. The joint efforts of MIPLAN and the sectoral ministries during October led to revisions in the original control figures and the first draft of the program as a whole. Work during November involved further revisions, the drafting of the state budget, and the presentation of the plan to the JGRN. Finally, on 10 January, Plan 81 was formally published.

The general approach to drafting the economic plans established during 1980 for 1981 appears to have remained the standard approach through 1985. Control figures in the form of "material balances" for the major agroexport, domestic food, and industrial products were drawn up by MIPLAN and were then revised in discussions with the various sectoral ministries. Targets for such goals as employment, investment, and necessary foreign exchange were determined. The impact of projected policy measures, such as wage and salary scales and the government budget, was estimated. Finally, "global balances" of aggregate supply and demand, external payments, and finance were calculated for the economy as a whole.

When applied to the drafting of Plan 81, the following target growth rates were established: 18.5 percent for GDP (compared to an actual rate of 10.7 percent in 1980); for "material production," 22.3 percent (compared to 3.8 percent in 1980); and, for services, 14.6 percent (18.5 percent in 1980). Thus, Plan 81 was seen as the culmination of the economic reactivation begun in 1979 and carried through 1980.

The four problems that received particular emphasis in the economic program for 1981 were the external sector, productivity, consumption, and "surpluses." As mentioned before, 1980 saw a widening trade gap generated by exports and imports that were, respectively, lower and higher than both programmed and historical levels. Part of this gap was determined by continuing declines in Nicaragua's external terms of trade (down 16 and 3.7 percent in 1979 and 1980, respectively). However, it was also the case that *quantum* export production levels remained relatively low and imports exceeded projected levels (based on the lack of import controls in the context of an overvalued córdoba exchange-rate, restricted domestic supply, and the unchanged high import content of domestic production). It was estimated that labor productivity had dropped by more than 50 percent since 1979, especially in APP firms. In addition, all three areas of consumption had exceeded programmed levels during 1980: private "basic" consumption (up 23 percent over 1979), primarily due to the increase in employment and minimum wages; private "nonbasic" consumption (up 34 percent), based on increases in both middle incomes and profits; and government consumption (up 30 percent), from government consumer subsidies, the expansion of state sector employment, and investments in economic and "social" (especially hospitals and schools) infrastructure.

These three sets of problems combined to create both internal and external disequilibria that would only be solved over the medium term. They eventually became the focus of the JGRN's "Economic Policy Guidelines 1983–88": economic development over the next 5 years would be

> based on structural changes that will gradually eliminate internal and external imbalances and lay the foundation for sustained economic growth that make it possible to attain the basic objectives of the country's development policy: satisfaction of the basic needs of the entire population and growing self-sufficiency.[24]

The fourth major problem to which attention was directed in Plan 81 was that of the economic "surplus." Although nowhere specifically defined, MIPLAN's notion of the surplus appears to refer to the portion of GDP available for government expenditures and (state and nonstate) investment. In the nonstate sphere, MIPLAN observed that investment had not risen *pari passu* with enterprise profits.

> Although objectively profits have recovered much faster than wages and salaries, the cooperation of private entrepreneurs has been limited to raising production; their attitude with respect to investment has been ambiguous.[25]

In addition, according to MIPLAN, the investible surplus itself was less available: it had decreased in certain sectors (especially in the APP), it had been lost through capital flight, and it had been absorbed by government expenditures other than investment. This meant that the only remaining sources of surplus or investment funds were "external savings" in the form of foreign donations, credits, and loans. The resulting external debt had risen from $1.1 billion at the end of 1979 to $1.6 billion in 1980.[26] Debt service was expected to absorb some 28 percent of projected 1981 export earnings. According to the Economic Commission for Latin America, the debt-service ratio actually reached 31 percent, and the outstanding external debt rose to $2.1 billion.[27]

The virtual absence of private investment and the recourse to higher levels of external debt to finance state investment continued to force the issue of the role of the state in the new Sandinista economy.

"The state as the center of accumulation"

The original conception of the role of the new state in Sandinista political economy was based, in general, on planning and, in particular, on control of the economic surplus.[28] The state was to become the "center of accumulation" by centralizing the so-called surplus within the Nicaraguan economy and planning the use of that surplus in accumulation. The state was understood to have direct access to the surplus generated in the APP and to have indirect access to the surplus produced in nonstate (capitalist and noncapitalist) enterprises. Thus, this particular form of "primary socialist accumulation" was not to be based on the wholesale confiscation of previously private property. Rather, the nationalization of property would be limited to the holdings of the Somoza regime (the Somoza family and its closest allies) and any property that over time was abandoned or otherwise unproductively utilized.[29]

For the state to serve as this center of accumulation, it needed to mobilize sufficient finance. What this meant in concrete terms was that, on one hand, state enterprises had to achieve high levels of profitability; on the other hand, the state had to realize a surplus on its current account and to use other mechanisms, such as its control over credit and marketing to "siphon off" surplus realized in nonstate enterprises. Once the surplus was effectively captured, its planned use could serve as the basis for the reactivation and restructuring of the economy on the basis of state investment.

Obviously, this accumulation strategy is not without its own inherent difficulties. It may be stalled and/or undermined by so-called exogenous factors such as declines in the external terms of trade, foreign aggression, and natural disasters.[30] In addition, attempts to increase the size of the surplus in both state and nonstate enterprises, and to gain effective state control over that surplus, may themselves create problems. These attempts may, and probably will, involve the state in a wide range of political and economic (including class) tensions and struggles. For example, attempts to lower real wages (to increase the amount of surplus extracted) and/or to increase taxes on capitalist enterprises (in order to direct the surplus into fiscal revenues) may generate conflicts that imperil the central role of the state in accumulation. Such conflicts may also have the effect of undermining the transitional project itself.

In the concrete case of Nicaragua, the attempt to construct a state that serves as the center of accumulation has been subject to precisely such tensions and difficulties. The short-term strategy to overcome these problems has been an important source of the increased levels of internal and external debt in the past 6 years. The success of the Sandinista transitional project depends, crucially, on finding additional means of resolving the political and economic contradictions inherent in making the state the center of accumulation.

One way to approach these potential problems and difficulties is to consider the finances of the Nicaraguan state. In general, any state can be expected to have a heterogeneous source of revenues and pattern of expenditures. The revenue of a typical state in a transitional society can be expected to include some combination of the following: current income from the profits of state enterprises, taxes on the profits of, and the exchange of, services with capitalist and noncapitalist enterprises outside the state, and taxes on the incomes of all other individuals, as well as state borrowing.[31] At the same time, the state is engaged in making expenditures that secure those sources of revenue: payments such as managers' salaries and interest payments that directly secure enterprise profits; financing a legal system, infrastructure, and certain types of education that maintain the state's access to some portion of profits appropriated elsewhere; and consumer subsidies, hospitals, etc. to secure all other revenue sources. Thus, the state in a transitional society is characterized by a wide variety of class and nonclass revenues and expenditures.

One of the objectives of the Sandinista state may be considered from this perspective as an attempt to open up some political "space" for the new state initiatives or to create a certain "relative autonomy" for the state by lessening its dependence on the tax portion of private sector profits to carry out its projects. One of the dangers of attempting to tax private capitalists and, instead of making expenditures that serve to maintain those particular revenues, to divert them to accumulation within the state sector, would be to lose that original source of revenue. For example, private capitalists might compensate for losing the state-provided expenditures by diverting another portion of their gross profits from accumulation to secure those conditions. They might also decide to create new positions for themselves, possibly by depositing those funds in financial institutions and purchasing assets in other countries. In both cases, private domestic capital accumulation and, hence, future sources of such revenues might suffer as a result. This has been one of the dilemmas of the Nicaraguan "mixed economy."

In principle, the surplus of the APP and the revenues from activities such as state credit and marketing were expected to provide sufficient alternative resources to carry out proposed state projects. However, such a strategy also entails political and economic difficulties. On one hand, increased state enterprise profits generated from, for example, decreases in real wages might generate struggles between state sector enterprise managers and workers. On the other hand, "expensive" state credit and wide price differentials for state-marketed commodities would threaten the participation of nonstate enterprises and poor citizens in the economic reactivation. Hence, additional sources of state revenues through such mechanisms have been limited.

Over the past 6 years, current government revenues and expenditures have risen dramatically in Nicaragua (see Table 4.2). The current revenue/GDP ratio has grown from approximately 12 percent during the 1970s to a little more than 36 percent in 1984. Similarly, the current expenditure/GDP ratio has increased from 8.7 to 37.7 percent during the same period. Neither APP profits nor state "savings" have turned out to be an adequate source of funds for state accumulation.

However, state accumulation (measured here as officially classified "capital expenditures" minus amortization payments) has expanded from 6.2 percent of GDP during the 1970s to 20.4 and 15.6 percent in 1983 and 1984, respectively.[32] With state "savings" being negative and debt service payments averaging 4.8 percent of GDP during the 1980–84 period, the only short-term alternative was in the form of internal and external borrowing.[33] Thus, the Nicaraguan fiscal deficit to be financed rose from 9 percent of GDP in 1980 to 21.2 percent in 1984. The mix of internal and external borrowing has also changed during that period. Although external loans available to Nicaragua for government deficit financing more than doubled between 1980 and 1984, their participation in financing the deficit fell from 48 to 26 percent. The increased importance of internal borrowing – mostly from the Central Bank – has become, in turn, an important factor in creating a highly monetized and inflationary economy.

Table 4.2 Government finance (percentage of GDP)

Year	1970–1978[a]	1979	1980	1981	1982	1983	1984[b]
Current revenues	12.1	13.1	20.6	21.7	24.6	29.9	36.2
Current expenditures[c]	8.7	15.0	19.6	22.3	26.3	34.2	37.7
State "savings"	3.3	–1.9	1.0	–0.6	–1.6	–4.3	–1.5
Capital expenditures[d]	6.2	1.7	5.6	5.0	4.0	20.5	15.6
Debt service[e]	1.7	3.1	4.4	4.7	6.5	4.2	4.2
Fiscal balance	–4.5	–6.8	–9.0	–10.4	–12.1	–28.9	–21.2
Financing (as percentage of total financed)							
Internal		22.6	85.8	52.1	66.4	80.5	83.2	74.1
External		77.4	14.2	47.9	33.6	19.5	16.8	25.9

Sources: author's calculations based on: 1970–82, Inter-American Development Bank (1983); 1983–84, Comisión Económica para América Latina (1985)

Notes
[a] Yearly average
[b] Preliminary
[c] Excluding interest payments, internal and external
[d] Excluding amortization payments, internal and external
[e] Interest plus amortization payments, internal and external

This "fiscal crisis" means that one of the conditions whereby the Nicaraguan state has become the center of accumulation has been on the basis of internal and external debts. The external debt situation is, of course, critical. Recent "austerity" programs in Latin America provide graphic examples of the tensions created by attempts to service the outstanding debt. At the same time, recourse to this particular segment of state income, instead of other revenues – such as further increasing taxes on income and services, increasing profits produced by state employees or "squeezing" capitalists, agricultural cooperatives or independent agricultural producers – has been an important factor in building and maintaining the complex alliances upon which the Sandinista project rests, and with which the current foreign aggression may be successfully fought.

Conclusions

The economic program for 1985 included a specific set of "austerity" measures designed, in part, to deal with the problems and difficulties generated by the state in its multiple roles in the Nicaraguan economy.[34] For example, state subsidies for consumer products would be gradually eliminated, state investments would be sharply curtailed, central government employment would be frozen, and new taxes would be applied.[35] The measures publicly announced and put into place on 8 February 1985 also included a devaluation of the córdoba, wage increases, and improved distribution of consumer products for "formal" sector employees.[36]

As of mid-1985, it was too early to formulate a final analysis of the consequences of these new policies; their effects would continue to develop over the course of 1985 and into 1986. However, the SPP's analysis of the results of the first trimester led to a revision of the initial estimates contained in the economic program.[37] Overall economic growth, instead of rising at a rate of 2 percent, was projected to fall by 1.3 percent. Industrial production was down 5.3 percent compared with the first trimester of 1984 (and down 8.8 percent with respect to the programmed level) and, in agriculture, the actual area planted was only 81.8 percent of the total initially programmed. Inflation of official consumer prices during the first 6 months of 1985 was calculated at 281.3 percent, whereas the official average monthly salary increased by only 146.2 percent. Both the fiscal deficit and the deficit on current external account were expected to reach levels at least as high as those in 1984.

The initial control figures for 1986 were based on an extension of the stabilization policies enacted during 1985.[38] The importance of the continuing external "gap" was represented by the fact that all of the targets for production – trade, government finance, etc. – were calculated in three variants, depending on the availability of foreign exchange. Thus, for example, estimates for overall economic growth varied between 4.5 and –0.1 percent. Similarly, total investment was projected to fall by an amount between –10.5 percent and –18.7 percent over projected levels for 1985. Of course, all of the estimates contained in these control figures were highly dependent on the results of the remainder of 1985, any new stabilization measures enacted, the response of state and nonstate producers, and the outcome of the war. The overall impression is that Nicaraguan economic planning, although never particularly long term and never allowed to escape the influence of external aggression, has been increasingly oriented toward short-term policymaking and putting the economy on a wartime footing.

One of the effects of this "war Sandinismo" is that the role of the state and planning in the Nicaraguan transition has to be reconsidered. If, as some have argued,[39] the tendency is for the Nicaraguan "mixed economy" to become increasingly state run, this does not mean that the state has decreased its involvement in securing the economic, political, and cultural conditions under which capitalism is reproduced in Nicaragua. On the contrary, capitalist production (both outside and, especially, inside the state) seems to be strengthened, at least in the short term, by the expanded role of the state and planning under the Sandinistas.

However, this short-term movement has been accompanied by other changes (in areas as diverse as cooperative production, foreign policy, the status of women and ethnic minorities, popular education, and forms of mass organization) that may lead to a future situation in which the position of the state in the Nicaraguan political economy can be radically transformed. On one hand, it may be possible to restrict, and eventually eliminate, the role of the state in providing some of the conditions of existence of capitalism. On the other hand, it may be possible to revolutionize the state and create for it a new role in securing some of the conditions whereby alternative, perhaps communal, forms of production can emerge and develop.

In this sense, the contradictory roles of the state and planning in the Nicaraguan transition should not obscure the fact that major, epochmaking changes have occurred in that country since 1979.

(original version published in 1986)

Acknowledgements

I would like to express my appreciation for the assistance and support of Valpy FitzGerald, Xabier Gorostiaga, and many other individuals too numerous to list. The research for this chapter would not have been possible without their guidance and cooperation. The comments of Rose Spalding and James Dunkerley on an earlier draft are also greatly appreciated. I am, of course, responsible for the analysis and conclusions presented here. The research for this chapter was supported, in part, by grants from the Helen Kellogg Institute for International Studies, the

Institute for Scholarship in the Liberal Arts, and the Jesse Jones Faculty Research Travel Fund of the University of Notre Dame. All translations are by the author.

Notes

1 This is as true in orthodox neoclassical theories of the "centrally planned" or "administered" economy as in radical theories of "socialism" or the "transition to socialism." See, for example, the various approaches surveyed in Michael Ellman (1979). This market-versus-planning dichotomy ends up telling us very little about the class-specific nature of different economies.

2 See, for example, the World Bank (1981), the Inter-American Development Bank (1983), and the Kissinger Commission (1984).

3 This alternative theoretical approach to planning in transitional economies is elaborated in Chapters 2 and 3 of this volume.

4 In this sense, the state can be seen as one "site" within Nicaraguan society at which some historically specific set of social (including class) processes occurs and changes over time. Such an approach must be clearly distinguished from orthodox theories of the state as a class-neutral social wealth enhancer that exists as an expression of the will of its individual subjects. It must also be distinguished from so-called radical accounts of the state as a mere instrument to secure the political rule of one class over another (or, as sometimes in case of analyses of Nicaragua, of one individual over the rest of society). The alternative approach used here views the state as a specific location in society at which a particular set of economic, political, and cultural processes are performed, which in turn define it as a social site. This subset of the range of social processes that make up the wider society is, of course, constantly moved and shaped by the social processes that make up the other social sites (for example, enterprises, families, churches, etc.). At the same time, the state's "relative autonomy" derives precisely from the specific set of component social processes that give the state its particular structure and movement.

The fact that the state cannot, at least in this view, be reduced to some essential set of underlying political or economic processes means that any particular state comprises a historically contingent set of economic, political, and cultural processes. The state may be the exclusive site of some social processes (for example, as the source of legal tender or lawmaking); other social processes may be present in the state as well as in nonstate social sites (as in public and private education and moneylending). In addition, social processes may shift from one social site to another over time.

For a critical review of alternative theories of the state, and a fuller elaboration of the approach underlying the present analysis, see Stephen Resnick and Richard Wolff (1983b). The conception of the Somoza state as the dictatorship of one individual over the rest of society is offered by, among others, Jaime Wheelock Román (1979) and George Black (1981).

5 These and other "social services" have not only been performed by the state. Nonstate, so-called "mass organizations" have been an important site where some of these activities have been carried out – the best known being the 1980 literacy campaign.

6 See, for example, the essays on education, health, and social welfare in Thomas W. Walker (1985).

7 Comisión Económica para América Latina (1985).

8 Including the National Lottery, Telecommunications and Post Office,

Nicaraguan Energy Institute, Nicaraguan Water and Sewerage Institute, and National Electrical Energy Institute.

9 The nationalization of primary resource production was one of the few instances in which property owned by foreigners was directly affected by the state. The relevant state corporations are the Natural Resources and Environment Institute (IRENA), the People's Forestry Corporation (CORFORP), the Nicaraguan Mines and Hydro-carbons Institute (INMINEH), and the Nicaraguan Institute for Fisheries (INPESCA).

10 During the period between August 1979 and August 1980, 200 collective bargaining agreements were signed, covering 50,000 employees. During the 46 years of the Somoza regime, only 46 such agreements were signed. For a fuller discussion, see Carlos M. Vilas (1984).

11 Nor is it clear that any other so-called socialist economy involves economic planning that conforms to the textbook model. Michael Ellman (1983) notes the increasing acknowledgment of the diversity of planning systems and the burying of the myth of the single "Soviet-type economy."

12 See E. V. K. FitzGerald (1982a), World Bank (1981), and Comisión Económica para América Latina (1979).

13 Ministry of Planning (MIPLAN) (1980a).

14 The expected participation in total production of enterprises under the control of INRA varied, of course, by crop. For example, the corresponding figures for cotton and sugar cane were 12.4 and 40 percent, respectively.

15 See MIPLAN (1980a, 68).

16 "Material production," in the sense used by MIPLAN, refers to production in the so-called primary and secondary sectors; that is, all production except the "tertiary" or service sector (see Table 4.1).

17 Alfonso Robelo – a former president of the Nicaraguan Chamber of Industry (1972–75), the Nicaraguan Development Institute, and the Higher Council of Private Enterprise (COSEP, 1975–78) – was one of the leaders of the anti-Somoza Nicaraguan Democratic Movement (MDN) and a member of the original post-Somoza JGRN. He resigned from the JGRN after it was announced that the FSLN and Sandinista mass organizations would have a working majority on the Council of State. Robelo and Violeta Chamorro (the other conservative member of the JGRN, who resigned a few days earlier than Robelo "for reasons of health") were eventually replaced by Arturo Cruz (director of the Nicaraguan Central Bank) and Rafael Cordoba. This crisis in the FSLN's attempt to maintain "national unity" continued throughout 1980. Robelo and Cruz are now prominent leaders of the major Contra group, the Nicaraguan Democratic Front (FDN).

18 Ministry of Planning (1980b and 1981b).

19 See, for example, the description of planning in the USSR by Edwin Haflett Carr and R. W. Davies (1969, Vol. 1, part 2, 787–808).

20 In the case of Nicaragua, MIDINRA Minister Jaime Wheelock (1983, 115) expressed his doubts about the feasibility of MIPLAN's approach to economic planning in the following way: "[The] introduction of a system of overall planning did not work because society, which has strong mercantile tendencies, does not lend itself easily to planning."

21 MIPLAN (1981a, 154).

22 For a fuller discussion of these and other changes in the agricultural sector, see Carmen Diana Deere, Peter Marchetti, and Nola Reinhardt (1985).

23 MIPLAN (1981a).

24 National Reconstruction Government of Nicaragua (JGRN) (1983, 1).

25 MIPLAN (1981a, 121).

26 Economic Commission for Latin America (1983, 571).

27 Comisión Económica para América Latina (1985).

28 This conception was implicit in the various published (1980a and 1981a) and unpublished (1982, 1984, and 1985) economic plans, explicit in other MIPLAN documents and theorized by E. V. K. FitzGerald (1982b and 1985b) and George Irvin (1983).

29 This was the logic that ruled the early nationalization decrees (Nos. 3 and 38) and the Agrarian Reform Law of July 1981.

30 The fall in the terms of trade had been noted previously. The impact of foreign aggression has been analyzed by Comisión Económica para América Latina (1985). The effects of the May 1982 floods are also discussed in Comisión Económica para América Latina (1985).

31 In Marxian terminology, enterprise profits consist of surplus-value directly extracted from state workers (SV); the direct transfers of surplus labor extracted in nonstate enterprises are subsumed class revenues (SCR); whereas all other revenues, including debt, include neither the extraction nor the distribution of surplus labor and are therefore classified as nonclass revenues (NCR). State expenditures can be similarly understood in class terms: the state makes ΣSC, ΣX, and ΣY expenditures to secure SV, SCR, and NCR revenues, respectively. Therefore, assuming that state revenues and expenditures are equal, $SV + SCR + NCR = \Sigma SC + \Sigma X + \Sigma Y$. There is no necessary one-to-one quantitative correspondence, however, between the respective revenue and expenditure terms on the left- and right-hand sides of the equation. For a fuller explanation of these categories, see Resnick and Wolff (1982).

32 Although no exact current data exist, private investment appears to have been minimal throughout the period since 1979. According to Inter-American Development Bank (1983), private investment averaged little more than 1.7 percent of GDP during the years 1980–82 (compared to 12.8 and 9.0 percent in 1977 and 1978, respectively).

33 An alternative, longer range policy that has been pursued with the aim of increasing the amount of surplus available has been to attempt to increase the productivity of state employees (within the APP) and of nonstate producers of basic foodstuffs.

34 Ministry of Planning (1985).

35 Such subsidies had hovered around 10 percent of total current government expenditures in preceding years.

36 The austerity measures were published in *Barricada* (9 February 1985) and are discussed by E. V. K. FitzGerald (1985a).

37 Secretariat of Planning and the Budget (1985b).

38 Secretariat of Planning and the Budget (1985a).

39 See, for example, Weeks (1986).

5 State, class, and transition in Nicaragua

The centrality of class in analyzing social change is one of the fundamental propositions of Marxian theory. Unfortunately, the revolutionary insights that can be gained from placing class at the center of analysis are often lost, particularly in transitional experiences. The problems of socialist development in Latin America and the Caribbean are rarely, if ever, viewed from the perspective of class. This is especially true when it comes to so-called economic questions. Key issues of the "peripheral socialist economy," such as the state, accumulation, and macroeconomic stabilization, are discussed as if they were general economic problems, without contradictory class conditions and effects. The danger, of course, is that the socialist project of class transformation may be curtailed, or even undermined, by not taking these class aspects into account.

Is there no alternative? One step in the direction of elaborating a specifically Marxian analysis of socialist development is to investigate the relationship between the state (including state economic policy) and class in the Nicaraguan Revolution. This analysis reveals some of the typical tensions and contradictions involved in carrying out a socialist project in the context of a small "mixed" economy faced with external aggression.

Peripheral socialist economy

The "peripheral socialist economy" is commonly characterized by two key elements:

1 significant state ownership of the means of production and state planning, united by a strategy of making the state the "center of accumulation"; and
2 the critical importance of the foreign trade sector.[1]

War and national defense are increasingly considered a third element to characterize at least the initial stage of development of peripheral socialist economies (see, for example, FitzGerald, 1985b). Additional elements of the definition of the peripheral socialist economy are offered by Vilas (1986).

The focus on the state encompasses many of the initial reforms enacted by revolutionary governments. For example, the nationalization of property in key sectors of the economy is a common early step in the building of what is considered to be a socialist economy. This change in the pattern of property ownership is, in large part, a reaction to concentrated ownership in those areas by a single individual (or small group of individuals) in the prerevolutionary period. It also represents an attempt, on one hand, to lessen the possibility of capital flight that threatens to disrupt the socialist project; on the other hand, its aim is to speed up the process of reconstruction from the destruction caused by the insurrection against the old regime. Other early measures regarding the state include organizing a system of national economic planning and increasing government expenditures, especially on investment projects and social services.

The importance of the foreign trade sector is a legacy of the particular form of capitalist development characteristic of the prerevolutionary period. Key sectors of the peripheral economy, especially large-scale capitalist producers, are highly dependent on international markets for both exports (in particular, primary agricultural and/or mineral products) and imports (both capital goods and luxury consumer goods). Other, noncapitalist producers and consumers are also affected in important ways by the extreme "openness" of the economy. The external sector of the peripheral economy will have an indirect impact on smaller-scale, noncapitalist producers of domestic consumption goods through, for example, the seasonality of wage-labor employment, the availability of land for nonexport production, and the demand for wage goods by workers in the export sector. Also, imports will typically find their way into the consumption bundles of wage and salary-earners, especially in urban areas.[2]

Finally, the integration of war into the definition of the peripheral socialist economy involves the recognition that widely varying revolutionary experiences have been subject to similar cases of external aggression by alliances of ousted domestic groups and foreign powers.

These three elements would be recognized by a wide group of observers as typical of the Nicaraguan revolutionary experience since 1979. Much of the discussion of the new Nicaraguan "mixed" economy has concentrated on the conflicts, tensions, and contradictions generated by the key role of the state in the context of a small, open economy in the midst of war (e.g., Weeks, 1986). Here, this discussion is extended by introducing a particular notion of class into the analysis of the role of the state in the so-called peripheral socialist economy of contemporary Nicaragua.

State and class

Not unlike other cases of peripheral socialist development, the emergence of a "mixed economy" in Nicaragua since 1979 has been accompanied by both qualitative and quantitative changes in the nature and role of the state (for more detailed analysis, see Chapters 3 and 4 of this volume).

According to certain well-known indicators (for example, the percentage of gross domestic product [GDP] produced within the "public sector"), there has been a quantitative increase in the role of the state in the Nicaraguan economy and society, compared with its role under the Somoza regime (although somewhat less than is commonly believed). In this sense, the Nicaraguan "mixed economy" is characterized, as would be expected, by a general extension of the state into areas previously restricted to private enterprise and other nonstate institutions.[3]

In a qualitative sense, the restructuring of the Nicaraguan state has involved, on one hand, the maintenance and/or extension of some activities previously performed in and by the state. Thus, for example, the state has increased its participation in such activities as health and education. On the other hand, the Nicaraguan state has been transformed by the shifting of traditionally nonstate activities to the state itself. This is true in the case of, for example, the state's near-total control over foreign trade and banking and the production of commodities by state enterprises.

These qualitative changes raise the question of whether or not the current Nicaraguan state exhibits a class structure which differs from the one that characterized the prerevolutionary state under Somoza. An analysis of the class nature of the state in peripheral socialist economies has traditionally been quite elusive (compare with Saul, 1986, 225). (For a critical review of alternative theories of the state, and a fuller elaboration of the Marxian class-analytic approach that informs the present analysis, see Resnick and Wolff, 1983b.) One way of addressing this question is to consider the class (and nonclass) processes that can be said to make up the current Nicaraguan state. To this end, a few definitions are in order. According to a Marxian framework of analysis, different societies can be distinguished by the mode in which surplus labor is pumped out of the direct producers. This process of performing and extracting surplus labor may be called the "fundamental class process." Thus, the feudal fundamental class process, to take one familiar example from history, involves the performance and extraction of surplus labor in the form of feudal rent. This process of surplus-labor appropriation may be distinguished from the "subsumed-class process," the process whereby surplus labor, once appropriated, is distributed. Again, to use a well-known example, the feudal subsumed-class process means that, once the rent is extracted from feudal serfs, it is distributed to a variety of other feudal classes – other feudal lords, the king, the church, and so forth – so that the social conditions for extracting feudal rent are reproduced over time. Finally, "nonclass processes" refer to all other social processes that include neither the performance/appropriation nor the distribution/receipt of surplus labor.

These class concepts can be used to analyze a peripheral socialist society, as well as any one of the institutions or "sites" in such a society. In the case of Nicaragua, the state, after the fall of Somoza, has continued to be the site of a variety of nonclass and subsumed-class processes; it has also become the site of a fundamental class process. In other words, the state is involved in activities that include:

1   the process of extracting surplus labor (the fundamental class process);
2   the process of distributing and receiving already extracted surplus labor (the subsumed-class process); and
3   a variety of other economic, political, and cultural (nonclass) processes.

More concretely, the Nicaraguan state, according to this view, has become the site of the capitalist fundamental class process by virtue of extraction of surplus labor in the form of surplus-value within firms that make up the Area of People's Property. The nationalization of the vast holdings of Somoza and his closest allies has meant that a significant number of capitalist enterprises have passed from the private sector to the public sphere. However, the new location of these enterprises does not mean that the extraction of surplus-value has ceased to exist. A radical change in the political process of property ownership does not lead, in any automatic way, to the elimination of the capitalist form of extracting surplus labor. Many other changes would have to occur in order to conclude that the capitalist class process had been eliminated and some other, perhaps communal, process of appropriating surplus labor had emerged.

At the same time, this conclusion does not imply that private and state capitalist enterprises are the same, that they exhibit the same structure or have the same dynamic. In the case of Nicaragua, two differences are quite apparent. Directors of state enterprises must be appointed to their positions by state officials (including members of the predominant party: the Frente Sandinista de Liberación Nacional [FSLN]) and state enterprises have generally widened the scope of worker participation in the overall running of the enterprises (Ortega, 1985). Without leading to the elimination of the capitalist fundamental class process, at least in the short run, such changes do produce new contradictions and developments in these new sites of surplus-value appropriation.

The Nicaraguan state has also become the site of a wide variety of nonclass economic, political, and cultural processes. For example, the state is involved in economic processes such as the marketing of commodities and credit allocation, in political processes such as lawmaking and law enforcement, and in cultural processes such as education and the dissemination of information in newspapers. Many of these processes have been carried over from, and even strengthened since, the prerevolutionary period. Others are relatively new. More importantly for the purposes at hand, some of these nonclass processes may be viewed as conditions that reproduce the various modes of extracting surplus labor throughout Nicaraguan society. Surplus labor is extracted in and through a variety of capitalist and noncapitalist fundamental class processes, both inside and outside the state – in privately owned and state-owned capitalist enterprises, as well as by individual and cooperative producers of agricultural and industrial goods. (Of the other possible class processes to which Marxists have traditionally directed their attention, slavery has not existed for quite some time and the feudal mode of surplus-labor appropriation has been virtually eliminated in Nicaragua since the downfall of Somoza.)[4] To the extent that the state participates in reproducing the different types of surplus-labor extraction, including its own position as extractor of surplus-value, it receives and distributes a portion of the extracted surplus labor and thereby participates in subsumed-class processes.

The Nicaraguan "mixed economy" is therefore characterized by a state with a qualitatively new class structure. Viewing the state in this way means that state employees participate in a variety of class and nonclass processes; they occupy a variety of class and nonclass positions. Some state employees occupy the two positions of extractor and distributor of surplus-value as the directors of state capitalist enterprises. Other state employees perform the surplus labor that is extracted in the form of surplus-value. Still other employees within the state receive distributions of the surplus labor, extracted in both state and nonstate enterprises. This is the case, for example, for managers of state capitalist enterprises and recipients within the state of taxes, merchant fees, and interest payments from capitalist and other fundamental class extractors of surplus labor. The state also has a large number of employees who do not perform, extract, distribute, or receive surplus labor. They include military personnel, employees of nonindustrial capitalist enterprises (such as banks and marketing firms), secretaries, judges, and so forth. Thus, a large number of state employees hold nonclass positions.

It should be emphasized that the new class structure of the Nicaraguan state, along with the new class positions of state employees, is defined with respect to the processes of surplus labor appropriation and distribution. It is expressly not based on the amount of income received or on the political power that the state or individual members of the state may wield. Individuals may hold considerable political power and yet occupy nonclass positions. The president of the republic and the heads of ministries exercise considerable political power; indeed, they hold power over occupants of both fundamental and subsumed-class positions, both inside and outside the state. That power has even become more concentrated in recent years.[5] However, at least under the current arrangement, they do not exploit workers or others, whether inside or outside the state; they occupy nonclass positions. Similarly, unless the incomes received by members of the state include either directly extracted or initially distributed surplus labor, the income-producing position is a nonclass position. The fact that a relatively large number of individuals occupy class positions – fundamental and subsumed – in the current Nicaraguan state, compared to the prerevolutionary state under Somoza, is due, in large part, to the existence of capitalist enterprises within the Area of People's Property.[6]

This quantitative and qualitative restructuring of the Nicaraguan state naturally involves a new set of tensions and struggles over the range and nature of the social processes that make up the state. Consider the noneconomic example of state involvement in the "New Education." Since 1979, Nicaraguan education has experienced a large number of changes, including the teaching of anti-imperialist views of history, the integration of military and productive tasks with classroom teaching, and the transformation of traditionally lucrative, individual professional studies like medicine into areas of social responsibility. Therefore, it is not surprising that there has been intense struggle over the nature and effects of the new educational system. Moreover, the struggles that have emerged have involved complex alliances that often cut across the lines of social groups such as workers, capitalists, and state officials. For example, members of the church hierarchy in opposition to secular education are joined by other supporters of private religious education. These allies (at least on this issue) include capitalists, who see the new public education as producing ideas that undermine capitalist exploitation, and workers on the Atlantic Coast who see state education as calling into question regional autonomy. At the same time, capitalists and subsumed-class enterprise managers, both inside and outside the state, support state officials in their attempt to foster a type of mass education that continues to produce trained productive laborers.

In general, all the social processes that make up the state will have contradictory effects on the class processes of the wider society. State involvement in the cultural process of education (to continue the preceding example) serves to reproduce and/or alter the fundamental class processes; it involves the training of potential workers as well as the dissemination of conceptions of work, life, and so forth. Therefore, state-sponsored education provides some of the cultural conditions whereby one or another mode of appropriating surplus labor is reproduced over time. The provision of mass education, for example, positively affects the productivity of laborers who produce surplus-value, thus providing a condition of existence for capitalism. However, the process of education may, and probably does, affect this fundamental class process in contradictory ways: while training productive laborers, educators may disseminate ideas about social life that are in opposition to capitalist exploitation. New ideas may even be produced that foster the emergence of alternative ways of organizing production and social life. Some of the cultural conditions of existence of collective or communal class processes may be fostered in this way. Other social processes performed in and by the state will have similarly contradictory class effects; thus they can be expected to be the objects of tension and struggle on the part of social groups, both inside and outside the state.

In the case of Nicaragua, such complex tensions and struggles have emerged over a wide range of state initiatives in addition to education – including property ownership, marketing, price-setting, law enforcement, and national defense. The outcomes of these struggles will play a role in determining future changes in the class structure, both of the state and of the wider society.

Class and state finances

Another way of accessing the qualitative structure of the new state and therefore of the tensions and struggles that impinge on the state in the Nicaraguan "mixed economy" is to consider the class nature of state finances. The current income of the Nicaraguan state can be viewed as a combination of different, class-specific flows of revenue. First, the state receives capitalist fundamental class revenues, that is, the surplus-value extracted from productive laborers within commodity-producing enterprises located within the state. These surplus-value revenues should be distinguished from, on one hand, the profits of non-commodity-producing enterprises, such as marketing boards and banks, and, on the other hand, mere state ownership of land and other means of production or assets. Since state enterprises, such as banks and marketing boards, do not involve the process of extracting surplus labor, their profits do not represent fundamental class revenues. As shown below, those profits will be either subsumed-class or nonclass revenues, depending on the particular kind of moneylending and marketing that takes place. Similarly, mere state ownership of the means of production or assets of an enterprise does not mean that the state receives fundamental class revenues. For example, the state may own land that is rented to nonstate agricultural producers or it may purchase or otherwise acquire stock in nonstate capitalist enterprises. In those cases, the state receives a distributed portion of the surplus labor extracted outside the state. Only in the case where

1   the enterprise produces capitalist commodities, and
2   the enterprise is located within the state, such that state employees occupy the fundamental class positions of performers and extractors of surplus-value,

does state income include capitalist fundamental class revenues.

The second category of Nicaraguan state income includes a variety of subsumed-class revenues – that is, taxes and other deductions from the various types of surplus labor appropriated in enterprises located both inside and outside the state. These subsumed-class revenues encompass, in turn, distributions of surplus-value (from state and nonstate capitalist enterprise), as well as transfers of noncapitalist forms of surplus labor: the surplus labor of independent producers of agricultural and manufactured goods (hereafter, following Marxian terminology, "ancient" producers) and of producers involved in communal arrangements.[7] For example, the state receives subsumed-class revenues from interest payments on credit allocated to capitalist enterprises. In such cases, the capitalists extract surplus-value from the productive laborers and then distribute a portion of that surplus-value to the state-owned banks. The state generates other subsumed-class revenues from such diverse activities as renting land, marketing commodities, selling foreign exchange, and taxing the income of the range of capitalist, ancient, and communal enterprises that make up the "mixed economy." In this sense, the peripheral socialist state is subsumed to a variety of different fundamental class processes.

Finally, the Nicaraguan state receives a third category of income: nonclass revenues. These are revenues that involve neither the extraction nor the initial distribution of surplus labor. For instance, these include taxes on the incomes of all other individuals, groups, and institutions (taxes paid not by capitalists but by productive laborers being one example) and state borrowing from domestic and foreign lending agencies. For a fuller explanation of these categories, see Resnick and Wolff (1982).

Turning now to the opposite side of the budget, the Nicaraguan state must make expenditures to secure the revenues from the various class and nonclass positions it occupies. The state pays managers' salaries and makes interest payments that secure revenues from the fundamental class position. State spending also includes the costs of a legal system, infrastructure, and certain types of education that lead to revenues from its various subsumed-class positions. Finally, state subsidies to consumers, the construction of hospitals, and social security are related to income generated by the state's nonclass positions.

From this perspective, the Nicaraguan state since 1979 has created a *new* source of revenue based on its position of capitalist commodity producer; therefore, it must also engage in expenditures that reproduce that position. The state has also *extended* its role in capturing distributed shares of surplus-value and in making expenditures that provide some of the conditions of existence of the process whereby surplus-value is distributed in capitalist enterprises both inside and outside the state. Together, these revenues and expenditures mean that the nationalization of banking, trade, and commodity-producing enterprises has expanded the role of the Nicaraguan state in reproducing the various economic, political, and cultural conditions of capitalism – both of its own position as capitalist commodity producer and that of capitalists outside the state. In addition, this dual role of the state implies that, even if the state loses some of its capitalist subsumed-class revenues and decreases the expenditures that secure those revenues, Nicaraguan capitalism would not therefore be weakened. This would be the case if the state matched the decline in those subsumed-class revenues and expenditures with an increase in the direct extraction of surplus-value from state workers and expenditures – in other words, if the state expanded and strengthened its own capitalist fundamental class position.

The contradictory tendencies of state financing in the Nicaraguan peripheral socialist economy are also apparent from the state's other class positions. For example, to the extent that the Nicaraguan state captures subsumed-class revenues from other noncapitalist fundamental class processes and makes expenditures that reproduce those sources of revenue, it is involved in securing simultaneously the conditions of existence of radically different, and perhaps directly contradictory, fundamental class processes (including its own). That this is the case in Nicaragua may be seen from the fact that its subsumed-class revenues include, in addition to transfers of surplus-value, revenues from ancient and communal producers of agricultural and industrial goods.

Therefore, the Nicaraguan state will normally be caught up in the competing claims of different class processes. State expenditures and state policy in general will have differential effects on the various class processes that exist throughout Nicaraguan society. For example, the expansion of ancient forms of production, through the agrarian reform and associated policy initiatives, has probably decreased the availability of seasonal labor power to capitalist producers of agricultural exports.[8] All state policy in the Nicaraguan peripheral socialist economy, even policies not explicitly designed to affect class processes, will have such differential class effects.

Two additional observations are in order. First, any particular activity performed within the Nicaraguan state – the activity of a ministry or other state entity – will probably include more than one class-specific type of expenditure. This is the case, for example, in state marketing. The role of the state as merchant (purchasing commodities from enterprises and selling them to other producers and/or consumers) means that the state can earn different subsumed-class revenues from, for example, capitalist and ancient commodity producers, in the difference between purchase and sale prices; state expenditures then include two class-specific types of expenditures as it carries out the activity of capitalist and ancient marketing.[9] Similarly, state participation in areas as diverse as the protection of private property, national defense, money-creation, and health care include a variety of class and nonclass expenditures.

Second, there is no necessary quantitative correspondence between the respective revenue and expenditure terms of the state's class-structural finances. Thus, for example, the total amount of surplus-value extracted from state employees need not be equal to the expenditures that secure those revenues; rather, such revenues may be used to secure the other, subsumed-class and/or nonclass positions of the state – or to create new positions. Indeed, this lack of quantitative correspondence is especially relevant to the relationship between the state and transition in Nicaragua. It may be possible for the state to use revenues from various *existing* sources to change its own class structure and that of the wider society by creating *new* fundamental, subsumed, and nonclass positions. This is an extremely important element of state policymaking in a peripheral socialist economy with an eye on transition and viewed through the perspective of class.

What is the state's flexibility in using its fundamental, subsumed, and nonclass revenues for purposes other than reproducing the positions that generate those revenues? Obtaining subsumed-class and nonclass revenues from the state monopoly of foreign trade, for example, still requires that the state make expenditures that reproduce its monopoly. Such spending cannot be ignored. The state, by eliminating such expenditures, would run the risk of losing that monopoly position and therefore the revenues that accompany it. With a fall in the world prices of Nicaraguan exports, the state monopoly on foreign trade has even become a net drain on state finances, since it has sought to subsidize the difference between the lower world prices and the prices paid to the domestic producers of exports in order to stem the fall in export production. At the same time, the socialist goal of transforming the Nicaraguan class structure requires that revenues generated from one class source be used to foster the conditions of existence of new class processes.

This problem of contradictory state finances has, in fact, been one of the sources of the current "fiscal crisis" of the Nicaraguan state and, hence, one of the key dilemmas of the state in the Nicaraguan "mixed economy."

State, class, and accumulation

One of the short-term problems of the state in the Nicaraguan peripheral socialist economy has been to create "relative autonomy" for new class initiatives on the part of the state. This is the goal that seems to have been encompassed by the original conception of the state in the Nicaraguan "mixed economy." In particular, the state was to become the "center of accumulation" by centralizing the various forms of surplus labor within the Nicaraguan economy and coming up with a plan to use that surplus for a new strategy of accumulation. The state was conceived to have *direct* access to the surplus generated in the nationalized enterprises of the Area of People's Property and to have *indirect* access to the surplus produced in nonstate enterprises through state control over such areas as credit, domestic and foreign trade, and taxation. Increased state accumulation was to be based, in others words, on the revenues generated from the new capitalist fundamental class position and from the extension of the subsumed-class positions of the state.

For the state to serve as this center of accumulation, it had to mobilize sufficient finance. In concrete terms this meant, given the changing Nicaraguan class structure, that:

1   capitalist commodity-producing enterprises in the state had to achieve levels of profitability by extracting surplus-value from state workers;
2   the subsumed-class distributions of state surplus-value had to remain within the state and not be transferred to entities outside the state; and
3   the state had to use other mechanisms to "siphon off" surplus labor extracted in other, nonstate enterprises.

Once these fundamental and subsumed-class flows of surplus labor were effectively captured, their planned use could serve as the basis for reactivating and restructuring the economy on the basis of state investment.

Obviously, this accumulation strategy is not without its inherent difficulties. It may be stalled and/or undermined by so-called exogenous factors, such as declines in the external terms of trade, natural disasters, and foreign aggression. All three factors have had significant influence in Nicaragua since 1979. Falling relative prices of exports mean that imported capital goods become relatively more expensive. They also discourage domestic agroexporters from increasing, or even maintaining, physical production levels. Natural disasters, such as the 1982 floods, hurt the production of domestic goods and exports. In both cases, subsumed-class distributions of surplus labor from private producers to the state have declined. The US-backed war of attrition has also negatively affected the state's accumulation strategy by further discouraging rural producers, destroying infrastructure, and absorbing more than 50 percent of the state budget in recent years. In addition, attempts to increase the amount of surplus labor in both state and nonstate enterprises and to gain effective control over that surplus will themselves create problems. They will involve the state in a wide range of cultural, political, and economic struggles. The outcomes of the ensuing tensions and struggles will shape the path of development of the peripheral socialist economy.

In the specific case of Nicaragua, the attempt to construct a state that serves as the center of accumulation has been subject to precisely such difficulties. For example, the attempt to expand the Area of People's Property, in order to generate an increase in the number of performers and the amount of surplus-value, has met with little success. Alternative attempts to increase the surplus-value component of state revenues have generated tensions and conflicts within the Area of People's Property over such issues as the level of real wages, working hours, the intensity of labor, and absenteeism. This situation has been complexly affected by a wide range of other state initiatives: cultural processes, such as explaining that the current situation requires sacrifices on the part of workers, implying, in turn, that worker associations should become less "trade unionist"

(Tirado López, 1985); political processes, including temporarily making strikes illegal and expanding worker participation in enterprise decision making; and economic processes, for example, the official wage and salary scale (SNOTS), increasing the "social wage" through expenditures on health and education, and rationing some basic foodstuffs in an attempt to guarantee minimum quantities of such goods to the entire citizenry.

One of the effects of such policies, and of the generalized economic crisis of recent years, has been a fall in the price of labor power below the value of labor power. That is, wages have been allowed to fall to a level below the customary standard of living of the class of wage-earners. A subsequent decline in the value of labor power – a lowering of the customary standard of living itself – then leads to an increase in the total amount of surplus-value appropriated through the state enterprises. A fall in the value of labor power for both private-sector and state workers means that capitalist enterprises outside the state also experience a rise in the rate of exploitation. The state, then, is also able to capture a higher level of subsumed-class transfers of surplus-value and thereby increase the capitalist subsumed-class component of state revenues.[10]

It is not surprising that productive workers would fight back by pressuring the state to reject wage controls and other policies that have led to the decline in the value of labor power. They might, for example, seek an alliance with nonproductive workers (laborers who do not perform surplus labor) whose wages have fallen in a similar fashion. The effectiveness of this type of reaction has been weakened in Nicaragua, however, by various constraints, including the "production-mindedness" of the largest trade-union confederation in response to the external aggression and temporary state restrictions on strike activity. An alternative strategy of Nicaraguan workers has been to leave the labor market of the "formal sector" entirely, to find wage employment or other sources of higher real income in the "informal sector."

When individual workers carry out this strategy on any significant scale, the number of workers from whom a surplus can be extracted diminishes. Again, various responses and complex alliances are possible. In the case of Nicaragua, both state and private enterprises have, at times, allied with workers to keep those workers in formal-sector employment. They have attempted, for example, to circumvent the official wage and salary scale by paying a price for labor power *above* the lowered value of labor power and by various payments in kind. Similarly, subsumed-class managers of unproductive laborers in the state have reacted to the general shortage of formal-sector workers by enticing government employees either to remain where they are or to relocate from other areas in the state by offering them higher salaries and/or nonmonetary perquisites. That is, there has been a struggle *within* the state over subsumed-class and nonclass revenues to encourage the stability of employment and the availability of certain kinds of skilled workers.[11]

The movement of workers from "formal" to "informal" employment, coupled with other factors that increase the shortage of formal-sector workers (such as the drafting of workers for national defense), has threatened both surplus-value and subsumed-class components of state revenues. One response to this situation has been to increase the other portions of subsumed-class revenues (for example, transfers of surplus labor from noncapitalist producers) and the remaining nonclass components of state revenues. This has been accomplished, for example, by tightening up control over the informal sector itself, in an attempt to capture some of the surplus labor appropriated by ancient producers from themselves (for example, by fostering more easily identified and taxed cooperative associations of such producers) and to increase nonclass revenues from informal-sector merchants. However, even when such control is possible, unless the corresponding expenditures are made, there is strong resistance to such measures. The complex alliance that forms the political support for other state initiatives, including national defense, is also weakened.

An alternative response to the threatened loss of fundamental and subsumed-class revenues has been to reduce the size of the informal sector itself. In this case, the state has been able to enlist the support of productive and unproductive laborers (whose real wages and salaries have been eroded by high prices for wage goods in the informal sector) for a program to discourage informal-sector activities.[12] This program has included decreasing the availability of inputs to small-scale urban informal-sector producers and closing down unlicensed vendors. It has also included attempts

1   to improve the system of distribution of wage goods at official prices to workers (both productive and unproductive) in the formal sector;
2   to encourage the flow of labor out of the urban informal sector and into the urban formal sector; and
3   to attract labor into agricultural production from urban informal-sector activities by increasing the general distribution of goods in rural, as opposed to urban, areas.

Still other problems in attempting to make the state the center of accumulation arise from changes in the pattern of state revenues that do not match changes in its distribution of expenditures. For example, expenditures directed toward securing the conditions of existence of private-sector capitalists may fall, without a corresponding initial decrease in the tax share of surplus-value. This inequality between revenues and expenditures might force capitalists to secure the conditions of existence originally produced by state expenditures by diverting a larger portion of extracted surplus-value from, for example, the accumulation of capital. Some Nicaraguan "patriotic" capitalists have responded in just this manner. They have continued to produce commodities without purchasing the additional labor power and/or means of production necessary to reproduce or expand their productive capacity. Thus, they continue to produce on the basis of simple rather than expanded accumulation. Other capitalists have reacted by disinvesting and even diverting appropriated surplus-value away from securing their positions as capitalists in Nicaragua to the creation of new class positions for themselves outside the country. This lower level of accumulation on the part of some and "disaccumulation" (and capital flight) on the part of others have had all manner of significant secondary consequences, including negative effects on state revenues from private-sector capitalists.

They have also left the state as the major accumulator of capital. In this sense, the Nicaraguan state has become the center of accumulation by default.

State and transition

There are various features of the peripheral socialist economic experience that have now become accepted features of the landscape. For example, short-term economic problems and policies can no longer be considered merely "technical issues," to be relegated to second-tier concerns. The central role of the peripheral socialist state (whether by strategy or by default) requires that attention be paid, not only to changes in property ownership, but also to such areas as monetary policy, alternative modes of financing the government budget, and exchange-rate regimes. This is clear, in general, from the work of Griffith-Jones (1981) and, in the specific case of Nicaragua, from my discussion above.

Similarly, a wide group of commentators has acknowledged that the peripheral socialist project is at least initiated, and carried out for some time, in the context of a mixed economy (for example, see Horvat 1982, 483). Such references to the mixed economy, defined in terms of the coexistence of different forms of property, are generally accompanied by discussions of the merits and/or possibilities of coordinating the economy through centralized planning or markets. Nove (1983) opts, in general, for the extensive use of markets, ostensibly because they (and not the central planners) are most capable of allocating "scarce" resources to alternative ends.[13] Harris and Vilas have argued, in the specific case of Nicaragua, that the "adoption of a mixed economy schema under conditions of continued insertion in the world market reduces considerably the capacity to plan the economy" (1985, 227). They presume, however, that a planned economy would exhibit "greater economic and social rationality" (1985, 227) and that eventually, in the transition to socialism, a system of national planning will be constructed.

Alternative positions in these discussions concerning macroeconomic policy, the mixed economy, and accumulation strategies in the peripheral socialist economy tend to share a general view that there are more or less obvious differences between the prerevolutionary capitalist society and the socialist or communist society that will be constructed after the downfall of the old regime. In terms of the economy, while the old society was a market-oriented one, built around the pursuit of profits, the new society will be planned according to social needs. Holders of private property made the key accumulation decisions before the revolution; after the revolution, the state will become the center of accumulation. At the political level, the focus is on the absence of democracy under the old regime and the emergence of democratic forms of decision making during the transition to the new social order.

Alongside these presumed differences, there are certain similarities that are said to characterize the two societies. Savings have to be generated and accumulation decisions made in both societies. Production has to be carried out with a certain degree of efficiency. And accumulation and production decisions have to be made in the context of the scarcity of resources. That is, there is a set of characteristics that are presumed to be common to both societies, conditions that transcend otherwise great social differences between the two orders.

Finally, these differences and similarities are brought to bear on the question of the transition to the new social order (what is called the "transition to socialism," the "preliminary transition to socialism" or another such label, depending on the commentator). The transitional order is characterized by both the emergence of the characteristics of the future socialist/ communist society (planning, democracy, etc.) and the maintenance, or perhaps even improvement, of the characteristics that are considered to cut across the two social orders (accumulation, productive efficiency, etc.).

It is obvious that most, if not all, of the participants in this emerging debate concerning the peripheral socialist economy and society share a commitment to establishing a new socialist/communist society that will be fundamentally different from the capitalist society that the revolutionary forces seek to radically alter. What is missing from the alternative positions in this debate, however, is a discussion of the class dimensions of both the socialist or communist society that is the revolutionary goal and the nature of the transition to that radically new society. In this sense, the crucial class insights of Marx's original contributions to revolutionary theory tend to be set aside or even ignored.

The debates about planning systems, markets, accumulation strategies, efficiency, short-term economic policies, and the like tend to be based on the presumed differences and similarities of capitalist and communist societies discussed above. Because of this, participants in such debates tend to miss the complex connections between those issues and the class transformation of existing peripheral societies. The danger inherent in disregarding these connections is that peripheral socialist strategies may reproduce the social conditions of class processes that are diametrically opposed to the goal of eventually creating a communist society.

If the revolutionary objective is to destroy the social conditions under which the capitalist class process and other forms of private exploitation have traditionally existed, and simultaneously to foster the social conditions under which the communal class process can eventually emerge and become predominant, then class has to be placed at the center of analysis. A strategy of socialist transition can then be defined in terms of creating the economic, cultural, and political conditions of the communal class process in a social context where that class process is not yet predominant.

There are two questions concerning the nature and role of the state (and state policies) in that context: first, how can the state eliminate its noncommunal (capitalist, ancient, etc.) subsumed-class positions and expand its new communal subsumed-class position? Second, how can the state eliminate its capitalist fundamental class position and itself become a site of the communal class process? That is, the long-term success of the revolution in Nicaragua and elsewhere in Latin America and the Caribbean will depend on a socialist transitional strategy that involves radically transforming the state in such a way as to eliminate the role of the state (and of all other nonstate sites) in reproducing the social conditions under which private forms of exploitation exist and fostering the development of other, especially communal, ways of organizing production and social life.

(original version published in 1988)

Acknowledgements

An earlier version of this article was presented to the XIII International Congress of the Latin American Studies Association (October 1986). The comments of Richard Wolff, Michael Zalkin, and Richard Harris and the financial support of the Helen Kellogg Institute for International Studies are gratefully acknowledged.

Notes

1   See, for example, FitzGerald (1985b and 1985c) and Irvin (1983). Along somewhat different lines, see Thomas (1974) and Harris (1986).
2   This runs counter to the presumption of many development economists that imported consumption goods in the periphery are entirely, or mainly, luxury goods. In the Nicaraguan case, many "basic" goods (from beer bottles to machetes) have traditionally been imported.
3   However, this should not be seen as a simple, unilinear process of increasing state involvement in areas previously restricted to private (i.e., nonstate) institutions. There are many recent examples of land being transferred from state enterprises to both private cooperatives and individual peasant producers. Thus, the proportion of agricultural land owned by the state grew from zero under Somoza to 23 percent in 1982 and had fallen to 13 percent by 1986.
4   This would appear to be the case, at least for prerevolutionary agricultural enterprises, in which feudal rent was extracted from peasants. There is still the

question of whether or not traditional Nicaraguan households represent sites in which surplus labor is extracted from some members by others in the form of feudal rent. Analyzing the class structure of Nicaraguan households, however, would take us beyond the limitations of this essay.

5   It has also become more democratic through, for example, the 1984 elections and the deliberations of the national assembly (see Coraggio and Irvin, 1985).

6   This brief comparison of the class structure of the Nicaraguan state before and after the downfall of Somoza suggests a number of areas that require further research, including the definition of the state itself. The multiple positions occupied by Somoza himself complicate the issue of defining the state. On one hand, Somoza occupied a number of different class positions in what may be considered nonstate social sites, for example, as extractor of feudal rent and surplus-value and recipient of subsumed-class revenues from banking and merchanting through enterprises in the private sector. On the other hand, he held a number of nonclass positions in the state itself. Obviously, the simultaneous occupation by Somoza of these various class and nonclass positions was not unrelated as his holding one position reinforced the holding of other positions. It is also probable that nominally state and nonstate revenues and expenditures were closely intertwined under Somoza. Somoza's actions, then, tended to blur the distinction between the state and nonstate sites in Nicaraguan society. It is therefore likely that the broad coalition of anti-Somoza forces could agree on the need to restructure the Nicaraguan state, while disagreeing on the particular nature – including the class structure – of the new, post-Somoza state. In this sense, the definition of the state is both a crucial theoretical and political question.

7   To be clear, the ancient fundamental class process involves the private extraction of surplus labor by individual producers from themselves. The communal fundamental class process refers to the collective extraction of surplus labor: the direct producers form part of the collectivity (or commune), which both appropriates and distributes the surplus labor. In both cases, surplus labor is performed, appropriated, and distributed. The difference lies in the specific class nature of surplus-labor performance, appropriation, and distribution: the individual self-appropriation (and distribution) of the ancient class process versus the collective appropriation (and distribution) of surplus labor of the communal class process. An interesting case where the ancient and/or communal fundamental class processes may be present is the cooperative organization of producers in Nicaragua. Some cooperatives are based on the association of ancient producers to acquire credit and other services as a group; surplus labor in such cooperatives continues to be extracted by separate, individual producers. In other cooperatives, surplus labor is appropriated and distributed by the unity of direct producers (or by a communal board designated by the direct producers). Many cooperatives in contemporary Nicaragua probably include both ancient and communal class processes.

8   Solon Barraclough (a world expert on peasants, land reform and rural development, who died in 2002) cautioned me that the widely observed decline in the availability of seasonal wage laborers in Nicaraguan agriculture is not only a product of the distribution of land to landless and smallholding peasants. The scarcity of goods that wage income can be used to purchase has also contributed to this decline. This is another important dimension of the "classical" problem of the town–country terms of trade.

9   State marketing may also represent a drain on state revenues, as it was in the form of consumer subsidies in Nicaragua until the end of 1984. Such subsidies represented nonclass expenditures on Nicaraguan workers and other consumers. However, the nonclass nature of these expenditures does not mean

that they did not have important direct and indirect class effects. For example, the ability of capitalists to pay a price of labor power (a wage that covered a subsidized wage bundle) that was less than the value of labor power (that same bundle of commodities at nonsubsidized prices) allowed them to realize higher profits. Also, ancient producers of foodstuffs were able to sell a larger portion of their total productions to the state at one price and purchase subsidized consumer goods at a lower price, thus increasing their real income.

10   This would be the case, for example, if we consider the subsumed-class component of state revenues as a percentage of surplus-value appropriated by private capitalists: $SCR^k = t_k SV^k$, where SCR^k represents subsumed-class revenues from capitalists outside the state, t_k is the constant tax rate on surplus-value, and SV^k is the amount of surplus-value appropriated by capitalists in the private sector.

11   This struggle for state revenues has encouraged individual state entities (ministries and other administrative units) to find alternative sources of income, such as the running of individual enterprises.

12   This response by formal-sector workers has been complicated by the positions that they occupy in the family. Many such workers have family members who earn incomes in informal-sector activities. Thus, the fall in the value of labor power has been somewhat compensated, at the level of family income, by the participation of other family members in ancient production and marketing in the so-called informal sector.

13   Readers will recognize the affinity of Nove's argument with the orthodox, neoclassical economists' discussion of planning and markets as merely alternative allocative mechanisms. The assumption is that markets and planning systems solve the "same" economic problem. They are merely alternative mechanisms for allocating scarce resources among alternative ends. Such discussions presume that scarcity is a transsocial phenomenon; that it is the same in all societies. They also ignore the fact that planning systems and markets may serve as the conditions of existence of radically different class processes. For a general discussion of these issues, see Chapters 2 and 3 in this volume. Mandel (1986) has criticized Nove's argument for markets, although in a manner quite different from the discussion here and below.

Development

Another area of my writings over the past 20 years is Third World development. If the discussion of socialism and planning had (at least until recently) virtually disappeared, development has been fundamentally transformed – from one of the most interesting areas of economics, where many important debates have taken place, to a more or less complete adoption of the theoretical terms and policy conclusions of mainstream economics. When I first got started, development economics represented a fundamental critique of mainstream economics, a politically radical and theoretically interdisciplinary alternative to the methods and presuppositions of conventional microeconomics, macroeconomics, and international trade. Today, development economics is focused almost entirely on traditional themes – promoting macroeconomic stability, fostering economic growth, and alleviating poverty – exactly when a whole series of new contributions are being made that could breathe new life into development studies. Certainly this is true in disciplines other than economics, with the emergence of postcolonial literatures, postmodern anthropologies, and so on. And in the region I know best, Latin America, the discussion of alternative forms of development has been rejuvenated with the emergence of a host of new social movements and left-wing parties and governments.

But what is the role of specifically Marxian class analysis in this area? In my case, I thought it important to start (working with a philosopher colleague at Notre Dame) with the radical theoretical debates out of which my own work emerged in college and graduate school: the work of André Gunder Frank, the modes of production debate, and the writings of Samir Amin. This was the work that broke open traditional Marxism and challenged the terms of both existing radical thought and mainstream economic theories.

- Frank, who died in April 2005, challenged modernization theory – according to which "backwardness" was the result of noncapitalist development – to put forward the idea that underdevelopment in the Third World was both a condition and a result of capitalist development in the First World (i.e., the "development of underdevelopment," which involved the metropolitan center siphoning off the surplus from the periphery and, at the same time, making the periphery dependent on the center. Hence, the term "dependency theory.")

- The modes of production debate was based on the work of French anthropologists, such as Pierre-Philippe Rey and Claude Meillasoux, but also involved contributions from Ernesto Laclau, Harold Wolpe, and others. In their approach, the "articulation of modes of production" involved a relationship between pre- or noncapitalist modes of production in the Third World that were dominated by the expansion of the capitalist mode of production on a world scale, with underdevelopment the result. This approach differed from that of Frank and other dependency theorists, who saw capitalism everywhere from early on.

- And then Amin, who combines dependency theory with modes of production and adds the problem of unequal exchange. For Amin, all stages of capitalist development – mercantilist, competitive, and monopoly – create a core–periphery relationship, characterized by autocentric development in the center and dependent/disarticulated accumulation in the periphery, which prevents (especially in the third stage) any country from the periphery joining the core. Global capitalism thus creates a permanently unequal structure of development and underdevelopment.

This was a key set of debates within radical thought, which distinguished it from mainstream, modernization theory, then as now. The emphasis in all three cases is on the structure of capitalism on a world scale, with varying degrees of attention paid to conditions *inside* countries, of both the First and Third Worlds.

Our thinking at the time was that mainstream and radical theorists of the problem of underdevelopment arrived at different conclusions because they used different entry points and therefore held quite different conceptions of capitalism and its consequences. All of them counterposed to individual choice and harmony within markets a different structure: the circulation of commodities (Frank), capitalist and noncapitalist modes of production, and unequal national units (Amin). These radicals also challenged the unilinear process of modernization or development presumed by mainstream economists. Finally, they were also more open about their political commitments, in contrast to mainstream economists who hid behind the veil of science (but tended to support the status quo). But, in our view, these radical approaches also suffered from attempting to analyze everything in terms of one essential factor, which ultimately drew them closer to their mainstream counterparts.

In any case, we decided that we had to work our way through these debates in order to clear a space for determining what a Marxian analysis of Third World development can and should look like today.

My own way of approaching this topic was to return to Nicaragua and to carry out a Marxian analysis of the "costs of austerity." Nicaragua under the Sandinistas was, of course, similar to other relatively small, foreign-exchange-constrained countries. But, unlike other countries, Nicaragua had carried out an austerity program without the backing of the International Monetary Fund (and therefore without the infamous IMF conditionality) and with an avowedly revolutionary government. And one of the lessons of other socialist experiments, from Lenin's New Economic Program to Allende's Chile, was that revolutionary governments ignore the problem of macroeconomic instability – inflation, unemployment, current account deficits, and so on – at their peril. So, the issue could not just be dismissed (as it was by many at the time) as a problem created by the pre-revolutionary situation or by a counter-revolutionary external aggression.

I decided to use the idea of the "worker–peasant alliance" as my way into the problem. There were two reasons for putting class at the center of the discussion: because workers and peasants were key participants in the revolutionary movement, and because the worker–peasant alliance referred to a project, supported by other social actors, to radically transform the existing society. Thus, I entered the discussion by focusing, not on power or property, but on class. And, from that entry point, three key questions emerged:

1   Does austerity call into question support for the revolution by the popular classes in urban and rural areas?
2   Are there conflicts between workers and peasants in responding to a clearly difficult economic and political situation?
3   How are the long-term goals of the revolution affected by the costs of austerity?

My general thesis was that the revolution was forced to confront the twin problems of revolutionary change and macroeconomic stability from the start – what I call the knife-edge of transformation and balance.

By the time I conducted my analysis in 1987, 3 years of an austerity program had lowered economic growth, devalued the currency (especially in parallel and black markets), and provoked widespread inflation. I wasn't interested in these problems because they threatened instability, as if either the existing instability or the attempt to create macroeconomic stability were class-neutral issues. I wanted to investigate the effects on the worker–peasant alliance, and for that I had to carry out a class analysis of the austerity program.

For example, in the urban areas, I discovered that, first, managers and professionals were hurt (by import controls and the scarcity of foreign exchange) and, then, wage-workers (by the decline in real wages and the instability of formal-sector employment), which was accompanied by a tremendous growth in the informal sector. So, how were urban workers surviving? By finding a combination of formal-sector employment (to receive nominal wages and basic goods from commissaries) and marketing and production activities within households and small enterprises of the informal sector.

With regard to the rural areas, I found that there had been both a qualitative transformation (with the nationalization of the Somoza family properties and an ambitious agrarian reform) and a shift of the center of gravity from Managua to the countryside. But agriculture was a complex sector: it included capitalist agroexporters, new state and cooperative producers of domestic foodstuffs, and independent peasant producers of basic grains. And, as austerity was imposed, peasant producers (both those that existed before the agrarian reform and those who had recently received parcels of land) responded by threatening to starve the cities and support the contra forces.

My way of analyzing the response was to construct a crude indicator of the relative strength of the parties in the worker–peasant alliance in order to measure the terms of trade between town and country. What I found was the that terms of trade had turned against basic grain producers from 1981 through 1984, but then switched in 1985 and, by 1986, had turned back toward rural producers. My more general conclusion was that – in the context of inherited conditions, external aggression, and government mistakes – macroeconomic policy had involved series of measures to maintain and recompose the worker–peasant alliance, trying to walk the knife-edge between transformation and balance. As of 1987, the policy was hurting urban workers and trying to keep rural producers from supporting the contras.

That was how I approached the problem of austerity in the case of Nicaragua. But I wanted to investigate what Marxian theory had to say for the more general issue of stabilization and adjustment programs, especially for Latin America. I was dissatisfied with the usual left response, to oppose neoclassical and IMF (what later came to be called Washington Consensus or neoliberal) austerity programs and offer instead a Keynesian or structuralist program. As with the planning debate, my response was: is that all the Left had to offer, a return to fiscal policy and state regulation?

This question formed the basis of the piece eventually published in *World Development*. The first problem was to elaborate a Marxian alternative to both neoclassical and Keynesian/structuralist theories and policy alternatives – a Marxian open-economy macroeconomics, if you will. Then, how can we explain the pendulum swings back and forth between neoclassical and structuralist plans?[1]

I started out by analyzing the fact that neoclassical and structuralist economists shared the same criteria of success – full employment, price stability, and balance of payments equilibrium – but differed in terms of their policies for achieving that success. Why? My answer was, that they have different stories of the macroeconomy – based on theoretical humanism and structuralism – and therefore different explanations of why a national economy might experience unemployment, inflation, and current or financial account deficits (plus, of course, the always-present and ever-shifting middle position, so cherished by mainstream economists.) And the alternative? We can move beyond the essentialisms of both humanism and structuralism (in favor of the mutual constitution of individual agents and structures) and introduce class into the analysis.

Utilizing such a framework, I examined the experiences of three countries – Argentina, Brazil, and Peru – that, between 1974 and 1987, had enacted one form or another of all programs: orthodox, heterodox, and a combination of the two. My view of the oscillation from one approach to the other during that period was that each was attempted and, when declared to have failed, there was a turn to the other (often, of course, by electing new presidents). However, that wasn't the end but the point when things actually got interesting. What if they weren't failures, at least from a Marxian perspective? What if nonclass macroeconomic failures produced class successes?

Using Marxian class analysis, I show how, in four key areas – a more unequal distribution of income, overvalued exchange rates, inflation, and government deficits – what non-Marxian economists and politicians perceive to be failures actually, in different ways, foster the development of capitalism. They lead, in different ways, to the widening and deepening of the capitalist appropriation of surplus-value. Thus, what others see as nonclass failures are, in fact, class successes. And it is that commitment – to capitalist class successes, in one form or another – that keeps the stabilization and adjustment debate confined to the terms of neoclassical and structuralist macroeconomic theories. That was the commitment underlying the debate in Latin America, just as it serves as the basis of the mainstream debate concerning the current crises of capitalism in the United States and around the world.

And, of course, as I was writing about stabilization and adjustment during that period, I also became interested in issues of foreign debt. Once again, the question was, what does Marxism have to offer that is different from both mainstream and heterodox approaches? The mainstream approach was, not surprisingly, to avoid moral hazard and to make sure countries facing a debt crisis would adopt an IMF-style structural adjustment package. The heterodox alternative was that countries should just refuse to repay the debt (and thus cut themselves off from international credit markets) and/or accept the bail-outs proposed in the Baker and Brady plans. Later, the focus shifted to debt forgiveness, especially for the most impoverished countries. So, the existing debate was between seeing debt as part of the normal resource transfer between countries and analyzing debt as a form of power wielded by one group of countries over others.

From a Marxian perspective, there are obvious problems on the part of both sets of claims. What was missing was an analysis of the class relations within and between countries, and the role that debt played in that complex national and international class structure. So, I used some basic concepts from Marxian value theory to show how debt and debt service might be introduced into the class revenues and expenditures of industrial capitalist enterprises, demonstrating the effects on capital accumulation (and therefore capitalist economic growth) of external debt and debt servicing. I then expanded on that framework to investigate the class structure of a country's external debt, depending on the class position of the borrower and the class nature of the interest payments (whereas the existing radical analyses had focused on the nature of the lenders). Then, I showed that nonclass debt (a nonclass revenue to private and public borrowers alike) has significant class effects, as in all purportedly nonclass stabilization and adjustment programs.

I also analyzed the class nature of capital flight (the equivalent then to the role that corruption plays now in development and international political economy), an attempt to blame Third World countries for their plight. What I show is that borrowers used capital flight to create new nonclass and subsumed-class positions for themselves elsewhere (e.g., in the United States). I was able to demonstrate, first, that domestic (Third World) borrowers can use nonclass revenues in the form of foreign loans to create or extend domestic and foreign class positions and, second, that the resulting debt crisis led to new class conflicts and alliances within and between countries.

Of course, this class approach to debt is part of a larger class analysis of Third World development, different from both mainstream and radical analyses. Here, in a more popular piece (for the URPE reader published in 2000, a revised version of an essay published earlier in the Italian journal *A Sinistra*), I take up the problems occasioned by the "turn to markets" in displacing a radical rethinking of development. First, I explore two of the ironies that accompany this neoliberal orthodoxy: it represents what many consider to be an Americanization of economic thinking at a time when the United States – measured in terms of income and wealth distribution, the percentage of the population in prison, the growth of poverty, and so forth – serves as a poor model for the expansion of markets; and new discoveries within orthodox economic theory – post-Walrasian microeconomics, the new trade theory, the role of the state in the East Asian miracles – served (if followed through) to undermine the existing free trade orthodoxy.

I then examine some of the problems inherent in the assumption that export-led industrialization is the only viable path to development in the Third World:

- the worsening distribution of income within those countries destroyed any potential domestic market based on mass consumption;

- the freeing up of markets exacerbates that distribution problem; and
- the privatization of state enterprises swells the ranks of the unemployed and the informal sector, thus creating downward pressure on formal-sector wages and making the distribution of income even more unequal.

And, if export-led industrialization is "successful" (just as the earlier import-substitution industrialization was, in fact, successful in terms of developing capitalism), what are the punishments meted out in the name of making it successful? What are the implications for workers, women, the environment, and so on?

Most importantly, what are the alternatives? Introducing class into the discussion allows us to see the existence of exploitation, and to make a break from both market-centered and state-centered poles of the existing debate. It encourages us to imagine taking areas out of capitalist competition and creating nonexploitative – collective, community-oriented – enterprises and forms of development.

I had been concerned with the issue of Third World development since my first trip to Brazil in 1970. It was, as I explain in the first chapter of this volume, an exciting area of study, both intellectually and politically. But then, when development economics was hijacked by neoclassical economics, it lost much of that excitement, at least for me. Later, however, postdevelopment theory – the critique of modernization pioneered by Arturo Escobar and others – succeeded in making new openings in that hardened edifice. (This occurred at the same time that I was writing about postmodernism, which culminated in my book with Jack Amariglio [2003]). Therefore, I was pleased to work with Julie Graham and Kath Gibson to take a critical look at what the postdevelopment theorists were up to. One of Escobar's great accomplishments was to extend the work of Michel Foucault into the field of development issues, mostly outside the discipline of economics (since, unfortunately, very few people in economics, mainstream or heterodox, have ever studied Foucault's work).[2]

As Chapter 11 makes clear, I am quite sympathetic to the postdevelopment critique. The basic argument is that, in the name of modernization, the development industry – the collection of theories and institutions designed to combat "backwardness" and underdevelopment in the postwar period – actually created a set of problems to which it provided the answers. In other words, the problems of illiteracy, unemployment, poverty, and so on were discursively and institutionally created – not given, preexisting problems – that needed to be overcome through modern development.

So far, so good. However, from a nonessentialist Marxian perspective, the key problem that besets the work of the postdevelopment critics is that it is focused entirely on capitalism and everything else – all forms of noncapitalism that have existed, continue to exist, or could be brought into existence – is rendered either missing or insignificant. That is what we call capitalocentrism, which (like logocentrism and phallocentrism for reason and masculinity) places capitalism on top of a hierarchical dichotomy, as the central referent of development. Thus, all instances of noncapitalism – feudalism, slavery, ancient forms of production, communism, and so on – become the same as, the opposite of, the complement to, and/or located inside capitalism itself.

The effect on postdevelopment thinking is that it becomes virtually impossible to imagine noncapitalist forms of economy and society, either as they currently exist within the social totality or as they might be fostered through alternative development policies. Capitalocentrism makes them all irrelevant.

The alternative is to use a language of class to create a diverse, heterogeneous economic landscape, in two ways:

- by rereading the economy outside the hold of capitalocentrism – for example, by seeing how modernization destroys some noncapitalist class processes and yet brings others into existence: inside households, in agriculture, in the urban economy, and so forth; and
- by opening the economy to new possibilities by theorizing new connections between social movements and class processes – for example, by retheorizing markets, money, enterprises, etc. outside the frame of capitalism, such as when women's cooperatives and nongovernmental organizations create forms of noncapitalist craft production that sell to the world market or when community stakeholders manage to get capitalist enterprises to distribute portions of surplus-value into community projects of environmental sustainability or new forms of production.

In this way, the Marxian language of class can be used to challenge the hold of capitalism and create a new, noncapitalist imaginary.

Harole Wolpe was a remarkable figure: a South African Marxist, deeply involved in the antiapartheid movement, who was arrested and put in prison in 1963 and spent 30 years in exile in England. He returned to South Africa in 1990, and died there in 1996. I had read some of his work, especially his edited collection on modes of production, but it wasn't until I was invited to a conference in South Africa that I had the opportunity to engage with the entirety of his contributions to Marxian theory and South African political economy.

In the final essay in this section (Chapter 12), I delve into three main themes of Wolpe's writings – class analysis, capital accumulation, and the role of the intellectual – and compare what he was trying to do, in opening up and applying Marxian class analysis to concrete problems in South Africa, to the project of many of us associated with *Rethinking Marxism*.

The parallels between the two projects are remarkable: each sought to open up Marxian theory by rigorously defining key concepts and, at the same time, eliminating any and all forms of essentialism and "iron laws" of necessity.

In Wolpe's case, it was clear that capitalist class exploitation (and not just racial segregation) was an important part of the apartheid regime. This focus on class allowed him both to analyze the relationship between the structure of capitalism and racial oppression and also to rethink the forms of political agency that might eliminate the apartheid regime and transform the South African political economy. Similarly, Wolpe's approach to the accumulation of capital eschewed the deterministic approach handed down by the Marxian tradition to, instead, focus on the contingent, conjunctural ways in which South African racial capitalism was both reproduced and changed over time, thus creating new openings to challenge the regime. Finally, Wolpe thought a great deal about the "relative autonomy" of critical intellectuals, with respect to both the state (they needed to resist any and all attempts on the part of the state to direct or curtail critical research) and the antiapartheid movement ("theory and analysis" needed to be a site of contestation within national liberation struggles).

In my view, the work Wolpe left behind serves as an example and a reminder that Marxian class analysis is always a "ruthless criticism of the existing order." The task of Marxist intellectuals therefore involves turning a critical gaze on our existing modes of thought as well as on the existing structures of social life.

Throughout this section, I show how a nonessentialist language of class serves to disrupt the existing terms of debate within economic develop-ment. In the third and final section of this book, I carry out a related project with respect to the debate about globalization.

Notes

1   Once that piece was completed, I wrote a more "popular" version for the journal published by the North American Congress on Latin America (Ruccio, 1993). That's something I try to do on a regular basis – to give talks and write articles in a form different from my more academic presentations and essays. As it turns out, more people no doubt read the NACLA version than the *World Development* article. Today, I have a blog (anticap.wordpress.com) in which I offer an occasional commentary on a variety of contemporary issues.
2   Keith Tribe (1978) and Jack Amariglio (1988) are two remarkable exceptions.

6 Radical theories of development: Frank, the Modes of Production school, and Amin

(with Lawrence H. Simon)

The past 400 years have witnessed the growth and global expansion of capitalism. In the minds of many, the development of capitalism is synonymous with the expansion of increasingly complex industrial, economic, and social structures into ever wider areas of the world. At least since Adam Smith, bourgeois theorists of capitalism have triumphantly heralded this expansion as progressive and unilinear, limited only by the emergence, in the twentieth century, of socialist regimes. Insofar as there remain in the world today differences in levels of development and national wealth, these can best be overcome, according to orthodox theory, through the further growth of capitalism. The job of neoclassical development economics is to chart this path of growth for the so-called less developed countries (LDCs).

The view from the Left is very different. Where bourgeois theorists see a story of triumph and progress, radical theorists see one of domination and exploitation in both imperialist and neocolonialist modes on one hand and struggles for independence on the other. Radicals are unanimous in rejecting the orthodox view as theoretically false and politically inadequate.

From afar, this radical approach might be thought to be a unified theoretical position that can be fairly easily differentiated from its orthodox opposite. To some degree this is true. But, in the past two decades, the Left has also generated complex theoretical debates and opposing positions; that is, radical theorists differ on basic issues in their story. Is the development of capitalism a necessary, if unfortunate, step in the path of development for any country? Are the economic structures that have developed in the various nations that were formerly colonies best characterized as capitalist? If so, is it capitalism in the same form as developed in Europe and North America, or a new and indigenous form of capitalism? If not, then how should the economies of the LDCs be characterized?

While most radical analyses accept the existence of a world capitalism system, they differ on how to understand the basic dynamic of this system and on how to describe the relations between the more- and less-developed nations within this system. Again, while most, but not all, radical analyses question whether the present economic structures of LDCs will allow development, they differ with regard to how to characterize the barriers preventing growth. Radical interpretations also disagree in terms of how much is to be accepted from the theories of Marx and the Marxist tradition. The spectrum runs from what might be considered orthodox Marxist theories of development to theories that, while acknowledging the importance of Marx, in effect reject nearly all of his important claims about the status and development of the colonial world.

In this essay, we analyze three of the theories that have emerged as contending positions on the Left. These three – Dependency Theory as formulated by André Gunder Frank, the Modes of Production school, and the theory of Samir Amin – by no means exhaust the radical perspective. This analysis, then, is not a survey of radical theories of development.[1] Rather, we hope that, by looking in depth at three of the alternative views, the issues around which much of the debates have revolved will be clarified.

The three positions we have chosen are not only major contenders in the debate, but they are related in important ways, both historically and conceptually. Theories arise at least partly in reaction to other existing theories that are judged inadequate by those seeking a new departure. The new theory takes up and recasts the challenge of the old one and is best understood in the light of this challenge. A theory, then, has at least two tasks: a negative or critical one of arguing against its predecessors, and a positive or constructive one of providing an alternative account of the issues in dispute and of raising new questions. To understand a theory, then, requires it to be placed within the narrative of the debates in which it arose and developed.

The three theories we have selected have this relationship. Frank's work can be taken as the beginning of the modern debate on the Left concerning development.[2] The Modes of Production school arises in direct response to what were seen as inadequacies in Frank's theory of underdevelopment. Amin's work represents an attempt to incorporate and synthesize into an encompassing theory of the world capitalist system various of the theoretical insights of Dependency Theory, the Modes of Production position, and more orthodox Marxist treatments.

This essay is intended to be, for the most part, an introduction to these three positions and is therefore primarily analytic and expository. Its aim is to clarify the structure of the different theories and the issues of contention among them in order to allow those unfamiliar with the material a way into what has become a complex and sophisticated literature.[3]

The essay proceeds as follows. In the second section, we present Frank's theory of underdevelopment, focusing on the structure of his theoretical model and how it departs from the model of development in neoclassical economics. The third section is a discussion of two critics of Frank – Sanjaya Lall and Robert Brenner. Both Lall and Brenner are sympathetic critics, at least to the extent that they agree with Frank that the neoclassical position must be rejected and a radical alternative provided. Their criticisms illustrate some of the theoretical disagreements that Frank's version of Dependency Theory has generated.

In the fourth section, we provide an analysis of the Modes of Production school. We analyze this position in terms of three distinguishable approaches: the articulation of modes of production, the colonial or peripheral modes of production, and the internationalization of capital. The focus of the discussion is not only on the basic claims of the three approaches, but also on the interrelations and differences among them. We also situate the overall Modes of Production position in the context of the general debate by analyzing the background and motivation for its emergence. In the fifth section, Amin's theory is presented. We end this section with a brief discussion of a recent reply by Amin to his critics, in which points of contact and disagreement between his theory and the others we discuss are further clarified.

Frank and Dependency Theory

André Gunder Frank is generally credited as the father of Dependency Theory.[4] *Capitalism and Underdevelopment in Latin America*, written in the early sixties and published in English in 1967, was the first important statement of the theory.[5] While Frank certainly had predecessors, as he readily acknowledges, his book can still be used to mark the opening salvo in the debate over Dependency Theory, in part because this book continues to be highly influential and is widely cited by both exponents and critics of Dependency Theory. To understand the structure of Frank's argument, however, it is necessary to keep in mind its antecedents, both the positions Frank critized and the authors upon whom he relied in formulating his own position.

Frank's work grew out of a reaction to both orthodox neoclassical work on development and to the views of certain traditional orthodox Marxists, in particular, those prevalent among the Communist Parties in Latin America. According to Frank, both of these opposing positions shared, in certain important regards, theoretical theses that were faulty. Positively, Frank's views were influenced by the structuralist theory of Raúl Prebisch and others in Latin America and by the work of the so-called neo-Marxists, especially that of Paul Baran.[6] In fact, in the theoretical configuration of development economics, Dependency Theory is perhaps best located on the continuum somewhere between orthodox structuralist theory and Marxism.

A central thesis shared, according to Frank, by both neoclassical and orthodox Marxist theories of development, and of which he was critical, was that capitalism was a normal and necessary stage of development. This conception of capitalism was part of a more general view of development as occurring through a series of stages. In addition, according to Frank, both of these positions accepted a general dualistic view of so-called Third World societies. Of course, these theses were expressed by each position in very different theoretical language and supported by antithetical theoretical arguments. And, needless to say, the implications each drew from these theses could not be more different. For the neoclassical, capitalism was the end of development, while for the Marxist, it was a necessary, if regrettable, stage to be transcended by socialism. But both agreed that any (nonsocialist) country that needed to develop had to do so within the framework of capitalism and, moreover, that the operations of the capitalist system (of course, conceived differently by the two positions) would lead to higher levels of development in the normal course of things.

In particular, Dependency Theory was defined in opposition to the prevailing neoclassical position.[7] That view starts from the assumption that the economies of all countries can be arranged on a scale from least to most developed (from backward to advanced, or from low-income to high-income, modified perhaps by the degree of oil reserves). Development is taken to be a unilinear process, and all nations have undergone and will continue to undergo essentially the same process. Presumably, according to this approach, at some point in the past all countries were at a stage of economic development that would now be considered undeveloped. For reasons generally taken to be extraneous to the theory, at some point certain countries began to develop economically, while others lagged behind or failed to develop at all. Different levels of development reflect different starting points and different growth rates. The presently undeveloped countries, then, have yet to undergo this process, and they should see their future in the past course of the presently more developed countries.

The orthodox measure of development is the accumulation of wealth (or "use-values"). According to this measure, most countries in the world are obviously relatively undeveloped in comparison to the so-called First World; but, at the same time, most countries have at least sectors of their economies that are relatively developed in comparison to the overall economy.

Neoclassical theory typically understands the condition of less-developed countries in terms of what is called a dualistic economy. According to the theory of dualism, an economy of an undeveloped nation has two sectors: one traditional and one relatively modern and developed. The two sectors are taken to be largely independent of each other. They may be linked during the transition to modern growth, however, in that the traditional sector may provide labor and an agricultural surplus to the modern sector. The modern sector, moreover, is intertwined in the world capitalist market, while the traditional sector is, in effect, precapitalist and more or less untouched by capitalist market relations. The dynamic of growth is due to trade and general economic activity, so the process of development of the whole economy is seen to involve the modernization or transformation of the traditional sector so as to bring it into the sphere of the market and thus expose it to the possibilities of trade and development offered by the free market.

Methodologically, neoclassical theory claims to present a model of economic backwardness and development that is based on empirical observation and certain theoretical assumptions about the nature of market activity and economic rationality. The market is taken as the central institutional structure that organizes economic activity and rewards efficiency. Individual actors in the market are taken to be rational, or at least capable of rational decision making in light of given needs, desires, and possible rewards. Neoclassical theory is essentially methodologically individualist in that it seeks to understand economic development ultimately in terms of the market behaviors of individual actors. Instances where development has failed to occur are explained either in terms of the absence of certain necessary conditions or in terms of local conditions that distort the proper operation of the market mechanism, preventing actors from behaving rationally.

Frank's original formulation of Dependency Theory begins with a rejection of two of the central theses of this neoclassical dualism. First, Frank rejects the dualist model of the economies of the undeveloped nations in which there are two sectors, only one of which, the more developed, is capitalist. Rather, according to Frank, during the era of European capitalist expansion, most areas, even the geographically remote, were incorporated within the network of capitalist relations. As a result, all parts of the economies of undeveloped nations should be seen to be within the web of capitalism. Not to see them as part of the capitalist system is to misunderstand their nature and operation. Frank (1969, 5) puts this claim forward as an empirical thesis: "A mounting body of evidence suggests, and I am confident that future historical research will confirm, that the expansion of the capitalist system over the past centuries effectively and entirely penetrated even the apparently most isolated sectors of the underdeveloped world."

The second thesis of dualism that Frank rejects is that the present condition of the undeveloped countries is similar to some original, predevelopment stage of the presently developed nations. Rather, Frank asserts, despite certain surface similarities (noncomplexity, nonindustrialization, and/or poverty) between the present condition of the undeveloped nations and the reconstructed past of the now-developed nations, neither the colonial past nor the present of the undeveloped nations resembles in any important respect the past of the developed nations. If we accept the assumption, which Frank seems to accept that, at some point in the past prior to the emergence and expansion of capitalism all countries were more or less the same developmentally (that is, that there was some kind of "original stage" the exact nature of which is never specified by Frank), then it follows that the present condition of the undeveloped nations is not original, primal, or traditional; rather, this state is itself a product of the historical development of capitalism on a world scale.

This point has two important implications. First, there is no single universal trajectory for development that is followed by all nations, for obviously the discrepancy between the more- and less-developed nations today is a result of at least two different developmental paths. Second, if we call the original, predevelopment stage one of undevelopment, then it is no longer correct to refer to the present condition of the less-developed nations today as undeveloped, since their present condition is itself a product of an historical, developmental sequence. Thus, Frank introduces a new term, "under-developed," to characterize the condition of the presently less-developed countries: "The now developed countries were never underdeveloped, though they may have been *un*developed" (Frank 1969, 5, original emphasis; see also Frank 1967, 3–6).

Frank shows little concern for the condition he calls undeveloped. The only relevant history for Frank concerns the "development of underdevelopment," and this process only begins with the penetration of capitalism. What came before is of little concern to Frank, and he has a good theoretical reason, within his model, for this attitude. Whatever the conditions that characterized various areas, regions or countries in their original (i.e., precapitalist) state, these conditions had little or no impact on subsequent development. Whatever the differences, if any, in their original conditions, all countries that are underdeveloped today are characterized by essentially the same conditions, so that the crucial variables explaining this present condition cannot include the original state.

Frank does discuss conditions in underdeveloped areas before the penetration of capitalism in explaining why some countries became developed and others underdeveloped. The kinds of conditions that enter into the explanation at this point, however, concern natural or physical factors, such as natural resources, climate, soil fertility, and so forth. They do not include facts about the economic and social structures that predominated in these areas. Thus, if underdevelopment is, in the first instance, a description of an economic and social condition, then the analogous original conditions (i.e., economic and social) do not enter crucially into the explanation. There is, however, one important historical case where Frank would admit that the original, precapitalist conditions do enter crucially into the explanation. This, of course, is the explanation of the original emergence of capitalism in Europe. But this case is, for the most part, an element of the story of the development of development, and not that of underdevelopment. It follows from what has been said that the process of development for Frank is the process of capitalist development, and that the history of development is the history of capitalism.[8]

Underdevelopment is a condition that characterizes the entire economy of a country, regardless of the different levels of sectoral development. It is a condition, moreover, that characterizes all the presently developing nations. This suggests (although by no means entails) that underdevelopment cannot be explained simply in terms of factors internal to the social and economic histories of the underdeveloped nations, for it seems highly unlikely that the histories of so many nations in different parts of the world with different initial conditions would have been such as to have led to the same outcome. Rather, what is suggested is that there is some common, external causal factor. The theoretical task that Frank undertakes is to identify this factor and incorporate it into a theory that explains the nature and development of underdevelopment.

To accomplish this task, Frank constructs a theoretical model that claims to show how the present condition of underdeveloped countries came about historically and is maintained today. This model employs certain theoretical concepts and posits the existence of certain entities or processes. The concepts are theoretical in the sense that their full meaning can only be grasped in the context of their role in the theoretical model. The posited entities or processes are theoretical in a somewhat different sense. First, their natures can be explained fully only in relation to the model and the theoretical concepts it uses. Second, they cannot be perceived or picked out independently of the theoretical model. They are observable, that is, only through the "lens" of the model. At the same time, the explanatory acceptability of the theoretical model depends, at least in part, on the acceptability of the theoretical concepts. As we shall see below, much of the critical reaction to Frank and, indeed, much of the debate concerning Dependency Theory, revolves around the acceptability of various theoretical concepts and their utilization in explanations of development.

The key concept in this model is dependency, hence "Dependency Theory." This concept is used to pick out and characterize the object of study, namely, the present condition of developing nations. That is, an initial distinction is assumed between developed and developing countries. What are initially identified as developing countries are supposedly selected through a comparison with the developed countries in terms of certain indices, for instance, an index of wealth, both as to its level and distribution.[9] The so-called developing nations, Frank then suggests, are better considered as *under*developed rather than *un*developed in order to distinguish states of development historically produced from those that can be considered in some sense "original" conditions. These underdeveloped nations are then characterized as participating in a relation of dependency. It is because of their dependency relationship, which is to be elaborated in the model, that these countries are underdeveloped. That is, dependency causes underdevelopment.

Dependency relations, in Frank's view, require two parties: one dominant and the other dependent. For Frank, the central dependency relationship exists between the various countries of the developed world and those that are underdeveloped. Historically, the relationship was between a colony and the imperial power that conquered it. Today, it is more a matter of an underdeveloped country and those developed countries with which it has primary economic relations. Various names have been given to the parties to these relationships: metropolis/satellite, core/periphery, or center/periphery.

The metropolis–satellite relationship, to use the term preferred by Frank, is one of dependency because of two features. First, the development of the satellite is dependent on the development of the metropolis, that is, on forces external to the satellite's economy and society. The suggestion in the model is that it is an asymmetrical relationship, with the development of the metropolis being for the most part independent, that is, determined by factors largely internal to the metropolitan economy and society. Thus, dependency in the first instance is a relation of unequal power. The metropolis has power over the course of development in the satellite, but not vice versa. It should be noted that this power need not be consciously realized or exercised, but might be (and generally is) the unintended result of structural relations and operations.

Frank sees the determining relationship as one-sided. Especially in his early work, he does not pay much attention to the reciprocal influence of the satellite on the metropolis. He has, that is to say, an insufficently dialectical understanding of the dependency relation. To say that the metropolis exercises greater power in the sense that Frank stipulates need not commit one to the denial that there is a sense in which the metropolis is also dependent on the satellite. The key to the relationship is control. The metropolis exercises greater power in that it has greater control within the relationship, in the way that a slavemaster who has control of slaves exercises greater power over those slaves, even while he or she may be very dependent on the slaves and, in general, on the master–slave relationship to reproduce him- or herself as slavemaster.

The dependent development of the satellite is such as to disadvantage it further and exacerbate certain problems it experiences, such as poverty and distorted development. The loss for the underdeveloped nation is twofold. Not only is it not in control of its own development, but it does not materially benefit from the relation of dependency. It is worth making this second point because a more sophisticated version of neoclassical theory might argue that developing countries do, at times, enter into dependency relations with developed nations due to certain types of market asymmetries, but that this dependency (here seen as just loss of control in some respects or to some degree) benefits the developing countries because it fosters development per se. It is this latter point that Frank denies. Dependency, for Frank, is a relation of exploitation, and, like "exploitation," "dependency" has a definite negative normative force as well as a descriptive role in Frank's theory.[10] It is also worth pointing out that the object of benefit or harm for Frank is the nation-state as such rather than, for instance, classes. Frank does discuss the fact that certain classes (local ruling classes) can and do benefit, in the short term at least, from underdevelopment, but this benefit is understood against the back-drop of the harm done to the nation as a whole.

While the locus of dependency relationships in Frank's model is the nation-state and relations between nations, the scope of the theory is prop-erly the world capitalist system. Nations are taken to be component parts of this system. To understand the development of underdevelopment in a particular country, it is necessary to place that country's history in the context of this larger system. It is important, according to Frank, to see capitalism as a world system and to understand its central structures. To fail to do so might well lead one both to misidentify the important struc-tures within the underdeveloped countries and to misunderstand the nature of the dependency relation. Dependency, as we shall see, is explained in terms of its function within the larger system, and the theo-retical model used in the explanation must, obviously, correctly charac-terize the system if the explanation is to be successful. A complete explanation of underdevelopment, then, would require nothing less than a full account of the origin, nature, and development of capitalism, for, as Frank (1967, 9) writes, "one and the same historical process of the expan-sion and development of capitalism throughout the world has simultane-ously generated – and continues to generate – both economic development and structural underdevelopment."[11]

By specifying that the scope of his theory is the world *capitalist* system, Frank has, in effect, raised the issue of the definition of "capitalism" that he is using. As various commentators have noted, Frank does not explic-itly define "capitalism."[12] Nevertheless, it is a fairly straightforward task to discern how he uses the term. As we have said, Frank takes capitalism to be a world system, one that has existed since at least the sixteenth century. It has gone through three stages: mercantilist, industrial, and financial capitalism. What has remained constant through all the stages is a certain kind of exchange relationship characteristic of metropolis–satellite relations:

> Whatever we may wish to say about its mercantilist, then industrial, then financial capitalist metropolis, in the peripheries of the world capitalist system the essential nature of the metropolis–satellite rela-tions remains commercial, however "feudal" or personal seeming these relations may appear.
>
> (Frank 1967, 20; see also 14–15)

If the periphery has been capitalist since the first European incursions and, if what has remained constant across the various stages is the nature of the exchange relations, then capitalism must be defined in terms of this rela-tion.[13] Ernesto Laclau (1971, 24–25) fills out this definition attributed to

Frank in the following way: Frank understands by capitalism "(a) a system of production for the market, in which (b) profit constitutes the motive of production, and (c) this profit is realized for the benefit of someone other than the direct producer, who is thereby dispossessed of it."

If capitalism is defined in terms of market exchange relations of a certain kind, we should specify more exactly what kind they are. As we have seen, according to Laclau's interpretation of Frank, the essential capitalist relation is a market exchange whereby profit is realized for the benefit of someone other than the direct producer. We have also seen that dependency relations in general for Frank involve power relations where one party is disadvantaged to the gain of the other. Third, we have noted that, for Frank, the dependency relations that generate underdevelopment must be understood in terms of the capitalist world system. Putting these points together, we can conclude that, for Frank, the essential capitalist relation is a dependency relation and thus a relation of unequal power. In other words, capitalism in the first instance is to be regarded as a system of power; power exercised through a particular form of relation, namely, a market exchange relation.

In what sense are capitalist market exchange relations relations of power? According to Frank, dependency relations in general, and metropolis–satellite relations within capitalism in particular, are best characterized as monopolistic and extractive. The metropolis exerts monopolistic control over economic and trade relations in the periphery. Monopoly domination within a market is, of course, a position of power. This position of power allows the metropolis to extract an economic surplus from the satellite. The appropriation of this surplus and its accumulation, in and under the control of the metropolis, is the central factor that deprives the underdeveloped nation of the ability to control its own growth, and thus leaves it dependent. The monopolistic, extractive relation was initially established by force of arms but, once in place, subsequent development perpetuates it through the structures of dependency and underdevelopment.

Two points should be noted about the monopolistic-extractive nature of the metropolis–satellite relation. The first is that any theory that attempts to conceptualize economic exchanges, in what Frank considers the underdeveloped nations in terms of equivalent market exchanges, necessarily, from his point of view, distorts the nature of what transpires. The outstanding theoretical issue is, of course, how to verify the existence of monopolistic market distortions and the "exploitative" transfer of surplus. This is a fundamental point of contention between neoclassical theories and Dependency Theory. In general, where a neoclassical theorist would see a free market and mutual advantage, Frank sees a structure of monopolistic relations and surplus transfer.

The second point to note is that Frank's concept of economic surplus is taken more or less directly from the work of Paul Baran. Frank appears to believe that Baran's concept is the same as that used by Marx in his analysis of "the surplus value created by producers and its appropriation by capitalists."[14] Many commentators have pointed out, however, that, according to Marx's theory, the extraction of surplus takes place by virture of the capital–wage-labor relation within production while, for Frank, the extraction is a function of exchange relations in the market. The two concepts are, therefore, not the same. One difference to be noted in this context is that Marx emphasizes that, for the purposes of his model, he is assuming that market relations are exchanges of equivalents while, as we have seen, Frank takes them to be monopolistic power relations involving the exchange of non-equivalents.

If Frank does conceive of capitalism in terms of a certain kind of market exchange relation, with production oriented towards the market, then three points should be noted that will be relevant to later criticisms of Frank. First, if the nature of the metropolis–satellite relationship remains a constant, then the analysis of the "development of underdevelopment" is, in a certain sense, ahistorical (Frank 1967, 12). The central dynamic and structures are the same at all points in the history of the phenomenon. For Frank (1967, 6), the focus of his theory, therefore, is "the continuity and ubiquity of the structural essentials of economic development and underdevelopment throughout the expansion and development of the capitalist system at all times and places." What is to be emphasized is continuity, not change.

Second, what defines the essential nature of an economic relation is its relationship to the larger system and, in particular, whether it is caught up in a commercial market exchange network that is connected to metropolitan development. Thus, Frank can say, in the quotation given above, that however "feudal seeming" a relation may be, if it is part of such a market network, then the relation is capitalist. Among the things to be noted here is the implication for the theory-ladenness of the possible observations involved. Merely observing a relation in a supposedly theory-neutral way would not allow the correct characterization of the relation. A relation that might, at first observation, be "seen" as feudal is really not feudal. Only by viewing it in terms of the theory can the relation be "seen" correctly.

The third point to be noted in light of Frank's definition of capitalism is that he focuses on exchange relations and pays relatively little attention to the so-called relations of production. This emphasis is especially obvious in his early work. The concept of the relations of production is one that is traditionally prominent in many Marxist analyses. Therefore, some Marxist critics in particular take exception to Frank on this point. And, as we shall see, the dispute over where the theoretical emphasis should be placed – on exchange or on production relations – is one of the key points in the Dependency Theory debates. In part, the dispute is over what is to function as the key explanatory variable or, in terms of the theoretical model, over what is to be taken as an independent and what as a dependent variable.

In our discussion of dependency relations thus far we have focused on the form of the relation of metropolis to satellite at the level of nation-states. This relation is the primary one within Frank's model. However, the nation–nation relation is not the only form of a metropolis–satellite relation for Frank. Rather, there is a chain of such relationships, all of which manifest the same form or structure. At the pinnacle of this chain is the nation–nation relationship of metropolis–satellite. But within the satellite itself, the structurally identical relationship is repeated on lower, and increasingly local, levels of the economy. The theoretical model, then, can be seen as a series of steps, each connection from step to lower step reiterating the same structural relations. As Frank (1967, 16) puts it:

> It is a major thesis of this essay that this same structure extends from the macrometropolitan center of the world capitalist system "down" to the most supposedly isolated agricultural workers, who, through this chain of interlinked metropolitan–satellite relationships, are tied to the central world metropolis and thereby incorporated into the world capitalist system as a whole.

There may seem at first to be real differences among the variety of metropolis–satellite dependency relationships; for instance, a nation–nation relationship seems very unlike that between an owner of a latifundium and a dependent sharecropper. Nevertheless, Frank maintains, they are essentially the same in structure, and it is their structure that determines their nature, despite the ready and apparent surface differences. This point, of course, can only be appreciated by "seeing" the relationships through the lens of the appropriate theory.

One last feature of Frank's theoretical model needs to be mentioned. The model has definite implications for the type of political developments and, in particular, for the nature of the class structure that one can expect to accompany the development of economic underdevelopment. It is necessary for Frank to address the issue of political development in order to provide some mechanism to account for how the policy of underdevelopment, as he calls it, is put into effect and maintained, especially after an underdeveloped colony achieves de jure independence, thus making the option to use the open coercion of an imperial power less feasible (see Frank 1972, 13).

Within the model, classes are understood, in the first instance, in terms of structural positions within a system of power relations. At each point in the metropolis–satellite chain, the structure of the chain creates certain objective interests with the most important being the interest in controlling the monopoly relationship at that point in the chain so as to be able to benefit from the extractive power available at that position. The group that coheres around that interest is, in effect, the ruling class of that area, region or nation. Since the ruling class at each point in the structure is dependent on the entire structure remaining more or less the same, so that the monopoly relationships can be maintained, each ruling class, in effect, bolsters every other ruling class. All ruling classes thus have an interest in perpetuating the development of underdevelopment, for that is precisely the structure that allows them to satisfy their interests as they discover them. As Frank (1967, 94) puts it:

> My thesis holds that the group interests which led to the continued underdevelopment of Chile [as a case in point] and the economic development of some other countries were themselves created by the same economic structure which encompassed all these groups: the world capitalist system . . . It was in the nature of the structure of this system to produce interests leading to underdevelopment in the countries of the periphery, such as Chile, once they had already been effectively incorporated into the system as satellites.[15]

Frank does not explicitly address the question of why the same groups that were economically powerful were also politically dominant, so that they could implement politically the policies that would benefit them economically. Any attempt on the part of Frank to fill in this gap, either in terms of an instrumental version of the Marxist theory of the state, or in terms of a general theory of the convergence of economic and political elites, would only push the problem back one level.

The theoretical model sketched above is to be found in Frank's early work. His later work carries the model forward in most of its essentials, but there are a few points of theoretical development, especially in *Dependent Accumulation and Underdevelopment*, that deserve a brief mention. In this book, Frank announces that he is responding to three criticisms of his earlier work. The three criticisms amount, in effect, to the charges that Frank did not pay sufficient attention to relations of production and thus overemphasized external as opposed to internal variables in his explanation of underdevelopment; that he was insufficiently historical and thus failed to appreciate and account for important differences across stages of the development of underdevelopment; and that he did not succeed in demonstrating the interconnections between metropolitan development and the dependent underdevelopment (Frank 1979, xii). In response, Frank admits that a complete theoretical model of underdevelopment would have to pay more attention to the mode of production within the underdeveloped nation and to how it changes, or does not change, through the different stages of capitalist development. Furthermore, it would have to be more sensitive to the ways in which the dynamic of the development of underdevelopment can help to determine the nature of metropolitan development, which, in turn helps to determine the further course of the development of underdevelopment; or, in a word, Frank admits that his model should be more dialectical. He thinks that these changes can be incorporated by refocusing the model more on the accumulation process seen from the point of view of the world system.

We cannot go into a thorough analysis of how Frank amends his theoretical model to account for these criticisms. It will have to suffice to say that, while his focus in *Dependent Accumulation and Underdevelopment* is somewhat different from that of his earlier work in that more attention is paid to accumulation on the world scale, the essentials of his model still remain more or less as they were and as we outlined them above. Despite discussions of the accumulation process, his work still seems to focus on capitalism as, in the first instance, a process of exchange and not of a certain form of relations of production. Frank does, in this later work, use the concept of mode of production, but he offers no real analysis of the concept and it seems to function less as an explanatory concept and more as a way of indicating awareness of historical difference. "Mode of production," as used by Frank, allows him to mark off different ways in which dependent economies have been organized. But, to the degree that the concept is focused on the organization of production, it remains subordinated to the notion of exchange relations. Whatever the mode of production within the dependent country, the satellite is still considered to exist within the world capitalist system and thus, in the last analysis, to be capitalist. In the end, we believe that Frank's theoretical model and its explanatory force remains basically the same in his later work.

Before going on to discuss other positions in the Dependency Theory debates that developed out of or in opposition to Frank, it is worth examining some of the criticisms of Frank. In particular, we will look in detail at the arguments of two critics, Lall and Brenner. They can be seen as two representative positions which are critical of the original formulation of Dependency Theory by Frank. Lall concentrates on the adequacy of the concept of dependence. Brenner casts a wider net, questioning Frank's use of concepts such as capitalism and class, and arguing that Frank has the order of explanation wrong. The arguments of a third critic, Laclau, will then figure in our discussion of the Modes of Production approach. While those are only three among the many critics of Frank, they raise interesting and important theoretical issues that help to illuminate Frank's approach to development.

Two methodological critics of Frank

Lall

Sanjaya Lall provides a somewhat limited but methodologically interesting criticism of Frank.[16] Lall's focus is the use of the concept of dependence. His concern, as a sympathetic critic of Dependency Theory, is that the central concept of the theory, that of a dependency relation or, as he puts it, dependence, has not been adequately formulated. In particular,

Lall (1975, 800) thinks that the concept sometimes seems to be defined in a circular or question-begging manner:

> Less developed countries (LDCs) are poor because they are dependent, and any characteristics that they display signify dependence. In such tautologous definitions, "dependence" tends to be identified with features of LDCs which the economist in question happens to dislike, and ceases to offer an independent and verifiable explanation of the processes at work in the less developed world.

Lall suggests two criteria that should be used to construct an adequate concept of dependence. The first criterion stipulates that the concept should "lay down certain characteristics of dependent economies which are not found in non-dependent ones." The second criterion stipulates further that the characteristics so designated "must be shown to affect adversely the course and pattern of development of the dependent countries" (Lall 1975, 800).

To understand what Lall's point is in suggesting these criteria, it is important to keep in mind a central thesis of Dependency Theory, namely, that dependence causes underdevelopment. If this thesis is interpreted as an ordinary causal claim, then its claim is that there is a correlation that supports a causal relation between two variables – the condition of being dependent and the condition of being underdeveloped. Now, if we are to verify this thesis, it must be possible to identify these two conditions independently. If, as Lall suggests happens, the condition of being dependent is "identified with features of LDCs which the economist in question happens to dislike," then there is a considerable chance that the same characteristics used to identify one condition will be used to pick out the other. This is especially true given that dependency theorists conceive of underdevelopment as a condition that is the result of, and results in, adverse effects. For example, if being poor is taken to be an essential characteristic of economies that are underdeveloped, then if "dependence" is defined in terms of, or picked out by, the state of being poor, it becomes true by definition that dependent economies are underdeveloped. But if this proposition is true by definition, it cannot be taken to be expressing a causal relation.

For the same reasons that it is necessary to identify the condition of being dependent independently of the condition of being underdeveloped, it is necessary to be able to differentiate dependent from nondependent economies. Again, consider the thesis that dependence causes underdevelopment. Assume that all economies in the world can be (roughly) categorized as either dependent or nondependent. If the thesis is to have any explanatory merit, given our assumption, then it must be true that an economy is underdeveloped if, and only if, it is dependent. This is to say that the condition of underdevelopment is caused by, and only by, the condition of dependence. What if, however, the characteristics used to pick out the condition of dependence were also true of some or all economies that are taken initially to be nondependent? If this were the case, then obviously the causal thesis could not be coherently applied and tested.

However, this is simply Lall's view of the case. He surveys a variety of attempts to differentiate dependent from nondependent economies, attempts that include the use of economic and noneconomic as well as static and dynamic characteristics. In all instances, Lall concludes, the attempt fails. Whatever characteristic or set of characteristics is used, either it applies to some nondependent economies as well as to dependent ones, or it fails to apply to all dependent ones. Lall's conclusion is the strong one that:

> the concept of dependence as applied to less developed countries is impossible to define and cannot be shown to be causally related to a continuance of underdevelopment. It is usually given an *arbitrarily selective definition which picks certain features of a much broader phenomenon of international capitalist development*, and its selectivity only serves to misdirect analysis and research in this area.
>
> (1975, 808–9, original emphasis)

In our opinion, Lall's conclusion is a little overstated, or at least a little premature. We do find much of his analysis of the use of the concept of dependence convincing as a criticism internal to Dependency Theory. Dependency theorists do need to pay more attention to the construction of their concepts, especially that of dependence. However, even if all attempts so far to construct an adequate concept have failed, that does not prove that the project, as such, is wrong-headed and that all future attempts will fail.

An additional point should be made concerning Lall's criticism. Consider again his claim that all attempts to construct a concept of dependence have failed to provide a concept that applies to all dependent economies, and only to them. This claim, however, seems to presuppose that there is a way of initially distinguishing all economies as either dependent or nondependent so as to be able to determine whether a concept does or does not apply to them. In other words, the denial of the adequacy of all concept candidates so far seems itself to presuppose an adequate concept. This may be stating the point too strongly, however. We might interpret Lall's claim in the following way: there are certain economies, let us say those of the very poorest LDCs, that everyone can agree initially are dependent.[17] Likewise, there are certain economies that everyone can initially agree are nondependent. Let us attempt to construct a concept of dependence by generalizing from what seem to be the salient characteristics of these clear cases. Lall's claim, thus interpreted, is that no concept that will be adequate can be constructed in this way. Again, we feel that this claim has an a priori ring about it that Lall's argument, which is essentially inductive, cannot substantiate.

Further, a determined dependency theorist has available the following reply to Lall:

> Even though my concept of dependence seems to you [Lall] to pick out some economies that you consider to be nondependent, I disagree. I have carefully constructed my concept and it is a coherent and convincing one, stipulating conditions that, if true, must demonstrate the existence of dependence. Thus, I consider as dependent all economies to which it applies, even those that you, given your initial intuitions, want to claim are non-dependent. That is, I use my concept to overrule your (and perhaps my own) intuitions. That is part of the way science progresses.

Lall obviously has a reply to his critic, and the discussion goes on. We cannot follow it any further here. Lall's criticism is a methodologically important one, but not one that leaves the determined dependency theorist bereft of moves.

Brenner

Robert Brenner presents a more wide-ranging and extensive criticism of Frank than that of Lall. Brenner (1977, 83) concedes that Frank's descriptions of the mechanisms of surplus transfer from the underdeveloped periphery to the developed core and of the resulting distortion of the economies of the periphery "clearly capture important aspects of the functioning reality of underdevelopment." But, in Brenner's opinion, while Frank's account may have descriptive adequacy, it fails to explain anything. In particular, it fails to explain the origins of underdevelopment. That is, Brenner rejects Frank's thesis that the development of underdevelopment is part of, and necessitated by, the development of capitalism in the metropolis.

Most of Brenner's argument is directed against the work of Paul Sweezy and Immanuel Wallerstein rather than Frank.[18] Since, however, Brenner sees Wallerstein's project of discovering the roots of development in the core as a continuation of and complement to Frank's work, the criticisms can be taken to apply to both theorists. The major problem that Brenner has with the Frank–Wallerstein position has to do with the definition of capitalism it assumes. As we saw above, Frank (in common with Wallerstein) conceptualizes capitalism in terms of a system of power exercised through exchange relations and involving production oriented toward profit in the market. The essential relation marking an economy as capitalist, the point at which power is exercised in the first instance, is a certain type of market exchange within a world system of metropolis–satellite dependency relations.

According to Brenner, it follows from this conception of capitalism that the accumulation process is centrally concerned with the generation of absolute surplus-value, value that is extracted by casting a wider and more intensive net over labor. It also follows from this starting point that the issue of the origins and development of capitalism primarily concerns the rise of a world commercial network and an expanding world market. In addition, Brenner argues that Frank and Wallerstein's model of capitalism leads them to understand class structure as determined in a rather mechanistic fashion by market relations. Market opportunities determine the nature of economic development in a given area and, in particular, the nature of production. The resulting requirements on production, in turn, determine the nature of the class structure. The classes that arise are structured by the dominant production process, and the production process that arises is the one best suited in a given area at a given time to allow the maximum extraction of absolute surplus-value by the ruling class. This model, and the explanation of both development and underdevelopment that it supports is, according to Brenner, theoretically inadequate and leads to empirically false explanations.

To appreciate why Brenner takes the Frank–Wallerstein position to be theoretically and explanatorily inadequate, it is necessary to contrast it with Brenner's understanding of capitalism. For Brenner, the defining and unique characteristic of capitalism is its tendency, not simply to develop, but to do so by way of expanding the productive forces. In other words, capitalism is a system of production involving, in particular, the extraction of relative surplus-value.

> For capitalism differs from all pre-capitalist modes of production in its *systematic* tendency to unprecedented, though neither continuous nor unlimited, economic development – in particular through the expansion of what might be called (after Marx's terminology) relative as opposed to absolute surplus value.
>
> (Brenner 1977, 30, original emphasis)

Expansion of productivity through technical innovation, Marx's revolutionary expansion of the forces of production, can occur only where it is possible to move labor in and out of the production process as best suits the available technology. Otherwise, the incentive for innovation would be lacking. But this form of labor mobility, according to Brenner, can only occur within a certain class structure, namely, one where labor is free wage-labor that is at the mercy of market forces; in other words, where labor power is a commodity. Thus, in Brenner's view, capitalism as a system of production oriented toward a specific form of accumulation (based on the extraction of relative surplus-value) necessitates a specific class structure. But, in contrast to the Frank–Wallerstein view, Brenner's position is that capitalism does not create the class structure it requires. Rather, capitalism can only exist within the confines of this class structure. The initial emergence of this class structure is thus a necessary condition for the emergence of capitalism, and the reproduction of this class structure is a necessary condition for the continued reproduction of capitalism. The problem of the origins of capitalism for Brenner, then, is not the development of a world market system, as it is for the Frank–Wallerstein position. Rather, the problem for Brenner is the emergence of the necessary class structure or, in other words, the genesis of labor power as a commodity.

Brenner's model of capitalism, then, leads to the result that the crucial explanatory variable in his account of underdevelopment is the class structure. Capitalism can exist only where the class structure accommodates it. And what ultimately determines the class structure are the outcomes of class struggles. The outcomes of class struggles, however, according to Brenner, cannot be determined in advance; it is not a matter of a mechanistic, deterministic process. Rather, in each instance under study, the particular conditions of class conflict, especially the opportunities available to the "ruling class" to exploit labor through extraction of either absolute or relative surplus-value, must be analyzed in order to understand the possibilities inherent in the situation that could, but did not have to, be realized. Market opportunities do not determine class, as in the Frank–Wallerstein view. Rather, the outcomes of class struggle condition the kind of market relations that are to be engaged in, for example, whether profit-maximization is to be pursued. In Brenner's view, and contrary to Frank and Wallerstein, "neither economic development nor underdevelopment are *directly* dependent upon, caused by, one another. Each is the product of a specific evolution of class relations, *in part* determined historically *'outside'* capitalism, in relationship with non-capitalist modes" (Brenner 1977, 61, original emphasis).

Development and underdevelopment, therefore, are explained by Brenner in terms of the particular opportunities for surplus extraction made possible by the different class configurations, free wage-labor, in the case of development, and forced feudal or slave labor, at least initially, in the case of underdevelopment. In particular,

the onset of a capitalist dynamic of development was thus, in the first appearance, made possible as an unintended consequence of class conflicts – conflicts in which the peasantry freed themselves from the extra-economic controls of the ruling class, while the latter secured ownership of the land. The resulting overall class structure of production and reproduction made possible an unprecedented degree of correspondence between the needs of surplus extraction and the *continuing development* of the productive forces through accumulation and innovation.

(Brenner 1977, 82–83, original emphasis)

Similarly,

the development of underdevelopment was rooted in the class struc-ture of production based on the extension of absolute surplus labour, which determined a sharp *disjuncture* between the requirements for the development of the productive forces (productivity of labour) and the structure of profitability of the economy as a whole.

(Brenner 1977, 85, original emphasis)

Brenner, then, presents a model of capitalism that contrasts with that of Frank, not so much in terms of the description of underdevelopment, as in the account of the origins of the structures that produce the conditions of underdevelopment. The two positions start off with different conceptions of capitalism. This initial difference leads to differences concerning the central dynamic of capitalism: in particular, the nature of the characteristic accumulation process. Given these differences, Brenner and Frank arrive at contrasting conclusions about the importance of class structure as an explanatory variable. For Brenner it is central; for Frank it plays, at best, a minor explanatory role. It is important to reiterate that, for Brenner, class structure is the outcome of class struggles and the outcome of class strug-gles cannot be determined in advance; or, at least, the outcome is a vari-able, the determination of which falls outside the theoretical model in question.

We have, then, two contrasting models and an important difference in the form of explanation involved in each. How might we decide between them? We cannot give a complete answer to this question here, but it is instructive to summarize the nature of the criticisms that Brenner makes of the Frank–Wallerstein position. First, as we have seen, Brenner contends that the Frank–Wallerstein view is empirically inadequate. Brenner pres-ents case studies of development in Poland, France, England, the Caribbean, and Virginia. In each case, Brenner argues, historical events can better be accounted for by his model of capitalism than by the Frank–Wallerstein model. On this level, joining the argument would require that both parties agree on some initial description of what actually occurred in each case history. Each side would then have to attempt to demonstrate in detail why its theoretical redescription and explanation of the history were superior to those of its rival. This process obviously does not admit of a clear way to establish the superior position, and it has the possible imme-diate problem of the two sides' not agreeing even on a common initial description of the subject matter.

The second form of criticism is based on conceptual analysis. Here, the important claim made by Brenner is that the definition of capitalism used by Frank and Wallerstein is inadequate. The argument is that their definition gives a necessary, but not sufficient, condition for the existence of capitalism. Brenner admits that "there is no doubt that capitalism is a system in which production for a profit via exchange predominates." However, "production for exchange is perfectly compatible with a system in which it is either unnecessary or impossible, or both, to reinvest in expanded, improved production in order to 'profit'" (Brenner 1977, 32). The claim is that production for exchange for profit is compatible with, and indeed takes place in, systems that even Frank and Wallerstein would have to admit were not capitalist. They could reply, of course, by denying that such systems were capitalist or by claiming that it is a matter of degree and, therefore, that once production for exchange for profit becomes the dominant relation, the claimed compatibility is no longer possible. A second criticism follows from Brenner's claim that there are problems with Frank and Wallerstein's understanding of some of their basic concepts. This charge is that the difficulties inherent in correctly conceptualizing the object of study prevent Frank and Wallerstein from being able to raise certain questions that Brenner considers important. And, in turn, not being able to raise certain questions further prevents Frank and Wallerstein from being able to confront and explain certain facts that Brenner holds as central to his account.[19] This charge, of course, could be countered by denying the importance of the contended questions and facts.

The third form of criticism has to do with explanatory adequacy. Brenner makes a number of points in this regard. For example, the Frank–Wallerstein model, Brenner contends, assumes that the individuals who control the means of production have the motivation, the rationality, and the freedom to pursue profit-maximization. That is, as Brenner (1977, 58) interprets it, the model assumes "the extra-historical universe of *homo oeconomicus*, of individual profit maximizers competing on the market, outside of any system of social relations of exploitation."[20] But there are at least two related problems with this assumption. First, this assumed universe is not some abstract, extra-historical realm; rather, it is the world of capitalism. The conditions specified by this model exist in, and only in, the capitalist market. Insofar as this model is used to explain the initial emergence of capitalism, and insofar as it assumes in its explanatory framework conditions that only exist within capitalism, it obviously begs the question.[21]

This is a familiar criticism, made first by Marx of Adam Smith. It is because Brenner finds Sweezy, Frank, and Wallerstein all guilty of this same fundamental mistake, as well as guilty of sharing "individualistic-mechanist presuppositions" with Smith, that he labels them "neo-Smithians." They are, however, neo-Smithians with a twist, or rather, an inversion, for "it has been their [Sweezy, Frank, and Wallerstein's] intention to negate the optimistic model of economic advance derived from Adam Smith" (Brenner 1977, 27). Smith's model of economic development is inverted to become Frank's model of the development of underdevelopment. The result of this inversion, according to Brenner (1977, 27) is "an alternative theory of capitalist development which is, in its central aspects, the mirror image of the 'progressist' thesis they wish to surpass."

The second problem with the assumption of rational profit-maximization is that it reflects the failure on the part of both Frank and Wallerstein to understand adequately the relations between individuals and social structures, in particular, class structures. In Brenner's view, the individual is much more produced by and constrained by class structures than Frank or Wallerstein seem to allow. This criticism is of a piece with Brenner's contention that Frank and Wallerstein do not accord class structure its proper explanatory role as a variable. As Brenner reads them, Frank and Wallerstein make class structure (reflected first of all in the relations of production) a consequence of the behavior of rational individuals in the market. For Brenner, this view has the relationship completely backwards. Individual rationality and behavior must be understood as conditioned and constrained by the existing class structure. Not to see the relation in this way, Brenner implies, is to have a fundamental mistake as the very basis of one's social theory.[22]

This discussion does not exhaust the criticisms that Brenner makes of the Frank–Wallerstein model, to say nothing of criticisms made by other commentators in the debates over Dependency Theory.[23] The criticisms we have mentioned do reflect, however, some of the levels on which the issues are joined and some of the more methodological considerations that enter into the debates. We now proceed to examine some of the positions that have emerged out of these debates with Frank.

The Modes of Production school

The debate concerning Dependency Theory entered a new stage with the emergence of the Modes of Production (MOP) school. The various approaches encompassed by this rubric represent both a criticism of the early forms of Dependency Theory, chiefly as represented by the writings of Frank (and, later, Wallerstein) and an extension of the basic problematic of Dependency Theory. The focus of the explanation of the persistence of underdevelopment is shifted by the MOP theorists away from what they understand to be the excessive emphasis in traditional Dependency Theory on a global scheme that exaggerates the role of external relations and markets. Instead, while not denying the importance of macro phenomena, relations between nations, and flows of commodities, they have focused on developing the concept of mode of production in an attempt to construct an alternative understanding of the phenomenon of underdevelopment.

Despite the shift of focus, the object of investigation remains the specific forms of development of what is taken to be the periphery of the world economy. Moreover, the concepts of dependency and underdevelopment, although defined differently, are not themselves challenged. In this sense, the MOP school represents, not a break from but, rather, an alternative formulation and extension of Dependency Theory itself.

Within the MOP school, three basic approaches can be distinguished. The "articulation of MOP" approach, as it has been termed, tends to explain the phenomenon of underdevelopment in terms of the relationships among and between the capitalist and other, noncapitalist modes of production existing within underdeveloped economies.[24] A second related approach, that of the "colonial or peripheral MOP," has sought to develop a set of concepts of modes of production that are specific to the colonial experiences and peripheral status of the developing countries.[25] According to this group of theorists, the concepts of modes of production that should be used to analyze the societies of the periphery are fundamentally different from those that have been used to investigate the countries of the center. Finally, there are MOP theorists who focus on what they call the "internationalization of capital" or the laws of motion of the capitalist mode of production.[26] In this view, international development (including development within specific nations) is analyzed in terms of the presumed dominance of the capitalist mode of production in the world economy. Each one of these approaches has staked out a different position in the dependency theory debate. The starting point in all cases is a concept of mode of production; however, they represent three alternative ways of constructing a theoretical model in terms of which an explanation of the past and present economic and social structures of developing countries can be generated.

Background

Although the work of many of the MOP theorists has been relatively well-documented,[27] the theoretical sources of this attempt to analyze development by using concepts of modes of production are less well-known. There are five major points that should be briefly elaborated. First, the various efforts to construct a theory centered on concepts of modes of production grew out of attempts to provide a link between Frank's relatively global model of metropolis–satellite relations and the ethnographic detail that emerged from detailed, especially anthropological, studies of developing countries. Many researchers found it difficult to relate the wealth of empirical detail generated in the course of fieldwork to the overarching logic of patterns of surplus transfer between the core and periphery of the world economy that form the focus of Frank's model.[28] The concepts and conceptual strategies of a group of French anthropologists who analyzed African underdevelopment in terms of modes of production represented one attempt to bridge this gap between existing theory and empirical research.[29]

A second factor that gave rise to the proliferation of MOP approaches to development was the reaction against Frank's seeing "capitalism everywhere," that is, that commodity flows or markets were present and such markets were sufficient to characterize the society in question as capitalist. Laclau's *New Left Review* article (1971) is the *locus classicus* of this criticism of Frank's work. Frank was accused of making all of the underdeveloped countries' social structures capitalist, from the sixteenth century onward, because he mistakenly identified markets or trade relations with capitalism. Laclau's alternative was to emphasize the primacy of the conditions of production over those of exchange.

To this end, Laclau (1971, 33) proceeded to define a concept of mode of production as a combination of four factors: the pattern of ownership of the means of production, the form of appropriation of what he called an economic surplus, the degree of the division of labor, and the level of development of the forces of production. In addition, Laclau distinguishes between a "mode of production" and an "economic system" to take account of the participation of *precapitalist modes of production* in a world *capitalist economic system*. An economic system is generally defined by Laclau as an articulated (or combined) set of different modes of production. In particular, the world capitalist system is not conceived to be a uniform production system – that is, a system with one exclusive mode of production. Rather, it is conceived to be an economic system in which both capitalist and noncapitalist modes of production coexist and which is characterized by the predominance of the capitalist mode of production. According to Laclau, Marxist theorists should attempt to understand underdeveloped countries in terms of the system of relations – the articulation – between the capitalist and other, noncapitalist modes of production, rather than in terms of Frank's homogeneous capitalist relations.

Third, the use of the concept of mode of production in Laclau's critique of Frank, and as the basis of an alternative framework of analysis that displaces Frank's focus on commodity flows, was itself predicated on a return to the work of Marx through the writings of Louis Althusser and Étienne Balibar.[30] These two French theorists had taken up the project of reformulating the basic concepts of historical materialism. Among their primary concerns was to combat what they considered to be various non-Marxist forms of "essentialism" within the Marxist theoretical tradition.[31] In particular, the explanation of social phenomena in terms of an essential human nature or an economic determinism was criticized. Their effort to formulate a concept of mode of production, along with the concept of overdetermination, and to produce a nonessentialist Marxist social theory was central to the emergence of the concept of mode of production as an object of theoretical attention.

A fourth source of the MOP school was the reexamination of Marx's own analysis of the so-called original accumulation of capital and the transition from feudalism to capitalism. Marx's account of the emergence and development of some of the economic, political, and cultural conditions of capitalism in a noncapitalist, feudal setting is filtered through the Dobb-Sweezy "transition debate" to become an additional component of the MOP analysis of the transition to capitalism in developing countries.[32] The relevance of the transition debate is twofold. First, the MOP analysis of underdevelopment is concerned with the emergence, or lack thereof, of the capitalist mode of production in the developing countries and hence, implicitly or explicitly, with a comparison with the European experience. Second, once the idea of transition (e.g., to the capitalist mode of production) is analyzed, the combined existence of different, capitalist and noncapitalist modes of production during the period of transition becomes an object of theoretical attention.

Finally, the work of Barry Hindess and Paul Hirst (1975) deserves a brief mention. Although not explicitly addressed to the question of developing countries, theirs is arguably the most sophisticated attempt to construct a set of concepts of noncapitalist modes of production. Their analyses of primitive communal, ancient, slave, and feudal modes of production were particularly instructive. However, their subsequent rejection (1977), based on both methodological and epistemological considerations, of the concept of mode of production has received much less attention in the MOP literature.

These are some of the historical and theoretical conditions, among others, out of which the MOP school emerged and to which it has responded over time. We turn now to a brief summary of the three approaches that have used the concept of mode of production as their entry point into the analysis of dependency and underdevelopment.

Articulation of modes of production

Laclau's critique of Frank announced the beginning of a Marxian reconceptualization of Dependency Theory based on the articulation of modes of production. Taking the concept of modes of production as their starting point, articulation of MOP theorists have sought to analyze the relations among and between the various possible capitalist and noncapitalist modes of production. The overriding objective has been, following Laclau, to produce a general theory of the articulation of modes of production within a capitalist economic system. The central focus of the articulation of MOP theorists is, in particular, the system of relations between the capitalist mode of production and the set of preexisting noncapitalist modes of production in the developing countries. A principal methodological concern in understanding this approach, then, is the constitution and use of the central concepts of mode of production and articulation within their theoretical model.

How can different capitalist and noncapitalist modes of production be combined or articulated in a single social formation within the context of capitalist development? In general, three alternative forms or models might be used to answer this question. The two salient variables of these models are the form of interaction and the degree of dominance by one mode of production over the others. One possibility is that the various modes of production are seen to exist alongside, but essentially independently of, one another. This position has traditionally been called "dualism" and Frank's original rejection of it is shared by the articulation of MOP theorists. A second answer is that the various modes of production in any particular society are interrelated under the dominance of one of these modes of production. One mode of production (for example, capitalism) would be understood to dominate the others in the sense of determining the nature of their existence – their reproduction over time, any changes they may undergo and their eventual demise. A third possible model holds that the modes of production are combined in such a way that there is, in general, no dominant mode of production. Thus, there would be no general outcome of the articulation of modes of production in the sense of one mode necessarily "winning out" over all others. The only way to understand the particular outcome of articulation (for instance, capitalist development) would be in terms of the analysis of the specific factors involved in the concrete combination of modes of production in any particular society.

The second alternative (that of capitalist dominance) still allows two possibilities that should be noted. On one hand, the articulation of modes of production may be such that capitalism clearly and quickly overwhelms and determines the outcome of other modes of production. The result is that the transition to the exclusive existence of capitalism would be of relatively short duration. On the other hand, the transition to capitalism may be understood as a long and complex process, such that any society in transition can only be understood in terms of different stages of articulation between the capitalist and noncapitalist modes of production.

The first variation of this position of the general dominance of the capitalist mode of production is usually attributed to the early theorists of imperialism, writers such as Lenin (1933) and Luxemburg (1951). The articulation of MOP theorists, in contrast, adopt the second variation of the second alternative. Central to this latter view is an understanding of the transition to capitalism as long and problematic, and thus in need of detailed analysis in each case.

It is necessary, then, to understand the notion of articulation in this light. "Articulation," as it is used to analyze the combined presence of different capitalist and noncapitalist modes of production during the course of transition to capitalism, takes on the dual meaning of "joining together" and "giving expression to."[33] Modes of production are conceived to be articulated in a social formation such that:

- the development of each mode of production is closely connected with (in the sense of being both dependent on and/or determined by) the other modes of production; and

- the way that one mode of production is manifested or expressed cannot be analyzed independently of how others are manifested.

Pierre-Philippe Rey (1971, 1973, and 1975) is one theorist who has attempted to produce a general theory of the relations among modes of production within a peripheral capitalist economic system using the concept of articulation.[34] His theory specifies three distinct and successive stages of articulation. In the first stage, the capitalist mode of production is "imported" into the noncapitalist peripheral society and proceeds to *reinforce* and, in some instances, to *create* noncapitalist modes of production. Second, capitalism "takes root" and *uses*, from its dominant position, the noncapitalist modes of production. Finally, at some point not yet reached by most developing countries, the capitalist mode of production *supplants* all noncapitalist modes of production: noncapitalism disappears. The often violent and prolonged nature of these stages of articulation in peripheral societies serves, in Rey's framework of analysis, to distinguish the articulation between capitalist and noncapitalist modes of production in the periphery from the articulation between capitalism and feudalism in Western Europe. Rey's unidirectional sequence of stages is more or less shared by all members of the articulation of MOP approach.

A more concrete, albeit schematic, example will serve to illustrate some of the salient features of this articulation of MOP approach and to compare it to the other two approaches discussed below. Postcolonial nineteenth-century Peru can be analyzed in terms of the articulation between capitalist and noncapitalist modes of production. In particular, Peruvian society during that period of time can be understood as comprising at least the primitive communal, feudal, and capitalist modes of production. The primitive communal mode of production was a more or less direct descendant of the precolonial Incan *ayllu* or clan-based community. The Peruvian hacienda can be conceptualized in terms of the lord–serf relations of the feudal mode of production. Finally, the incipient development of the capitalist mode of production within Peru could be found in the organization of the recovery of guano (bird droppings used as fertilizer) for eventual export to England.

Two aspects of the articulation between these capitalist and noncapitalist modes of production, while not exhaustive, illustrate the approach. First, the initial instance of capitalist development was a product of capitalist development in England; the capitalist mode of production did not emerge within any of the Peruvian noncapitalist modes of production. Guano was commercialized by British capital exports and served as a cheap raw material for further capitalist development in England. This form of capitalist export production led neither to the development of a domestic capitalist class nor to the expansion of the internal market for further capitalist development. Second, this form of dependent capitalist development served to reinforce the predominance of the feudal mode of production in the rural areas. For example, a combined strategy of debt, purchase, and forcible expropriation led to the destruction of the communal *communidades indígenas* and allowed the increased concentration of land in feudal latifundia. Neither capitalist agriculture nor capitalist industry developed to any significant degree at this time. The (noncapitalist) feudal mode of production was first created (in the colonial period), then reinforced (in the nineteenth century), and only gradually supplanted (well into the 1960s) by the development of the capitalist mode of production. The result of this articulation of modes of production was continued dependency and underdevelopment at the periphery of the world economy.

The articulation of MOP approach, then, is meant to provide a conceptual framework to analyze the interrelations between capitalist and noncapitalist modes of production as they manifest themselves in peripheral societies. The particular concern is to map out the development of capitalism from entry to hegemony where it was imposed initially from the outside. The central dynamic is the development of capitalism, understood in terms of the laws (or tendencies) governing its development and involving certain "needs" that come to be met by the noncapitalist modes of production – for instance, a need for a large pool of landless laborers. The development of the noncapitalist modes of production is explained in terms of their ability to satisfy the needs of capitalism. In turn, the development of the capitalist mode of production is understood to be enabled or hindered in terms of the ability of the noncapitalist modes of production to satisfy capitalism's posited needs.

It can be anticipated, then, that a major controversy resulting from such investigations into the articulation between the capitalist and noncapitalist modes of production has concerned the "needs" of capitalism during the course of reinforcing, using, and eventually supplanting noncapitalism. On one side of the controversy, there are theorists who tend to stress the unchanging process of capitalist development.[35] Capitalism is inherently expansive according to these accounts; its internal dynamic forces it at all stages to engulf and inevitably destroy all noncapitalist forms of production. This conception of capitalist expansion results in a single general theory of the articulation between capitalist and noncapitalist modes of production. On the other side of the controversy, some argue that the capitalist mode of production involves different problems and contradictions according to its various forms and stages of development.[36] Therefore, the articulation between the capitalist and noncapitalist modes of production is founded on a changing pattern of capitalist expansion. For example, according to Barbara Bradby (1980, 95), "capitalism has different needs of precapitalist economies at different stages of development, which arise from specific historical circumstance, e.g., raw materials, land, labor-power, and at times of crisis, markets." As a result of this latter mode of analysis, capitalism is considered inherently expansive, but there is no general theory of the forms of the system of relations between capitalist and noncapitalist modes of production.

Whether or not the stress is on the changing nature of capitalist expansion, the general conclusion of the articulation of MOP theorists is that the development of capitalism on a world scale involves, first, the creation and maintenance and, then, the breakdown of noncapitalist modes of production. However, at the same time that noncapitalist forms of production are understood to be dominated and, at least tendentially, supplanted by capitalism, an additional conclusion of the work of the articulation of MOP theorists is that the full, nondistorted development of the capitalist mode of production in the underdeveloped countries is itself blocked by its dependent relation to capitalism in the developed nations.

Thus, underdevelopment and dependency have somewhat different meanings in this framework compared to what we have seen in the case of Frank. For the articulation of MOP theorists, underdevelopment is caused by the persistence of precapitalist modes of production as they are reproduced in their articulation with the dominant capitalist mode of production. Full-fledged capitalist development is itself arrested by relations of dependency between core and periphery. On one hand, the peripheral capitalist mode of production is imposed from the outside in the midst of preexisting non-capitalist modes of production, not a direct outgrowth of a Western European-like feudalism. The implication is that Western European feudalism provided a better "breeding ground" for capitalist development than did the noncapitalist modes of production that pre-existed or that were subsequently created by colonial expansion in peripheral social formations. On the other hand, once in place, the peripheral capitalist mode of production is conceived to be reproduced in a dependent status vis-à-vis the capitalist mode of production in the center.

There has been an additional concern in the various attempts to analyze the articulation of MOP. It involves the thesis of the continued coexistence of the capitalist and noncapitalist modes of production and the portended eventual demise of those noncapitalist modes of production. According to Bradby (1980, 93), "the establishment of capitalism in a social formation necessarily implies the transformation, and in some sense the destruction of formerly dominant modes of production." It is generally accepted that the societies or social formations of peripheral countries comprise both capitalist and noncapitalist modes of production, at least at some stage in their history. Theorists differ, however, as to the manner and cause of the destruction of the noncapitalist modes of production. Are they destined to disappear because of pressures induced by the coexisting capitalist mode of production, or will their own developmental dynamic cause their destruction?

This debate parallels the earlier transition debate between Dobb and Sweezy over whether the demise of feudalism in Western Europe was caused primarily by internal factors (Dobb) or external factors (Sweezy). Wolpe formulates this distinction in the context of the articulation of modes of production in peripheral social formations by noting that "it is one thing to argue that precapitalist relations of production may be transformed into capitalist relations; it is quite another to assume that this is both an inevitable and necessary effect of the CMP [capitalist mode of production]" (1980a, 41). In general, the dynamic of peripheral social formations that comprise both capitalist and noncapitalist modes of production has been analyzed in terms of the external relations – conflicts, tensions, etc. – among these modes of production. Social change is understood to occur as one mode of production (generally the capitalist mode of production) grows at the expense of other, noncapitalist modes of production. As a result, the sources of change internal to each mode of production have received scant attention.

However this controversy is resolved, the general thrust of the literature has been to argue that, although these peripheral social formations comprise both capitalist and noncapitalist modes of production, the arrival of the capitalist mode of production from outside stamps these societies with its unique mark. The logic of articulation tends to be analyzed in terms of the functional needs of the reproduction of the capitalist mode of production. Thus, we have Anibal Quijano's characterization of this articulation as a

> combination of capitalist and precapitalist relations of production, under the hegemony of the first and serving its interests. The movement of the whole configuration is directed by the first and, from this point of view, it is fundamentally capitalist but not homogeneously capitalist.
>
> (Quijano 1980, 255).

To appreciate the appearance and further elaboration of the articulation of MOP approach, it is helpful to note the critical tension that exists between this approach and other frameworks of analysis. The articulation of MOP theorists in some ways agree with, and at the same time are quite critical of, other frameworks in regard to certain key points. It has already been stated above that this approach was, in part, a response to Frank's original formulation of Dependency Theory in which peripheral societies were characterized as capitalist from the time they were first inserted into what he termed the "capitalist world economy." In contrast to Frank's seeing capitalism everywhere, the articulation of MOP theorists have focused on the continued existence of various noncapitalist modes of production and their articulation with the capitalist mode of production. However, they have also taken a page from Frank's book by insisting that the capitalist mode of production was originally introduced from outside the periphery and that it continues to take its dynamic from the capitalist mode of production in the center. In this sense, the articulation of capitalist and noncapitalist modes of production in the developing countries is a different formulation of the original notion of dependency. As Aidan Foster-Carter has stated it, "the 'history of capital itself' continues to be 'written outside such social formations'" (1978, 23).

The articulation of MOP approach also shares with Frank and the remainder of the Dependency Theory school a criticism of the orthodox "dualist" conception of the developing countries. Giovanni Arrighi (1970), for example, has analyzed what orthodox economists understand to be the labor-surplus economy (for instance, the Lewis model) as a product of capitalist development, not as some original state. However, his criticism is distanced from that of Frank in the sense that Arrighi reconceptualizes what others consider to be dualism as a structured combination of capitalism and noncapitalism, as an articulated combination of modes of production.

Not surprisingly, a traditional interpretation of the Marxist theory of development has also been the object of criticism in the work of the articulation of MOP theorists. Two aspects of this critique deserve at least brief mention. First, many of the articulation of MOP theorists have argued against the notion of a necessary or inevitable succession of modes of production.[37] Thus, they react against the mechanistic-deterministic tendency often found in some traditional Marxist analyses which hold that there is a unique path of development for all countries. Articulation of MOP theorists maintain that the transition to capitalism in peripheral societies has noncapitalist origins which differ from those involved in the transition in Western Europe. This means that there is no single succession of stages of development in all countries.[38]

The criticism of traditional Marxist theories of development made by the articulation of MOP theorists often has a second aspect. The question here is whether the transition to capitalism in peripheral societies is fundamentally distinct from the transitions that have occurred elsewhere, especially in Western Europe. The traditional Marxist answer is taken to be that there is no fundamental distinction to be drawn here. The articulation of MOP theorists, on the other hand, argue that something different has been occurring in the peripheral transition to the capitalist mode of production. In particular, the development of capitalism in the periphery is seen as an *uneven* process taking place over an *extended* period of time. As we mentioned above in relation to Rey, the assumption here is that the European transition was, in contrast, relatively smooth and rapid. This attempt to portray peripheral capitalist development as unlike the supposedly smooth, short development of capitalism in Western Europe is then used by Rey to argue that violence and other aspects of formal colonialism are inherent in the development of the capitalist mode of production in the periphery.

While critics of the articulation of MOP approach can agree that the development of capitalism in the peripheral countries is uneven and prolonged, they can also point out that it is evident that the transition to capitalism during, say, the period 1100–1850 in Western Europe was neither smooth nor of short duration. In support of their position, these critics can point out that the work of historians as diverse as Dobb (1947) and Henri Pirenne (1937) has demonstrated the extended, often violent nature of the Western European transition to capitalism. Therefore, without denying that there are certainly differences between the transitions to capitalism in the so-called core and periphery countries, critics of the articulation of MOP approach can maintain that it is probably mistaken to attempt to distinguish these transitions on the basis of their relative unevenness or the length of time over which they occur.

In summary, the articulation of MOP theorists construct their understanding of the developing countries in terms of a system of relations between capitalist and noncapitalist modes of production. In particular, the concepts of dependency and underdevelopment are adopted from Dependency Theory and reinterpreted as the persistence of noncapitalist modes of production and the less than full development of the capitalist mode of production in that context. The articulation of MOP approach differs from specifically Frank-like interpretations of Dependency Theory, then, because of the focus on the relationship between capitalism and noncapitalism within the periphery. However, it still takes as given the notion, shared by Dependency Theory, that there are fundamentally different schemes of development which define a core and periphery of a world economy.

Peripheral modes of production

A second approach within the MOP school criticizes the specific set of concepts of modes of production that the articulation of MOP theorists have tended to use in their analyses. This alternative approach has sought to specify the concepts of "peripheral modes of production" or "colonial modes of production," a set of *sui generis* modes of production that are said to correspond better than the "classical" concepts of capitalist and noncapitalist modes of production to the conditions of underdevelopment and dependency in the peripheral countries of the world economy.

The modes of production picked out by these new concepts are considered to be qualitatively distinct from those that are used to analyze the development of capitalism in Western Europe and elsewhere. The operative assumption is that the forms of development in the core and periphery are fundamentally different and that different concepts must be used to understand these different forms of development. According to the peripheral MOP theorists, the fact that colonialism changed the precolonial pattern of development – in particular, the precolonial modes of production – in the colonized countries means that what is required is a separate set of concepts of modes of production with which to analyze their colonial and postcolonial experiences. This argument is best summarized by C. F. S. Cardoso:

> The specificity of internal colonial structures and of their historical genesis implies the inadequacy of such categories as "feudalism" to explain them. What is required is the elaboration of a theory of colonial modes of production, starting with the notion that such structures are specific and dependent.
>
> (1974, 86, our translation)

Here, then, the concept of mode of production is modified by the notion of dependency to produce a framework of analysis based on a set of concepts of peripheral or colonial modes of production. The presupposition seems to be that a mode of production that is affected to some more or less significant degree by conditions external to the social formation where that mode of production is located, is fundamentally different from an "independent" mode of production. For example, according to this approach, the existence of slavery in Brazil during the colonial period would make it a different mode of production, by virtue of its colonial ties with Portugal, from the slave mode of production of ancient Rome. Thus, despite what might at first appear as important similarities, different concepts are needed in each case to conduct a proper analysis. This presumption that external influences serve as the criterion for a separate set of concepts of peripheral modes of production is also the origin of the well-known Alavi–Banaji *et al.* debate on India (Alavi 1975, Banaji 1972).[39]

Again, a more concrete example will help to illustrate this particular version of the MOP interpretation. Returning to the case of Peru, it will be remembered that our hypothetical articulation of MOP analysis utilized "classical" concepts of modes of production and conceptualized dependency in terms of the specific articulation among these modes of production. The present, alternative approach would dispense with the notion of different modes of production articulated in a single social formation. Rather, it would emphasize the colonial origins and general dependent nature of economic and social relations in Peru. Indeed, all of those relations that would be picked out by the articulation of MOP theorists as elements of the "primitive communal," "feudal" or "capitalist" modes of production would be understood as different aspects of a single peripheral mode of production, as distinct social relations that were specific to the peripheral status of the Peruvian social formation. It follows that one would not expect this peripheral mode of production to develop along the same path as the classical modes. This peripheral mode of production would generate a path of development which differed fundamentally from what would have existed in a nondependent setting. In relation to our example, the role of Peru's economy as a subordinate mode of production within the world capitalist system precluded the development of capitalism in Peru in the same form as that in which it emerged from nondependent, noncapitalist modes of production in the core countries. The peripheral status of this mode of production, not the articulation between capitalist and noncapitalist modes of production, explains dependency and underdevelopment in Peru.

It is interesting to note that the advocates of these concepts of *sui generis* modes of production for analyzing the developing countries tend to accept the use of the classical concepts of the modes of production of slavery, capitalism, and so on for the countries of the core. However, it would be difficult to argue that the modes of production of the colonizing countries, especially the capitalist mode of production, were less affected by colonialism than those of the colonized countries. Was the development of capitalism in Britain any less conditioned by the existence of colonial ties with India than the existing modes of production in India itself? If not, then why, on their theoretical assumptions, should the classical concepts be thought to be applicable to core countries across the precolonial, colonial, and postcolonial periods? And if these concepts of modes of production are not applicable across periods, how do we demarcate new and changing modes of production? There seems to be a problem of concept specification here.

This attempt to draw a sharp distinction between peripheral and classical modes of production does make it quite evident, however, that the focus of this form of analysis is on the external relations of domination that shape and otherwise determine what are conceived to be the subordinate modes of production of the peripheral countries. In this regard, then, the work of the peripheral MOP theorists is continuous with the earlier work of Frank. They agree with Frank that the dependency condition of the developing world is a result of the domination of economic forces (for the most part) outside the developing countries themselves. Where they differ from Frank is over how best to analyze the internal structures of dependency; whether, for instance, underdevelopment should be analyzed in terms of capitalist relations or whether it should be seen as the result of the logic of development of a different, peripheral mode of production.

Internationalization of capital

The third major approach to the MOP analysis of dependency and underdevelopment focuses on the internationalization of capital as part of a world system that is to be understood in terms of the laws of motion of the capitalist mode of production. In many ways, Frank's most recent works on "world accumulation" reflect this new focus (e.g., 1978 and 1979). Attention is shifted both from the articulation between capitalist and noncapitalist modes of production and from the specification of specific peripheral modes of production to an analysis of the structure and logic of development of the capitalist mode of production itself. According to the internationalization of capital theorists, the other two MOP approaches do not pay sufficient attention to the "real" dynamic determining world development (i.e., the capitalist mode of production). This mode of analysis presumes the dominance of the capitalist mode of production within the international economy; that is, it implies that the fundamental structure of the world economy is that of the capitalist mode of production and that the logic of world development reflects the laws governing that mode of production. In this way, the internationalization of the capitalist mode of production becomes the new demiurge, propelling the world economy forward and driving a larger and larger wedge between core and periphery.

This focus on the structure and effects of the capitalist mode of production on a world scale may be seen as either a critique or an extension of the two other MOP approaches surveyed in previous sections. It represents a critique to the extent that noncapitalist and peripheral modes of production are replaced by a single global capitalist mode of production. For example, units of production that would be analyzed as feudal or peripheral in the other MOP frameworks would be placed inside a single process of capitalist accumulation by the internationalization of capital theorists. On the other hand, it represents an extension insofar as some theorists argue that the historical period when the other modes of production approaches were applicable has passed. There may have been, and probably were, either noncapitalist or peripheral modes of production at one time in the developing countries – so they might argue – but these modes of production have been supplanted by a single capitalist mode of production on a world scale. Interpreted in this way, the various MOP approaches would represent a historical sequence at the level of theory that corresponds to the stages of development of the world economy.

However understood, whether as a break from or an extension of the other MOP frameworks, the basic unit of analysis of the internationalization of capital approach is the structure and movement of the capitalist mode of production. Partly in response to the debate between theoretical approaches, which argued over the predominance of circulation (Frank) versus that of production (Laclau), the internationalization of capital theorists have defined capitalism in terms of a particular interpretation of Marx's three circuits of commodity-capital, money-capital, and productive-capital. In other words, capitalist production is conceived of as a unity of production and circulation. The focus is, in particular, on the global nature of these circuits as they transcend the confines of the nation-state. The symbol of this global process of accumulation is, of course, the transnational or multinational corporation. These corporations embody the logic of the third stage of the international expansion of the capitalist mode of production, intertwining the various parts of the world economy into a single entity and subordinating these parts to the needs of capitalist accumulation.

Within this framework, how is what appears to some as the articulation between capitalist and noncapitalist modes of production to be understood? David Barkin responds:

> We can examine the problems of the relationship between peasant and capitalist production by determining if and how surplus value is generated and the ways in which it is appropriated by different segments of the capitalist class. In this way, the complex productive structures within individual countries can be analyzed in terms of their particular contributions to the global process of articulation.
>
> (1981, 157)

The articulation *between modes of production* within peripheral social formations is replaced by a notion of *articulation within the capitalist mode of production* itself. According to Christian Palloix,

> this new type of articulation characterizes the different chains of dependence in the self-expansion of capital, in particular with the underdeveloped countries, which is no longer an articulation of the capitalist mode of production at the centre with other modes of production, but an articulation within the world CMP [capitalist mode of production] itself, among differing processes of self-expansion of capital and increasingly accentuated differentiation of this expansion as between the centre and the periphery.
>
> (1975, 83)

To return once again to our Peruvian illustration, the internationalization of capital theorists would tend to explain Peruvian development in terms of the logic of the development of the capitalist mode of production on a world scale. No capitalist production was initiated within the Peruvian social formation during the colonial and immediate postcolonial periods because the global expansion of capitalism took the form of the extension of predominantly commercial relations. That is, Peru was a site for exports (of gold, sugar, etc.) to the core countries. In a second stage, the export of money-capital financed a certain development of infrastructure and involved Peru in a web of international debt relations. In neither of these stages was capitalist production itself initiated in Peru. Only with the internationalization of the circuit of productive-capital did Peru embark on a path of capitalist development per se. For some, it would be described as dependent capitalism, with Peru occupying a subordinate position in the international division of labor; underdevelopment would be reproduced as a result. For others, this capitalist development, although incipient, would be characterized as a break from dependency, which was characteristic of the noncapitalist phases, and thus the end of underdevelopment. In both cases, the explanation of Peruvian (under)development is based on the effects of the development of the capitalist mode of production on a world scale.

Thus, while they all focus on the internationalization of the various circuits of capital, and therefore of the capitalist mode of production itself, the various internationalization of capital theorists reach different conclusions concerning the continued existence of dependency and underdevelopment. Basically, as exemplified in the preceding example, there are two positions. On one hand, it is argued that the new international division of labor produced by the internationalization of the capitalist mode of production serves to perpetuate conditions of underdevelopment and the dependency of the peripheral countries on the core countries (where the multinational corporations are based).[40] Underdevelopment and dependency are no longer associated with the persistence of noncapitalist modes of productions, as they are with the articulation of MOP theorists, or with the dependent status of developing countries, as in the peripheral MOP approach; they are effects internal to the capitalist mode of production itself.

On the other hand, James Cypher (1979) and, even more so, Bill Warren (1980) argue that underdevelopment is associated only with the continued existence of noncapitalist modes of production and that these are entirely supplanted by the expansion of the capitalist mode of production. The expansion of the capitalist mode of production on a world scale, particularly within what others would term the periphery, induces a process of unqualified capitalist development. Here, the break with the conclusions of Frank and other theorists of the "development of underdevelopment" or "dependent development" is virtually complete.

Even among those who assume the first position and choose to retain terms such as "dependency" and "underdevelopment," many tend to analyze the development of so-called Third World countries solely in terms of the logic of expansion of the capitalist mode of production. A typical statement is the following:

> International markets and economic power structures are increasingly determining the individual decisions made in ever more isolated parts of national economies, even when "noncapitalist" productive groups are involved, such as peasant producers in many Third World economies.
>
> (Barkin 1981, 158)

Two factors appear to be lost here. Any dynamic inherent in the particular economic structure, capitalist or otherwise, of a developing country is overlooked in favor of international forces. Second, noncapitalist modes of production recede into the background or disappear completely; thus, we are faced with the collapse of the notion of articulation and an ironic return to Frank's original position, this time in terms of "seeing the capitalist mode of production everywhere."

Amin

The various conceptualizations of dependency and underdevelopment analyzed in the previous sections are synthesized and recast as a distinct version of Dependency Theory in the work of Samir Amin. Basically, Amin combines notions of the world capitalist system, the articulation of modes of production, and the internationalization of capital with a theory of unequal exchange. The result is a theory of development in which the core and periphery are conceived as complementary opposites within a world capitalist social formation. This relation between core and periphery promotes capitalist development in the former while blocking the same path of development in the latter. This conception of dichotomous economic development serves, in turn, as the basis of what Amin considers to be the central political contradiction of the world capitalist system.

Amin begins his theory of development with the presumption of a world capitalist system that is divided into two fundamentally distinct parts – a core and a periphery – which are functionally related. In a manner obviously consistent with Frank's approach, he argues that "the structures of the periphery are shaped so as to meet the needs of accumulation at the center, that is, provided that the development of the center engenders and maintains the underdevelopment of the periphery" (1976, 104).

Going beyond Frank, however, Amin realizes the importance of providing a more detailed analysis of the internal structures of the countries of the periphery. Amin shares with the articulation of modes of production theorists a structural explanation of the underdevelopment of the periphery in terms of the system of relations between the capitalist and various noncapitalist modes of production. In general, for Amin, "social formations are . . . concrete, organized structures that are marked by a dominant mode of production and the articulation around this of a complex of modes of production that are subordinate to it" (1976, 16).

The particular social formations of the world capitalist economy are analyzed in terms of the dominance of the capitalist mode of production and the subordinate existence of various noncapitalist modes of production. Finally, Amin follows the internationalization of capital theorists in analyzing the various parts of his world economy in terms of the globalization of the capitalist mode of production.

> The predominance of the capitalist mode of production is also expressed on another plane. It constitutes a world system in which all

formations, central and peripheral alike, are arranged in a single system, organized and hierarchical.

(1976, 22)

These three notions (world capitalist system, articulation of modes of production, and internationalization of the capitalist modes of production) are combined, as we show below, with a theory of unequal exchange to constitute Amin's particular theory of blocked development in the periphery.

Amin's work is characterized, then, by this synthesis of other Dependency Theory approaches to produce an alternative model of dependency and underdevelopment. His work is also characterized by the importance it places on history. This focus on history is thematic in at least two senses. First, much of Amin's published work – in fact, some would argue, the best of that work – consists of historical writing. His accounts of the different paths to capitalism in the social formations of the periphery, especially in Africa, are among the best available (Amin 1966, 1967, 1971, and 1973). Second, Amin conceives of history as providing the "correct perspective" for carrying out the analysis of the developing countries. The terms of his own particular analysis are said to correspond to a perspective that emerges from the history of the developing countries.[41] Theories that have been generated from perspectives that represent the histories of the core countries – in particular, neoclassical and traditional Marxist theories of development – do not correspond, according to Amin, to the reality of the developing countries.

The basic terms of Amin's version of Dependency Theory are by now quite familiar: concepts of modes of production, social formation, center, periphery, and the accumulation of capital seem to be borrowed, more or less intact, from other theorists and used to construct a theoretical model. This model is then deployed to explain the process of development of the world capitalist system. The particular use of such concepts would appear to make Amin's mode of analysis a straightforward Marxist one. However, at least two difficulties arise in this connection. On one hand, commentators have noted the relative lack of precision in Amin's use of these concepts. Explicit definitions of concepts are rarely offered and, because of their shifting meanings from passage to passage, implicit definitions are difficult to construct. This is especially troublesome given the vastly different meanings of such concepts throughout the Marxian tradition. Thus, it is difficult to pinpoint exactly which interpretation of the concepts and method of Marxist theory is at work in Amin's writings. On the other hand, Amin self-consciously distances his analysis from that of Marx, if only because the latter's theory was limited by his perspective which, in turn, corresponded to the historical period in which he wrote. In this vein, Amin writes that in fact, the monopolies, the rise of which Marx could not imagine, were to prevent any local capitalism that might arise from competing. The development of capitalism in the periphery was to remain extra-verted, based on the external market, and could therefore not lead to a full flowering of the capitalist mode of production in the periphery.

(1976, 199)

The central element of Amin's model of the world economy is the relation-ship between the two groups of core and periphery countries as comple-mentary opposites. These two poles are created by the history of capitalist expansion from the core. According to Amin, a core and periphery exist at all of the three stages into which he periodizes capitalist development: mercantilist, premonopoly/competitive, and monopoly/imperialist capi-talism. However, the dichotomy becomes "hardened" in the third, imperi-alist stage: from that point on, no country of the periphery or semiperiphery is capable of joining the core.

The reason for this hardening of the core and periphery is that Amin considers these two parts of the world economy to be governed by funda-mentally different laws of development. The contrast is between *autocen-tric* and *extraverted* accumulation. "I maintain that the dynamic of the core is autonomous, that the periphery adjusts to it, and that the functions the periphery fulfills differ from one stage to another" (1982, 168–69).

Amin is quite specific in stating that autocentric accumulation does not mean autarchy. Rather, autocentric development is a result of the dynamic of development originating in the core itself. The nature of development in the core is such that it determines its own development as well as that of the periphery. The key relation making for a pattern of autocentric accu-mulation in the center is the balance between increases in productivity and wages.[42] This results in an expansion of the internal market and the balanced development of industries specialized in the production of both producer and consumer goods (or, in Amin's terminology, Departments I and II). This balance between changes in productivity and wages in the center is also supported by surplus transfers from the periphery on the basis of unequal exchange.

The periphery, however, is barred from achieving such a balance. Its pattern of accumulation is characterized as extraverted, deformed, and dependent. The pattern of accumulation is fundamentally different in the periphery, where the coexistence of capitalist and noncapitalist modes of production means that there is no necessary relation between the levels of productivity and wages. Increases in productivity, even in the "modern" export sector, are not translated into corresponding improvements in wages because of the existence of a Lewis-like surplus labor force. The sources of this "surplus labor" are those parts of the economy in which noncapitalist relations are still strong. This imbalance between produc-tivity and wages leaves the domestic market "limited and distorted," so that the key result is a link between production in the export sector and luxury goods consumption.

According to Amin, the peripheral economy is considered to be "disarticulated."[43] It should be emphasized that this concept of disarticulation is quite different from what it might mean for the articulation of modes of production theorists. "Articulation" and "disarticulation" in Amin's sense refer to the economic conditions that give rise to a balance or imbalance between changes in productivity and wages. The result of disarticulation, then, is that the possibility of autocentric accumulation in the periphery is blocked.

The three main "distortions" of the periphery, with respect to the development of capitalism in the core that derive from this model of disarticulation, concern the main sectors of economic activity. The peripheral economy is biased toward export production, service activities, and, in the choice of branches of industry proper, toward light industry with modern technology. This pattern of investment or accumulation reproduces what Amin calls the "marginalization of the masses," a level of unemployment that ensures a minimum wage in all sectors far below the level of productivity. This minimum wage serves, in turn, as the basis of a restricted internal market. The final result of this fundamentally distinct pattern of accumulation in the periphery is that development is blocked.

> None of the features that define the structure of the periphery is thus weakened as economic growth proceeds: on the contrary, these features are accentuated. Whereas at the center growth means development, making the economy more integral, in the periphery growth does not mean development, for it disarticulates the economy – it is only a "development of underdevelopment."
>
> (Amin 1976, 292)

Amin's conceptions of dependency and underdevelopment are thus quite clear: underdevelopment means both that noncapitalist modes of production are reproduced and that the expansion of the capitalist mode of production is distorted in the periphery of the world economy. Insofar as these conditions are maintained, they continue to serve as the basis for the dependency of the peripheral countries on the core countries. In the end, the periphery does not have the power to control its own development.

The key mechanism in Amin's model whereby the two patterns of autocentric and dependent development are reproduced is the process of unequal exchange between core and periphery. Amin takes over and subsequently modifies Arghiri Emmanuel's (1972) original theory of unequal exchange. Emmanuel takes as given, and bases his analysis on, differences in real wages between center and periphery. Amin argues that the essential condition for unequal exchange is not merely wage differentials, but rather that these real wage differences are larger than productivity differences. The result, however, is the same as that in Emmanuel's model: the prices (of production) at which the goods of the center and periphery exchange are such that a surplus is transferred to the former from the latter. This surplus transfer means that there is an external drain on internally generated investment funds and the reproduction of a limited internal market. These results then serve to reproduce the general conditions of accumulation that, in turn, give rise to the wage-productivity differentials that are the basis of unequal exchange.

Given this relationship between the phenomenon of unequal exchange and the conditions that give rise to unequal exchange, a question immediately arises concerning the pattern of cause and effect between international prices and unequal wage levels. Amin responds:

> The question is pointless. Inequality in wages, due to historical reasons (the difference between social formations), constitutes the basis of specialization and a system of international prices that perpetuate this inequality.
>
> (1982, 151)

That is, once some initial wage-productivity differences between the core and periphery historically emerge, a pattern of unequal exchange is produced whereby these initial differences continue to be reproduced over time.

Amin's theory of unequal exchange, like that of Emmanuel and others, has elicited comments and criticisms from many quarters.[44] The most damaging criticism to his general model of the unidirectional transfer of a surplus from the periphery to the core concerns the real wage-productivity disparity between center and periphery. According to Amin, this transfer of surplus requires that production in the periphery be based on a higher rate of exploitation than that in the center. Amin's own equations bear this out. If this is so, critics respond, why is it the case, assuming as Amin does the full mobility of capital, that all production in the core is not transferred to the periphery? Amin's answer is twofold. First, capitalists respond to different profit rates, not to different rates of exploitation. And, since Amin's model of unequal exchange assumes the existence of a single, general rate of profit across all industries, there is no apparent reason for capital to be shifted from the core to the periphery. Second, Amin has argued that the absence of a large domestic market in the periphery keeps industry in the core countries. This second response is less than satisfactory because there is no reason that the location of production must coincide with the location of the final market. His own assumption of the existence of international exchange shows this.

His first answer, concerning the difference between profitability and exploitation, is also beset with difficulties. On one hand, Marx's theory of prices of production and a general rate of profit, which Amin says that he adopts, was part of Marx's attempt to analyze the dynamic nature of capitalist competition.[45] Marx used the concept of price of production as a hypothetical *equilibrium* to illustrate the ceaseless *movement* in the direction of the formation of a general rate of profit. Flows of capital between industries in response to unequal rates of profit so change the conditions of profitability that the hypothetical general rate of profit itself changes. This general rate of profit can be thought of as a shifting equilibrium, an elusive goal that is never reached. Its only purpose in Volume 3 of *Capital* is to illustrate the dynamics of capitalist competition by momentarily abstracting from that movement. On the other hand, even assuming a general rate of profit *across* industries does not mean that the rate of profit is equal *within* each industry. The existence of a range of "efficiencies" among firms that make up each industry at any point in time implies that there will be a similar range of profit rates among those firms (Wolff 1978, 50). The competitive dynamic that forces less efficient producers within an industry to innovate (for example, by moving to a location where rates of exploitation are supposed to be higher – in the periphery, according to Amin), is not brought to a standstill even if a general rate of profit is imposed across industries.

In general, then, the existence at any given moment of a set of prices does not ensure that the underlying conditions that give rise to those prices will be reproduced over time. In fact, the opposite conclusion is more likely; namely, that the existence of unequal prices of production will cause movements of capital within and between industries so that the conditions of profitability within those industries are changed. The nature of these changes in the conditions of profitability cannot, of course, be predetermined. However, there is no reason, even on the basis of Amin's assumptions, for such capital movements to unilaterally promote capitalist development in one set of countries (the core) and prevent such development in another group of countries (the periphery). Unequal capitalist development in both core and periphery, rather than the "development of underdevelopment," would be the more likely result.

Amin's model of the world capitalist economy starts with a fundamental distinction between core and peripheral patterns of accumulation. This relation of complementary opposites is reproduced over time by the mechanism of unequal exchange. The result, then, of Amin's economic analysis is that the development of capitalism on a world scale is radically dichotomized: while continuing apace in the core countries, the development of capitalism is substantially blocked in the peripheral countries. This underdevelopment means, for Amin, that noncapitalist modes of production continue to exist in the periphery and that the peripheral capitalist mode of production cannot serve as the basis for a process of autocentric development.

This model of economic development (and underdevelopment) serves, in turn, as the basis for Amin's analysis of what he considers to be the central contradiction of the world capitalist system, to wit, the conflict between what Amin calls the world bourgeoisie and the world proletariat. The implicit notion of contradiction in Amin's work is that of a pair of opposing forces, each of which is generated by complementary processes of accumulation within a single world capitalist system. The central nucleus of the world bourgeoisie is located in the core countries. Because of the existence of "superexploitation," within the periphery, Amin finds the central nucleus of the world proletariat there. Amin explains the superexploitation of the peripheral proletariat in the following manner:

> [Unequal exchange] means that the bourgeoisie of the center, the only one that exists on the scale of the world system, exploits the proletariat everywhere, at the center and at the periphery, but that it exploits the proletariat of the periphery even more brutally, and that this is possible because the objective mechanism upon which is based the unity that links it to its own proletariat, in an autocentric economy, and which restricts the degree of exploitation it carries out at the center, does not function at the extraverted periphery.
>
> (1976, 196)

According to Amin, the relationship between capitalists and workers in the core countries is characterized by a "social democratic alliance." Capitalists are said to benefit from the continued existence of profitable production while workers share both in increases in productivity at home and in transfers of surplus from the periphery. Workers in the periphery are subject to superexploitation. Therefore, the principal set of opposing interests that is the basis of the contradiction of the world system is between the world bourgeoisie (of the core) and the world proletariat (of the periphery).

Amin's framework of analysis has, of course, not escaped the criticisms of writers both inside and outside the Dependency Theory tradition.[46] His most recent, comprehensive reply, responding to the critical commentaries of Warren, Smith, and Brewer, serves to highlight the main elements of his interpretation of Dependency Theory (Amin 1983). Amin's points are basically three. First, he seeks to clear up what he considers a misinterpretation of his notion of the blocked development of the periphery. "Blocking" does not mean stagnation or the absence of change. Rather, capitalist development in the periphery is considered to be blocked because it "does not reproduce the model of that of the developed world" (1983, 365). What this means for Amin is that peripheral development is subject to periods of growth and crisis because of an external impetus, and this uneven process continues to create inequality in the distribution of income.

Amin's critics would be hard-pressed to disagree with the notions that the developing countries continue to experience income inequalities and that economic crises are transmitted internationally. However, it is not clear how these phenomena serve to block peripheral development or serve as the basis of his radical dichotomy between the patterns of accumulation in the core and periphery. This means that Amin's conclusion concerning the complementary and opposite nature of the relationship between the core and periphery depends crucially on his presumption of such a dichotomy as the starting point of his analysis. Amin begins his investigation, and thus ends that investigation, with the division of the world capitalist system into two groups of core and periphery countries.

This is Amin's second point. All attempts to deny, as a point of departure, this core–periphery dichotomy are fundamentally mistaken: "the 'theory' which rejects the analysis of capitalist expansion in terms of centre and periphery stops at the threshold of the real questions" (1983, 377). This is not just one among other entry-points into an analysis of development for Amin, one that has its attendant consequences for the subsequent conclusions of that analysis. Rather, it is the entry-point that is determined by "history." In this sense, Amin is merely reasserting that one of the defining characteristics of Dependency Theory – the presumption that there is a world system divided into a core and periphery – is also his and that this starting point is the correct one from which to analyze dependency and underdevelopment.

Finally, Amin reiterates, in the face of the protestations of his critics, the basic theses of his previous analyses. Unequal exchange, the social democratic alliance between workers and capitalists in the core, and so on, remain his basic arguments. He also redefines the relationship of his framework of analysis to that of other versions of Dependency Theory. On one hand, the modes of production debate is not "decisive" because it avoids an analysis of the insertion of noncapitalist modes of production into a "world system which can only be termed capitalist" (1983, 376). On the other hand, the work of Frank and Wallerstein continues to be valid. In particular, Amin reaffirms that "the development of some [countries] is the cause of the underdevelopment of others" (1983, 371).

It should be relatively clear from our and other summaries of Amin's work that his analysis of the world capitalist system begins and ends with the fundamental dichotomy between the modes of accumulation in the core and in the periphery. Distinct processes of accumulation are posited at the beginning of his analysis and reproduced over time, through the mechanism of unequal exchange, so that the fundamental differences between these complementary opposite forms of development are present in his conclusions. In addition, the fundamental political contradiction of the world system – between the capitalists of the center and the superexploited workers of the periphery – corresponds exactly to this economic distinction between core and periphery.

The key mechanism that is both cause and effect of this dichotomy – unequal exchange – has been called into question above. Our point is not the substantive one that unequal exchange cannot or does not take place in international trade. Rather, our criticism indicates that the existence of unequal exchange, and the accompanying flows of profits among enterprises within and between industries, cannot ensure the reproduction of the two fundamentally distinct patterns of accumulation that are presumed in Amin's analysis. In addition, it is only the presumption of this essential economic dichotomy between core and periphery that allows Amin to make the fundamental political conflict of the world system that between capitalists located in the core countries and workers located in the periphery. To so reduce the political dynamic within the world system, if such a system can be presumed at all, serves only to "forget about" the other conflicts and contradictions that emerge in the course of world development.

Conclusion

There is a wide variety of theories that serve as alternatives to orthodox, neoclassical approaches to development. We have presented three of those theories in this chapter: the Dependency Theory of Frank (and, by extension, Wallerstein), the Modes of Production school, and the approach elaborated by Amin.

All three theoretical approaches are explicitly put forward as dependency and/or Marxian alternatives to bourgeois development theory. Using different concepts, they arrive at conclusions in stark contrast to those put forward by neoclassical economists and other social scientists. Where bourgeois theorists see the development of capitalism as propelling a process of modernization from traditional or backward forms of economic and social organization to modern growth and development, the radical theorists see imperialist domination and exploitation. Thus, these radicals "see" a different reality in the currently less-developed or underdeveloped countries. The difference in the very names used to designate these "poor" countries by the alternative approaches – less-developed vs dependent and/or underdeveloped – betray these different realities.

Orthodox and radical theorists arrive at different conclusions because their analyses of development start in different places; they have different conceptual "entry-points." Orthodox theorists tend to focus on individual decision making and begin their analysis with a particular model of human behavior. In neoclassical theory, capitalist economic growth and development are understood in terms of individual utilities or preferences (together with exogenous technology and resource endowments). Prices, the distribution of income, and all other economic phenomena are derived from this utility model of behavior. Individual utilities, taken as given within the model, are considered the principal factor determining the economic forces leading to development. From this perspective, the development of capitalism is generally understood to bring about an increase in individual freedom. This greater freedom, in turn, is seen to help guarantee the accumulation of wealth and social modernization by providing the incentives for rational market behavior. This is true for all countries in which capitalism takes root.

The radical approaches arrive at different conclusions because they start with different concepts. In the case of Frank (and Wallerstein), the circulation of commodities serves as the conceptual entry-point for the analysis of world capitalist development. Laclau and his followers begin with concepts of modes of production to describe and analyze development in the core and periphery of the world economy. Different and unequal national units within a world capitalist social formation are the starting point for Amin's theory of development. Many radicals have attempted to use all three standpoints, by synthesizing concepts of commodity and capital flows, modes of production, and the world capitalist system into a single framework of analysis. Thus, radical approaches tend to replace the model of human behavior of orthodox theory with one of a variety of different concepts (or a combination of them).

It is natural, then, that capitalist development will look very different to these radical theorists in comparison with the bourgeois outlook. Where the orthodox theorists see freedom, the radicals see unequal power relations. The orthodox notion of economic growth for all countries becomes, in radical theories, economic growth for some countries at the expense of growth for all the others. The orthodox theory of a unilinear process of development from traditional to modern societies is similarly challenged by radical theorists: development occurs in the center while underdevelopment or dependent development occurs in the periphery. In this sense, capitalism is the problem, not the solution.

These radical theories are certainly alternatives to the orthodox approach to development, both in terms of their conceptual entry-points and the conclusions they generate about the process of development. However, they share with their orthodox opposite one crucial element: they tend to reduce the analysis of development to a single decisive factor. That is, just as the neoclassical conception of development explains all social phenomena in terms of a particular model of human behavior (psychological utility), the radical theories we have presented tend to explain development in terms of international commodity circulation, the mode of production, or the world capitalist social formation, respectively. The result is that quite different theories end up agreeing on the methodological point that the rest of society can be explained in terms of one essential factor. What they disagree about is what that factor is.

The difficulty with all such approaches is that they attempt to reduce the explanation of a complex and diffuse phenomenon – world development in the past 400 years – to one ultimately determining factor. One can be justifiably wary of whether any theory of this sort can provide an entirely convincing account.

Orthodox and radical approaches also share another key aspect. They are both directly and indirectly connected to political agendas. Radical theorists tend to be more upfront about their political interests. Orthodox theorists, concerned to claim the mantle of science, tend to shy away from stating explicitly the political dimensions and implications of their approach. Nonetheless, we should recognize that such contrasting theories of development will lead to significantly different consequences for the actual course of development.

(original version published in 1987)

Acknowledgements

We want to thank Charles Wilber, Kenneth Jameson, Vaughn McKim, and Rhoda Halperin for their helpful comments on an earlier draft of this material. The research on this article was supported in part by a grant from the Institute for Scholarship in the Liberal Arts of the University of Notre Dame.

Notes

1   For three recent attempts to survey this literature, see Brewer (1980), Palma (1978), and Griffin and Gurley (1985).
2   What might be called the classic debate took place in the first decades of the twentieth century and largely involved issues of how to interpret and extend Marx's theory to the questions of imperialism and the colonial world. The major figures included Lenin, Luxemburg, Bukharin, and Hilferding. The works listed in note 1 all discuss this material. Paul Baran's *The Political Economy of Growth* (1957) preceded Frank's work by a decade and was very influential in setting the stages for the modern debate.
3   For discussions of a more critical nature, focusing in particular on methodological issues, see two of our essays (Ruccio and Simon 1986a and 1986b). Some of the material in the present chapter has been adopted from those two essays.
4   Fernando Henrique Cardoso, it should perhaps be noted, differs somewhat from this view. See his 1977 article.
5   Frank's other major works include *Latin America: Underdevelopment or Revolution* (1969), *Lumpenbourgeoisie: Lumpendevelopment: Dependence, Class, and Politics in Latin America* (1972); *World Accumulation 1492–1978* (1978), *Dependent Accumulation and Underdevelopment* (1979), and *Critique and Anti-Critique: Essays on Dependence and Reformism* (1984).
6   For a discussion of the structuralist position, see Jameson (1986).
7   For example, Rostow (1960). For a recent restatement of this orthodox approach, see Herrick and Kindleberger (1983).
8   This point should not, of course, be taken to imply that Frank does not admit the possibility or desirability of socialist development; quite the contrary. But socialist development is a relatively recent phenomenon and cannot be part of the explanation of underdevelopment.
9   As we shall see in our discussion of Lall's criticism of Frank below, this initial distinction is open to damaging criticism.

10 It should be noted that not all Dependency Theorists would agree with this last point. For instance, dos Santos (1970) defines "dependence" in the following way:

> "Dependence is a conditioning situation in which the economies of one group of countries are conditioned by the development and expansion of others. A relationship of interdependence between two or more economies and the world trading system becomes a dependent relationship when some countries can expand through self-impulsion while others, being in a dependent position, can only expand as a reflection of the dominant countries, which may have *positive or negative* effects on their immediate development." (emphasis added)

The trouble with this definition is that if, in fact, the dependency relation has positive effects on the development of the dependent country, then it is hard to see how the theory can serve the critical function that Frank, at least, wants to give it. Three possible replies to this point are

1 that the positive effects are *immediate* and not long-term, and that the long-term effects of dependent development are, and must be, negative;
2 that even if there are positive effects on development, as long as the dependent country is dominated from without and does not control its own development, there is a violation of national autonomy, if not sovereignty, and this is to be criticized; and
3 that the theory is not meant to be critical, but only descriptive.

The problems with these replies are that the first makes it unclear why the short-term positive effects should ever be mentioned; the second reply, if it is intended to support a critical theory, requires an additional argument to the effect that the loss of autonomy is worse than the gain in economic development, and this would be a controversial claim; and the third reply is not accurate, at least in relation to Frank. This entire problem can be sidetracked by building the normative dimension into the concept of dependence from the beginning. Sanjaya Lall (1975) also makes the point that "dependence," as used by the Dependency Theory school, has a definite normative dimension – namely, that the future development of the dependent economy is adversely affected by its being dependent. For an additional discussion and critique of Frank's use of the concept of dependence, see Brewer (1980, 164 and 177–80).

11 It should be noted that, while Frank's view requires a complete account of the origins and development of capitalism (and he acknowledges as much), his early work only gestured at such an account. In more recent work, however, he has attempted to develop more fully this side of his project. See, especially, Frank (1979). It should also be mentioned that Immanuel Wallerstein shares Frank's view of capitalism as a world system and more or less agrees with Frank's understanding of what capitalism is and how it works. Wallerstein's work has, of course, concentrated on the historical development of the capitalist world system, and in many ways the projects and perspectives of Frank and Wallerstein complement each other. Thus, many of the points we make about Frank could easily be adapted to fit Wallerstein's work. See Wallerstein (1974 and 1979).

12 See, for instance, Laclau (1971, 24) and Brewer (1980, 160).
13 Brewer (1980, 160) makes this point.
14 This point is made by Laclau (1971, 22) and Brewer (1980, 160). This criticism is one to which Frank responds in his later work; see Frank (1979, xii).
15 Also see Frank (1979, 123).

16 The article under discussion is Lall (1975).
17 Notice that even putting the point this way circumscribes the audience to which the claim is addressed, for only those theorists who are predisposed to be sympathetic to the concept of dependence in the first place will have any initial notions or intuitions concerning the use of the concept; but, without such intuitions, it is impossible to agree or disagree with the initial distinction. Without initial notions as to concept boundaries, no economies are obviously dependent or obviously nondependent.
18 In particular, Brenner cites Sweezy (1976) and Wallerstein (1974).
19 See Brenner (1977, 31–32 and 68) for examples of this criticism.
20 There might seem to be an initial tension between the claim that the explanation generated by the Frank–Wallerstein model at the same time is deterministic and yet relies on the free choice of rational individuals. If the individuals are really free, surely it is possible that they won't choose to act as the model determines they will. This tension, we think, can be dissolved by two considerations. First, the explanation is deterministic, not in the strong sense of metaphysical necessity, but rather in the sense of a lawlike natural relation. Second, it is important that the free individuals involved are also rational, where this is a strong condition. Given their assumed motivation – profit-maximization – and their assumed rationality, the individuals really do have no choice. For an individual to fail to act in the way the model stipulates would mean either that one of the initial assumptions was violated, or that some other variable was involved that the model failed to take into account. Thus, if the model is correct, and given the nature of human beings as assumed by the model and the initial conditions, it follows that the behavior predicted by the model obtains.
21 Brenner makes this point in several ways and in several places, directed variously against Smith, Sweezy, Wallerstein, and Frank. See, for examples, Brenner (1977, 34, 45, 55, 58, 67, and 83).
22 Brenner (1977, 48–50 and 79–82) also makes this criticism in various ways.
23 Among the other interesting critics see especially Palma (1978).
24 The individuals whose work exemplifies the articulation of MOP approach include Laclau, Rey, Arrighi, and Bradby. The most comprehensive surveys of this approach are Foster-Carter (1978) and Taylor (1979).
25 C. F. S. Cardoso, Banaji, and Alavi are among those who have developed this particular interpretation of MOP analysis. See Foster-Carter (1978, 63–64) and Brewer (1980, 268–72).
26 The work of Palloix, Cypher, Warren, and Barkin is representative. Unfortunately, the tendency is to submerge this approach within a more comprehensive MOP school of thought; see, for example Cypher (1979). Our brief survey is an attempt to demonstrate the specificity of this internationalization of capital interpretation of Dependency Theory.
27 For example, in the surveys by Foster-Carter, Taylor, and Brewer.
28 Palma (1978) is one who has commented on the problem of "operationalizing" the concepts of Frank's formulation of Dependency Theory.
29 The most famous are Rey, Meillasoux, and Terray.
30 Many of the MOP theorists have acknowledged their intellectual debt to the work of Althusser and Balibar. A central text in this tradition is Althusser and Balibar (1975).
31 Essentialism is defined by Althusser and Balibar as a form of analysis in which the relations among social processes are understood in terms of essence – phenomenon relations. It is more or less synonymous with reductionism and determinism. According to Althusser and Balibar, the two most common forms of essentialism in the Marxist theoretical tradition are economic determinism

and theoretical humanism. In both cases, an essence (the economy or human nature) serves to ultimately determine all other aspects of society (politics, culture, etc.) as the phenomenal forms of that essence. See, in particular, Althusser (1970). This critique of essentialism and the project of formulating a nonessentialist interpretation of Marxist theory have been extended more recently by Stephen Resnick and Richard Wolff (1983a).

32 The debate was initiated by the publication of Maurice Dobb (1947). The actual debate between Dobb and Paul Sweezy in *Science and Society*, along with other contributions, was published as *The Transition from Feudalism to Capitalism*.

33 Cf. the discussion by Foster-Carter (1978, 53).

34 Rey's work is analyzed by Barbara Bradby (1980).

35 The classic example is Luxemburg (1951).

36 A position elaborated by Bradby (1980).

37 Conceptions of historical development based on more or less inevitable successions of MOP are criticized by Umberto Melotti (1974).

38 Certainly, many of Marx's oft-quoted summary statements on historical development can be interpreted as laying out an inevitable succession of stages; one example is the following: "In broad outline, Asiatic, ancient, feudal and modern bourgeois modes of production can be designated as epochs marking progress in the economic development of society" (Marx 1970, 21). However, Marx himself made clear that his objective was not to present "an historic-philosophic theory of the general path every people is fated to tread" (Marx and Engels 1959, 440). Stalin's interpretation, to take one example, is exactly such a "philosophy of history"; see his "Anarchism or Socialism?" and "Dialectical Materialism" in Stalin (1952).

39 See, also, the discussion by Brewer (1980, 270–72).

40 See, e.g., Frobel, Heinrichs, and Kreye (1981).

41 This point, concerning the epistemological status of history in Amin's work, as well as the more general analysis of this section, shares much with the more extensive critical analysis of Amin's theory of development by Medley (1981).

42 This model of autocentric and, below, of extraverted development is presented by Amin in summary form in Amin (1974) and explored at length in Amin (1975).

43 Similar concepts of "social articulation" and "social disarticulation" are used by de Janvry and Sadoulet (1983).

44 See, for example, the comments by Charles Bettelheim published as Appendices I and III to Emmanuel (1972) and the survey article by David Evans (1984).

45 This interpretation of Marx's theory of value is presented at length by Bruce Roberts (1981).

46 See, for a representative sample, the following: Jonathan Schiffer (1981), Sheila Smith (1980 and 1982), and John Weeks and Elizabeth Dore (1979).

7 The costs of austerity in Nicaragua: The worker–peasant alliance (1979–87)

Adjustment programmes carry costs, which raises the question of who bears the burden of adjustment. It is a sad comment on the state of economics that the statistics necessary to give a definitive answer to this question are usually unavailable; nonetheless, with the use of some imagination, one can hazard a guess as to the answers.

Victor Bulmer-Thomas (1987, 302)

We have sacrificed the working class in favor of the economy as part of the strategic plan.

Tomás Borge (Jameson 1987, 58)

Austerity and revolution

The ongoing economic crisis in Nicaragua has been comparable in severity and duration to the desperate situation in the remainder of Central America.[1] Since at least 1980, all five countries have experienced deteriorating external accounts and domestic stagflation. Although the immediate economic problems faced by these countries have been similar, their causes have been different. Some factors of external origin (increased real international interest rates, declining external terms of trade, etc.) have negatively affected all of these countries; at the same time, United States foreign policy, war, and domestic political upheaval have had less uniform consequences in the region. Naturally, then, all countries in the region have been forced to adopt programs of economic stabilization and adjustment; however, because these programs have been forged under radically different economic and political conditions, they have had contrasting effects on domestic social sectors and classes.[2]

One of the distinguishing characteristics of the Nicaraguan case is that an economic austerity program has been carried out without the backing of the International Monetary Fund (IMF). This sets it apart from much of the rest of Central – and South – America.[3] The Nicaraguan government has apparently not needed IMF support to enforce its particular austerity program. In addition, the weight of the United States in the IMF and

Nicaraguan attempts to redefine national sovereignty would have made any official IMF program difficult to implement. Still, the similarities between the Nicaraguan program of stabilization and adjustment and traditional IMF conditions have been the focus of attention since the February 1985 announcement of the Nicaraguan policy package.[4]

The general issue of the relationship between traditional austerity programs and the nature of austerity in a revolutionary situation clearly needs to be addressed. We might expect, on one hand, that a revolutionary government would carry out a macroeconomic program quite different from those of right-wing military dictatorships or clearly pro-capitalist civilian regimes. On the other hand, we would probably expect a relatively small peripheral country to share with other foreign exchange-constrained economies the limitations imposed by the short-term inflexibility of restructuring either demand or supply (cf. Helleiner 1986). How do the various forms of austerity manifest themselves under their respective regimes, and how can these differences be explained? How much room for maneuver is there – especially in the context of a crisis-ridden world economy, not to mention continuing external aggression? Can the revolutionary project stay alive under such conditions? Unfortunately, these questions have tended to be neglected.

This relative lack of attention is explained, at least in part, by the presumption that austerity is a singular phenomenon in all economies, generally associated with traditional IMF-style programs. Orthodox austerity policies are often aimed at restoring the conditions of profitability in the domestic economy by changing the balance of power between classes. The differential consequences of these programs for different social sectors and classes have long been suspected; they are now being explored in some detail.[5]

Still, the general problem of stabilization and adjustment, and the costs of austerity, cannot be dismissed in the Nicaraguan revolutionary context by assuming that the government in power represents the popular sectors or that the economy is centrally planned or, finally, that the economic problems are all externally generated. First, notwithstanding appeals to the "logic of the majority" (whereby economic policy is designed to satisfy the basic needs of the majority of the population instead of the interests of the ruling minority, as under the previous regime),[6] the early revolutionary economy is still characterized by a complex combination of capitalist and other forms of production and distribution; the pre-revolutionary class structure has been transformed, not abolished. Second, there is generally much less central economic control than is presumed by the Ministry of Planning, economic advisors, or outside observers.[7] Finally, even if the causes of the economic crisis can be attributed to the pre-revolutionary economic legacy and external "shocks" (whether international economic conditions or the war, or both), the revolutionary program itself can be expected to create its own share of economic imbalances. Moreover, these internal and external disequilibria, regardless of origin, have effects that need to be addressed. Thus, the revolution "forgets about" the problem of stabilization and adjustment at its peril. This is certainly one of the lessons to be learned from Chile under the Popular Unity government; it is also an issue that goes back at least as far as Lenin's New Economic Policy.[8]

In the case of revolutionary regimes in the Third World, it is important to assess the costs of austerity through the lens of the "worker–peasant alliance." The worker–peasant alliance has a twofold meaning in this context. On one hand, workers and peasants are key participants in the tensions and conflicts that provoke a revolutionary crisis in society; they are also the projected beneficiaries of the policies and programs of the revolutionary government. On the other hand, the worker–peasant alliance refers to the project, supported by an even wider constellation of social forces, of transforming social relations – especially the class aspects of those relations – in both urban and rural areas of the country.

The use of the worker–peasant alliance as an "entry point" into the problem of austerity in a revolutionary context has the advantage of focusing on precisely those class dimensions of austerity that are usually left out of typical economic and political analyses. Attempts to understand austerity in terms of simple private-sector/public-sector or party/non-party dichotomies view the problem in terms of competing claims on resources based on property ownership or the ability to wield political power. Property and power are placed at the center of the analysis; they are substituted for class. The result is that many of the issues that arise in the course of building, maintaining, and redefining the worker–peasant alliance – the complex class dynamic of a society undergoing revolutionary change that, in turn, affects and is affected by changes in property ownership and the ruling political party – tend to fade into the background, or disappear completely.

At the same time, maintaining the revolution's bases of peasant and worker support and its goal of class transformation cannot just be assumed, especially within the context of economic crisis and the government austerity measures. Does austerity call into question short-term support for the revolution by popular classes in urban and rural areas? Are there conflicts between workers and peasants that emerge in the course of responding to difficult economic and political conditions? What about the long-term goals of the alliance: how are they affected by the costs of austerity? The present chapter begins to answer these questions for the Sandinista Revolution in Nicaragua.

The nature, scope, and consequences of austerity for the Nicaraguan Revolution cannot be understood without an analysis of the main features of the Nicaraguan economy and economic policy since the overthrow of the Somoza regime; such an analysis appears in the first section of this chapter. The second section involves a relatively brief discussion of the costs of the insurrection and the economic situation within the revolution through 1984. In the third section, I present a critical assessment of the austerity program that was adopted in early 1985. The fourth part of the analysis focuses attention on the costs of austerity in the cities and in the countryside. Finally, the immediate and long-term consequences of these costs are addressed in the last section.

Adjustment and stabilization (1979–84)

The worker–peasant alliance attempts to transform the key features of the inherited model of development. The initial measures taken by the government, together with the gains made by social movements outside the state, tend to alter the macroeconomic balances of the pre-revolutionary economy. In addition, the insurrection against the old regime disrupts "normal" economic life. This chapter's first general thesis, therefore, is that a revolution is forced to confront the twin problems of revolutionary transformation and macroeconomic balance from the moment it is ushered into power.

In the case of Nicaragua, the knife-edge of transformation and balance has been further sharpened by the inherited economic situation, a general deterioration of world economic conditions, and the military and economic aggression sponsored by the US government. From the outset, then, the Nicaraguan Revolution has been forced to devise an appropriate program of stabilization and adjustment. The changing response to the economic crisis during the past 8 years may conveniently be divided into three phases. The first phase, covering the 1979–81 period, involved a recovery from the pre-1979 depression. Starting in 1982 and lasting until the elections in 1984, the second phase was characterized by central economic controls and state-led growth – the Nicaraguan attempt at "stabilization with equity." The subsequent austerity phase was provoked by the accumulated imbalances and the escalation of the war; it was officially announced in 1985 and continues to the present.

Phase 1 (1979–81)

Many of the early measures of the Government of National Reconstruction were aimed at reviving the "stagnationist" Nicaraguan economy.[9] The last years of the Somoza regime witnessed a balance-of-payments crisis caused, in large part, by capital flight. Beginning in 1977 and continuing through the first year of the new government, the "flight to safety" for wealthy Nicaraguans totaled $685 million.[10] These capital exports, officially classified as short-term for balance-of-payments accounting purposes, were presumably converted into a unilateral, long-term movement once the Somoza regime was deposed. Therefore, although long-term capital inflows totaled $811 million during the same period and the accumulated external debt had reached $1.6 billion by the time Somoza left the country, only $3 million remained in the official reserves of the Central Bank when the new government assumed power.

Strict capital controls are arguably the most effective mechanism for stemming capital flight. One of the first acts of the new government was, in fact, nationalization of the banking and foreign trading systems. However, by that time, the bulk of the capital flight had already taken place. This is certainly one of the macro policy dilemmas of revolutionary governments: it is possible to close the floodgates, but only after government institutions have been seized from the old regime – and by then the level of capital outflows has already crested.

In the end, the Nicaraguan economy had already "adjusted" to this pre-revolutionary balance-of-payments crisis: although total exports exceeded pre-insurrectional levels, imports fell by approximately 22 percent in both 1978 and 1979. The immediate cause was the depression generated by the destruction and general disruption of the insurrection itself. Real gross domestic product (GDP) dropped by 7.1 percent and by 25.5 percent in 1978 and 1979, respectively (ECLA 1982, 565).[11]

Against the backdrop of intense political struggle for control of the revolution, Nicaragua was able to begin the process of recovering from the damages and disruption caused by the insurrection. The economic slide was reversed and, although GDP growth rates were below the overly optimistic expectations of the first two economic plans, national product grew at an annual average rate of 5 percent during 1980–81.[12]

The three key features of the stabilization during this period were an inflow of external resources, an expansionary fiscal policy, and liberal credit distribution. Net long-term capital inflows rose from $120 million (in 1979) to $343 million (1980) and $596 million (1981), the product of widespread support from official donors and creditors around the world (ECLA 1982).[13] The importance of fiscal expenditures more than doubled during this period, rising from an average of 8.7 percent of GDP during 1970–78 to 15 percent in 1979, 19.6 percent in 1980, and 22.3 percent in 1981 (see Chapter 4). However, the growth of tax revenues fell behind that of expenditures; therefore, the fiscal deficit increased steadily during the same period (6.8, 9, and 10.4 percent of GDP for the same years, respectively) (see Chapter 4).[14] The third leg of the recovery passed through the nationalized banking system: total credit grew by 46.7 percent from 1979 to 1980 (and again by 26.8 percent in 1981), with the largest part aimed at rural producers.[15] In addition, the combination of negative real interest rates and the low rate of loan repayment magnified the expansionary impact of the credit bonanza.

The general increase in national output was accompanied by an increase in basic consumption, as employment and real standards of living of peasants and workers increased. Unemployment, which had risen to 22.9 percent in 1979 (from a level of 14.5 percent in 1978), fell to 17.8

percent in 1980 (ECLA 1982, 575). In addition, workers experienced increases in wages. These increases were mostly the result of raising, enforcing, and narrowing the differential between rural and urban minimum wages. Even in this first phase, however, no attempt was made to allow the total real monetary wage bill to rise significantly. Rather, the emphasis was on expanding social services (the "social wage") through state-sponsored programs in health and education, and on the buying power of individual incomes, in the form of government subsidies to basic consumer goods and services and decreased housing and land-rental rates.

The success of these measures in raising national output and basic consumption expenditures, together with the 1980 renegotiation of the inherited external debt, won plaudits from foreign and domestic observers alike. However, the growth-oriented stabilization of the Nicaraguan economy was not a uniform success. Already, at this early stage, cracks were beginning to appear in the armor of economic recovery. The availability of foreign finance to cover the fiscal deficit (47.9 percent of the deficit in 1980) was beginning to fall off (see Chapter 4); continued expansion in government programs would require increasing use of domestic borrowing, especially new Central Bank funds. Still, the domestic inflation rate fell by 50 percent between 1979 and 1981.[16] The effects of the expansion were felt, instead, on the external account: whereas exports fell by 26 percent from 1979 to 1980 (and continued to oscillate around levels far below the pre-revolutionary peak), imports jumped by 78 percent in 1980 and slackened only slightly in 1981. The result was a deficit on current account of $491 million in 1980 and $563 million in 1981. New adjustment measures were therefore necessary.

Phase 2 (1982–84)

The first flush of success in consolidating a worker–peasant alliance and in growing out of the pre-revolutionary recession was followed by a series of attempts to control the growing imbalances in the domestic economy and the external sector.

Import controls and export incentives were introduced with the aim of closing, and reducing the need to finance, the persistent current-account deficit. Measures such as multiple exchange-rates, import surcharges, and foreign-exchange rationing succeeded in lowering total imports by 20 percent in 1982.[17] Exports, however, continued to decline, even in the face of increases in guaranteed export prices. Part of the problem was the slowdown in nontraditional (mostly manufactured) exports to the Central American Common Market, caused in turn by the economic crisis in the remainder of the isthmus. At the same time, Nicaraguan agroexporting capitalists responded less enthusiastically than expected to the class compromise offered by the revolutionary government. Traditional super-profits in agroexport production had probably declined as a result of the combined effect of the fall in labor productivity (as agricultural laborers shortened their workday) and the appreciation of the real exchange-rate. Presumably, exporters were also reacting to their now limited access to foreign exchange, the 1981 agrarian reform law, and political changes in the country as a whole.[18] The export–import imbalance did, however, fall by 20 percent during 1982.[19] This decrease, in turn, slowed the rate of growth of external debt.

On the domestic side, the government attempted to prevent inflation by continuing to limit increases in nominal wages and salaries. Any increase in standards of living would come from government social welfare programs and access to consumer goods at official prices. The aim was to increase the percentage of domestically produced goods provided by the state itself through the intermediary of institutions such as the Nicaraguan Enterprise for Basic Foods (ENABAS) at official (and therefore subsidized) prices. The rate of increase in food prices was slowed to 23.9 percent (from 25.9 percent in 1981), whereas the overall inflation rate remained at less than 25 percent.

One of the immediate effects of this second phase of adjustment was a decline in GDP of 0.8 percent in 1982. Total consumption fell by a comparable amount, although the consumption "mix" continued to change: "social consumption" (basic plus public consumption) barely decreased, whereas nonbasic consumption fell by almost 30 percent (see FitzGerald 1985d 203). Instead of traditional retrenchment, the government was attempting to carry out a program of "stabilization with equity."[20]

The second nontraditional element was the boom in state spending during this period. The government was not going to let economic activity slow to a standstill in order to solve the accumulating disequilibria. Rather, decisions were taken across the various government ministries to expand public-sector spending, not only on defense but also on new investment projects.

The emphasis on state investment was established with the initial flood of foreign funds during 1980 and 1981; it continued to be justified both by the near disappearance of private capitalist investment and by the objective of transforming the existing productive structure of the country. The strategy from the beginning was for the state to serve as the "center of accumulation."[21] The majority of new investment projects was centered in the agroindustrial sector.[22] The result was that investment as a percentage of GDP rose from negative 9.3 percent in 1979 to 19.5 percent in 1980, falling back to the more reasonable 15.9 percent in 1983.[23]

Although investment ratios reached levels unmatched in the rest of Central America, the remainder of the economy was subject to more typical policies designed to curb inflation and close the current-account deficit. Wages and salaries were kept constant in nominal terms; with an inflation rate slowly climbing to above 30 percent, real remuneration continued to decline. The responsibility of maintaining standards of living fell on government programs, both health and education expenditures, and subsidies for basic consumption goods. As a result, transfer payments for such welfare programs reached 7 percent of GDP in 1984.

Government attempts to balance the external account also contributed to the fiscal deficit. The official exchange-rate was kept pegged at 10 córdobas to the dollar (the level established in an IMF agreement just before Somoza was deposed): high-priority inputs and basic consumption goods were offered at the official rate, while export proceeds were surrendered at rates somewhat higher (each product had a different rate) – implying a de facto devaluation for exporters while the external terms of trade continued to decline. Again, the effect was to add an additional component to the fiscal deficit. Although government revenues increased every year, the rate of increase did not match that of expenditures; the resulting public-sector borrowing requirement peaked at 30 percent of GDP in 1983, falling back to 24.8 percent in 1984 (see Table 7.6 in note 13).

Notwithstanding the price incentives, exports continued at levels far below both the pre-revolutionary period and the current level of imports. Nonbasic consumption items (including nonbasic food) had been squeezed out of the import bill, but the attempt to maintain domestic industrial production, the state investment program and import-intensive exports (especially cotton) meant an increasing deficit on the current account.[24] The accumulated result was a growth in external debt from $2.6 billion in 1981 to $4.4 billion by the end of 1984 (see the table in note 13). The scarcity of foreign exchange and the "overheating" of the domestic economy were finally exhibited in the widening gap between the official and black-market exchange-rates: whereas the official rate remained pegged at 10 córdobas to the dollar throughout this phase, the number of córdobas for each dollar on the black market soared from 29 in 1981 to 276 during 1984.

The final destabilizing tendency throughout this period was external aggression. The war with the Contras represented both a direct shock to the fiscal deficit and a direct and indirect factor that disrupted production throughout the country. The most recent data, through the middle of 1987, are presented in Table 7.1.[25]

The "exhilarationist" tendencies of the Nicaraguan economy were increasingly visible in 1984. In macroeconomic terms, these tendencies meant that capacity and foreign-exchange limits were such that continued economic expansion resulted in growing internal and external disequilibria, especially inflation and a current-account deficit. In fact, the 1984 economic plan (drawn up at the end of 1983) called for a series of macroeconomic adjustments. However, the necessity of calling for national elections in November 1984 deferred any change in economic policy until 1985. On 8 February, newly elected President Daniel Ortega announced the initial measures of an economic austerity package.

The austerity program (1985–87)

The aim of the new economic policy was obvious: a general policy of "belt-tightening" was called for and special attention would be given to so-called strategic sectors. Thus, the government assigned the highest priority to the war effort – in particular, to the state's defense budget and, in matters of distribution, to the combatants and residents of the war zones. The "formal sector" of the economy, oriented toward the production of goods and services, both rural and urban, received the next highest priority; finally, government policy would attempt to squeeze the urban "informal sector."

The policy that drew the most attention was the change in the foreign exchange-rate: for the first time since 1979, the córdoba was officially devalued, declining from 10 to 28 (with multiple rates rising to 50 córdobas) to the dollar. The devaluation was aimed, in part, at reducing the foreign exchange losses of the Central Bank: by 1984, total losses from purchasing dollars (from exporters) at a price greater than they were sold (for imports) reached 5.5 percent of GDP; these losses were reduced to 2.8 percent of GDP in 1985.[26] It was also aimed at closing the current-account deficit by changing the relative prices of imports and exports. Additional incentives to exporters included an increase in guaranteed prices for cotton and coffee, and the first step of a complicated policy of surrendering a portion of export earnings in dollars to cattle-ranchers.

The fiscal deficit was attacked from both sides of the ledger. New taxes were imposed on capital gains and the incomes of independent professionals; however, the revenue generated by these direct tax increases tended to be offset by the decline in enterprise profits and the growth of the nontaxed "informal" economy. The main source of new revenues was indirect (consumption and excise) taxes. On the expenditure side, the government instituted a hiring freeze, a cutback in the state investment program, and the elimination of consumer subsidies. This last measure contributed to a rise of 376 percent in the 1985 price index for food – compared to 220 percent for the overall consumer price index.[27]

There was a simultaneous attempt to tighten monetary policy; for example, interest rates, which ranged from 5 percent (for loans to rural cooperatives) to 19 percent (for 5-year deposits) in 1984, were raised to 6 and 27 percent, respectively, in 1985. The percentage of production costs covered by state credit was also lowered from 100 to 80 percent.

These traditional (in terms of typical IMF programs) austerity measures were accompanied by less traditional moves to stem the fall in real wages and salaries. The official wage and salary scale was adjusted upward in February 1985, and then again in both March and May. This attempt to index wages and salaries was designed both to protect deteriorating standards of living and to attract workers back into formal-sector employment. As we shall see, however, wages and salaries did not keep pace with accelerating inflation.

Table 7.1 The costs of war in Nicaragua (1980–87): direct material and financial losses, effects on GDP (in millions of dollars)

Years	Material			Financial			Total of direct losses	Effects on GDP
	Destruction of wealth[a]	Production losses	Sub-total	Blocked loans	Commercial blockade	Sub-total		
1980	0.5	1.0	1.5	–	–	–	1.5	–
1981	4.0	3.4	7.4	8.2	–	8.2	15.6	241.0
1982	11.0	21.2	32.2	38.3	–	38.3	70.5	326.0
1983	58.6	106.6	165.2	61.3	14.0	75.3	240.5	331.0
1984	27.7	170.2	197.9	92.1	15.0	107.1	305.0	458.0
1985	18.4	97.8	116.2	73.0	79.4	152.4	268.6	682.0
1986	14.2	89.8	104.0	92.0	79.4	171.4	275.4	783.0
1987[b]	10.1	41.5	51.6	–	–	–	51.6	779.0
Total	144.5	531.5	676.0	364.9	187.8	552.7	1,228.7	3,600.0[c]

Source: unpublished data from the Nicaraguan Institute of Statistics and Censuses

Notes

[a] Capital stocks and inventories
[b] To 30 April 1987
[c] Estimated, to end of 1987

The results of the new policy package were mixed: the fiscal deficit continued to fall from the 1983 high of 30 percent of GDP to 23.3 percent in 1985, even as defense expenditures soared to 35.6 percent of total government expenditures.[28] Imports grew at a slower pace than in 1984, but total exports continued to fall, leaving a current-account deficit of $627 million. Finally, the recession induced by the new measures meant that 1985 GDP fell by 4.1 percent.

The overall decline in economic activity was the expected result of the war-economy package. The other effect of the 1985 "shock" was a spiraling inflation rate: the general price level, which had been increasing at an average annual rate of 50 percent through mid-1985, was growing by 334 percent by the year's end. Typical explanations of inflation, based on fiscal deficit financing and escalating wage costs, are clearly not applicable. The government deficit, as noted above, had declined during both 1984 and 1985; real wages, not withstanding the nominal adjustments, also fell (as discussed in detail below). The immediate causes must be sought elsewhere – in the elimination of consumer subsidies and the freeing of the prices of consumer goods, in the redirection of consumer goods away from civilians and toward combatants, and in the increased prices of imported goods.

This heterodox austerity program continued to be applied in the subsequent two years. In 1986, the official exchange-rate was devalued once again, to 70 córdobas per dollar. Dollar incentives were extended to cotton and coffee exporters. Interest rates on loans and deposits were again raised; in addition, payments by check were required for large transactions. The official wage and salary scale was increased in both January and March. Finally, the government responded to the shortage of consumer goods by raising producer prices on basic grains and other domestic foodstuffs.

According to the available preliminary data, the fall in real GDP actually slowed in 1986, to –0.4 percent.[29] Similarly, the fiscal deficit fell to 17 percent of GDP, with the largest part continuing to be financed by credit from the Central Bank. The external sector gap, however, widened even further: exports fell to $274.5 million whereas imports rose to $1.1 billion. Thus, the accumulated external debt, as expected, reached $7.2 billion by the year's end.[30] The unemployment rate continued to hover around 22.5 percent while inflation skyrocketed to 681.6 percent. Nicaragua's successes in the war against the Contras were clearly taking their toll on the domestic economy.

The economic plan for 1987 called for a continuation of the austerity program. All sectoral programs were based on the continuing difficulties caused by the foreign-exchange bottleneck. Production targets were set by calculating the guaranteed availability of foreign exchange and the need to negotiate additional foreign loans and donations. The economic plan also demonstrated the difficulty of planning in a situation in which economic survival and military defense meant making unforeseen decisions in an ever-changing context. For example, the drafting of the 1987 plan was based on three key presumptions:

1   there would be an increase in wages and salaries;
2   coffee prices would rise (by 13.5 percent); and
3   the córdoba would not be officially devalued.

The situation during 1987 evolved in a dramatically different way. International coffee prices remained constant while nominal wages and salaries were allowed to rise. On 1 March, the official scale was increased by 56 percent (on average) and the scale itself was expanded from 28 to 39 categories. Additional increases were granted in June, July, and August. It was finally announced that wage and salary increases would be granted on a monthly basis, according to the percentage increase in the official prices of a basket of 54 products. Additional measures to make the official scale more flexible included the payment of bonuses based on length of service, technical qualifications, and productivity increases that, according to recent estimates, trebled the actual salary base.

Finally, the córdoba continued (and continues) to face downward pressure in the desperate attempt being made to close the current-account deficit. Surcharges have been applied that raise the import exchange-rate from 70 to 170 for essential imports (such as fertilizers and medicines) and to 370 for goods classified as nonessential imports. Export prices were also raised to the extent that the average implicit exchange-rate fell to 560 córdobas to the dollar. The growing scarcity of foreign exchange, by mid-year, had driven the parallel exchange-rate to 6,000 and the black-market rate to 9,500.

The costs of austerity

The Nicaraguan economic crisis and the macroeconomic policies that have been followed in the past 8 years have had predictably severe costs. For example, GDP per capita, after rising slightly between 1979 and 1983, fell by more than 15 percent during the 1984–86 period. That trend should continue for 1987. However, in the context of the Nicaraguan Revolution, the decline in the average availability of goods and services for the population as a whole tells us little about the effects of austerity on the class composition of the country and, therefore, about the class dynamics of the revolution itself. An analysis of the consequences of austerity in the cities and the countryside focuses attention on the current status of the worker–peasant alliance. It is also a key ingredient in assessing the tensions that the revolution will have to confront in the postwar period.

Austerity in the city

Important crosscurrents have affected the urban class structure in Nicaragua during the 1979–87 period. The fact that the struggle to overthrow the Somoza regime had been based, in large part, on urban social groups meant that the workers' struggles earned them a share of benefits from government policy that, at least in the early years of the revolutionary process, probably surpassed the workers' percentage (or numerical weight) in the population as a whole. It also meant that the population of the cities, especially Managua, swelled considerably during that past 8 years, on the basis of rural to urban migration.[31] However, the period of austerity proper (1985 to the present) has witnessed a shift in priority away from the cities to the countryside, as the program of adjustment and stabilization has responded to the exigencies of the war.

The early measures of the revolutionary government, together with the postinsurrection economic recovery, led to an improvement in conditions in the urban centers. The combined effect of the nationalization of Somoza's enterprises, the creation and expansion of government-sponsored social services, and the general resurgence in economic activity, was an increase in jobs for the urban unemployed. Although increases in nominal wages were kept low, urban workers benefited from new health and education programs and the organization of new trade unions, as well as from the availability of domestic and imported consumer goods distributed through the state marketing system at officially controlled prices. It may also be inferred that, except for the few domestic capitalists whose enterprises were nationalized along with those owned by the Somoza family, other urban social groups (shopkeepers, owners of small industry, state employees, and urban professionals) also benefited from the program of economic recovery during the early years of the revolution.

Beginning with the first phase of adjustment and stabilization in 1982, the relative benefits began to shift. Import controls, the scarcity of foreign exchange, and the first assault on nonbasic consumption, negatively affected the traditional living standards of such urban groups as managers and professionals. At the same time, the state responded to their threat of emigration by offering them incentives in the form of housing, vehicles, and other goods. Although inflation remained at manageable levels, the slower increases in nominal wages and salaries meant that, by the end of 1982, their purchasing power had declined by 19 percent with respect to 1980 (see Table 7.2).

The economic situation of the urban working class has provoked numerous tensions within the revolutionary process. For example, the purchasing power of individual wages and salaries could be allowed to decline as long as the state was able to distribute basic consumption goods and maintain the social wage in the form of health and education services to the majority of the population. However, the increased scarcity of goods

Table 7.2 Nicaragua: real wages and salaries, 1980–86

	1980	1981	1982	1983	1984	1985	1986
Nominal wages and salaries	100.0	113.0	125.2	141.3	182.8	460.6	1,223.6
Consumer price index	100.0	123.9	154.6	202.6	274.4	876.7	6,852.5
Real wages and salaries	100.0	91.2	81.0	69.7	66.6	52.5	18.0

Sources: ECLAC (1987b) for nominal wages and salaries; and unpublished data from the Nicaraguan Institute of Statistics and Censuses for the consumer price index

Notes: 1980 = 100 for all indices. Data on nominal wages and salaries are based on monthly averages for workers registered with the Nicaraguan Social Security Institute. The consumer price index covers Managua; it represents the average for each year. Real wages and salaries were calculated by the author as the ratio of nominal wages and salaries to the consumer price index

available at official prices through the state distribution system, as well as eventual cutbacks in state welfare expenditures, reduced the ability of workers to achieve their customary standard of living by purchasing goods in nonstate markets at prices many times higher than the official ones. The decline in purchasing power and the instability of industrial employment (as production declined due, among other factors, to the shortage of imported inputs) led to a fall in productivity, higher levels of absenteeism, and, eventually, to increased participation in so-called informal-sector activities.

The organization of an official wage and salary scale (SNOTS) in February 1984 was aimed, not at stemming the decline in purchasing power but, rather, at equalizing the level of remuneration for similar types of work. Employers responded to the movement of workers from formal- to informal-sector activities by offering payment in kind and other incentives.[32] In the state sector, the movement of employees between different government agencies soared as administrators competed for skilled workers by offering positions that were in a higher SNOTS category and other "perks." Industrial capitalists, in both state-owned and private enterprises, reacted by supplying a portion of output (shoes, textiles, etc.) to compensate for the decline in the purchasing power of wages in order to keep workers from shifting to informal-sector activities.[33]

The urban sector that has suffered the greatest increase throughout this period had been the so-called informal activities sector. Both the movement of urban workers pushed out of formal-sector employment because of the decrease in real wages and rural-to-urban migrants have swelled Managua's informal sector. The estimates of the Secretariat of Planning and Budget of the relative size of nonagricultural informal-sector employment are presented in Table 7.3.

Table 7.3 Nicaragua: formal and informal sector employment (percentage of total employment in each category)

	Formal sector	Informal sector
Manufacturing	53.2	46.8
Energy and water	98.8	1.2
Construction	70.2	29.8
Commerce	19.5	80.5
Transport and communication	62.3	37.7
Finance	97.9	2.1
Services	63.0	37.0

Source: Secretariat of Planning and the Budget (SPP) (1986, 145)

Though significant in terms of its role in urban economic life, the informal sector is also the subject of numerous myths. For example, it is common in Nicaragua to claim that all participants in the informal sector have acquired great wealth in comparison to the rest of the population. In fact, the rate of depreciation of the córdoba is evidence that large incomes can be earned through speculative activities – not only on imported goods but also on domestic foodstuffs. An internal study by the Ministry of Foreign Trade concluded that the activities of a typical *buhonero* (a government-licensed private importer) would earn a 32 percent rate of return on a single transaction. However, the number of private importers has been drastically reduced, and, although no reliable data have been produced, low-income "proletarian" informal-sector workers probably far outnumber those whose activities are the source of elevated incomes.

The other powerful myth concerning the informal sector is that all activities are speculative, commercial ones. Again, exact data are not available. However, the merchants of Managua's Eastern Market coexist, there and elsewhere in the city, with a large number of producers of goods and services (furniture, shoes, car repair, etc.). Government attempts to "squeeze" the informal sector have been hampered by the role of both informal-sector incomes and goods and services in stemming the decline in the standards of living of working-class families.

The austerity program has particularly affected the role of women in the Nicaraguan economy. In part as a result of the equal-rights movement and of the drafting of men for the armed forces, but also as a consequence of the deterioration in the real wages of traditionally male jobs, the participation of women in the labor force has increased dramatically. Unfortunately, the data presented in Table 7.4 do not permit a precise demarcation of the changes before and after 1979.

The general situation in Managua has changed rapidly since the new economic policy was initiated in 1985. The shift in priorities from Managua to the countryside has involved a freeing up of the prices of domestic foodstuffs and the movement of goods (both domestic manufactured and imported goods) that were previously available to the countryside and to the smaller urban areas located in the war zones. This attempt to close the town–country "scissors" has had the effect of increasing the supply of food to the cities, but at significantly higher free-market prices. The widening gap between the rate of inflation and increases in nominal wages and salaries has meant that purchasing power had declined by the end of 1986 to less than 20 percent of its 1980 level (see Table 7.4).

At the same time, the government responded to workers' demands by indexing the SNOTS scale to a basket of 54 goods, opening up a network of Workers' Distribution Centers (CATs) and factory-level commissaries, and allowing employers to pay bonuses above the official SNOTS scale.[34] However, the fact that wages and salaries are indexed to the official prices of a basket of goods that does not represent their "typical" consumption pattern, and the fact that goods in the official distribution centers are limited in availability, means that workers' living standards will continue to decline, albeit at a slower pace than before. Although precise data are not currently available, the economic plan for 1987 noted that most social services – in particular, the "social wage" that was designed to stem the

Table 7.4 Nicaragua: economic participation of women

	1971	1985
Women of working age	614,657	1,002,129
Economically inactive women	504,215	683,547
Students	107,913	200,730
Homemakers	329,135	434,718
Retired	4,252	8,193
Incapacitated	–	29,014
Others	62,915	10,892
Economically active women	110,442	318,582
Employed	106,923	309,039
• full-time	–	172,168
• sub-employed	–	116,210
• others	–	20,661
Unemployed	3,519	9,543
• laid off	1,601	4,494
• looking for first time	1,918	2,642
• others	–	2,407
Participation rate	17.9	31.8
Rate of employment	17.4	30.8
Rate of unemployment	3.2	3.0
Rate of underemployment	–	36.4

Source: unpublished data from the Secretariat of Planning and Budget fall in real individual wages and salaries – have stagnated or decreased during the past 3 years (Secretariat of Planning and the Budget (SPP) 1986).

This deterioration in customary standards of living in the context of wartime austerity raises a final question: how are the urban workers surviving? Recent research has discovered a wide assortment of survival strategies in the more "popular" neighborhoods of Managua.[35] Basically, working-class families have been forced to find a combination of formal-sector employment (so as to receive nominal wages and, more importantly, access to the goods available in the CATs and commissaries), informal-sector marketing, and the production of goods and services in informal-sector activities.

Austerity in the countryside

Agriculture was the key economic sector within the Somozaist pattern of capitalist development. This leading role has not been challenged thus far by the revolution. Moreover, as a result of the concentration of the Contra war in the countryside, the rural areas have acquired additional prominence during the past 8 years. At the same time, government policy and rural social movements have achieved a qualitative transformation of the Nicaraguan countryside.

The nationalization of the properties of the Somoza family (1979–80) and the first agrarian reform (1981) were the initial steps in recharting the course of agriculture. The reorganization of these lands into state farms (the Area of People's Property, or APP) and agricultural cooperatives still left the bulk of both domestic-use and export-oriented land and production in the form of peasant smallholder and capitalist enterprises.[36] Other early measures that directly affected the class landscape of the countryside included the nationalization of export marketing, the reduction of land rental rates, the attempt to replace traditional rural merchants by state marketing boards, the provision of credit from the nationalized banking system, and the expansion of agricultural extension programs.[37]

The key role within the first phase of economic recovery was assigned to the APP; specifically, to the state capitalist farms. Although these state enterprises occupied only 21 percent of the land under cultivation (and although they participated in agricultural production in roughly the same percentage), it was planned that they should occupy center stage in reactivating agricultural production.[38] This emphasis was reinforced by the raising of rural minimum wages (in an attempt to attract landless laborers and small peasant producers to state farms), by the extension of credit to the enterprises directly under the control of the Ministry of Agriculture, and, later, by the state investment program in agroindustrial projects. These measures were complemented by state support for agricultural producers organized into production, credit, and service cooperatives.[39]

Other forms of production have generally occupied a less prominent role in state policy, and there has been no attempt to eliminate them. Together, peasant producers of basic grains and capitalist enterprises, in both export-oriented production and the production of domestic food-stuffs, have accounted for about 65 percent of land and 74 percent of total agricultural production.

From the outset, capitalist producers have been squeezed between, on one hand, the decline in international commodity prices and their political role as the "class enemy" and, on the other hand, their traditionally strategic position in the production of agricultural exports and some domestic foodstuffs. One option would have been to eliminate them entirely. However, neither the 1981 agrarian reform nor a subsequent reform law in early 1986 has eliminated capitalist production. Rather, the various phases of adjustment and stabilization during the past 8 years have maintained capitalist producers through a combination of state credit and support prices. In the case of agroexporters, increased price guarantees have meant an implicit rate of exchange above the official rate. These producer prices began to be supplemented in 1985 with a complex procedure of surrendering export proceeds directly in dollars. By 1986, the implicit exchange-rate ranged between 1.68 (for coffee) and 7.08 (for sugar) times the official exchange-rate.[40]

In the case of peasant producers of basic grains, the situation has been similarly complicated. Again, although the emphasis of government policy has been on state farms and cooperative forms of land tenure, there has been no attempt to eliminate individual peasant producers. Rather, the state has supplied credit, technical assistance, and the legalization of individual land titles in return for state purchases of their marketed output. Thus, between 1981 and 1982, ENABAS was able to increase its purchases of grain (corn, beans, and rice) from 33 to 50 percent of total marketed output (Zalkin 1987, 970). However, this apparent success masked the emergence of a significant problem: the total level of marketed grain production decreased by 29 percent during the same period.

The first attempts to increase grain production were oriented toward the strengthening of cooperative producers (for example, under the aegis of the Nicaraguan Food Program, or PAN, established in 1981) and state production (within, for example, the 1983 Contingency Plan). This emphasis on state and cooperative farms, which was successful in raising the level of domestic-use agricultural production, failed to address the problems of peasant smallholder and capitalist producers of basic grains. The effects of economic stabilization led, therefore, to the formation of a new multiclass organization of agricultural producers – the National Union of Farmers and Cattlemen/Ranchers (UNAG). The UNAG has lobbied for expanded individual land reform, increased support prices, and the distribution of consumer goods to the countryside.

The reaction of UNAG bears a close resemblance to the pre-revolutionary response of both peasant and capitalist producers to the monopsonist position of private merchants and banks under the Somoza regime. Its conflict with the Sandinista state – over ENABAS's purchases of basic grains at prices below those that the black market would yield, the privileging of state and cooperative ownership of land, and the lack of availability of consumer goods – led its members to resist marketing basic grain output at official prices and, especially in the most remote zones, to their limited support for the Contras.

This dual threat – to starve the cities and to support the Contra forces – led to a significant reorientation of state policy within the 1985–87 austerity program. First, there has been an expansion of land distribution (including the transfer of state lands) to individual producers. Second, the state has attempted to improve the distribution of consumer goods (including imports) to rural producers.[41] Finally, the official prices offered to agricultural producers have improved, in part because support prices have been increased (beginning in 1986) and, in part, because producers have been allowed to market their output through nonstate, private channels (starting in 1987). As a result, the terms of trade, which declined through 1985, began to turn in favor of basic grain producers; a particular reading of the data presented in Table 7.5 makes this clear.

The terms of trade facing basic grain producers can be traced through row A for the years 1981 to 1985 and then in row B for 1985 and 1986. This jumping from one index to another can be explained in the following way: because manufactured goods at official prices were generally unavailable to rural producers, they had to purchase these goods in private markets; thus, the consumer price index is the relevant terms-of-trade deflator for the 1981–84 period. The result was that the prices at which producers of basic grains could offer their output through official channels declined steadily relative to the prices at which they could buy goods from the cities. Between 1985 and 1986, however, support prices rose and manufactured

Table 7.5 Nicaragua: town–country terms of trade

	1981	1982	1983	1984	1985	1986
A	1.00	0.94	0.80	0.72	0.43	0.37
B	1.00	1.03	1.13	0.97	0.63	1.13

Source: author's calculations based on data from the International Monetary Fund (1987)

Notes: A is the ratio of basic grain support prices (a simple average of the price index for corn, beans, and rice) and the consumer price index (1981 = 100 for both indices). B is the ratio of the basic grain support price index and the national accounts industry deflator (1981 = 100 for both indices) goods became increasingly available at the official prices; hence, the national accounts price deflator for industry should be used as the basis of the relevant terms-of-trade index. According to this measure, government policy has succeeded in shifting the town–country terms of trade in favor of producers of basic grains.

Austerity and the worker–peasant alliance

The Nicaraguan Revolution has captured the imagination of economists and many other observers. Policymakers' flexibility in responding to the ongoing economic crisis and the multiclass nature of the revolutionary movement are two of the reasons why Nicaragua has attracted so much attention.

Flexibility in responding to different class demands has been the hallmark of many government strategies, including the various programs of stabilization and adjustment since 1979. In this sense, macroeconomic policy has been based on a series of changing class compromises. The aim of economic policy has been to cement the worker–peasant alliance and to ally other domestic social groups to the dual processes of revolutionary transformation and national defense. Thus, what may appear at first to be a series of "concessions" to social groups other than workers and peasants – the army, capitalist producers of agroexports, and so on – may be interpreted as a series of compromises designed to maintain the worker–peasant alliance under difficult and changing conditions.

The austerity program announced in early 1985 may be seen against this background as a response both to the war and to the problems generated by earlier economic policies. Among these "mistakes," two were especially significant in terms of the relationship between the role of the state and the conduct of macroeconomic policy. First, state planners and economic policymakers appear to have been guided by the presumption that market relations had been effectively removed from a large part of the Nicaraguan economy. Macroeconomic balance could be achieved, so it was thought, precisely because private merchants had been ousted and replaced by a state trading system.

A related problem was the presumption that the "correct" functioning of the administrative, banking, and commercial system of the state could control the development of the economy and, ultimately, the terms of the worker–peasant alliance. Implicit in this presumption was the mistake of ascribing a decisive role to the state's economic organs and of one-sidedly emphasizing the development of agroindustry, based on investment directly controlled by these organs. This focus on state control has had the opposite effect of putting private and, until recently, illegal commerce and production into an advantageous position. Since efforts to develop the role of the state presumed the existence of more resources than the state could effectively mobilize, private traders and producers were able to step in and replace the role of the state in key economic activities. Minister of Internal Commerce, Ramon Cabrales, has noted the role of state policy in creating conditions that led to the strengthening of private markets:

> One of the most serious errors was that during each agricultural cycle we obligated the peasants to sell us their production at official prices and in a coercive manner, in an attempt to resolve the distribution problem of everyone in the country. As the peasantry learns that the only thing that matters are the revenues from selling the harvest, it filches the harvest and refuses to sell its products to the state. Therefore, the state enterprise ENABAS is no longer able to collect those products.
>
> (Cabrales 1987, 3)

This emphasis on the key role of the state, and the tendency to "forget" about the other marketing and production relations in the Nicaraguan economy, ended up driving a wedge between workers and peasants. Peasant producers of basic grains were compelled to increase their self-sufficiency and to market their output through parallel and black markets.[42] Many producers were drawn toward the UNAG in an effort to bargain with the state over higher prices, over the ability to market their output in nonstate markets, and over the improved distribution of industrial goods to the countryside. Others joined with landless rural laborers in demanding more land reform.[43] Workers, on the other hand, were faced with deteriorating living standards as wage goods become increasingly scarce in official channels and available, at much higher prices, only in "free" markets. Calls for increased work discipline and productivity proved ineffective. Instead, wage-earners responded by pressuring the leadership of the Sandinista Worker Confederation (CST) and by moving into the informal sector.

In brief, post-1985 austerity policies have benefited peasants and rural capitalists (through higher food prices, the distribution of consumer goods, etc.) at the expense of the urban population, consisting of both workers and nonworkers alike.

The government's response to this situation, especially in 1987, may be seen as an attempt to recompose the worker–peasant alliance on new terms. The data are not yet available to analyze whether the peasants are responding to the new policies by expanding the area planted and marketing their output to the urban areas. The workers, however, are still struggling just to survive.

The political costs of this austerity are difficult to gauge. At least one observer has concluded that the counterrevolution has gained at least "passive support" from the peasantry (Marchetti 1986). The situation in the cities is somewhat different. Tensions have increased in the trade union movement and within such mass organizations as the Sandinista

Defense Committees (CDS), but there is little evidence of urban support for the Contras. On the contrary, the bulk of the blame for the current situation seems to have been placed squarely on the invading forces. Again, according to at least one report,

> there is no relation between the popular sectors' criticisms of the economic situation and their political position. The economic crisis these people are living through is not translated into domestic political criticism.
>
> The ideology of Managua's popular classes included the clear image of a government which began to aid them in a variety of ways until the war cut off the possibilities for further advancement. This is the base of their understanding of the government's economic campaign.
>
> (Department of Sociology, Central American University, 1986, 55)

The short-term solution for this crisis depends, in large part, on the course of the war and the current regional negotiations for peace. Recent economic problems and the severity of the austerity program imposed on the country also raise questions about the medium- and longer term strategy for the Nicaraguan Revolution. If the worker–peasant alliance – both the participation of workers and peasants in the revolution and the project of transforming the class structure of society – is to survive in the postwar period, developmental solutions beyond the mere continuation of austerity will have to be forged.

(original version published in 1989)

Acknowledgements

This chapter could not have been completed without my access to the data and observations offered by a large number of individuals and institutions. Special thanks are due to colleagues in the Nicaraguan Institute of Economic and Social Research (INIES), the Center for the Study of the Agrarian Reform (CIERA), the Nicaraguan Institute of Statistics and Censuses (INEC), the Nicaraguan Central Bank (BCN), and the Economic Research Team of the Regional Coordinator of Economic and Social Research (CRIES) in Managua. Research assistance was provided by Jimmy Campbell and Stephen Francis. The Helen Kellogg Institute for International Studies provided partial travel support. An earlier version of this chapter was presented at the fourteenth International Congress of the Latin American Studies Association, Yale University, and the University of Chicago. Comments from Michael Conroy, Michael Zalkin, and an anonymous reviewer are gratefully acknowledged. I am responsible for the translations and, finally, for the analysis itself.

Notes

1 The economic situation across the Central American isthmus is discussed by the United Nations Economic Commission for Latin America (1984).
2 The different adjustment programs adopted by the five Central American countries are surveyed by Bulmer-Thomas (1987).
3 The coverage and effects on Latin America of IMF-sponsored programs are analyzed by Manuel Pastor, Jr. (1987a).
4 For example, see Rodolfo Delgado (1985) and Roberto Pizarro (1987). A similar debate was provoked by the new austerity program adopted in mid-February 1988. The latest measures include a substantial devaluation of the córdoba, a currency conversion (1,000 old córdobas to 1 new córdoba), price increases, a wage and salary adjustment, and a 10 percent cut in the state budget. This chapter was completed in late 1987; there is no attempt to analyze the impact of the 1988 measures.
5 See Manuel Pastor, Jr. (1987b).
6 "Simply stated, the core economic problem of the transition is how to transform the inherited economic structure of underdevelopment into one that benefits the majority of the population and at the same time generates acceptable levels of economic growth" (Fagen *et al.* 1986, 17).
7 The role of the state and planning in the Nicaraguan economy is discussed in Chapters 4 and 5 of this volume.
8 For the Chilean case, see Stephany Griffith-Jones (1981) and, for the Soviet experience with the New Economic Policy, see Charles Bettelheim (1976).
9 "Stagnationist" is the term used by Lance Taylor (1987, 12).
10 This is the sum of net short-term capital movements and errors and omissions for the 1977–80 period. See the United Nations Economic Commission for Latin America and the Caribbean (1986a, 182–83).
11 United Nations Economic Commission for Latin America (1982, 565). The total of damage and lost production for the 1978–80 period was estimated to be $2 billion, equivalent to the 1980 Nicaraguan GDP. See World Bank (1981, 2).
12 The plans had predicted growth rates of 22.5 and 18.5 percent for the two years, respectively. For a comparison of the planned and actual values for a wide variety of economic indicators, see Hugo Cabieses (1986, 96).
13 The mix of multilateral and bilateral loans and credit lines changed considerably during the 1979–81 period: multilateral financing fell from 78.4 percent of the total in 1979 to 11.4 percent in 1981. The sources of bilateral external

Table 7.6 Nicaragua: selected economic indicators, 1980–86

	1980	1981	1982	1983	1984	1985	1986
Gross domestic product (GDP)[a]	100.0	105.4	104.5	109.3	107.6	103.2	102.8
GDP per capita[a]	100.0	102.1	98.0	99.1	94.3	87.5	84.2
Exports[b]	495	553	447	463	430	338	292
Imports[b]	909	1,037	829	925	890	973	955
External debt[b]	1,825	2,556	3,139	3,788	4,362	4,936	5,773
Fiscal deficit/GDP	9.2	12.4	13.6	30.0	24.8	23.3	15.8

Source: ECLAC (1987b)

Notes
[a] 1980 = 100, [b] In millions of dollars, [c] In percentages

financing also changed during that period: the socialist countries (including Cuba) increased their participation in total bilateral credit from negligible amounts in 1979 to 26 percent in 1981. (My calculations were made on the basis of data in Stahler-Sholk [1987, 162].) The strategic importance of external finance for the initial stage of socialist transition in peripheral societies is argued by Barbara Stallings (1986).

14 These percentages differ only slightly from the corresponding entries in the longer data series presented in the table in note 13.

15 For a discussion of the rural credit program, see Laura J. Enriquez and Rose J. Spalding (1987).

16 The annual average rates of inflation were 48.1 percent (1979), 35.3 (1980), and 23.9 percent (1981); see ECLA (1982, 582).

17 See the table in note 13.

18 One of the forms of class compromise offered by the Somoza regime had been the free convertibility of foreign exchange. After the revolution, foreign-exchange earnings have been controlled by the state, and capitalists' access to foreign exchange has been allowed for either rationed inputs at the official rate of exchange or, at rates considerably higher than the official rate, in the parallel market.

19 See the data on export and imports in the table in note 13. Nonetheless, because of the continued payment of interest on the outstanding external debt, the deficit on current account fell by only 8.7 percent during 1982. See ECLAC (1986a, 183).

20 The logic of "stabilization with equity" is explained by FitzGerald (1985d, 191–204).

21 The theory of the transitional state serving as the center of accumulation is presented by FitzGerald (1985b) and Irvin (1983). I critically discuss the theory in Chapter 5.

22 For a comprehensive list of these investment projects, many of which are still under way, see Cabieses (1986).

23 These figures refer to gross domestic investment, including changes in inventories. For 1979 and 1980, see ECLA (1982, 568); for 1983, see ECLAC (1984, 474).

24 On the evolution of food imports, see Utting (1987).

25 A more detailed analysis of the costs of the Contra war is presented by FitzGerald (1987). The evolution of the war and of US policy toward Nicaragua is discussed by Peter Kornbluh (1987).

26 International Monetary Fund (1987, 31). This report, an internal document prepared by a May 1987 staff mission, was made available for consultation by my colleagues in Nicaragua.

27 See Table 7.2 for data on the increase in the overall consumer price index during 1985. The price index for food covers eight agricultural products: rice, beans, sugar, coffee, corn, beef, eggs, and milk products. The Nicaraguan Institute of Statistics and Censuses graciously supplied the unpublished global indicators for this data from Chapter 2 of *Nicaragua en Cifras* (INEC 1986).

28 For data on the fiscal deficit, see Table in note 13; data on defense expenditures as a percentage of GDP are taken from ECLAC (1987b, 16).

29 Unpublished data supplied by Nicaraguan Institute of Statistics and Censuses (INEC) (1986).

30 The accumulated external debt includes the capitalization of payments in arrears. See Sevilla *et al.* (1987, 46).

31 Unless otherwise stated, information about conditions in the cities refers to Managua. According to recent estimates, Managua's population is growing at an annual rate of 7.04 percent (compared to a national population growth rate

of 3.36 percent); the current population stands at 1.3 million (out of a total population of 3.3 million). See *Monitoreo*, No. 3 (August 1987), a publication of the Nicaraguan Institute of Economic and Social Research (INIES).

32 According to unpublished data provided by colleagues in the Secretariat of Planning and Budget, job rotation in the Ministry of Transportation (workers who left the ministry as a percentage of total ministry employment) reached 57.9 percent during the period from September 1986 and February 1987. For the government as a whole, job rotation (by the same definition and for the same period) was 9.5 percent.

33 These attempts to circumvent the SNOTS scale by making payments in kind were declared illegal by the government in June 1985. See Stahler-Sholk (1985).

34 The state has also bowed to pressure from professionals and other higher-income formal-sector employees to open up a CAT specifically for those groups. It remains to be seen if the professionals will be successful in achieving their other demand – to release them entirely from the SNOTS scale.

35 The research was conducted by the Department of Sociology at the Central American University in Managua (1986).

36 The complex class structure of the Nicaraguan peasantry is discussed by Michael Zalkin (1987).

37 The Nicaraguan agrarian reform and associated policy measures are discussed in detail by Carmen Diana Deere *et al.* (1985).

38 Throughout this section, land and production figures are based on Cabieses (1986, 131).

39 The cooperative sector covered approximately 15 percent of farm land in 1983. This figure grew to 21 percent by the end of 1986, the last year for which data are available. The figures for production are 9 and 26 percent for the 2 years, respectively. Production cooperatives are distinguished from credit and service cooperatives by the degree of collective ownership of both land and machinery and the collective organization of work. Credit and service cooperatives tend to gather together peasant producers for the purpose of sharing state credit and technical assistance; however, property ownership and the responsibility for organizing work remain at the individual family level. A third, "intermediate" stage of cooperative production is the *surco muerto*, in which barriers between individual plots of land have been eliminated. However, their weight in terms of total land use and production is negligible.

40 These figures are based on calculations made by the International Monetary Fund (1987, table 35, 57).

41 The state has guaranteed to distribute the following nine products through the Centers of Rural Distribution at official prices: batteries, lighters, blankets, flashlights, light bulbs, boots, ponchos, grain mills, and kerosene lamps.

42 Parallel markets are legal markets (involving both state and private merchants) in which goods are exchanged at prices higher than the official ones. Black markets are strictly illegal. To the extent that goods and services can be channeled through official and parallel markets, transactions can be accounted for (i.e., for planning purposes) and taxed. Black-market activities tend to undermine both state planning and government tax revenues.

43 The demand for land reached a peak in the region around Masaya during 1985. According to unpublished data (Ministry of Agricultural Development and Agrarian Reform, Region IV, "Plan Masaya"), land redistribution has affected 13,356 acres, benefitting a total of 1,490 families – 460 in individual land-tenancy arrangements and the remainder in cooperative form. The land was

redistributed from diverse sources: 22.4 percent from APP enterprises, 50.8 percent from negotiated sales involving private landowners, and 26.8 percent expropriated from a single landowner, Enrique Bolaños Geyer (head of the Superior Council of Private Enterprise and outspoken critic of the government).

8   When failure becomes success: Class and the debate over stabilization and adjustment

It is said that two out of three stabilizations fail.

Michael Bruno *et al.* (1988, viii)

"Success" and "failure" are relative notions.

Lance Taylor (1988b, 148)

What *have* we learned from stabilization and adjustment in developing countries (Dornbusch 1982)? Both orthodox and heterodox policy packages have been put to the test in recent years and, according to many economists, they have failed. These failures, however, have not led to the abandonment either of the policies or of the theories that gave shape to the policies. Instead, the debate over stabilization and adjustment continues to move within the strict limits set by neoclassical and structuralist economists.

This debate is consistent with the tradition of standard development economics. Neoclassical and structuralist economic theories determine the parameters of debate and, when the policies of one theory are said to have failed, economists and policymakers turn to the policies advocated by the other theory. In this sense, the current debate over stabilization and adjustment does not represent a departure from, but a continuation of, a longer and more general debate between neoclassical and structuralist economics over economic development in the postwar period.[1]

Economists and policymakers of both schools continue to discuss the relative merits of their respective development theories and policies. While there has been a shift in focus from long-term growth to shorter term stabilization and adjustment (Arida 1986), the outer bounds of the debate are still set by neoclassical and structuralist economic theories. In recent years, developing countries have implemented a variety of orthodox and heterodox stabilization and adjustment policies, connected in turn to neoclassical and structuralist theories. As in the past, both sets of policies are seen as failures; many observers acknowledge that the developing world continues to suffer widespread unemployment, inflation, and balance-of-payments difficulties as policymakers move back and forth between orthodox and heterodox policy packages.

What, then, have we learned? There is a curious anomaly in the commitment on the part of development economists to existing theories and policies even when they appear, on their own terms, to have failed. What if, however, these failures turn out to have been successes, not with respect to employment, price stability, and the balance of payments – variables on which both neoclassical and structuralist economists choose to focus their attention – but in terms of increasing exploitation, which it generally falls to Marxists to point out? The standard policies may not have been able to achieve internal and external balance, but they may have strengthened the class dimensions of capitalism. Thus, although failures from a neoclassical or structuralist perspective, both orthodox and heterodox stabilization and adjustment policies can be considered to be successful from the perspective of a theory that focuses on class.

Theoretically, a failure from the perspective of one theory may be a success when viewed in terms of another, and vice versa. The criteria for success and failure would then be internal to each theory. The implication for development *policy* is that the "failed" development policies of neoclassical and structuralist theories – and the continued oscillation between their different failed policy packages – may combine to increase exploitation and, in general, to promote the successful development of the class aspects of capitalism.

In this chapter, I explore these ideas with respect to the ongoing debate over stabilization and adjustment. The theoretical contributions and policy recommendations of neoclassical and structuralist economists are reviewed in the second section. The two theories are connected to their respective "humanist" and "structuralist" underpinnings. I also show that both theories tend to place the class aspects of stabilization and adjustment outside the present debate. In the third section, I look at the recent experience of three countries – Argentina, Brazil, and Peru – where first orthodox and then heterodox policies have been implemented. By most accounts (both neoclassical and structuralist) those policies have failed. In the fourth section, an alternative theoretical approach is employed and the opposite conclusion is reached: instead of failures, both orthodox and heterodox policies can be seen as successes in terms of promoting capitalist class processes. The conclusion suggests that the so-called failures of recent stabilization and adjustment policies are part of the successful development of capitalist class processes in Argentina, Brazil, Peru, and the rest of Latin America in the postwar period.

Success according to neoclassical and structuralist theories

Stabilization and adjustment typically refer to those macroeconomic policies designed to solve internal and external disequilibria – such as unemployment, accelerating inflation, and balance-of-payments deficits – in the face of what are considered "shocks" to an economy; that is, unforeseen events such as a decline in export earnings (or, conversely, a foreign exchange bonanza), an increase in external debt payments, and financial panics. While most traditional economists concur on the need to stabilize and adjust the domestic economy after such shocks, they disagree on what the appropriate set of policies should be (Fishlow 1981). Some economists advocate tighter monetary policy, lowering government deficits, and liberalizing internal and external trade and capital markets; other economists dismiss this market-oriented, orthodox policy package and, instead, argue for increased controls over markets.

These different recipes for success derive, in large part, from the use of different economic theories. Both neoclassical and structuralist economists agree that success entails moving the economy to a position of low unemployment, price stability, and balance-of-payments equilibrium. They disagree, however, about the appropriate policies to achieve such success.

Although development specialists are generally familiar with many of the elements of the debate between neoclassical and structuralist economists, it is useful to review briefly their respective theoretical approaches and policy recommendations. The focus here is on an especially important but less familiar aspect of that debate, namely, that the differences between neoclassical and structuralist theories and policies are explained by their varying theoretical starting points: individual human nature for the neoclassicals; given economic and social structures for the structuralists. Their different approaches to stabilization and adjustment, therefore, are ultimately grounded in a debate that pits humanism against structuralism. They also tend to ignore the important class implications of their theories and policies.

Neoclassical theory

The starting point for the present debate lies in the theoretical underpinnings of so-called orthodox stabilization and adjustment policies.[2] As is well-known, according to neoclassical development economists, the need for such policies is based on the persistence of unsustainable internal and external disequilibria. These problems are, in turn, caused by a series of imperfections that prevent internal and external markets from clearing. For example, accelerating inflation is said to be caused by excess aggregate demand that can often be traced to government decisions to increase current expenditures beyond the level of revenues. Similarly, balance-of-payments difficulties are tied to, among other things, overvalued exchange-rates and the existence of exchange controls. In both cases, the problem is caused by an unwarranted government (or other) intervention that keeps markets from clearing and therefore gives improper market signals to individual economic agents. Without such microeconomic imperfections, macroeconomic imbalances cannot arise or, if they do emerge (e.g., as the result of an unanticipated shock), stability will reappear as soon as the appropriate individual decisions are taken and market adjustments are made.

How then can a situation arise at which the price level is too high and/or a balance of payments deficit exist? Transitory disequilibria may appear if one of the underlying determinants of the model changes as a result of an internal or external shock (for example, an unanticipated increase in import prices or a severe drought) and markets have not yet had time to adjust. Once the appropriate adjustments have been made, however, the disequilibria disappear and macroeconomic stability is once again established.

If internal and external balance is automatically restored by individual decisions, persistent disequilibria can only be explained by the existence of barriers to the carrying out of such decisions, that is, market imperfections. Thus, for example, if a government decides to manage the exchange-rate "float" by not allowing the full depreciation necessary to eliminate a balance-of-payments deficit, the resulting overvaluation will prevent domestic factors of production from shifting in the requisite proportions from non-tradables to the production of import substitutes and exports. This obstacle will be further complicated by other possible market imperfections such as downwardly rigid wages, trade barriers, capital controls, a government decision to overexpand the money supply to satisfy the demand for real cash balances, and so on. In this sense, maintaining such imperfections can be thought of as irrational, since they prevent a country from achieving what it would otherwise be able to achieve – namely, the maximum wealth for its citizens.

The orthodox set of policy measures advocated by neoclassical economists to solve such persistent disequilibria is equally well-known: balancing the fiscal budget, real wage adjustments, exchange-rate depreciation (either by devaluing the overvalued currency or by instituting flexible exchange-rates), external trade and exchange liberalization, and so forth. All of these policies are designed to eliminate the obstacles that prevent individuals from making the appropriate adjustments and to bring government actions into line with the results of allowing markets to operate freely. In other words, in the face of macroeconomic imbalances, policymakers have two choices:

1   do nothing, and let individuals make the appropriate microeconomic decisions, or
2   if market imperfections exist and/or if there is government mismanagement of policy, dismantle market barriers and restrict the government to its role in maintaining free markets and other minimal guarantees of engaging in individual economic activity.

Success is indicated when, on the basis of individual decisions, the economy reaches a point of full employment, price stability, and balance-of-payments equilibrium.

This formula for success can be explained by the neoclassical economists' use of human nature as the ultimate determinant of the economy. They base their argument on the idea that there is a macroeconomic equilibrium position (of full employment, price stability, and balance-of-payments equilibrium), consistent with resource endowments, technology, and individual choice, which individuals will find if allowed to make rational decisions in microeconomic markets. Consumers, producers, and owners of factor endowments will both keep the economy at that full equilibrium and, in the aftermath of a shock, return the economy to that point. Individuals, not government policy, will stabilize and adjust the economy.

The neoclassical economists' celebration of market-oriented stabilization and adjustment is therefore grounded in a humanist logic, according to which all economic structures can be reduced to individual choice. Macroeconomic results are determined within microeconomic markets, and market behaviors are reflections of (constrained) individual choices. These choices are, in turn, tied to the given preferences and expectations of individual human beings. For example, according to neoclassical economists, the balance of payments is determined by individuals' decisions concerning their willingness to hold stocks of money or interest-bearing assets. Once the individually desired targets are reached, there is no need to adjust their balances any further and external payments equilibrium is restored. The results of all other markets can be similarly reduced to individual decisions. In this sense, the exogenous rational maximizing behavior of individual economic agents – human nature – is considered the irreducible essence of the macroeconomy.[3]

Structuralist theory

Structuralist economists criticize the neoclassical story and the implied policy of little or no state intervention.[4] They argue instead that markets are inherently imperfect stabilizers and that, if left to themselves (i.e., without state intervention), they will *not* be successful in restoring internal and external balance.

Structuralist criticisms of orthodox stabilization and adjustment policies of the sort indicated above are now widely known.[5] They fall under three main categories:

1   orthodox policies are stagflationary – that is, they cause short-term recessions and often provoke more, not less, inflation;
2   such policies sacrifice long-term growth for short-term stability; and
3   they redistribute income from poor to rich and lead to an increased concentration of assets.

These criticisms are based on an alternative, structuralist macroeco-nomic story in which non-neoclassical economic and social structures play a significant role. For example, structuralist economists argue that prices, instead of being determined by supply and demand equilibria in competi-tive markets, are the result of markup-pricing behavior by individual firms. In addition, the various components of the pricing equations are either determined institutionally (e.g., wages) or are not perfectly substi-tutable (e.g., labor and capital-output, or domestic and imported input-output, coefficients).[6]

A typical situation in a structuralist world is exemplified where the economy is at less than full employment, the price level (or the rate of inflation) is unacceptably high, and the balance of payments is in deficit. Because of the prevailing economic and social structures, there is no auto-matic market adjustment in these circumstances: wages can remain at their current level even in the presence of significant unemployment, prices need not fall, even if output is below capacity; and the balance-of-payments deficit can persist, at least until foreign exchange reserves are exhausted. This scenario contrasts sharply with the automatic tendency to move toward full equilibrium posited by neoclassical economists.

Based on this alternative model, structuralists tell a different story, both of the effects of orthodox policies and of the kinds of policies that should be adopted in their place. As mentioned above, neoclassical economists often advocate exchange-rate depreciation as a way of correcting a balance-of-payments deficit. From the structuralist perspective, such a policy is doomed to failure: not only may it not lower the current account deficit (except over the long term, when trade structures become less inelastic, and only in conjunction with other – e.g., industrial – policies), it may also cause both increased inflation and recession.

Not surprisingly, this model also leads to an alternative, so-called heterodox policy package. Whereas neoclassical economists focus on free markets, structuralists argue that market imperfections are inherent in real world conditions and that development policy must contend with them – not magically dispose of them, as in the neoclassical story. Thus, structuralist economists advocate increased controls over (imperfect) markets:

- to solve the structural problems inherent in inertial inflation, they favor income policies;
- to overcome sectoral complementarities and trade inelasticities, industrial policies;
- to orient microeconomic investment decisions in the face of uncer-tainty, capital controls;
- to surmount the decline in lending and increased debt service payments, external debt relief; and
- to eliminate unemployment, an increase in government expenditures.

From the structuralist perspective, these policies, and not unregulated markets, can ultimately lead to success in combatting unemployment, inflation, and balance-of-payments difficulties.

This alternative approach to the success of structuralist development economics can be explained by a structuralist methodology that is as deterministic as its neoclassical counterpart. The direction of determination used by neoclassical economists, however, is reversed: structuralists consider individual economic behaviors to be determined by a set of given economic and social structures. In this sense, reference to the "structuralism" – the antihumanism – of structuralist economic theory might be confusing, but that term is probably even more appropriate than many believe.[7]

According to structuralist economists, the macrorelationships of an economy are determined, not by individual decisions but by a set of "key forces" (Taylor, 1983, 6) that governs production, financing, and other economic activities. These economic and social structures include oligopolistic industries (which give rise to markup-pricing behavior), institutionally determined wages (tied, in turn, to the existence of surplus labor and/or capital-labor conflict), fixed coefficient production functions, "animal spirits" and uncertainty, and incomplete or poorly articulated credit and transport systems. Given these structures, individuals are prevented from generating full employment, price stability, and external-payments balance. Instead the macroeconomy may reach an equilibrium at which one or more, or any combination, of these conditions will not be satisfied. Starting with these structures, structuralist economists argue that the free operation of markets will only generate more unemployment, inflation, and balance-of-payments difficulties. Markets are therefore a problem, not a solution. Structuralists contend that success lies with another structure: government policies and controls. The government is needed to coordinate and guide individual choices to the point where full equilibrium, price stability, and balance of payment equilibrium are reached. The market behavior of individuals is thus determined by the irreducible structures – institutions, power relationships, and so on – of the society in question.

The middle position

There is, of course, a third approach, which combines elements of both neoclassical and structuralist stories.[8] In effect, it serves to cement the two poles of the debate – individuals and structures, free markets and government controls.

Like the structuralists, the economists of the middle position observe the possibility of less-than-full employment equilibrium and balance-of-payments deficits in the absence of government intervention. Like their fully neoclassical counterparts, however, they argue that violating the "fundamentals" of markets will ultimately prevent the macroeconomy from reaching a sustainable full equilibrium. Depending on the time and place, the advocates of this middle position move back and forth between neoclassical markets and structuralist government interventions. Their view suggests a perfectly neoclassical world in which internal and external balance could be maintained by individuals operating through free markets, although the immediate elimination of all market imperfections is not proposed. Their position implies a kind of managed transition from a short-run structuralist world to a long-run neoclassical one.

Those who occupy this middle position argue, for example, that both excess aggregate demand and high wages are sources of inflation (and, therefore, in the long run, excess government spending and labor market imperfections should be eliminated), but that lowering both would, in the short run, introduce such high costs that it is necessary to create a breathing space through income policies and other government programs. There is room then for discretionary macroeconomic policies, but also an important role for individual decisions within microeconomic markets.

This middle position is therefore based on an ever-changing compromise between humanism and structuralism. At times, the tendency to reduce all economic phenomena to human nature is apparent; at other times, given economic and social structures play a significant role. At present, this middle ground is caught between the neoclassical resurgence in development economics and the widespread criticisms of the neoclassically inspired stabilization packages of recent years.

An alternative

Notwithstanding their differences concerning the necessity for and the nature of appropriate policies, neoclassical and structuralist economists can and do find room for agreement on at least two counts. First, they agree that the problem of stabilization and adjustment is inherent in nature. For the neoclassicals, the problem derives from human nature: stabilization and adjustment are automatic if economic agents are allowed to act in free markets; they require government intervention to dismantle market imperfections if such obstacles prevent the rational decisions of individuals from producing the desired result. Structuralists, in contrast, reduce the problem to a set of naturally existing economic and social structures: the rigidities and other "imperfect" features of an economy prevent the automatic achievement of full equilibrium. The presence of such structures requires government intervention in order for society to achieve the desired macroeconomic objectives. Second, they agree that the relevant criteria for success of stabilization and adjustment programs are internal and external balance, that is, low unemployment, price stability, and balance-of-payments equilibrium. Despite their different explanations of why such programs fail (or succeed), they share a definition of what constitutes failure (and success). Ultimately, this shared conception of the objectives of and the criteria for evaluating stabilization and adjustment programs is what allows neoclassical and structuralists to agree on the limits of the present debate.

The implications of each of these two areas of agreement are far-reaching. First, since both neoclassical and structuralist economists presume an ultimately determining factor or essence to which all economic behavior can be reduced, they leave no room to extend the analysis further – to investigate the conditions that, in turn, produce the individuals and structures of their respective theories of stabilization and adjustment. One alternative to this debate between competing essences (and their related policies) is to use a "nonessentialist" theory, in which microeconomic individuals and macroeconomic structures each participate in constituting the other. Elaborating such a posthumanist/poststructuralist – what has come to be called a postmodern[9] – approach would also involve analyzing the mutual constitution of, on one hand, individuals and structures and, on the other hand, all the other social processes that exist at any point in time. As such, each individual or structure would be considered as both the product of and, in turn, as a constitutive component of the ever-changing ensemble of economic, political, and cultural processes that make up a society. Neither would be a "given" in the analysis and therefore neither could function as the essence to which all other events and relationships could be reduced. In particular, neither could serve as the given determinant of the need for and the effects of stabilization and adjustment policies.

The second point – the fact that both groups of economists agree that the relevant criteria for success consist of the level of employment, inflation, and the balance of payments – leads to theories of stabilization and adjustment in which macroeconomic changes within capitalism are seemingly unrelated to the existence of exploitation. Neoclassical and structuralist economists tend to focus on three nonclass aspects of capitalism to the exclusion of all else, including the class processes that, in part, make up a capitalist society. Therefore, neither group sees how the existence and reproduction of capitalist classes are related to the problem of stabilization and adjustment.

This tendency to "forget about" class is reinforced by the humanist and structuralist terms of the debate. The reduction of employment, prices, and the balance of payments to given individuals or structures means that class can be effectively displaced from the center of analysis. Class either does not exist in those theories, or it is defined in a manner that rules out any consideration of the processes in and through which surplus labor is performed/appropriated and then distributed/received. In particular (for the purposes of this chapter), neoclassical and structuralist economists tend to ignore the capitalist class processes of extracting and distributing surplus-value. Classes, if they play a role at all (as in some structuralist accounts), merely designate groups of individuals who can claim distinct flows of money income (with their respective wage, profit, consumption, savings, etc. behaviors).[10]

This relative neglect of class within both neoclassical and structuralist theories serves as the basis of policy prescriptions which, although aimed at producing full employment, price stability and balance-of-payments equilibrium, may – and often do – have class effects that increase exploitation and, in general, strengthen the class aspects of capitalism. This trend may occur even when the original objectives are not achieved. In such cases, nonclass failures become class successes.

Failure in Argentina, Brazil, and Peru

The implications of the nonclass neoclassical–structuralist debate on stabilization and adjustment can be seen in the recent experiences of Argentina, Brazil, and Peru. These countries have served as a kind of economic laboratory for economists of both schools (and, of course, the middle position) during the past 15 years. Both orthodox and heterodox policy packages (and combinations thereof) have been applied in order to solve the macroeconomic disequilibria associated with inherited domestic policies and the turmoil within the world economy. In all three cases, the policy prescriptions of neoclassical and structuralist economists (and of advocates of the middle position) have been attempted and, eventually, declared failures.

The approximate chronology of Table 8.1 indicates the changing nature of policies in the three countries under different governments and economic advisors. For example, various combinations of orthodox and middle-position stabilization and adjustment policies were used in Argentina, Brazil, and Peru from the first oil price shock in the early 1970s to the mid-1980s. Then, in 1985 or 1986, the governments of all three countries enacted heterodox policy packages.

Argentina

The most orthodox case among the three is Argentina, which (along with Chile and Uruguay during the same period) formed part of what came to be known as the Latin American experiments in neoconservative economics.[11]

Table 8.1 Stabilization and adjustment policies, 1970s–80s

Argentina	Orthodox (1976–83)	Middle position (1983–85)	Heterodox (1985–86)
Brazil	Middle position (1974–79)	Orthodox (1979–85)	Heterodox (1986–87)
Peru	Orthodox (1975–80)	Orthodox (1980–85)	Heterodox (1985–86)

Under the guidance of Economy Minister Martínez de Hoz during the Videla military regime (1976–81), Argentina entered into an agreement with the International Monetary Fund (IMF) and began a full-scale neoclassical policy program: external trade and capital market liberalization (including significantly lower tariff barriers and export taxes), devaluation of the nominal exchange-rate through preannounced adjustments (the so-called *tablita*), elimination of domestic subsidies, the raising of public sector prices and domestic interest rates, and the privatization of public enterprises. These reforms were designed to create a relative price structure that would provide the "correct" signals, both to lower inflation and to direct domestic and foreign factors of production into the areas consistent with Argentina's international comparative advantage. The Martínez de Hoz New Political Economy was followed by similarly orthodox packages under subsequent ministers and military governments through 1983.

Argentine attempts to stabilize and adjust on the basis of freeing up markets and allowing individuals to take the lead were initially successful (see Table 8.2); the rate of inflation was lowered (from 443.2 percent in 1976 to less than 150 percent on average for 1977–81), real output grew (by 12.9 percent for 1977–80), and a current-account surplus was generated (until the end of 1979). These improvements were accompanied, however, by an increase in external debt (from $6.5 billion in 1976 to $14.4 billion in 1981) and capital flight, an eventual deterioration in the current account balance (a deficit that reached 3.8 percent of GDP in 1981), and a decline in real wages (especially during 1976–78). The continued application of orthodox policies finally led to a steep recession in 1981–82: most of the real output growth during the preceding 4 years was reversed during half that time.

Table 8.2 Argentina: selected macroeconomic data

1975	1976	1977	1978	1979	1980	1981	1982	1983	1984	1985	1986	1987
Inflation[a]												
182.3	443.2	176.1	175.5	159.5	100.8	104.5	164.8	343.8	626.7	672.1	90.1	131.3
GDP growth[b]												
–	–5.3	5.6	–5.3	11.1	1.5	–6.7	–5.0	2.9	2.5	–4.4	5.4	1.8
Current-account balance[c]												
–3.2	1.2	2.2	2.8	–0.5	–3.1	–3.8	–4.1	–3.8	–3.2	–1.4	–3.6	na
Urban real minimum wage[d]												
na	–48.2	–4.1	–18.8	13.7	17.3	–4.8	1.8	41.1	26.0	–32.5	–5.1	9.6

Sources: International Monetary Fund (1988), ECLAC (1986b, 1987a, 1989)

Notes
[a] Consumer price index, percentage change over previous year
[b] GDP at constant prices, percentage change over previous year
[c] As percentage of GDP
[d] Percentage variation from previous year

With the economy mired in recession, and the military forced to relinquish control to the civilian Raúl Alfonsín, Argentina entered a middle position phase of "gradual adjustment" in late 1983. The new civilian economic team instituted price controls with full indexation, increased social welfare expenditures, and agreed to large wage increases. The result was that the preceding declines in real output and real wages and the growth in the current-account deficit were all reversed. Less than one year after assuming power, however, Alfonsín signed a stand-by agreement with the IMF that was similar in content to the conditions agreed to in 1976 by the military government. By 1985, the growth of real wages had turned around once again (a decline of 32.5 percent compared to a 26 percent gain in 1984), real output fell by 4.4 percent, and annual inflation soared to more than 600 percent.

Finally, in June 1985, the Alfonsín government unveiled its heterodox Austral Plan. The rationale of the plan was that previous stabilization and adjustment programs did not conform to the structural problems of the Argentine economy, particularly the inertial quality of inflation, and that government controls were necessary to bring the economy back to full equilibrium. Preceded by a series of price adjustments (for instance, devaluation of the foreign exchange-rate and an increase in tariffs and public sector prices), the new plan consisted of an immediate price–wage freeze (the so-called heterodox shock), deindexation of all contracts and their conversion to a new currency (the austral), and a series of reforms aimed at reducing the fiscal deficit. The initial results, from mid-1985 to mid-1986, were dramatic: inflation slowed to less than 100 percent, real output grew (although GDP fell during 1985 as a whole), and a trade surplus led to an improvement in the current account (from –3.2 percent of GDP in 1984 to –1.4 percent in 1985). Inflationary pressures were never eliminated, however, and the continuing wage freeze, more strictly enforced than the price freeze, led to a sharp drop in real wages. After various phases of the original plan and the "australito" of early 1987, inflation accelerated, external deficits increased, and output growth began to slow. By mid-1989, the failure of heterodox attempts to control the adjustment path back to stability was finally publicly acknowledged in the early transfer of power to Carlos Menem, the opposition Peronist candidate in the presidential elections.

Brazil

Brazil followed a different path to the implementation (and eventual failure) of its own heterodox plan in the mid-1980s.[12] By 1974, after 10 years of harsh military rule, the military government of General Geisel began a 5-year program of stabilization and adjustment, best characterized as a middle position between orthodox and heterodox. The program included large government investments (in such sectors as energy, mining, and heavy industry), liberal price controls (which allowed the adjustment of prices based on increased costs) and wage increases, import controls and export subsidies, and encouragement of external borrowing.

This combination of government controls and market activity produced moderate levels of both inflation (approximately 45 percent on average for 1976–79) and real wage growth (3.5 percent for average wages and salaries during the same period): it also maintained uneven but relatively high rates of output growth (4.6–9.8 percent per annum for 1976–80). These positive macroeconomic developments were accompanied, however, by correspondingly negative trends, especially in the foreign sector – in external debt (which grew from $23.4 billion in 1976 to $46.1 billion at the end of 1979) and in current-account deficits (which, notwithstanding strong export growth, reached 4.7 percent of GDP in 1979).

In the wake of the second oil-price shock, Brazilian macroeconomic policy took an abrupt orthodox turn. Both at the end of 1979, and in 1980, the João Figueiredo administration opted to decrease government control and let individuals adjust and stabilize the Brazilian economy through market activity. Beginning with a maxi-devaluation of the foreign exchange-rate in December 1979, Brazil enacted a number of orthodox reforms – including additional mini-devaluations, decreases in public sector expenditures (especially investments) and a slowdown in the rate of growth of credit to the private sector, decontrol of interest rates, and limited upward wage adjustments – culminating in the signing of an agreement with the IMF in the wake of the Mexican external debt default in 1982. The effect of these measures was the deepest recession in recent Brazilian history: output declined by almost 5 percent during 1981–83 and

Table 8.3 Brazil: selected macroeconomic data

	1975	1976	1977	1978	1979	1980	1981	1982	1983	1984	1985	1986	1987
Inflation[a]													
	29.0	42.0	43.7	38.7	52.7	82.8	105.6	97.8	142.1	197.0	226.9	145.2	229.7
GDP growth[b]													
	4.2	9.8	4.6	4.8	7.2	9.1	–3.3	0.9	–2.5	5.7	8.3	8.2	3.7
Current-account balance[c]													
	–5.7	–4.3	–2.9	–3.5	–4.7	–5.3	–4.4	–6.1	–3.3	–	–0.1	–1.7	–1.5
Urban real minimum wage[d]													
	na	na	na	na	–0.2	2.6	6.1	0.7	–10.2	–8.8	1.7	4.4	–0.4

Sources: International Monetary Fund (1988), ECLAC (1986b, 1987a, 1989)

Notes
[a] Consumer price index, percentage change over previous year
[b] GDP at constant prices, percentage change over previous year
[c] As percentage of GDP
[d] Percentage variation from previous year

real wage increases, which were first maintained, nosedived in 1983 (provoking widespread riots in that year). While the recession did eliminate the current account deficit, it failed to keep the domestic rate of inflation in check: it more than doubled between 1980 (82.8 percent) and 1984 (197 percent).

As in Argentina, the combination of the transfer of presidential power from the military to a civilian and the widely perceived failure of existing macroeconomic policies prepared the conditions for a third attempt at stabilization and adjustment. Even more so than its heterodox precursor in Argentina, the Brazilian Cruzado Plan, announced by President José Sarney in February 1986, was designed as an attack on inertial inflation. The main theoretical idea was that Brazilian contracts were heavily indexed, and that such indexation created a structure that transferred past inflation to the present. It was therefore necessary to control this form of structural inflation – through general price and partial wage freezes, the prohibition of indexed contracts of less than one year, the deindexation of financial instruments (especially treasury bonds) and the introduction of a new currency. The initial results were as swift and dramatic as in Argentina: inflation slowed (from 226.9 percent in 1985 to 145.2 percent in 1986), output growth was maintained (8.3 and 8.2 percent, respectively, for 2 years), and real wages increased. Nevertheless, current account deficits reemerged and, with the eventual acceleration of inflation and the continued necessity to service the external debt, the failure of the Brazilian attempt at heterodox stabilization and adjustment was gradually acknowledged. By late 1987, orthodox market reforms were once again promoted as the only macroeconomic solution.

Peru

Peru followed a third succession of stabilization and adjustment programs during the 1970s and 1980s.[13] The palace coup in 1975, which transferred power within the military government from Francisco Velasco to Juan Morales Bermúdez, was accompanied by a typically orthodox approach to macroeconomic policy. In this case, the drain on foreign reserves caused by persistent current-account deficits initially provoked the turn to a market-based stabilization and adjustment program. The series of devaluations of the foreign exchange-rate, initiated in late 1975, and the negotiations with the IMF during 1976–77 were supplemented by other orthodox measures: monetary restraint, more favorable treatment of foreign investment, the sale of some state enterprises, a relaxing of price controls, and attempts to lower the fiscal deficit by increasing taxes and eliminating subsidies. The net results of these austerity measures were felt during the course of 1977–78: the data in Table 8.4 indicate the extent to which the orthodox program reduced real GDP and real wages. They also show that price adjustments led to an acceleration in the rate of inflation and that the current account

Table 8.4 Peru: selected macroeconomic data

	1975	1976	1977	1978	1979	1980	1981	1982	1983	1984	1985	1986	1987
Inflation[a]													
	23.6	33.5	38.1	57.8	66.7	59.2	75.4	64.4	111.2	110.2	163.4	77.9	85.8
GDP growth[b]													
	2.4	3.3	−0.3	−1.7	4.3	2.9	3.0	0.9	−12.0	4.8	1.6	9.0	7.3
Current-account balance[c]													
	−11.3	−8.7	−7.3	−1.8	5.3	0.6	−8.6	−7.9	−5.4	−1.3	0.9	−1.2	−1.6
Urban real minimum wage[d]													
	na	na	−12.2	−23.2	11.7	27.5	−15.8	−7.6	2.4	−22.7	−12.6	3.7	1.4

Sources: International Monetary Fund (1988), ECLAC (1986b, 1987a, 1989)

Notes
[a] Consumer price index, percentage change over previous year
[b] GDP at constant prices, percentage change over previous year
[c] As percentage of GDP
[d] Percentage variation from previous year

balance gradually improved (especially in 1978 and thereafter due, at least in part, to an external terms-of-trade improvement). These conditions provoked a wave of strikes and demonstrations, including the first general strike in 20 years. By 1979, however, economic growth had resumed.

The transfer of power to the civilian Popular Action Party candidate, Fernando Belaúnde, in 1980 involved an extension of, rather than a departure from, the orthodox path charted by the military. The new government was committed to a program of market liberalization, including the removal of external trade harriers, an increase in domestic interest rates, and the freeing-up of all domestic prices. These new orthodox policies provoked further inflation and a decline in real wages during 1981; they also reversed the current account position from surplus to deficit. An extension of these measures under agreement with the IMF, coupled with a series of natural disasters, finally sent the Peruvian economy into a deep recession in 1983 (when real output declined by 12 percent) and to the brink of hyperinflation (as the annual rate of price increases reached three digits), while real wages began a downward spiral that lasted through the 1985 presidential elections.

The third phase of Peruvian stabilization and adjustment policy was the heterodox plan announced in July by Belaúnde's successor as president, the APRA party's Alan García. The so-called Inti Plan was designed more to reactivate the Peruvian economy than as an anti-inflation shock: it involved the introduction of a new currency, a price freeze and an increase in wages, tax cuts and subsidies to specific sectors, a lowering of interest rates, the introduction of multiple exchange-rates, an increase in agricultural credit, and the announcement of a cap on external debt servicing.

These measures did, however, have the dual effect of halving the inflation rate (from 163.4 percent in 1985 to 77.9 percent in 1986) and of boosting output (by 8 percent in 1986). Nonetheless, the current-account position worsened and inflationary pressures eventually resumed. The last gasp of the Peruvian heterodox program took the form of García's announcement of his government's intention to nationalize the country's banking system in mid-1987. Since then, internal and external instability have returned and the government has chosen to apply increasingly orthodox austerity measures.

When failure becomes success

It is not surprising that, based on the experiences of Argentina, Brazil, and Peru, both orthodox and heterodox stabilization and adjustment packages (and the policies of the middle position) have been considered failures by neoclassical and structuralist economists and policymakers. The explanations of failure are different according to the two groups. Neoclassical economists argue, for example, that heterodox programs ultimately fail because they place controls on markets which prevent individuals from reaching full equilibrium (e.g., Blejer and Liviatan 1987). Structuralist economists, in contrast, conclude that orthodox policies fail because they rely too heavily on individual decision making within free markets and do not recognize the existence of macroeconomic structures that undermine automatic adjustment (e.g., Singer 1989). Not surprisingly, both groups invoke their respective essences to discuss their own, as well as alternative, policy packages. The neoclassical explanation of the failure of orthodox neoclassical programs is based on governments' macroeconomic mismanagement of otherwise successful microeconomic reforms (e.g., Corbo and de Melo 1985), while structuralists contend that the failure of their heterodox programs can be explained by the continued existence of distributional conflict and the constraints imposed by the current political situation (e.g., Taylor 1988b).[14]

The respective failures of both policy packages often lead to an oscillation between them: when orthodox policies are perceived to have failed, there is a call for more heterodox policies, and the perceived failure of structuralist heterodox policies tends to produce a movement in the direction of neoclassical orthodoxy.[15] In general, because neoclassical and structuralist theories dominate the debate over stabilization and adjustment (not to mention the theoretical training of the economic teams and international agencies that participate in the formulation of policy), their respective policies – and the oscillation between them – tend to define the limits of that debate.

The claim that both sets of policies have failed, however, may well be premature – at least from the perspective of the alternative, class-theoretic approach mentioned above. Instead, neoclassical and structuralist policies may be seen as successes, when their effects on the rate of exploitation and other class features of capitalism are taken into account. Each policy package, in its own way and under different circumstances, may participate in strengthening important conditions within which surplus-value is appropriated from the direct producers. Thus, what may be a failure from the standpoint of achieving full employment, price stability, and balance-of-payments equilibrium can be considered successful in terms of promoting the widening and deepening of capitalist class processes.

Four examples serve to demonstrate the point that the nonclass macroeconomic failures, as they are defined and analyzed by neoclassical and structuralist economists, can be viewed as class successes, when the focus of theoretical attention is shifted to the class consequences of stabilization and adjustment policies.

Income distribution

A redistribution of income, among sectors but especially from poor to rich, is generally acknowledged as one of the failures of stabilization and adjustment policies. These distributional effects are noted, not only in the three cases discussed in the previous section, but also in the general literature on stabilization and adjustment (e.g., Demery and Addison 1987; Streeten 1987). Although such changes in the distribution of income are complex (in the sense that they can involve many different kinds of income), they often include a decline in real wages.[16] This lowering of real wages may, in turn, contribute to an increase in exploitation and, therefore, to a strengthening of the class aspects of capitalism.

Declining real wages mean that, in the first instance, the gross profits of capitalist enterprises rise. Then, if the lower real wages persist over time, there is an increase in the amount of surplus-value extracted by capitalists. These results can be explained by using the class analysis of Marxian value theory. The initial decline in real wages means that the market price of labor power falls below the value of labor power; capitalists are able to purchase the laborers' ability to work for a wage that is less than the value of the customary standard of living of wage-earners. Thus, capitalists receive a revenue in addition to the surplus-value extracted from the laborers. This advantage, of course, leads to an increase in the capitalists' rate of profit, an immediate class success created by the decline in real wages.[17]

If this situation continues for any length of time, then the customary standard of living of wage-earners can be expected to decrease – that is, the value of labor power will fall to the lower market price. The amount of surplus-value appropriated within capitalist enterprises increases. Another index of capitalist success – the rate of exploitation – rises as a result.[18] In both cases, then, what is considered a failure in terms of maintaining workers' real living standards may be judged successful when viewed from the perspective of strengthening capitalist class processes.[19]

Exchange-rates

The impact of stabilization and adjustment programs on foreign exchange-rates can also be analyzed in a different light if we focus on the class dimensions of the problem.[20] Overvalued exchange-rates are widely considered a failure because they undermine international competitiveness and exacerbate balance-of-payments difficulties. This nonclass failure, with respect to maintaining an equilibrium price of foreign exchange, however, can often be accompanied by a success in class-analytic terms.

Overvalued exchange-rates can contribute to the further development of capitalist class processes to the extent that they lead to a cheapening of the imported elements of constant capital. In the case of imports of both raw materials and means of production, the lowering of import prices contributes directly to decreasing the constant portion of the capital advanced by capitalist enterprises in order to engage in commodity production. Thus, overvalued exchange-rates increase the profit rates of capitalists who use imported inputs.[21]

The impact of overvalued exchange-rates on variable capital can also contribute to class successes. The cheapening of imported commodities (or, similarly, of commodities produced with imported inputs) that enter into the determination of the value of labor power, means that the amount of money capitalists need to advance in order to gain access to the commodity labor power decreases. As the value of labor power falls (assuming that nothing else has changed), the rate of exploitation rises. This is a reversion to the previous case of a decline in real wages.

Overvalued exchange-rates can therefore contribute to the strengthening of the capitalist class process of extracting surplus-value through cheapening imports of either the elements of constant capital or variable capital.[22] Once again, what is often perceived to be a failure of stabilization and adjustment policies with respect to one aspect of capitalism – in this case, the price of foreign exchange – can be termed a success when the focus is shifted to the class dimensions of capitalism.

Inflation

Another perceived failure of existing stabilization and adjustment policies is continued inflation or, as in the cases of Argentina, Brazil, and Peru, the emergence of hyperinflation. In what sense can inflation contribute to the strengthening of capitalist class processes? The existence of generalized price increases means, of course, that capitalist producers are successful at raising prices and are thus able to create a source of revenues in addition to the value of their commodities. From the perspective of Marxian value theory, inflation indicates precisely this positive deviation of prices from values and, therefore, the ability of capitalists to protect their position as capitalists.

Not surprisingly, additional class effects occur when there are differential rates of price increase included within a rise in the general price level. If real wages fall – as is the case in many inflationary situations, even under various wage indexation schemes – then we return to the results of our first example: the price and, eventually, the value of labor power decrease and the rates of profit and exploitation move in the opposite direction. Capitalist profits are also affected by other real price changes. This is the case, for example, with interest rates. If real interest rates fall, capitalists are required to distribute less of the appropriated surplus-value in the form of interest payments in order to gain access to money capital – one of the conditions of existence of capitalists' ability to continue to extract surplus-value. Similar results follow from changes in tax rates, the salaries of managers, rental rates, and so on that fall below the rate of price increases by capitalists. All of these real price changes affect the portions of surplus-value which capitalists are required to transfer to those who provide some of the important conditions of existence of the capitalist extraction of surplus-value.[23]

This examination of the class dimensions of inflationary situations that are either downplayed or ignored by both neoclassical and structuralist approaches to stabilization and adjustment indicates that inflation is not necessarily a sign of failure. There are, instead, various ways in which inflation can contribute to the successful development of capitalist class processes.[24]

Government deficits

A fourth failure attributed to stabilization and adjustment policies is the continued existence of government budget deficits. Once again, a class analysis of fiscal deficits leads to a quite different conclusion.

It is useful to consider two different dimensions of typical state activities that are often tied to fiscal deficits: state-owned enterprises and current government expenditures. First, from a class perspective, public enterprises that produce capitalist commodities – whether electricity, oil, or transportation – are capitalist enterprises.[25] Thus, maintaining or increasing the revenues to these state capitalist enterprises allows them to increase their expenditures on the conditions that maintain or increase the amount of surplus-value appropriated from state workers. The capitalist process of appropriating surplus-value is thereby strengthened within the state.

Running fiscal deficits can also contribute to the strengthening of capitalist class processes outside the state. This is true for a wide variety of government programs. Maintaining or increasing expenditures on these programs provides some of the cultural, political, and economic conditions whereby nonstate or private capitalists can continue to appropriate surplus-value. For example, public education disseminates ideas and provides skills that contribute to the training of laborers capable of producing surplus-value. The state also passes laws and maintains administrative and judicial bureaucracies which, among other things, protect the rights of capitalists to purchase the labor power of workers and sell the commodities produced by those workers. Finally, capitalist states provide some of the economic conditions – ranging from creating money to building infrastructure – that affect the ability of private sector capitalists to appropriate surplus-value. Fiscal deficits therefore allow the state to maintain or increase its participation in activities that reproduce the existence of capitalist class processes outside the state.[26]

These examples indicate that the state may be actively involved in shaping the existence of capitalist class processes both inside and outside the state. In this sense, the inability to control fiscal deficits may actually strengthen the capitalist class process of appropriating surplus-value.[27]

In general, the four cases considered here demonstrate that focusing exclusively on the failure of stabilization and adjustment policies with respect to nonclass aspects of capitalism such as real wages, exchange-rates, inflation, and fiscal deficits hides from view the extent to which such failures may be successful in terms of increasing exploitation and promoting the class aspects of capitalism.

Conclusion

The fact that the nonclass failure of some development theories may become class successes, when viewed from the perspective of another theoretical framework, suggests that adhering to the limits of the theoretical debate between neoclassical and structuralist economists, and to the oscillation between orthodox and heterodox stabilization and adjustment policies, may condition the growth and development of capitalist class processes where these theories and policies are practiced. What are often seen as development failures may, in fact, be part of a more general process of the successful emergence and strengthening of capitalist class processes in Latin America and the rest of the developing world.

This conclusion stands in sharp contrast to recent pronouncements that class analyses and Marxian theory are irrelevant in discussing contemporary development issues. In order to confront this challenge, it is necessary to consider briefly two additional issues. First, the idea that the development of capitalist class processes has been successful does not mean that it occurs evenly or that all existing capitalists gain as a result. As noted in the four examples above, individual capitalist enterprises or groups of capitalist enterprises (e.g., producers of wage goods in the case of declining real wages or exporters in the case of overvalued exchange-rates) may be weakened and/or cease to exist as a result of policies that otherwise promote the development of the capitalist class process.[28] Such a phenomenon would be consistent with the Marxian approach to capitalist development. Consider, for example, the case of capitalist competition. The process of extracting surplus-value may well be strengthened at the level of society as a whole together with, or as the result of, the concentration and centralization of capital that allow some capitalist enterprises to grow at the expense of others. The important point is that tensions and struggles between different groups of capitalist enterprises – which serve, in turn, as the basis for divergent and conflicting interests on the part of capitalists with respect to specific stabilization and adjustment measures – can, and often do, occur alongside a general strengthening of the process of capitalist exploitation.

A second caveat to the analysis presented here is that there is no presumption that there is some set of necessary conditions (whether economic, political, or cultural) for the successful development of capitalist class processes. It would be a mistake to conclude that the particular experiences of Argentina, Brazil, and Peru – or of any other group of countries – could be simply generalized or extended to another area of the world. East Asia is a good example. The distribution of income there, for example, as measured by Gini coefficients, is more equal than in Latin America (Evans 1987). Does this difference mean that capitalist class processes are any more or less developed in Singapore, Taiwan, South Korea, and Hong Kong than in Latin America? Furthermore, does it mean that a class analysis is invalidated by the East Asian experience, an issue recently taken up by Chakravarty (1987)?

In the case of the newly industrializing countries of East Asia, it is their success – not their failure, as in Latin America – that is the subject of debate between neoclassical and structuralist economists. Balassa (1988) and many other neoclassical economists have claimed that East Asian success is based on the existence of free markets. Structuralist economists (e.g., Kim 1985) have criticized this view and responded that state intervention has been the key to success.[29] Again, both schools of thought focus on the nonclass aspects of capitalist development, to the exclusion of class. They therefore tend to ignore key ingredients of class success in East Asia, such as the creation of a pool of wage-laborers through land reform, the length of the work day, and the control of the wage-setting process through the suppression of trade union activity. Furthermore, as shown in the discussion above, a rise in real wages can be (and often is) accompanied by an increase in exploitation. In these terms, the relative success of East Asia during the turmoil of the 1970s and 1980s with respect to some of the nonclass aspects of capitalist development – unemployment, inflation, and balance-of-payments equilibrium – has been accompanied by success in terms of the widening and deepening of capitalist class processes.

A detailed investigation of the strengthening of the other important economic (not to mention political and cultural) conditions of capitalist exploitation in East Asia throughout the postwar period is beyond the scope of this chapter. Such an investigation would contribute to challenging the limits of the existing development debate along the lines suggested by what we *have* learned about stabilization and adjustment; namely, that the widely perceived failure of stabilization and adjustment policies with respect to some of the nonclass aspects of capitalism in the cases of Argentina, Brazil, and Peru (and the much-vaunted success of East Asia on similar criteria), are consistent with the class successes registered in both groups of countries.

These class successes may, in turn, explain the fact that, while development economists and policymakers cannot agree on why stabilization and adjustment policies have variously failed and succeeded in different parts of the Third World, they are content to remain within the neoclassical and structuralist limits of the present debate.

(original version published in 1991)

Acknowledgements

I want to thank Stephen Resnick, Richard Wolff, colleagues in the Economic Development Workshop at the University of Notre Dame, and three anonymous referees for *World Development* for comments on earlier drafts. I also want to thank participants in the following conferences, where previous versions of this essay were presented: the Conference on Global Imbalances: Alternative Perspectives on the International Economy (American University), the conference on Bringing Classes Back In (University of Kansas-Lawrence), and the Economic and History Workshop (University of Massachusetts-Amherst). The dismissive reaction of an anonymous referee for the Helen Kellogg Institute for International Studies (on a working-paper version of this chapter) fortunately arrived after this essay was accepted for publication.

Notes

1 See Arndt (1987) for a more detailed discussion of the debate among development economists in the postwar period.
2 The neoclassical theory presented here is synthesized from a variety of sources, including Polack (1957), the essays in International Monetary Fund (1977), Beenstock (1980), Balassa (1982), and Khan and Knight (1981, 1982); it is variously referred to in the literature as new classical, the monetary approach to the balance of payments, global monetarism, and rational expectations.
3 James (1984) is a good introduction to the reductionism of humanist or individualist theories. The humanist orientation of neoclassical microeconomics has been part of that tradition from the beginning. More recent are the various attempts to construct a humanist microfoundation for macroeconomics. Pissarides (1989, 3) is one representative example of this trend:

> I believe that the only way we can make progress is to think in terms of small, internally consistent, equilibrium models. In these models there are decisions that we generally represent by supply and demand functions. But to derive these functions we need to specify very carefully the

constraints facing the agents and their objective functions. Within these constraints, agents maximize their objectives and the variables of interest are equilibrium outcomes.

... The central part of the research strategy in macro is the correct specification of preferences and constraints.

Note, however, that humanist modes of explanation are not the sole province of neoclassical economic theory. Radical economics has also integrated various forms of humanism; see Resnick and Wolff (1992).

4 The various contributions to the structuralist story have been synthesized and further developed by Taylor (1983, 1988b, and 1989).

5 These criticisms have been elaborated by, among others, Cooper (1971), Krugman and Taylor (1978), Bruno (1979), Taylor (1981), Díaz-Alejandro (1981), Buffie (1984), and Van Wijnbergen (1986).

6 Other non-neoclassical elements in structuralist theorizing include rigid trade elasticities, a minimal level of investment determined by "animal spirits," complementarity between public and private investment, and economically consequential uncertainty on the part of different groups of economic actors.

7 To be clear, it is this antihumanism, and not the direct application of the so-called structuralist linguistic model, which serves as the structuralist basis of structuralist development economics. Structuralism is generally associated with a method of analysis tied to the linguistics of Ferdinand de Saussure and widely employed in anthropology, literary criticism, and cultural studies (see Pettit 1975). My argument is not, however, that structuralist economists such as Taylor are attempting to investigate a "sign system" in the economy in the way that structuralist linguistics treats language. Structuralist economics is related to the more general critique of humanism announced by Michel Foucault and Claude Lévi-Strauss in the 1960s and developed by the structuralist movement of the 1970s, according to which social structures are viewed as constitutive of human subjectivity. This analysis can be compared to the humanist thesis that whatever structures exist are ultimately accountable to the activity of given individual human subjects. For more detailed discussions of the structuralist movement in social theory, see Soper (1986) and Glucksmann (1974). Other methodological treatments of the so-called new structuralist macroeconomics are Jameson (1986) and Arndt (1985).

8 This middle position includes, among others, Dornbusch (1980), Porter and Ranney (1982), Islam (1984), and Foxley (1987).

9 Postmodern alternatives to both humanism and structuralism have existed for at least 20 years in such diverse areas as literary criticism, cultural studies, architecture, and philosophy. The discussion of postmodernism is now being extended to economics; see, for example, Amariglio (1990), Ruccio and Wolff (1989), and Ruccio and Amariglio (2003).

10 See Resnick and Wolff (1987b, Chap. 3) for a discussion of the differences between a class analysis based on surplus labor and other definitions of class.

11 Foxley (1983). For more detailed analyses of the Argentine case, from a variety of theoretical perspectives, see Canitrot (1981), Wogart (1983), Heymann (1986), Epstein (1987), Frenkel (1987), and Manzetti and Dell'Aquila (1988).

12 The Brazilian experience has been discussed in more detail by Wells (1979), Bacha (1986), Tyler (1986), Baer (1987), Bresser Pereira (1987), and Modiano (1988).

13 Further sources of information on the Peruvian case include Thorp (1979), Beckerman (1987), and Ugarteche (1988).

14 There is, of course, the middle position: orthodox policies are too harsh (because they attempt to eliminate all government controls) and heterodox

policies violate too many market fundamentals (because they are not accompanied by the necessary freeing up of markets); see, for example, Baer, Biller, and McDonald (1989).

15 To be clear, this movement from one to the other does not follow a regular or predetermined pattern. Instead, it may be seen as a result of the following dynamic: as each set of policies is enacted, and the conditions under which it is applied change – in part, because of the policies themselves – there is a case for another policy package. For example, one of the usual consequences of orthodox policies is, as structuralists note, to redistribute income. This tendency may, in turn, lower the demand for nontradables (even if, as neoclassicals would claim, it raises national income). Firms engaged in nontradable goods production therefore may, along with wage earners and other groups, press for incomes policies that moderate or reverse the change in income distribution. An analogous turn toward orthodox policies has occurred in recent years as the initial successes with heterodox policies have given way to significant macroeconomic instability.

16 This is certainly true of orthodox policies, as the three cases of Argentina, Brazil, and Peru confirm. The Argentine example, however, demonstrates that declining real wages can also be a consequence of heterodox incomes policies.

17 On this point, consider the following example: if capitalists pay a wage equal to the value of labor power, i.e., $W = V = eq$ (where W is the wage or the price of labor power, V is the value of labor power or the customary standard of living of the sellers of labor power, e is the vector of per-unit exchange values of the commodities that make up the value of the labor power bundle and q is the vector of use-values in that bundle) then, in traditional Marxian terminology, the capitalists appropriate an amount of surplus-value (S) equal to the difference between V and the total amount of value created by the laborers (the so-called value of labor). The capitalists' value rate of profit (r) can be expressed in familiar terms as $r = S/(C + V)$ (where C is the value of the raw materials and means of production, i.e., constant capital). If the real wage falls (while the customary standard of living remains the same), capitalists are able to purchase the commodity labor power at less than its value, i.e., $W_1 < V = eq$. Laborers are, in effect, paying a subsidy to the capitalists (equal to the difference between W_1 and V) in order to be hired. The capitalists are now able to appropriate the original S and, in addition, the revenue associated with purchasing labor power at less than its value ($R_1 = V - W_1$). The new profit rate is then $r_1 = (S + R_1)/(C + V) > r$.

18 This second effect can be simply illustrated as follows: capitalists now purchase the commodity labor power at the lower value of labor power ($V_1 = eq = W_1$). If the laborers create as much total value as before, the amount of surplus-value (S_1) and the rate of exploitation (S_1/V_1) increase.

19 Nothing in this analysis should suggest that lowering real wages is a uniform class success. The Marxian notions of contradiction and uneven development preclude such an approach. For example, the fall in real wages can be expected to lower the demand for wage goods, thereby creating a "realization" problem for the capitalist producers of those commodities. It is, therefore, possible for workers to join together with the affected capitalists and others (e.g., politicians who fear widespread strike activity, and so forth) in order to demand higher real wages. This turnabout in policy, however, can also be a class success to the extent that workers can now purchase capitalist wage goods and solve the realization problem. In addition, if the wage increase is accompanied by an increase in productivity, it is possible for the rate of exploitation to rise. In terms of the value theory of note 17, as Marx (1977) explains in some detail in Volume 1 of *Capital*, if the fall in e occasioned by the change in productivity is

proportionately more than the rise in q, V will decrease and the rate of exploitation will increase.

20 Note that, if the real exchange rate is defined (as, for example, in Dornbusch 1988) as the ratio of wages to the nominal exchange rate, the traditional (neoclassical or structuralist) economist's notion of an overvalued exchange rate is equivalent to a rise in real wages (i.e., the opposite of the first example of failure defined by declining real wages).

21 This result is straightforward: the cheapening of the elements of C leads to an increase in the value profit rate $r = S/(C + V)$.

22 Again, I am not claiming that overvalued exchange rates represent a uniform class success. Capitalists can also be hurt by overvalued exchange rates; this is especially true for exporters and for those who must distribute part of the appropriated surplus-value in the form of bribes and other payments in order to gain access to rationed foreign exchange. In such cases, capitalists can be expected to support government policies to lower the exchange rate. A devaluation may itself contribute to a class success, to the extent that it leads to more commodity sales for exporting capitalists and eliminates foreign exchange rationing.

23 This analysis is an extension of Marx's treatment in Volume 3 of *Capital* of the various distributions of surplus-value made by capitalists to landlords, financial capitalists, and others in order to secure some of the conditions of existence of their continued appropriation of surplus-value; see Resnick and Wolff (1987b) for a more detailed discussion of these "subsumed class" transfers of surplus-value.

24 To be clear, the continued existence of inflation can also undermine capitalist class processes. This may be the case, for example, when some capitalists are able to increase the prices of their commodities at a slower rate than the producers of the elements of constant capital (thereby decreasing their rate of profit), or when the managers of capitalist enterprises have to devote increasing resources to finding and manipulating money substitutes instead of providing the conditions for the appropriation of surplus-value. In such cases, capitalists may call for heterodox price controls or other, more orthodox measures to lower the rate of inflation.

25 They may differ from capitalist enterprises in the private sector in many ways: in terms of property ownership, the procedures for appointing managers, access to funds other than current revenues, and so on. If the state enterprises are sites where the process of appropriating surplus-value takes place, however, they are no less capitalist than capitalist commodity-producing enterprises that exist outside the state. For a more detailed discussion of state capitalist enterprises, see Ruccio (1987).

26 Another government program that is often considered a major factor in maintaining high fiscal deficits entails subsidies on consumer goods. Space limitations prevent a detailed class analysis of subsidies. The terms of such an analysis, however, are given by the previous discussion of a decline in real wages: first, consumer subsidies have the effect of keeping the price of wage goods below their value. Workers' real standard of living is increased (they can purchase use-values in addition to those included in the value of labor power), while capitalists continue to pay a wage equal to the existing value of labor power. If, then, capitalists succeed in reducing the value of labor power, workers are left with a standard of living, after the subsidies, equivalent to their presubsidy position and the rate of exploitation rises.

27 Policies that restrict the role of the state may also contribute to the strengthening of capitalist class processes. For example, selling state-owned enterprises and cutting government programs may be class successes to the extent that

they involve laying-off state employees, thus creating downward pressure on real wages.

28 See, for example, the discussions in notes 19, 22, 24, and 27 above.

29 There is, of course, the middle position, exemplified by Cline (1982), who argues that the East Asian model cannot work for all developing countries in a slow-growing world economy.

9 Power and class: The contribution of radical approaches to debt and development

> The individual capitalist who sends his money abroad and receives 10 per cent interest for it, whereas by keeping it at home he could employ a mass of surplus people, deserves from the standpoint of capitalism to be crowned king of the bourgeoisie.
>
> Marx, *Capital*, Vol. 1

The crises of debt and development

The total external debt of the developing countries at the end of 1990 was estimated at $1,246 billion, an amount equivalent to 123 percent of their total exports of goods and services.[1] Debt service (amortization plus interest payments) alone consumed 17.3 percent of their export earnings. Of the long-term guaranteed component of these debts ($949 billion), some 45 percent was owed to international private banks and other private creditors located in the advanced industrial nations of the West.

The increased importance of external borrowing during the 1970s, reflected in these figures, was more than matched by a decline in the quantitative significance of foreign direct investment in the total capital movements to developing countries. In 1960, for all developing countries, net direct foreign investment represented 47.9 percent of annual net long-term capital flows (World Bank 1980). The 1970 figure declined somewhat to 34.2 percent, but by 1977, it had fallen to 19.3 percent. Official lending suffered a similar relative decline during the same period. The share lost by those two items was taken over by debt-creating flows of capital on commercial terms, especially private bank lending.

Recent controversial debt repayment schemes, in turn, have focused attention on the sharp decline in economic growth rates and in most, if not all, indicators of standards of living in the developing countries. The abrupt end of relatively high "golden age" growth rates in the Third World – from 5.2 percent in the 1960s and 5.4 percent in the 1970s to 3.2 percent in the first half of the 1980s (World Bank 1988) – has been accompanied by widespread environmental destruction, growing poverty, and deteriorating conditions in health, nutrition, and education (Bell and Reich 1988; Cornia *et al.* 1988).

Faced with such information, few would deny that the international economic relations of developing countries have changed dramatically in the past decade, or that the external debt situation of those countries – in Africa, Asia, and especially Latin America – reached crisis proportions during the same period. However, it is not enough to cite shocking statistics on levels of external debt or income inequality – or, on the other hand, to report on successful cases of economic stabilization and structural adjustment – as if the facts could speak for themselves (cf. Bacha and Díaz-Alejandro 1982, 14). Rather, all economic "facts" are theoretical, in the sense that they only exist and make sense within theoretical frameworks. Different economic theories produce different sets of facts, and each, in turn, understands its facts – and those of other frameworks – differently, depending on the concepts used to produce and interpret them.

External debt is one case in point. The analysis of both external debt and the recent debt crisis has been dominated by work within the "orthodox" or neoclassical/Keynesian tradition. Even the data collected, as I show below, depend on the categories that make up this particular analytical framework. The orthodox tradition tends to view international flows of capital and commodities in terms of individual decision making and, in the aggregate, in terms of the ability of these flows to satisfy national development requirements. External debt is aggregated with other foreign capital flows and analyzed as a means to finance the so-called "foreign-exchange" and "savings" gaps, enhancing allocative efficiency. Alongside this orthodox tradition, an alternative "radical" analysis has emerged, focusing on unequal power relations among and within the various nations in the international economy. International economic relations, radicals argue, create and reproduce relations of dependency between developed and developing nations. External debt, in particular, is seen to involve a form of "debt-peonage" between developing nations and their creditors, especially private banks, in the developed nations.

Of course, such different perspectives on external debt, as well as on the other international aid, trade, and investment activities among nations, have provoked a narrow, two-sided debate about the role of developing countries in the world economy. Does international financial intermediation involve capital flows that directly or indirectly benefit individuals in both the advanced industrial nations and the less-developed Third World? Or do international loans to developing nations trap them in an exploitative web of financial commitments that distort their short-term development prospects and undermine the possibility of development in the long run?

A parallel debate concerns alternative "solutions" to the debt crisis. Some economists, especially the orthodox ones who dominate the discussion, debate the relative merits of domestic stabilization and adjustment policies, increased foreign aid and lending, and the resumption of world economic growth as means to the end of relieving the developing countries' heavy burden of external debt-service payments. The radical response is that such measures are inadequate, that the burden in any case falls disproportionately on the debtor countries (and on the poorer sectors in those countries), and that debt cancellation and other fundamental changes in the world economy are necessary for development to occur in the Third World.

This essay both critically analyzes and participates in this debate concerning the nature and effects of international economic relations. Considering external debt provides a way of focusing on, and entering into, the larger debate concerning economic development in the Third World. My critical review of orthodox and radical approaches to debt and development is, in turn, related to an extension of the radical analysis of external debt. While radical political economists have been remarkably successful in challenging many of the problematic presumptions and policy prescriptions of neoclassical and Keynesian economists, they have been less successful in elaborating an alternative approach. In particular, they have missed the opportunity to develop and extend the radical insights that can be gained by placing class at the center of the analysis. To begin the process of filling this gap, I present a class analysis of external debt, one that focuses on exactly those class aspects of the "debt crisis" that have been downplayed or left out by existing treatments. The specific implications of this class-theoretic approach to external debt are suggestive of some of the remaining problems and issues that the radical literature on economic development needs to address.

Alternative approaches to debt and development

The two basic approaches to external debt can be roughly grouped under the convenient shorthand terms "orthodox" and "radical." A brief discussion of the main elements of the orthodox approach helps to highlight the particular contributions of radical approaches to debt and development.

The orthodox approach

It is typically argued that borrowing from foreign banks and governments by Third World countries is one component of a larger transfer of resources from developed to less-developed nations. The purpose of foreign credit, together with private investment and (multilateral and bilateral) aid, is to finance the aggregate foreign capital requirement of developing countries. This requirement may take the form of a "savings gap" and/or a "foreign-exchange gap" (Chenery and Strout 1966). In the former case, the supply of domestic savings from all sources falls short of the demand for savings for investment purposes. An inflow of foreign capital can serve to bridge this domestic savings gap. In the latter case, the foreign-exchange gap is understood as the outcome of a shortage of foreign funds to finance the external balance of the national economy: a shortfall of foreign-exchange earnings (from exports of goods and services, etc.) with respect to foreign-exchange requirements (for imports, etc.). In both cases, foreign capital is understood to overcome "bottlenecks" that arise in the course of development, thereby contributing to further development.

The fact that foreign capital (whether as direct and portfolio investment, government aid, or loans) enters into the credit column of official national balance-of-payments statements lends support to the idea that such foreign capital represents a resource transfer to (and, therefore, a form of "national investment" for) developing countries. This is certainly the case, according to the orthodox perspective, when capital inflows and outflows are kept within certain "limitations" (no balance of payments crisis arises) and repayment (debt service) is not "excessive." In addition, international economic relations are understood to be structured in such a way that this flow of capital from developed to less-developed nations occurs more or less automatically. Orthodox economists start from the premise that "in the normal course of world development, capital should flow from advanced countries, where it is abundant and its return is relatively low, to developing countries, where capital is scarce and its return high" (Cline 1983, 9). Notwithstanding the existence of market imperfections, developing nations should be able to attract the foreign capital necessary to promote economic growth through the normal functioning of the institutions of international financial intermediation.

This orthodox approach insists, finally, that international capital flows not only directly promote the development of Third World countries but also indirectly promote growth and development throughout the world. Overcoming the foreign capital bottlenecks of developing countries increases international trade and thereby promotes growth and efficiency of the world economy. Thus, it is said, the availability of foreign credits for developing countries during the 1970s, especially after the first oil shock, averted an even deeper world recession than that which in fact occurred.

To summarize briefly, the orthodox approach views foreign loans and other foreign capital flows as

1 mutually beneficial to both developed and less-developed nations within the world economy and
2 a product of the more or less normal functioning of contemporary international economic relations.

This orthodox approach to foreign debt is, of course, linked to a more general theory of development that emerged in the early 1950s.[2] The aim of development, according to this approach, is to transform the small "modern sector" of developing countries into an "engine of growth." Orthodox development economists support the transfer of capital and technology through direct investment, aid, and credit from developed nations to this modern sector (with the goal, in some cases, of transforming the traditional sector itself). Growth then ensues, at least partly in response to this transfer, allowing the developing nations to pay back their benefactors, both directly and indirectly, especially through the acceleration of world trade. There have been differences, to be sure, concerning whether these capital flows would have to be concentrated and short-lived or a long-term necessity but, in either case, self-sustaining growth is said to be the result. Obstacles to this untrammeled flow of capital on either side – for example, through nationalizations or a decline in aid-giving – are understood to curtail world economic growth.

Certainly there has never been a consensus among orthodox economists on the myriad issues associated with international capital flows.[3] And the emergence of the debt crisis in the 1980s, especially in the aftermath of the Mexican difficulties in 1982, only served to exacerbate these differences, especially regarding the origins of the debt crisis and proposed solutions. With respect to the origins of the crisis, debate continues over whether recent problems of repayment can be attributed to debtor countries' living "beyond their means" (for example, using foreign loans to augment consumption instead of investment), to policy "errors" (such as maintaining overvalued exchange rates for too long), or to externally induced terms of trade, recession, and oil-price shocks.[4] Proposed policy measures, especially considering the role of International Monetary Fund (IMF) "conditionality" in many recent refinancing and rescheduling agreements, have produced even more diversity among proponents of the orthodox approach.[5] However, notwithstanding these specific differences, the orthodox approach to external debt remains committed to the view that loans and other foreign capital flows represent a positive resource transfer from capital-rich to capital-poor countries and, as such, a source of mutually beneficial economic growth.

The radical approach

Both of these points are contested by radicals. According to this alternative approach, external debt takes its place alongside other flows of capital from advanced industrial, "core" nations to less-developed, "peripheral" nations as a source of dependency of the latter on the former. Through these international capital flows, power is exercised by the core over the periphery. The result of these unequal power relations is that a surplus is extracted by the developed nations from the less-developed nations; development in the core on the basis of this surplus transfer, then, results in either underdevelopment or dependent and distorted development in the periphery.

This radical approach became prominent in the late 1960s and early 1970s as a critique of foreign aid and foreign direct private investment in the Third World. Such aid and investment were seen as mechanisms whereby development in the Third World was shaped and guided to benefit development elsewhere, in the nations where the aid and investment originated (see, for example, Richards 1977). Multinational corporate investment also resulted in profit repatriations and thus in the "foreign exploitation" of the periphery by the core. Supranational lending agencies (especially the World Bank and the IMF) were seen as partners in this exploitation (Payer 1974 and 1982). Finally, the "unequal exchange" of commodities and the decline of the external terms of trade of peripheral countries were additional mechanisms for the exercise of power over and the "exploitation" of Third World countries.[6]

During the late 1970s and early 1980s, with the relative decline of both the aid and investment components of total foreign capital flows to developing countries, external debt assumed, in the radical framework, the role of previous mechanisms as the primary means of foreign exploitation of the periphery by the core.[7] In the new situation, interest payments to private creditors in the dollar and Eurodollar markets take the place of profit repatriations in transferring a surplus from the periphery to the core and creating a form of "debt-peonage" (see DeWitt and Petras 1979; cf. Hawley 1979). And, in the case where countries fall behind on repayment of the debt, the conditions established by the IMF or by private bank creditors themselves are such that the "poor" are eventually forced to shoulder the debt burden. Whereas, in the orthodox view, external debt is a mechanism for increasing international wealth through resource transfers from developed to developing nations, for radicals it is a means by which core countries extract wealth from peripheral countries and, ultimately, from the "super-exploited" poor within the periphery.

This radical approach to external debt is, like its orthodox opposite, rooted in a more general theory of development and international economic relations. According to the radical framework, capitalist international economic relations are ruled by unequal power relations among and between countries within the world economy; indeed, capitalism itself is defined as a "deeply unequal system of domination of one class by another, of one nation by the ruling class of another" (Bagchi 1982, 39). In this view, then, global economic relations are structured in such a way that international flows of resources have differential effects on the nations involved. Where proponents of the orthodox approach see mutual benefit as the result of international economic relations, radicals see the exploitation of one group of nations by another. This exploitation, in turn, serves as the basis for complementarily opposite effects: development and social stability in the core, and underdevelopment (and/or dependent development) and instability in the periphery. These effects serve, finally, to reproduce conditions for these unequal power relations, as a low-wage, "extraverted" structure of accumulation and a high-wage, "autocentric" structure of accumulation emerge in the periphery and core, respectively (Amin 1974; 1988; cf. Chapter 6 in this volume). The result is that the free flow of capital and commodities in international markets, instead of leading to global economic growth as in the orthodox approach, serves to drive a deeper wedge between developed and underdeveloped, core and periphery nations. External debt represents merely the most recent form of this foreign exploitation of the periphery (see, for example, MacEwan 1985).[8]

We have, then, two diametrically opposite approaches to external debt based, in turn, on different theories of development in general. According to the orthodox approach, foreign loans represent one means for developing countries to close their savings and/or foreign-exchange gaps, a tool which, if "responsibly" used, serves to enhance development throughout the world economy. This view of external debt ultimately assumes that capitalist international economic relations provide an appropriate environment within which individual, rational decision making – individual choice – operates to secure growth and development for all nations. Developing countries benefit directly from the freedom of individuals to buy/sell commodities and borrow/loan capital in international markets but, finally, all nations are beneficiaries of this free international flow of capital and commodities.[9]

The radical story is, of course, quite different. From this perspective, external debt ties developing countries into an unequally structured world economy and, in the end, leads to a net capital outflow. This exploitative transfer of surplus in the form of interest payments enhances development in the advanced industrial countries but worsens the prospects for development in the Third World. Therefore, external debt (along with foreign aid, foreign direct private investment, and unequal commodity exchange) is a product of unequal power relations and a mechanism through which unequal power is exercised to produce an unequal international distribution of the gains from the world accumulation of wealth.

Debates within the radical approach

Radical political economists have succeeded in challenging many of the most cherished propositions of orthodox economists. Their approach, to borrow Evans's (1985, 149) phrase, is "no longer an upstart challenger from the periphery." In fact, the thesis that the metropolis is the "prime mover" behind poverty and underdevelopment in the periphery is no longer the sole province of dependency theorists; Taylor (1988a, 20), for one, has argued that "at root, the poor growth performance of the developing countries is caused by the economic slump of the industrialized world" (see also Singh 1986). There is, however, much debate among radicals about the appropriate framework for their alternative analysis of international relations and Third World development.[10]

The debate has surfaced most recently in the radical attempt to analyze the emergence of the so-called newly industrializing countries (such as Brazil and South Korea) during the past decade (Chakravarty 1987). Alternative radical analyses have used these various country experiences as examples of either "dependent development" (Landsberg 1979 and Hart-Landsberg 1984) or of the possibility of successful capitalist development in the Third World (Barone 1983 and 1984). Warren (1973 and 1980), in fact, provoked considerable consternation when he argued that imperialism had created the conditions, not for underdevelopment, but for successful capitalist development in the Third World.

This debate, however, has existed within the radical approach almost from the beginning. Much discussion has focused on the relationship between power and class, with critics maintaining that class has been subordinated to power in radical analyses of development and international economic relations. Jenkins, for example, takes Warren to task on the grounds that "the specific class structures and modes of surplus appropriation, which have permitted rapid capital accumulation in certain Third World countries (particularly the newly industrializing countries) are not analyzed" (1984, 38). This critique echoes points raised in the earlier "modes of production controversy," which emerged from Laclau's (1971) critique of Frank's version of dependency theory.[11] According to Laclau, early dependency theorists, such as Frank, focused on unequal power relations within homogeneous capitalist markets and failed to analyze the combination of capitalist and noncapitalist modes of production present in Third World settings. This criticism has led some (e.g., the various contributions to Wolpe 1980a and Taylor 1979) to reformulate the radical development approach on the basis of the "articulation of modes of production" or other versions (e.g., that of "peripheral modes of production") in which the mode of production played a central role in the analysis of world capitalist development.[12] This work was successful in bringing classes back into analytical focus within the radical approach. However, it ended up overemphasizing the external relations of dominance of the capitalist mode of production over other, noncapitalist modes of production. As a result, modes of production theorists downplayed the dynamics and complexity of the class processes within the various modes of production.

Another major debate within the radical approach was initiated by Brenner's (1977) critique of the emerging "world-systems" theory, associated with the work of Wallerstein (1974 and 1980; Hopkins and Wallerstein *et al.* 1982), Frank, and other radical development theorists. Brenner took issue with the world-systems theorists' definition of capitalism as a system of power exercised through exchange relations and involving production oriented toward profit in the market. Their definition led, in turn, to a type of analysis in which the emergence of a capitalist class structure was determined by market relations. According to Brenner, market opportunities could not determine class, as in the Wallerstein–Frank view. Rather, he argued, the origins of capitalist market relations had to be sought in the prior emergence of a specifically capitalist class structure.[13]

Gourevitch (1978) echoed Brenner's theme in observing that, according to the world-systems theorists, international market forces rely upon, and accentuate, inequality. Unequal power relations confine weak peripheral states to a subservient role, perpetuating their weakness. In this sense, Wallerstein and the other world-systems theorists reduce the various socio-economic (including class) structures within the world economy to unequal world market opportunities (Skocpol 1977).

More recently, Lipietz (1987) has criticized radical approaches that start with, or presume, a hierarchically structured world system, thereby emphasizing an unchanging structure of core–periphery relations. Because such approaches pay scant attention to the "concrete conditions of capital accumulation in the centre or on the periphery" (1987, 2), they have missed important changes, in center–periphery relations and within the periphery itself, over the course of the last century, and especially in the past 20 years.

Lipietz's observation strikes to the heart of the dilemma posed for radical development thought by the newly industrializing countries and other "unexpected" events in the Third World.[14] It coincides with the critical comments of others, such as Gunnarsson (1985) and Willoughby (1986), who argue that the various forms of capitalism recently emerging in the Third World require a framework of analysis that differs from existing radical approaches – one more sensitive to the variety of political and economic processes which integrate the different Third World social formations into the world capitalist system.

In response to this requirement, Evans has called for a "dependency approach but without the dependency label" (1985, 157). Others (such as Becker *et al.* 1987) have proposed a "postimperialist" framework of analysis. In general, they argue that radical development theory needs to be modified and extended by focusing on the class aspects of relations within and between the Third World and the advanced capitalist countries. This suggestion deserves to be taken seriously and, in the next section, I sketch the outlines of a specifically class-theoretic approach to development issues, focusing on the concrete problem of external debt.

A class analysis of external debt

A class analysis obviously requires clarity on the meaning of the term "class." Not surprisingly, Marx's writings are the most important example of class analysis for the radical tradition in development economics, but there are, of course, several possible readings of Marx's contributions. Richards (1986), for example, recognizes at least two interpretations of Marx's concept of class: one focusing on property endowments in a context of individual choice, and another defining class as a process of appropriation of surplus labor. Here, I adopt the latter approach.[15]

Class processes

The heart of Marx's approach to class was the distinction between necessary labor (labor necessary to reproduce the social existence of the direct producers) and surplus labor (labor performed above and beyond necessary labor). According to the present interpretation, Marx built on this distinction, defining the class process as the particular social process in which surplus labor is appropriated from the direct producers – the performers of that surplus labor.[16] This process of surplus labor appropriation is, in turn, complexly determined by the other economic, political, and cultural processes that make up social life. The various modes of surplus labor appropriation or class processes designated by Marx (primitive communal, feudal, slave, capitalist, etc.) are then produced by differing configurations of such nonclass social processes. Each particular class process is understood to exist only as an effect of its own uniquely constituted social context.

The capitalist class process, in particular, is defined as the appropriation of surplus labor in the form of surplus-value.[17] The source of this surplus-value is, as discussed at length in Volume 1 of *Capital*, the extraction of labor from labor power. Assuming that the commodity labor power is purchased at its value (the value of the commodities necessary to reproduce the social existence of the sellers of labor power), capitalists gain income only if the labor performed in the course of production creates new value greater than the value of labor power. This extra value – Marx's surplus-value – is (under "normal" conditions) realized in the sale of the commodities and appropriated by the capitalist. Thus, the process of performing and appropriating surplus labor in the form of surplus-value defines two class positions: creators of surplus-value ("productive laborers," in Marx's terms) and initial appropriators of that surplus-value (what Marx called the "functioning" or "industrial" capitalists). This process of performance and appropriation of surplus-value can be called the capitalist *fundamental* or appropriative class process.

It is also possible to extend the analysis of class to consider the distribution of surplus labor. In the case of capitalism, once surplus-value is appropriated, it is distributed to finance some of those social processes necessary for the reproduction of the capitalist fundamental class process. For example, portions of the appropriated surplus-value may be distributed to such individuals as merchants, moneylenders, stock owners, and state officials, all of whom participate in processes that secure some of the "conditions of existence" of the original appropriation of surplus-value. The surplus-value may be distributed directly by the industrial capitalist, as in the case of interest payments to moneylenders, or indirectly, when merchants realize part of the surplus-value through the differential between wholesale and retail prices. Regardless of the mechanism, this process of distributing and receiving distributed surplus-value (as distinct from the process of performing surplus labor and appropriating surplus-value), can be called the capitalist *subsumed* or appropriative class process (see Resnick and Wolff 1987b and the Introduction to this volume).

Finally, individuals may earn income or receive revenue in activities entirely separate from fundamental and subsumed class processes. Such flows of value, which represent neither the sale of productive labor power, the direct appropriation of surplus-value, nor the initial distribution of surplus-value, are termed *nonclass* payments.

To illustrate, consider a typical industrial capitalist enterprise, that is, one in which means of production (with value c) and labor power (of value v) are combined to produce capitalist commodities.[18] Surplus-value (SV), once appropriated from productive laborers, is distributed in the form of subsumed class payments (ΣSC). One of the particular conditions of existence of this enterprise, especially in the context of domestic and international competition, may be the accumulation of additional means of production (Δc) and labor power (Δv). Thus, one of the specific subsumed class distributions will be outlays for this accumulation of "productive capital." Therefore, the class revenues and expenditures of the industrial capitalist enterprise may be written as

$$SV = \Sigma SC = \Delta c + \Delta v + \Sigma \overline{SC} \qquad (9.1)$$

where $\Sigma \overline{SC}$ represents all other subsumed class distributions of appropriated surplus-value beyond those devoted to capital accumulation.

In general, the class structure of capitalism includes not only the fundamental class positions of productive laborer and industrial capitalist, but also numerous other subsumed class positions. Individual human beings may occupy one or more of these fundamental and subsumed class positions during the course of a day, a year, or a lifetime. Thus, the class analysis of a particular capitalist society must be capable of distinguishing positions in fundamental and subsumed class processes, as well as nonclass processes, in order to comprehend their constitutive effects. And, since each of these processes and positions is conceived to interact with and "overdetermine" all of the others, the goal of a class analysis is to construct an understanding of precisely this complex interaction.

The remainder of this section elaborates these basic concepts as they apply to the specific development problems associated with external debt. The case of loans to industrial capitalists is the first step in the presentation; other borrowers are then considered.

The industrial capitalist

I begin with the analysis of financial or interest-bearing capital in *Capital*. According to Marx, lender/borrower relations involve an unequal exchange of value in the form of money, M–M'. In the particular case of finance capital highlighted by Marx (1976, 566–652), an initial sum of money (M) is lent to an industrial capitalist who is obliged to repay a larger sum (M') in the form of amortization and interest payments. The original loan is itself a nonclass revenue to the industrial capitalist, but it alters the restrictions imposed by the strict equality between surplus-value and subsumed class payments assumed in equation (9.1). The subsequent flow of interest to the creditor represents a transfer of currently extracted surplus-value, funds lost to the industrial capitalist in return for the use of the money as capital. As receivers and payers of interest respectively, financial and industrial capitalists occupy what I have termed above subsumed class positions: a portion of surplus-value is distributed by the industrial capitalist to the moneylender to secure access to credit, one of the conditions of existence of the extraction of surplus-value. Therefore, following Marx's reconceptualization of the "Trinity Formula" (1981, 953–70), the flow of interest payments from industrial to financial capitalists involves, not a fundamental class process of extracting surplus-value, but a subsumed class process of distributing a portion of surplus-value already appropriated from productive laborers.

A class analysis of the interest payments on loans to an industrial capitalist in another country makes use of these distinctions. The unequal exchange of value in the form of money between, say, Citicorp and an Argentine industrial firm, establishes an international lender/borrower relation in which surplus-value is first extracted from Argentine productive laborers and then distributed as subsumed class revenue to the US bank. Therefore, the foreign profits, P_f, of the US (or German, British, etc.) lending agency represent subsumed class interest revenue, SCR, in return for providing an economic condition of existence of the exploitation of Argentine (or Mexican, Brazilian, etc.) workers; that is

$$P_f = SCR \tag{9.2}$$

Such flows of subsumed class revenue may be received by any of several sorts of lending institutions: private bank consortia, state-owned bilateral lending agencies – such as central banks, and multilateral lending agencies like the World Bank. As long as the loan is made to an industrial capitalist for use in securing one or another of the conditions of existence of the extraction of surplus-value, the interest payments represent a subsumed class revenue to the lending institution.

In the case where borrowed money capital is used for commodity purchases of means of production and labor power (that is, where productive capital is accumulated), if all other subsumed class distributions of surplus-value are constant, then the upper bound on the amount of interest payable is the extra surplus-value (ΔSV) extracted in production. Therefore, the rate of interest paid to the lender (i) cannot be greater than the rate of self-expansion of value based on this new debt (ΔD):

$$i \leq \Delta SV / \Delta D \tag{9.3}$$

Any deviation of i from $\Delta SV / \Delta D$ implies an increase or decrease in the other subsumed class distributions of surplus-value: for example, a lower interest rate on concessional borrowing will allow other subsumed class payments to increase. Alternatively, a rise in the rate of interest on variable-rate loans requires a decrease in other subsumed class payments, which include the enterprise's retained earnings. Therefore, even in the case where private external borrowing leads to increased extraction of surplus-value, the industrial capitalist enterprise may not be able to make the subsumed class payments necessary to secure the other conditions of existence of extracting surplus-value from Third World workers.

We can explore the further effects of such foreign borrowing on domestic capital accumulation in the following manner.[19] Assuming that the industrial capitalist borrower uses foreign loans to expand capital accumulation, equation (9.1) is rewritten to include, on the left-hand side, the newly created debt (ΔD) and, on the right-hand side, the subsumed class distribution of interest payments on total debt (iD) such that:

$$SV + \Delta D = \Delta c + iD + \Sigma \overline{SC} \tag{9.1'}$$

It can be shown (see Appendix) that a decision to increase the role of foreign debt in financing productive capital outlays can positively affect the long-term rate of capital accumulation if the interest rate is less than the net rate of return (net of other subsumed class distributions $\Sigma \overline{SC}$) on productive capital. It is also clear that, everything else being held constant, an increased interest rate will lower the rate of accumulation.

Balance of payments

This initial instance of external borrowing to finance productive capital accumulation requires, in addition, a reconceptualization of the traditional balance of payments statements. Based on the analysis above, the interest payment component of "services" on the current account includes subsumed class flows of value from Third World industrial capitalist enterprises to foreign creditors. This point has many important implications, three of which are noted here. First, debt service payments, because they do not involve the direct extraction of surplus-value, should not be seen as a form of "foreign exploitation." Rather, international money-lending secures a condition of existence of the exploitation of Third World productive laborers by *domestic* (Third World) capitalists; a portion of the surplus-value extracted from those workers is, in turn, distributed to *foreign* creditors for securing this particular condition of existence. Thus, we should distinguish the "cost" to the "nation," based on the flow of interest payments out of the country, from the "cost" imposed by the extraction of surplus-value. The different social tensions and conflicts set in motion by these two costs will have fundamentally different implications for such diverse phenomena as the process of democratization and the success of policies designed to solve the debt crisis (see Chapter 14 in this volume).

Second, since these foreign interest payments are predicated on prior extraction of surplus-value from Third World workers, a surplus in the remainder of the current and capital accounts will not, in general, solve the payments imbalance from such interest payments. Only in the case where merchandise exports realize surplus-value pumped out of the direct producers (and/or new borrowing directly finances debt service payments) can entries on the credit side of the balance of payments ledger be said to "solve" a balance of payments problem created by debt service payments.[20] External debt servicing is obviously not independent of net export performance; foreign interest payments must, in the end, be made in the form of foreign currency earnings.[21] However, an exclusive focus on net export performance and, hence, on *nonclass* balance of payments entries means that the performance, appropriation, and distribution of surplus-value – and therefore the class nature and effects of the debt service – are hidden from view. To "forget about" these class aspects of debt servicing is to miss the struggles generated by attempts to increase the extraction of surplus-value and/or modify its distribution among different subsumed classes. Such struggles may undermine the best-laid plans to service the debt.

Finally, even though debt service payments do not, in themselves, represent foreign exploitation, the rise in subsumed class interest payments may create the conditions for an eventual rise in the exploitation of domestic workers by foreigners. For example, domestic and/or international decision makers may react to a balance of payments "crisis" by requiring additional external payments entries on the credit side. As stressed by the orthodox approach surveyed above, foreign capital inflows in the form of foreign direct private investment represent such a credit entry. Therefore, attempts to solve an imbalance of external payments may take the form of policies to promote foreign direct investment, thereby increasing the extraction of surplus-value by foreign citizens (as in the case of Mexico, which relaxed restrictions on foreign investment as part of the "adjustment" policy package).

Other borrowers

The preceding analysis focused only on private industrial capitalists' borrowing of external funds, for the purpose of expanding the accumulation of productive capital. However, the current external debt of most developing countries has arisen with the participation of borrowers other than industrial capitalist enterprises and for purposes other than the accumulation of productive capital. There are at least three other major categories of borrowers that must be considered in analyzing the class structure of external debt: state-owned industrial enterprises, government administration (government agencies and enterprises other than industrial capitalist enterprises), and private nonindustrial enterprises (including commercial banks and other financial enterprises, merchant companies, etc.). Each of these other borrowers must be analyzed in order to determine the class nature of the revenue flows from interest payments to foreign lending institutions.

Following the logic of the analysis above, loans to state industrial capitalist enterprises generate subsumed class interest payments to foreign creditors in a way analogous to that of loans to private industrial capitalist enterprises. The provision of money capital in the form of loans provides a condition of existence of the extraction of surplus-value, now from state employees, and generates a direct distribution of surplus-value – a subsumed class flow of revenue – to the lending institution. Certainly, other conditions of existence of the exploitation of productive laborers differ in this case (for example, state ownership of the means of production) but the "unequal exchange" of value in the form of money with state industrial capitalist enterprises continues to generate foreign interest payments that represent subsumed class revenue. Again, the international lender/borrower relation involves a foreign distribution of surplus-value and not foreign exploitation.

So far, in my analysis, the foreign profits of lending agencies have been classified as a subsumed class income because those lenders occupy a class position subsumed to the capitalist fundamental class process in another country. More generally, though, the class nature of interest payments, foreign or domestic, depends on the class position of the *borrower* of money. This is, of course, largely irrelevant to the lender, for whom a successful loan is simply one that performs; the apparent irrelevance of the identity of the borrower is precisely why moneylending appears to be an independent form of capital. However, from a class-analytic standpoint, interest is a subsumed class distribution of surplus-value only when the borrower occupies the position of industrial capitalist, either in state or private enterprise. Foreign profits on loans to government agencies and private non-industrial enterprises have a different class content since, in these cases, neither the extraction of surplus-value nor its direct distribution as subsumed class revenue takes place. Because the borrowed funds are not deployed by the borrower to secure a condition of existence of the extraction of surplus-value, then, whether these funds are later lent to industrial capitalists or deployed for some other purpose, the lending agency occupies a nonclass position and the interest received represents a nonclass flow of revenue from borrower to lender. When neither the extraction nor the initial distribution of surplus-value is involved, the foreign profits of the lending institution must be categorized as nonclass flows of revenue (*NCR*); the expanded foreign profit equation for the creditor is then

$$P_f = SCR + NCR \tag{9.4}$$

An international lender/borrower relation continues to exist and interest payments across national boundaries continue to form part of the debits on the current account, but the class nature of those debt service payments depends on the class status of the borrower; the existence of external debt does not, by itself, indicate the class-structural form of that debt.

Typically, then, interest payments on the external debt of a capitalist developing country will involve both subsumed class and nonclass flows of value to foreign lenders. Similarly, the non-merchandise "service" export revenue of the country in which the lending agency is located includes both subsumed class and nonclass revenues. Therefore, typical balance-of-payments data need to be further reconceptualized to distinguish these different flows of value. In particular, the nonclass division of external debt and debt service payments into "official" and "private" accounts can be reinterpreted by means of this distinction between subsumed class (ΣSC) and nonclass (ΣNC) payments. Figure 9.1 represents a first approximation to this end: official debtors are broken down into state industrial capitalist enterprises (K^s) and other government agencies (G), while private debtors include nonindustrial (B) and industrial capitalist (K^P) enterprises.

Figure 9.1 Class structure of external debt and debt service

Borrower	Class nature of interest payments		
Official $\begin{cases} G \\ K^s \end{cases}$	ΣNC		ΣSC
Private $\begin{cases} B \\ K^P \end{cases}$	ΣNC		ΣSC

It is worth stressing that the nonclass nature of certain debt service payments does not imply that these flows are any less important for the general course of development of the country concerned or, in particular, for the reproduction over time of the capitalist fundamental class process. It is, in fact, the task of class analysis not only to distinguish the fundamental, subsumed, and nonclass aspects of social reality, but also to analyze their complex mutual interactions. For example, the nonclass status of interest paid on government agency borrowing (*G*) leaves open the question of the uses of the borrowed funds, any of which may have various important effects on the class (and nonclass) processes of the country in question. The government, among other possibilities, may lend the borrowed money or sell foreign exchange to industrial capitalists, or create infrastructure (such as roads and dams) that positively affects the extraction of surplus-value. These government moneylending, money-dealing, and infrastructure-building activities may secure conditions of existence of the capitalist fundamental class process and, therefore, create the basis for a governmental claim on appropriated surplus-value. These subsumed class payments to the government may take the form of interest payments, fees on sales of foreign exchange, or taxes on industrial capitalist income. Thus, even when governmental interest payments to foreign creditors represent nonclass payments, the source of revenue for those payments may be a subsumed-class position established by government expenditures financed by foreign borrowing.

As another example of the different class structural forms of debt, consider a government guarantee of the private debt of industrial capitalists. Such official guarantees are often important conditions for international borrowing by residents of developing countries. So long as the industrial capitalist borrowers meet their debt obligations, the interest payments remain as subsumed class distributions of appropriated surplus-value. Only in the event of a perceived failure by private borrowers to maintain debt service payments, when the government itself is forced to assume the servicing obligation,[22] do the interest payments become nonclass flows of value. Such a government "bailout" therefore implies that one claim on appropriated surplus-value, that of foreign creditors, has been eliminated. Unless the debt service is financed by taxes on industrial capitalist firms, the debt burden will tend to fall on individuals occupying other class positions in the country. Other subsumed class claimants on distributions of surplus-value (merchants, domestic moneylenders, corporate managers, etc.) may, in turn, support such a class transfer of the debt burden; a possibility suggestive of the complex tensions created by government guarantees.

A similar example involves the case of nongovernment enterprises, such as commercial banks, whose foreign interest payments on debt also represent nonclass flows of value. Their borrowing activity in international money markets may be motivated by the opportunity to capture a differential between the foreign interest rate at which they borrow and the domestic rate at which they can lend. They may expand their lending to domestic industrial capitalist enterprises which are unable to participate directly in international money markets, thereby providing access to foreign exchange and/or lowering the domestic interest rate to industrial capitalist borrowers through an increase in the supply of loanable funds. Here, the domestic commercial bank creates a subsumed class claim on domestically appropriated surplus-value as the means to finance its own international obligation to make nonclass payments.

Class and debt

The important point here is that "nonclass debt" may have significant class effects. In the recent literature, the examples most discussed (though not in the terms elaborated here) concern the conditions for debt rescheduling (e.g., Feinberg and Ffrench-Davis 1988). Foreign recipients of nonclass interest payments often form alliances with government officials, central bank officers, and industrial capitalists within their own country, with international multilateral lending agencies, and with capitalists, officials, and other groups within the debtor country to demand that the government of the latter country enact an "adjustment" policy as the condition for receiving "bridging" loans and a new debt repayment schedule. Immediate policy goals often include raising domestic interest rates, decreasing the government deficit, lowering the exchange-rate (devaluation), forcing down real wages in order to lower inflation and promote exports, and encouraging foreign investment. The most common measures advocated involve some combination of restrictive fiscal and monetary policies. But such policies may have contradictory effects, undermining certain conditions of existence of industrial capitalist enterprises, while making possible increased extraction of surplus-value.

A typical policy package will include, for example, higher real interest rates and lower import tariffs (see Canitrot 1980 and Ffrench-Davis 1983). Such measures may force industrial capitalist enterprises to distribute an increased share of their surplus-value in the form of subsumed class payments to domestic banks, even as heightened import competition undermines their domestic sales. The realized surplus-value of domestic capitalists may decline as a result. The combined effects of these conditions thus threaten the continuation of the subsumed class payments needed to secure the various conditions of existence of those in the class position of industrial capitalist. In particular, less surplus-value may be available in the form of retained earnings to distribute to managers of those enterprises for the purpose of accumulating capital. Ironically, then, policies enacted to maintain access to foreign credit lines – in the form of nonclass debt to the government and financial enterprises – may threaten the very existence of the industrial capitalists. Nowhere is the contradictory situation of the state in a typical developing country more evident.

Of course, other factors can, in part, offset this threat to industrial capitalists. If the wages (and, in time, the value of labor power) of productive laborers can be lowered enough, then the additional surplus-value extracted will enable industrial capitalists to continue their subsumed class distributions of surplus-value, including interest payments to domestic and foreign creditors. Various policies of Third World governments appear to have had just this effect. For example, restrictions on forms of labor association have contributed to reduced absenteeism and weakened trade union bargaining power. In addition, absolute decreases in the employment of both government and industrial workers have lessened pressures for nominal wage increases. In this sense, it is the increased exploitation of domestic workers – and not stand-by credits from the IMF, loans from private banks, or agricultural exports – that has "financed" the foreign debt problem.

Thus, the nonclass process of debt servicing produces a complex set of political and economic interactions that may lead to increased domestic exploitation and, with a rise in foreign investment, to foreign exploitation as well.[23] But there is another dimension of debt that deserves at least brief mention as a further demonstration of the class complexity of development problems in debtor countries.

Capital flight

Capital flight is frequently a major concern in attempting to manage a debt crisis. Cumby and Levich (1987), for example, used the World Bank method to estimate capital flight, ranging from 24 percent of Brazil's total external borrowing (during the period 1976–84) to 66 percent for Argentina (during 1979–82) and 68 percent for Mexico (1976–84). Interpretation of these data requires an extension of the analysis to allow for the use of external funds for purposes other than capital accumulation by industrial capitalist enterprises, domestic lending by financial enterprises, and the purchase of equity in other domestic enterprises by both industrial and non-industrial firms. Consider once again the example of industrial capitalist enterprises. If capital outflows are directed into purchases of stocks and bonds of foreign industrial capitalist enterprises, Third World residents, in effect, use their own foreign borrowing to create or extend subsumed class claims on surplus-value generated in other countries. In this case, foreign funds are not used to secure a condition of existence of any domestic fundamental class position; instead, the nonclass revenues from external borrowing flow out of the country to secure a condition of existence of the extraction of surplus-value by industrial capitalists in the United States and other countries. In return, the Third World investor receives a subsumed class distribution of surplus-value appropriated elsewhere.[24] The original foreign lenders – in all likelihood the same financial institutions that facilitated the capital flight – now receive nonclass interest payments from the developing country's industrial capitalist borrowers. Only in the case where debt is used to secure a condition of existence of the *fundamental* class position of the borrower do the interest payments themselves represent a subsumed class claim on surplus-value extracted from Third World workers.[25]

We can extend our previous analysis of the effects of external debt on the domestic accumulation of capital by including, on the right-hand side of equation (9.1'), the foreign portfolio investments made by the industrial capitalist enterprise (ΔA) and, on the left-hand side, the subsumed class revenue derived from such investments (*SCR*):

$$SV + SCR + \Delta D = \Delta c + \Delta A + iD + \Sigma \overline{SC} \tag{9.1''}$$

Again, it can be shown (see Appendix) that (all other variables being held constant) an increase in the interest rate on outstanding debt will reduce the rate of domestic capital accumulation. An increase in the ratio of external debt to the firm's productive capital can increase the long-term rate of domestic capital accumulation, if the interest rate on foreign debt is less than the overall rate of return (net of other subsumed class distributions $\Sigma \overline{SC}$) on total assets. Finally, an increase in foreign portfolio investment may itself have a *positive* effect on long-term domestic accumulation of productive capital if the rate of return on such foreign assets exceeds the net rate of return (net of interest payments and other subsumed class distributions) on the portion of domestic capital owned free of debt ($c + v - D$). That is, domestic productive capital accumulation may actually *increase* as a result of foreign unproductive capital accumulation if the rate of return to the latter is high enough and, of course, if the returns are repatriated. Otherwise, such capital flight will leave the domestic accumulation of capital unaffected or actually lower it.

An additional issue that arises here concerns the use of foreign subsumed class revenues to make expenditures, such as those sustaining capital accumulation, which reproduce a capitalist's domestic fundamental class position. Such a transfer of funds within the enterprise will lower the expenditures that secure the foreign subsumed class position of the capitalist and, thus, may jeopardize that position and the future receipt of subsumed class revenues.

It is also clearly possible for subsumed class revenues to be redirected to processes other than the accumulation of productive capital. The revenues from foreign portfolio investment may, for example, be distributed to internal managers, interest payments, dividends, or taxes. However, if the rate of return on foreign investment is less than the "internal" rate of profit derived from exploitation of domestic productive laborers, increased foreign investment may lead to a decrease in domestic subsumed class payments.[26] Such a situation may generate alliances among various domestic classes to restrict the capital outflow. Alternatively, domestic industrial capitalists may seek to ally themselves with other domestic classes to resist interest payments to foreign banks and to support a new government capable of rescheduling the existing debt burden.

Conclusions

The class analysis of external debt focuses on exactly those class processes which are left out of other accounts of international lender/borrower relations, both orthodox and radical. It provides a framework for analyzing interactions, since class processes are both shaped by and participate in shaping the other class and nonclass processes of the various socially diverse Third World nations. Such an approach allows us to reconceptualize the problem of external debt by investigating the class and nonclass processes operating, as it were, behind the official balance-of-payments statements.

As in the examples considered above, domestic borrowers can use nonclass revenues in the form of foreign loans to create or extend domestic and foreign fundamental, subsumed, and nonclass positions. For industrial capitalist enterprises, such nonclass revenues allow them to evade the restrictions imposed by the originally assumed equality between fundamental and subsumed class revenues and the expenditures made to secure those revenues. The class nature of the interest payments to creditors varies, however, depending on the specific class position(s) of the borrowers. Thus, for example, interest payments to private banks in New York by Third World industrial capitalist enterprises may represent subsumed class distributions of surplus-value or nonclass expenditures, depending on whether the debt is used to secure the fundamental class position of capitalist appropriator of surplus-value or a class position subsumed to other industrial capitalists. A similar class-analytic study can be made of other borrowers.

Distinguishing these various class-structural forms of debt is a necessary step in exploring the contradictory effects on class and nonclass processes typically experienced by capitalist developing countries. For example, "adjustment" policies (those designed to correct the external imbalance created, in part, by previous external borrowing), come into focus as a source of new contradictions within industrial capitalist enterprises and the state. One response by Third World industrial capitalists has been to engage in new foreign borrowing and capital exports to create or extend their foreign subsumed class positions.

Debt crises

To take this analysis a step further, consider the conditions under which a debt crisis might arise. To begin with, a domestic borrower can increase expenditures through external indebtedness only on condition that, first, the money returns to its original owner after a definite time interval and, second, it returns as a sum greater than the original loan. Leaving aside, for simplicity's sake, repayment of the principal, the borrower can avoid constraints on other expenditures only if expectations prove correct and the loan is used to generate additional revenue at least equal to the interest payments due. A payments crisis would emerge, then, if actual revenues fell short of those expected. For a typical industrial capitalist borrower, servicing external debt requires that the additional domestically appropriated surplus-value (ΔSV) and foreign subsumed class revenues (ΔSCR), free of all other claims, are not less than the subsumed class and nonclass interest payments on outstanding debt (iD). Success thus depends on avoiding unexpected depletions of either surplus-value appropriated at home or subsumed class payments from abroad. Should either circumstance occur, interest payments to foreign creditors would be threatened and a debt crisis would emerge.

There are, of course, numerous ways of attempting to overcome such a crisis, each with its own different class effects. Creditors might be induced to extend additional nonclass revenues by creating new loans. The industrial capitalist borrowers might attempt to decrease other subsumed class and nonclass payments, both inside and outside the enterprise. However, such cutbacks – a drop in the accumulation of productive capital, for example – would jeopardize their fundamental and subsumed class positions. Finally, borrowers might attempt to find other means of increasing their appropriation of surplus-value and subsumed class income receipts. Any of these changes could alter the conditions of struggle over production and distribution of domestic surplus-value. Thus, the debt crisis is likely to produce qualitative changes in the form of fundamental and subsumed class struggles.

Class and capitalist development

This class-theoretic analysis of external debt is one example of an emerging "new direction" in the radical analysis of international capitalist development. At the general level of theory construction, it shares the aims of recent efforts to rethink the central role of concepts of power in radical political economy (see, for example, Amariglio 1988 and Norton 1988b).

More specifically, reaffirming the centrality of class recasts a significant number of issues within radical development theory. Among its other effects is a different concept of development itself. Rather than defining development as the accumulation and distribution of wealth in the form of use-values – whether equal, as in orthodox theory, or unequal, as in existing radical accounts – development is reconceptualized in terms of class, as a matter of the differential effects produced by the various forms and types of class and nonclass processes that jointly make up both "developed" and "developing" nations and the international relations among and between them. The accent of this alternative approach, then, is not on "more" or "less" development – whether measured by the amount of use-values produced (Richards 1986), the level of development of the productive forces (Warren 1980 and Bardhan 1986), or an understanding of wealth as power (Chakravarty 1987) – but on the various class-specific forms of development. From the perspective of this approach, the analysis of development according to wealth is more appropriate for an approach based on Smith and Samuelson than for the tradition of radical development theory initiated by Lenin and Baran.

Still, the class-theoretic approach to debt outlined here is only a first step in rethinking some of the well-known arguments and conclusions of radical development thought. Brewer (1980) and Willoughby (1986), for example, have initiated the process of critically examining and, in some cases, rejecting the results of previous radical approaches to imperialism.

> Imperialism does not represent a special stage in the development of capitalism; uneven development does not always culminate in the breakdown of capitalist order, there is no necessity for the super-exploitation of the periphery by metropolitan capital; and consequently, it is possible for some Third World economies to develop sophisticated industrial capitalist structures.
>
> (Willoughby 1986, 80)

The political economy of the peasantry has been subject to similar critical scrutiny through a clarification of the class concepts that inform radical approaches to "peasant studies" (Deere 1986).

Finally, the collapse of existing socialist regimes in Eastern Europe and the ongoing turmoil of the Soviet Union and China have created a thoroughly spurious sense of the "correctness" of the orthodox approach which celebrates capitalism. It is therefore even more urgent to criticize the effects of orthodox development theories and strategies. As a result, the issues raised by class-analytic approaches to the state (Thomas 1984 and Bryan 1987) and socialism (Fagen *et al.* 1986 and Chapters 4 and 5 of this volume) are likely to be at the forefront of radical debates over the next few years. At least one orthodox development economist has recognized the need to develop a "theory of class formation and class conflict" (Lewis 1984, 8). Radical political economists have the opportunity to respond to this need and, even more importantly, to elaborate a class-analytic framework that builds on and extends their own approach to development.

Appendix

To explore the effects of external debt on domestic capital accumulation, rewrite equation (9.1′) in the text as:

$$\Delta c + \Delta v = SV + \Delta D - iD - \Sigma \overline{SC}$$

The rate of productive capital accumulation can be obtained by dividing through by the flow of value $(c + v)$:

$$\frac{\Delta c + \Delta v}{c + v} = \frac{SV}{c + v} + \frac{\Delta D}{c + v} - \frac{iD}{c + v} - \frac{\Sigma \overline{SC}}{c + v} \tag{A9.1}$$

Assume a given long-run ratio of debt to productive capital, $\alpha = D/(c + v)$. Given α, $\Delta D = \alpha (\Delta c + \Delta v)$. Define $K^* = (\Delta c + \Delta v)/(c + v)$, $p' = SV/(c + v)$, and $\mu = \Sigma \overline{SC}/(c + v)$. Substituting these expressions into (A9.1) yields

$$K^* = p' + \alpha K^* + \alpha i - \mu$$

which can be solved for:

$$K^* = \frac{p' - \alpha i - \mu}{1 - \alpha} \tag{A9.2}$$

The sustainable long-run rate of capital accumulation (K^*) thus depends on the rate of surplus-value appropriation (p'), the "gearing ratio" for debt (α), the rate of interest on foreign borrowing (i), and the ratio of other subsumed class distributions of surplus-value to productive capital (μ). Assuming that p', i, and μ are determined independently of α, the results referred to in the text can be derived by partially differentiating (A9.2) with respect to α and i:

$$\frac{\partial K^*}{\partial \alpha} = \frac{(-i + p' - \mu)}{(1 - \alpha)^2} \gtrless 0 \text{ iff } i \lessgtr p' - \mu, \, \alpha \neq 1$$

$$\frac{\partial K^*}{\partial i} = \frac{-\alpha}{(1 - \alpha)} > 0, \, 0 < \alpha < 1$$

To examine the additional effects of foreign portfolio investments, assume that the enterprise earns a rate of return r on its foreign portfolio investments A; then $SCR = rA$. Assume further a given long-run ratio of foreign portfolio investment to domestic productive capital, $\beta = A/(c + v)$. Substituting into equation (9.1′) in the text and solving for K^* yields:

$$K^* = \frac{p' + \beta r - \alpha i - \mu}{1 - \alpha + \beta} \tag{A9.3}$$

The sustainable long-run rate of capital accumulation thus depends additionally on the given "foreign portfolio weight" (β) and the subsumed class rate of return on foreign portfolio investment (r). Assuming again that p', i, r, and μ are determined independently of the enterprise's choices for α and β, the results in the text follow from partial differentiation of (A9.3) with respect to i, a, and β:

$$\frac{\partial K^*}{\partial i} = \frac{-\alpha}{(1 - \alpha + \beta)} < 0, \ \alpha - \beta \neq 1$$

$$\frac{\partial K^*}{\partial a} = \frac{-i(1 + \beta) + p' + \beta r - \mu}{(1 - \alpha + \beta)^2} \gtrless 0 \text{ iff } i \lessgtr \frac{p' + \beta r - \mu}{1 + \beta}, \ \alpha - \beta \neq 1$$

where $\dfrac{p' + \beta r - \mu}{1 + \beta} = \dfrac{SV + SCR - \Sigma\overline{SC}}{c + v + A}$

$$\frac{\partial K^*}{\partial \beta} = \frac{r(1 - \alpha) - p' + \alpha i + \mu}{(1 - \alpha + \beta)^2} \gtrless 0 \text{ iff } r \gtrless \frac{p' - \alpha i - \mu}{1 - \alpha}, \ \alpha - \beta \neq 1$$

where $\dfrac{p' + \alpha i - \mu}{1 - \alpha} = \dfrac{SV + iD - \Sigma\overline{SC}}{c + v - D}$

(original version published in 1992)

Notes

1   The estimates in this paragraph come from the International Monetary Fund (1990); they apply to the total debt of developing countries and include short-term debt.

2   On orthodox development theory, and the ways in which it differs from radical approaches, see Resnick, Sinisi, and Wolff (1985).

3   In fact, one longstanding critic of the benefits of foreign aid for developing country growth continues to plead his case; see Bauer (1984).

4   See, as an example, Fishlow's critique of Cline (1983) in Ruccio and Kim (1986).

5   This summary of the orthodox approach is not meant to imply that the differences among and between mainstream economists – in their explanations of the debt crisis and in their proposed solutions – are unimportant. The various strategies advocated by orthodox economists for overcoming the debt crisis (e.g., export promotion, currency devaluation, seizing foreign assets, and/or capping interest payments) would, if implemented, have radically different implications for the development of both advanced capitalist and Third World countries. The point here is that orthodox economists are biased toward the consideration of some kinds of development policies to the exclusion of others – toward

which radical economists would be equally, but differently, biased – because of their framework of analysis.

6 See the review by de Janvry (1981, 50–55). The unequal exchange debate began with Emmanuel (1972); critics of Emmanuel include Bettelheim (in Emmanuel 1972, 271–322), de Janvry and Kramer (1979), Evans (1984), and Szentes (1985).

7 The notion that capital-importing countries are "exploited" by capital-exporting countries has been developed most recently by Roemer (1988, 105).

8 Elsewhere, MacEwan (1987) has analyzed the external debt crisis as part of a more general "crisis of imperial decline."

9 There are, however, neoclassical models in which countries may not always gain from trade, as when "distortions" are present; for instance, if there are non-economic objectives or if "largeness" distorts product or factor markets (see Bhagwati and Srinivasan 1983).

10 Palma (1978) observes that radical development economists have been more successful in inverting the neoclassical paradigm – for example, in arguing that foreign trade, instead of promoting economic development, actually creates obstacles to development – than in formulating an alternative position.

11 Frank has elaborated his theory of dependency in numerous texts (1967, 1969, 1972, 1978, 1979, and 1984). Another version of dependency theory, originally published in Spanish in 1971, was presented by Cardoso and Faletto (1979); Cardoso (1977), in fact, challenged the originality of Frank's approach.

12 See the surveys by Foster-Carter (1978) and Chapter 6 of this volume.

13 For a more extended discussion of Brenner's further criticisms, see Chapter 6 of this volume.

14 For a discussion of both the positive contributions and the limitations of Lipietz's "regulation theory" approach, see Chapter 13 of this volume.

15 Wright (1985) and Resnick and Wolff (1987b) discuss the diverse interpretations of Marx's concept of class. Richards (1986) chooses to employ the property relations/individual choice approach to class; I (1988), in turn, have criticized that approach, associated with the "rational choice" school of radical economics.

16 Marx explicitly refers to class as a process in the *Grundrisse* (1973, 258): "Capital is not a simple relation, but a process, in whose various moments it is always capital." The stress here on class as a process is based on an interpretation of Marxian theory in which class refers to one particular social process among the many that comprise social life.

17 The feudal class process, in contrast, involves appropriation of surplus labor in the form of feudal rent (in kind labor, or money). Different class processes are defined by the different ways in which surplus labor is pumped out of the direct producers; see Resnick and Wolff (1987a, Chap. 3).

18 Here and throughout I assume, with Marx in Volume 1 of *Capital*, that commodities exchange at their values and that circulating capital alone (with yearly value $c + v$) is advanced in the production sphere. Consideration of the issues involved in transformation to prices of production, fixed capital, and so forth would modify, but not fundamentally change, the thrust of the analysis. See Wolff, Callari, and Roberts (1984) and Roberts (1987) for a treatment of value-theoretic issues in line with the approach taken here.

19 The choice here to focus on the process of accumulating productive capital should not be interpreted to mean that capital accumulation is the only, or most important, process involved in reproducing the fundamental class position of the industrial capitalist. It is only one of many conditions financed by subsumed class distributions of surplus-value; others include managerial supervision, access to the means of production, sales, and the adjudication of

contract disputes. The focus on capital accumulation is for illustrative purposes only.

20 In the former case, the prior exploitation of developing country workers must have occurred before the commodity is exported; export allows the enterprise to realize the surplus-value necessary to make the subsumed class payment of interest. In the case of new debts, extraction of surplus-value is merely postponed until a later date.

21 Thus, for example, changes in the external terms of trade will affect export earnings and, therefore, the foreign exchange available for debt service payments. Debt service may also depend on export earnings, as in the case where the borrower is also a producer of exports. In this case, the ability to realize the surplus-value contained in the exported commodities, and not the hard currency earnings per se, is a necessary condition for making interest payments.

22 As, for example, in Chile during 1983–84; see Ffrench-Davis and de Gregorio (1985).

23 For a fuller discussion of the class effects of orthodox (neoclassical and structuralist) stabilization and adjustment policies, see Chapter 8 of this volume.

24 Of course, such capital outflows may also be used to secure foreign nonclass positions, by purchasing the bonds and securities of institutions other than industrial capitalists (e.g., foreign governments and financial enterprises).

25 Equation (9.3) would be rewritten as $i \leq (\Delta SV + \Delta SCR)/\Delta D$. In addition, the term iD in equation (9.1'') now includes both subsumed class and nonclass interest payments to foreign creditors.

26 Third World capitalists may engage in foreign investment even when the rate of return is less than the "internal" rate of profit if there is uncertainty concerning future exchange rates or their control over domestic bank accounts, and foreign investments are considered more secure.

10 Capitalism and industrialization in the Third World: Recognizing the costs and imagining alternatives

The irony of free market ideology

The industrialization that has been achieved in the Third World during the postwar period has occurred largely under the aegis of extensive state involvement in the economy. Now, however, the situation has changed: more free markets (and less state involvement) are heralded as the appropriate environment for new forms and higher levels of industrialization. What are the prospects for this new industrialization? Can it be successful? Is there space within the global capitalist environment for the Third World – or the Fourth or Fifth Worlds – to industrialize? If not, is there an alternative?

It is, of course, ironic that the idea of free markets – together with privatization, deregulation, and so on – has acquired such prominence at this time. And not only among the usual neoclassical suspects (including the International Monetary Fund, the World Bank, and the economic advisors in the East who, we are led to believe, had been secretly reading Friedrich von Hayek and Milton Friedman under the noses of the central planners). This new, market-oriented development thinking is summarized by Joseph E. Stiglitz and Lyn Squire (1998). The *World Development Report 1997* (World Bank 1997) is devoted to shrinking and transforming the role of the state in development (but see Ha-Joon Chang and Robert Rowthorn [1995] for a critical review of the main components of the standard neoliberal view of the state). Many liberal and left-leaning economists have also come forward to, in the form of disciplinary rectitude, disavow the "excesses" and "mistakes" of their intellectual youth and proclaim their allegiance to the eternal verities of the market. As I demonstrate below, the ironies of such old orthodoxies and new conversions abound.

Irony I: is the United States a model to emulate?

The Americanization of world economic thinking has taken place at precisely the same time as the economic and social situation in the United States has deteriorated. Not for everyone, of course: the latest figures show that the richest 1 percent of Americans reaped three-quarters of the gains in average family income from the late 1970s to the early 1990s. By the middle of the 1990s, the net worth of these same households – all of them millionaires at a minimum – was greater than the bottom 90 percent of Americans put together. The increasingly unequal distribution of income and wealth in the United States, a tendency that began in 1969 and has persisted to the present, has been documented, using different methodologies, in a wide variety of sources. These include studies by the US Census Bureau (Weinberg 1996), Edward N. Wolff (1995, 1996), Paul Krugman (1992), the Center on Budget and Policy Priorities (1997), and United for a Fair Economy and Institute for Policy Studies (1998). The particulars are interesting, but it is the overall theme that truly stands out: the distribution of income and wealth in the United States (however measured) has been worsening for three decades and is by far the most unequal among the industrialized countries.

The United States is also "Number One" among industrial nations on many other unsavory scales: it now claims more than twice the average rate of intentional homicides (at 12.4 per 100,000 people), the highest incidence of poverty, the largest portion of the total population incarcerated, and a disgraceful degree of economic and social infrastructure in disrepair (including not only bridges and roads but also the traditional two-parent household enshrined on American television). The sight of "urban jungle vehicles" being maneuvered by American yuppies through city streets is reminiscent (albeit without the bulletproof plating) of chauffeur-driven all-terrain vehicles in San Salvador and Djakarta. In this case if in no other, the least industrialized have revealed, to the most industrialized, their future.

Irony 2: markets "get it wrong"

Interestingly, the hegemony of neoliberal development policy has grown at the same time that economic research and theory offer increased support for government intervention: nonmarket linkages are important for economic development; coordination failures play a key role in business cycles. For example, "post-Walrasian" approaches to microeconomic theory demonstrate the existence of significant informational asymmetries and problems with the enforcement of contractual exchanges, meaning that prices will not clear markets, thereby creating the justification for extramarket intervention (see, for example, Samuel Bowles and Herbert Gintis 1990 and 1993).

In addition, the "new trade theory" (now almost 20 years old) demonstrates the significance of noncomparative advantage trade: countries do not necessarily specialize and trade in order to take advantage of their (natural or given) differences. They also trade because there are increasing returns to producing a narrow range of goods and services, which makes specialization advantageous per se (see Krugman 1987 and Baldwin 1992 for summaries of this approach). The policy conclusion of the new models of international trade is that government can often improve on free-market outcomes (for instance by imposing import tariffs and/or offering export subsidies). However, the new trade theorists have been quick to back away from this implication, on political rather than economic grounds. As Krugman (1987, 132) explains, "There is still a case for free trade as good policy, and as a useful target in the practical world of politics, but it can never be asserted as the policy that economic theory tells us is always right." Robert Kuttner (1996) takes Krugman to task for "backpedalling" in favor of market outcomes.

Thus, most products that enter international commerce are created by imperfectly competitive industries. This means that the pattern of special-ization and trade around the globe is, in a fundamental sense, arbitrary: who produces what, is the result of history, "accidents," and past govern-ment policies; it is not dictated – as the strictly neoclassical, comparative-advantage theorists would have us believe – by given tastes, resources, and technology.

The so-called new trade theory is buttressed by the "discovery" that the industrialization success of the East Asian countries owes little to free markets and has been mostly the product of active government involve-ment. According to Wade (1995), the role of the government in the indus-trialization successes of countries such as Korea, Taiwan, and Japan went far beyond the neoliberal recipe. Alice Amsden (1989) and Ajit Singh (1995) have argued that the state – rather than free markets and "getting prices right" – has been a key factor in the industrialization experiences of Korea and India, respectively. The same, of course, is true of China.

The limited options of the South: trade (and poverty) or no trade (and poverty)

What is *not* ironic is that the export-oriented path of industrialization advocated by free-market economists and policymakers is the only viable path to industrialization left for much of the South. While many industrial countries have been somewhat sheltered from the "spillover" effects of world crises (the 1980s debt crisis in Latin America, and the 1990s financial crisis in East Asia), global economic forces have contributed to economic slowdown in much of the North and the decline in the rate of growth of world trade. In the Third World, both global economic problems and the policies that have been implemented to "solve" them have decimated domestic markets. Using current exchange rates, the International Monetary Fund (IMF) estimates the industrial countries' share of world gross domestic product (GDP) to be 73.21 percent and that of the devel-oping countries to be 17.71 percent; using an alternative measure – purchasing-power-parity rates – the shares are 54.44 and 34.38 percent, respectively. The latter approach to measuring inequality between nations has the effect of lessening the appearance of the gap between the incomes of the North and of the South (International Monetary Fund 1993). But the growth of poverty and income inequality *within* Third World nations has all but eliminated the possibility of relying on domestic mass consumption as the impetus for industrialization. The only remaining market for the growth of manufacturing and other industries lies outside the South.

A total of 33 percent of people in developing countries have annual incomes that place them below the average poverty line for such countries ($370 in 1985). The absurdity, as the World Bank (1990, 29) itself has shown, is that it would require a transfer of only 3 percent of total world consumption to these people to lift them all above poverty. An alternative way of looking at the problem is provided in the *Human Development Report 1997* (United Nations Development Programme [UNDP] 1997, 112). According to the UNDP, the price tag for eradicating poverty and providing basic social services in developing countries would be about $80 billion, which is less than 0.5 percent of world income or, even more dramatic, less than the combined net worth of the seven richest men in the world. So near, yet so far!

But the freeing up of markets will, if anything, shift assets from the poor to the rich; or, with recent and ongoing privatization efforts, from the state to (some) private hands. As state enterprises are sold to private – both domestic and foreign – investors, the state succeeds in eliminating an important source of fiscal deficits and in filling, on a one-off basis, state coffers, while wealthy individuals and corporations acquire assets for much less than it would cost them to build them up over time. According to the International Labour Office (1995), the proceeds from sales of state-owned enterprises in developing countries rose from just over $2 billion in 1988 to almost $20 billion in 1992.

The reorganization of the newly privatized enterprises involves, in many cases, the loss of labor rights (such as tenure in the company, strike and association rights, retirement and health benefits and the like) and the laying-off of employees (often under the auspices of "early retirement" and "voluntary departures" with severance pay) (Petrazzini 1996). According to a World Bank sample of the sale of state-owned enterprises in Africa (White and Bhatia 1998), employment in those enterprises fell by 15 percent from the date of privatization (between 1986 and 1995) to early 1996.

Such displaced workers are then "freed" to join the ranks of the reserve army, or (as it is now referred to in development circles) the "informal sector." Employment statistics for such people, precisely by virtue of the "informality" of the sector (including the fact that many units have very few employees and a large number are illegal or not officially recognized), are notoriously unreliable. However, the magnitude of the informal sector is quite clear. For example, according to the International Labour Office

(1997), of the 15.7 million new jobs created in Latin America between 1990 and 1994, 8.4 out of 10 were in the informal sector. In Asia, the informal sector absorbs 40 to 50 percent of the labor force, rising to 80 percent in countries such as Bangladesh. And, in Africa, the urban informal sector employs 61 percent of the urban labor force and is expected to account for 93 percent of all additional jobs in the region in the 1990s. And, since the public sector has been the major formal sector employer of women in many Third World countries, the loss of jobs associated with privatization and the contraction of the state has had a disproportionate effect on women. Given the low incomes that accompany work in this sector, the result is to further shrink that part of the domestic market devoted to mass consumption.

What lies ahead? Seeking development that develops hope

What, then, are the prospects for Third World industrialization? The other side of declining real wages and impoverished informal sector incomes is the growth of profits: both those that are retained by the enterprises and those that are distributed to company officials, bribed politicians, and investors in the rejuvenated or newly created stock exchanges. These profits are, of course, a source of demand, but rarely for the products of domestic industry. Instead, they are used either to employ personal servants (to cook, clean, or stand guard) or to import equipment and luxury goods from abroad. Wage-earners and those in the informal sector are, in turn, reduced to participating in mass consumption via television commercials – or actually purchasing goods in the cottage industries of the informal sector and food from the countryside. The only market for industrialization that remains is the international one.

Not surprisingly, the prophets of the "new competition" are waiting on the doorstep, with their slide shows illustrating new forms of organization and slick speeches about "flexible specialization" and the importance of CAD/CAM (computer-aided design/computer-aided manufacturing) and CNC (computer numerically controlled). There is no shortage of "experts" to advise enterprises about the best way to break into world markets, and academic treatises on industrial competitiveness are also plentiful (e.g., Best 1990, Lazonick and Mass 1995, and Lazonick *et al.* 1997). Some enterprises will, in fact, become successful exporters on the basis of such approaches – but mostly in countries where industrialization and the technical and social infrastructure have already reached a high degree of sophistication. For the rest, low-cost (low-wage, assembly) production is the only "arbitrary" advantage that can serve as a platform for export-oriented industrialization.

The fact is that, while some industries will be destroyed by import competition and others will never get off the ground, facing competition from low-wage *maquiladoras* and high-tech "growth poles," Third World

industrialization will continue to proceed apace. Not long ago, this development took place within the "hothouse" for industry created by protectionist barriers, government ownership, and more state forms of
capitalism. Now, the preferred model is that of free markets and more
private forms of capitalism. The question here is not whether such strategies can be successful but, instead, what are their effects, and is there a
better way?

The economic and social punishment meted out in the name of industrialization has been well-documented. There is the devastation of the
rainforests and other ecological disasters, women and children toiling in
multinational sweatshops, and men waiting in the parking lot for the poor
in Third World cities. It is increasingly difficult to argue that more industrialization is better than less – at least if it is the same sort of industrialization that has taken place in the past and that continues to be proffered as
the only possibility today.

But are there any alternatives? The first step in the direction of formulating a different way of organizing economic and social life is to challenge
the limits within which current economic thinking is confined. For
example, introducing class into the analysis of industrialization disrupts
the limits imposed by forms of economic discourse that move back and
forth between structures and human nature, between governments and
markets. Elsewhere (see Chapters 8 and 9 of this volume), I carry out such
a class analysis of external debt and macroeconomic stabilization and
adjustment policies in the Third World. The goal is to identify the various
ways in which the surplus labor of workers (their total labor minus the
necessary labor they receive in the form of products or money for their
continued existence) is, first, appropriated by nonworkers (capitalists as
well as feudal lords, slaveowners, and others) and, then, distributed to still
other groups (such as merchants, bankers, and the state) in the wider
society. The pattern of such surplus appropriations and distributions – not
the relative amount of government intervention and free markets – is what
makes up the class structure of any given society (see Resnick and Wolff
1987a and Gibson-Graham 1996 for general introductions to Marxian class
analysis).

This approach allows us to "see" the existence of exploitation in both
state-led and private-market forms of capitalist industrialization – and, of
course, to begin to imagine alternatives to that exploitation. And, when
class is brought in, it is necessary to carry out the investigation at all social
sites: not only in offices and factories, but also in other areas of social life,
such as the informal sector and households (see Fraad *et al.* 1994). Only on
this basis can we begin to recognize the (often unpaid) labor of women
and, even more important, the radical class restructuring within both the
informal sector and households, which is currently taking place as a result
of the process of Third World industrialization. It is in precisely such
sectors that the injuries meted out by capitalist industry are experienced

and, at the same time, that innovative, noncapitalist forms of production are being created.

Creative new approaches can challenge the limits within which economic policy is currently confined. For example, George DeMartino (1996) has suggested an emphasis on *competition-reducing* rather than *competitiveness-enhancing* approaches to trade and development. And much of economic and social life can be taken out of competition altogether. Rather than being structured according to the dictates of capitalist competition, whether foreign or domestic, areas as diverse as health care, housing finance, and manufacturing production can be reorganized as noncapitalist – either cooperative or community – activities. Or, on a national level, a tariff structure can be devised to govern the terms of trade between countries on the basis of various criteria of social welfare, such as human rights, environmental protection, and so forth, as proposed by DeMartino and Cullenberg (1994b) and DeMartino (2000).

Simply put, the time has come to break out of the pendulum swing between government intervention and free markets, to recognize the alien power that is created by both state-centered and market-oriented forms of industrialization and to leave them behind. They promise little success and, even when partial successes are achieved, the economic and social costs are too high. Instead of accepting the existing goals of industrialization and development, and the strategies presented by mainstream economists and policymakers to get there, we need to move beyond them, to begin to imagine and to create the conditions for alternative, communal, and collective forms of production – in agriculture and services, as well as industry.

(original version published in 2000)

Acknowledgements

An earlier version of this chapter was commissioned by the Italian journal *A Sinistra*, and appeared in the March 1993 issue. I would like to thank Ric McIntyre for helpful comments and, especially, Dawn Saunders for her encouragement to make the appropriate revisions for the URPE reader, *Political Economy and Contemporary Capitalism: Radical Perspectives on Economic Theory and Policy*.

11 "After" development: Reimagining economy and class

(with J. K. Gibson-Graham)

The postdevelopment project pioneered by Arturo Escobar and others represents a rich new source of ideas for radically transforming concepts and practices of development. Within this "antidevelopment" approach, the condition of the "Third World" – its underdevelopment as well as its need for development – is understood to be, in part, a product of the representations and knowledges deployed by the development profession as it emerged during the post-World War II period.[1] One of the primary goals of postdevelopment theory is to negotiate alternatives to development, to conceive and bring into existence new forms of economy and society within the Third World. To achieve this goal, theorists fix their attention on local cultural practices and models of social organization, especially those associated with new social movements (Escobar and Alvarez 1992).

In this chapter, we want to build on the pathbreaking contribution that postdevelopment theory has made to rethinking development. Our collaboration with this project begins, however, with the critical observation that the strategies used thus far to unmake the Third World and negotiate alternatives to development are weakened by the power still granted by postdevelopment theorists to "the economy."

Most postdevelopment theory attributes to the global capitalist system a naturalized role as the preeminent and self-regulating essence of development. Development is seen to have been created and disseminated as the discourse of capitalism, and global capitalism is the system of power against which local communities and new social movements are struggling:

> Local communities bring their material and cultural resources to bear in their encounter with development and modernity. The persistence of local and hybrid models of the economy, for instance, reflects cultural contestations that take place as capital attempts to transform the life of communities.
>
> (Escobar 1995, 99)

Despite recognition that "a universal model of the economy [has] to be abandoned" (1995, 97) and that "in rethinking development from the perspective of the economy . . . [there is a need] to make explicit the existence of a plurality of models of the economy" (1995, 98), in the work of Escobar and others, repeated references to "global capital," "global systems of economic, cultural and political production," and "capitalist megamachines" constitute an economic hegemony that cannot easily be dislodged. Local cultural formations are represented as only ever mediating the effects of external global forms of capital without, in turn, having any impact on capitalism itself (except in the cases where weak instances of noncapitalism serve to feed the voracious appetite of an expansive, powerful capitalism).

The discursive constitution of capitalist hegemony is so common in left approaches to, and criticisms of, development that its negative implications are often overlooked. What, we might ask, are some of the effects of allowing the "global capitalist economy" to escape the deconstructive techniques that postdevelopment theorists have so effectively turned on development? We want to suggest that one effect of this ubiquitous capitalist centering is to constrain the possibility of imagining – and bringing into existence – alternatives to development, including noncapitalist forms of economy. Another effect of this positioning is to understand noncapitalist economic formations (where such forms can already be seen to exist), not only as inherently unviable, but also as cultural practices or resistances that lack sufficient economic potential for development.

We propose to utilize an antiessentialist form of class analysis to reclaim some of the ground ceded to the capitalist economy and to dislodge the central role played by capitalism in conceptions of development. The approach to class analysis outlined here identifies a range of forms in which surplus labor is appropriated and distributed in a multiplicity of class processes that can be seen to constitute social structures and identities within Third World countries. By respecifying the relationship between multiple noncapitalist class processes and instances of capitalist class relations, we hope to contribute to a rethinking of the economy and to strategies for empowering different knowledges and practices "after" development.

Postdevelopment

The work of Escobar (1995, building on 1984 and 1992) is perhaps the best-known example of what has become a wide-ranging critique of Third World development as it has been understood and practiced throughout the postwar period.[2] This critique is a powerful discursive intervention, aimed at defamiliarizing the terms within which development has traditionally been construed. Its effect is to create the conditions for a relation to the economic and social practices of development that is radically different from that posited both by existing development practitioners and many left critics. In particular, it calls into question the idea that "development is always the cure, never the cause" (Crush 1995, 10) of the misery and inequality, authoritarian regimes and civil strife, ecological devastation and social deprivation that are visible in much of the Third World today.

The novelty of this critique of development stems from its appropriation of the work of Michel Foucault, its reading of Edward Said's "orientalism," and its use, more generally, of postmodern and poststructuralist modes of analysis to bracket (and thereby denaturalize) the terms in which development and underdevelopment have been conceived. The basic argument is that development, especially as it emerged in the postwar period, can be recognized as a discourse, a historically produced cultural and institutional space, within which both the problem of underdevelopment and its supposed solution – the enacting of Western-style development – were elaborated. Rather than seeing underdevelopment as an original state characterizing the countries of the Third World, to which the panoply of development projects and assistance offered by international agencies were the necessary response, Escobar and others view development as a way of producing a specific kind of knowledge of the Third World – literally creating (theoretically and socially) the condition of underdevelopment to which it alone offered the answer.

Development discourse arose out of the material conditions of post-World War II reconstruction in Western Europe, Asia, Africa, and Latin America, dominated as they were by the growing economic and political supremacy of the United States and the discursive positioning of economics as the preeminent form of social knowledge in the West (Arndt 1987, Oman and Wignaraja 1991, and Escobar 1995). As a response to socialist initiatives in the "old world" and postcolonial or anticolonial movements in the previously colonized areas of the "new world," it constituted the so-called Third World as a Cold War battleground where the future of capitalism and modern society was to be decided.

As a system of representations, development discourse served to universalize and homogenize Third World cultures, creating the possibility of subjecting developing countries to economic, cultural, and political transformations, offered in the name of eradicating underdevelopment and ushering them onto the path of development. The professionalization of development and the emergence of an array of development institutions (including universities, national and multilateral granting and lending agencies, specialized think tanks, and nongovernmental organizations) created a veritable army of development specialists (theorists as well as practitioners) who have defined the "symptoms" and "causes" of underdevelopment and devised the means to eradicate them. In this manner, power is exercised among and over the peoples of the Third World, not so much through repression (although that, too, has been present as the histories of Latin America, Asia, and Africa clearly show),

but through normalizing the condition of underdevelopment and naturalizing the need for development.

Development has produced forms of subjectivity through which people
have come to recognize themselves and others as developed or underdeveloped. It has portrayed and brought into being "abnormal" subjects,
such as the illiterate, the malnourished, small farmers, and landless peasants, who need to be "reformed" for development to "take off." It has
constituted what it means to be a villager, a Third World woman, a
member of the informal sector – the various others who populate the landscape of underdevelopment and in whose name development projects
have been formulated and carried out. The collective subjectivity and
sociospatial domain of the Third World – defined by overpopulation, the
threat of famine, and widespread illiteracy, to name but a few of the prevalent images – have been fabricated in the name of development.

Development was fashioned and disseminated as the only force capable
of destroying the archaic relations, institutions, and superstitions that
stood in the way of modernization. Codified most notably in development
economics, the project of development was centered on the economy (as
a distinct social space) and driven preeminently by capitalist industrialization.

It is, perhaps, not surprising that the postdevelopment critique has led
to a call for alternative regimes of representation and practice, discourses
and modes of intervention that both challenge and exceed the terms
imposed by the development/underdevelopment dyad. These alternatives can be recognized in the local knowledges and social movements
that have been marginalized in the name of development and that
are being foregrounded and fostered as it becomes possible to "marginalize the economy" and to imagine the "end of development" (Sachs
1992).

Clearly the strategy of postdevelopment theory stands in opposition to
mainstream modernization discourse. It also differs in important ways
from inherited left critiques of modernization. The unique focus on
discourse and the very different strategic alternatives it offers are telling
reminders of the novelty of this approach. But these distinctive features
should not blind us to some of the similarities between postdevelopment
theory and its others.

Oddly enough, one axis of similarity that links modernization theory,
left theories of dependency and underdevelopment, and postdevelopment approaches to questions of development is the positioning of the
economy within a realist epistemology. By this we mean the presumption
that economic knowledge reflects the true state of a real entity called "the
economy" (generally understood as a locus of capitalist dominance).
While not surprising in the context of modernist theories of development,
whether of the Right (modernization) or Left (dependency/underdevel-
opment) variety, this presumption contradicts the general epistemological

position of the postdevelopment theorists, who see knowledge as constitutive rather than reflective of reality. Such a positioning of the economy, we argue, places severe limitations on rethinking development, allowing the putative dominance of capitalism in the "real" world of the economy to go unquestioned and to continue to define and constrain the development potentialities of other economic and social practices.

"The economy" and discourses of development

The advocates of modernization, their left critics, and those who argue in favor of moving beyond development put forward quite different ways of understanding development as well as alternative strategies for achieving it. While we want to keep these differences in mind, so as to highlight the challenge that postdevelopment thinkers pose to the other two theoretical traditions, we also wish to explore the similar ways in which the economy is constituted in these related literatures.

In modernization theory, capitalist economic growth represents the necessary solution to underdevelopment. The particular strategies advocated for promoting capitalist growth have changed over the course of the postwar period: where, once, capitalist development was predicated on state intervention and aid transfers, now it is based on the freeing up of domestic markets and extensive integration into world markets. Capitalist development is seen to be preceded by backward, primitive, and – during the transition to development – dual forms of economy and society. Definitions of the dual economy have, however, changed over time, with "backwardness" originally conceived in terms of the predominance of agriculture and rural life, and associated today with protected markets and urban corruption. The role of the "informal" sector in the development process has similarly changed; once the target of active elimination, it is now seen as the seedbed of microenterprises that will be the building blocks of a fully developed capitalist economy (Lubell 1991). Despite slight changes in orientation and strategy, the modernization school positions the capitalist economy as the only viable and, ultimately, developmental form of economy.

In contrast, for much of the Left, the capitalist economy is the problem rather than the solution. The international spread of capitalism inaugurated the "development of underdevelopment." Until they were drawn into and subjected to the maelstrom of the capitalist world economy, a variety of precapitalist modes of production represented autonomous forms of development (Frank 1969 and Chapter 6 of this volume). It was the process of capitalist development itself that blocked or distorted this autonomous development trajectory. Thus, for development to occur, it is necessary to break from capitalism and to construct socialism.

The economy, as mapped by dependency and underdevelopment theories, is represented as either structured by duality or by an articulation of different modes of production. The international capitalist sector is seen as unevenly linked to remnant fragments of a feudal sector and a sector of independent commodity producers in the rural economy, and to a comprador capitalist sector and petty bourgeois sector in the urban economy. In the light of this representation of a diversified economy, left theorists (certain of the heightened power of the capitalist economy) have highlighted the impossibility of even development and have turned their attention to the unequal distributional consequences of the articulation of different sectors with a hegemonic capitalism.

Like left development theory, postdevelopment theory is critical of capitalism in the sense that development – which has served to colonize reality, to circumscribe local cultural constructions, to break down local communities and expose them to the vicissitudes of the global economy – has done so in the name of capitalism. The postdevelopment theorists call for a "semiotic resistance" to all discourses within which (under)development and the economy have become privileged terms of reference. Their project requires the creation or recognition of a world of difference, populated with a diversity of local economic practices and cultural constructions, a space whose identity is not fixed and singular but open and heterogeneous. This is a major contribution to the task of deconstructing the identity and fullness of existing development models, challenging their definitional closure, apprehending – and intervening to promote – alternatives to development.

But the critique of economic monism and the proliferation of antidevelopment possibilities, which we recognize in the work of Escobar and other postdevelopment thinkers, is constrained by the terms in which the concept of capitalism is invoked. Semiotic resistance eventually comes up against the hard realities of global capital and, in this confrontation, the cultural and social identities of local organizations may be seen to be insufficient to the task of true resistance:

> Global capital . . . relies today not so much on homogenization of an exterior Third World as on its ability to consolidate diverse, heterogeneous social forms . . . The global economy must . . . be understood as a decentered system with manifold apparatuses of capture – symbolic, economic, political.
>
> (Escobar 1995, 99)

> Some of these (new social) movements in structure and character strike me as populist . . . and hence as part of a long lineage within modernity itself, which raises the question . . . of their relation to class and forces of co-optation . . . At the very least there is a need for careful analyses of the relations between new social movements and the hegemonic class forces of capitalism.
>
> (Watts 1993, 268)

A powerful notion of capitalist hegemony situates capitalism at the center of development, thus limiting or closing off economic and social alternatives.

For traditional modernization and left approaches to development, the capitalist economy is an extra-discursive reality – something that can be cultivated wherever underdevelopment is found, or something that dominates and actively restricts the autonomy of other economic forms. For postdevelopment theory, the global capitalist economy is similarly positioned as somehow extra-discursive – something that contains and captures heterogeneous local practices and operates outside and beyond the forces of deconstruction. Since capitalism exists as the "real," it is not subject to destabilization in the play of intertextuality, as with other terms in the development discourse. It appears in postdevelopment theory as an ontological given, disproportionately powerful by virtue of its indisputable reality in a world of multivalent concepts, shifting discursive practices and unstable meanings.[3]

While the theorists of postdevelopment successfully shift our attention to local differences, movements, and forms of resistance, these turn out to be the weaker "other" to the dominant structure and larger force of capitalist development. The effect is to maintain capitalism as the central referent of development and indeed of what comes "after" development. This narrows the gap that separates the postdevelopment approach from the other two. Rather than representing the economy as a radically heterogeneous social space, postdevelopment critics reinforce the discursive hegemony of capitalism and thereby tend to marginalize the very alternative economic practices they seek to promote.

Capitalocentrism and its effects

It is not too far-fetched to say that development, in all three approaches, is governed by capitalism in the same way that writing is dominated by logos, gender and sex by the phallus, and exchange by money, in their respective discursive domains. In each case, difference and incommensurability are ultimately defined by and subsumed within the sphere of an apparently self-sufficient master term. Development discourse, including traditional, left, and postdevelopment approaches, is unified by capitalocentrism, in the sense that each of these three otherwise different approaches to development operates with a similarly centered and centering notion of capitalism.

Building on a feminist definition of phallocentrism (Grosz 1990), we identify capitalocentrism wherever noncapitalism is seen as either: (a) the same as, (b) the opposite of(c) the complement to, or (d) located inside capitalism itself (Gibson-Graham 1996).[4] We want to ask how a capitalocentric vision of the economy weakens or limits a radical rethinking of development. In what follows, we explore each type of capital-centering and the effects it has had on our conception of Third World economies.

Noncapitalist forms of economy and social life are frequently considered to be the *same* as or indistinguishable from capitalism.[5] Thus, independent commodity producers who have effective possession of (by owning or renting) the means of production, who appropriate and distribute their own surplus, and who buy and sell commodities on markets, are often considered to be either the same as capitalists, or the same as proletarians. It is mainly the market that is seen to homogenize different economic practices, binding them within the dense and expanding web of capitalism. Neoclassical economists, for example, are likely to view small coffee-growers in Central America or independent rice-growers in the Gambia as profit-maximizing economic agents, responding like capitalist enterprises to price (Schultz 1964 and Bliss and Stern 1982). Critics of orthodox development theory and policy might understand their behavior as obeying the same logic, albeit under different constraints (Bardhan 1984 and Basu 1990). At other times, left analysts see the force of the "capitalist" market as reducing such producers to the status of de facto proletarians, forced to intensify their labor on their plots to meet quotas imposed by marketing authorities (Pred and Watts 1992, 82).

The role of the market in rendering these producers the "same" as capitalists/workers is seen again in the case of the petty commodity producers of the urban informal sector. Because they operate in markets that, in the end, are seen to be tied into and governed by global capitalism, they become subsumed by the laws and identities of the capitalist sector. Most recently, this sector has been the subject of development initiatives to promote existing microenterprises under the assumption that entrepreneurship and capitalism are synonymous (Lubell 1991). The result in all these cases is that the specificities and differences of capitalism and noncapitalism are elided in favor of capitalism.

Noncapitalist practices are also often portrayed as being the *opposite* of capitalism as, for example, when they are seen to be primitive or traditional, stagnant, marginal, residual, about to be extinguished, or weak. Communal or tribal practices of hunting and gathering, craft activities, or indigenous agricultural production involving the production of use-values that are not commodified and/or of commodities that are not designed to garner profits in the market are viewed as incapable of growth and development in their own right (de Janvry 1981 and Sender and Smith 1986). Despite their resilience and viability over centuries of practice, these noncapitalist activities become the negative image of capitalism, which is characterized as dynamic, powerful, and endowed with the capacity for infinite expansion. Modernizers attribute to traditional activities the condition of backwardness – they must be eliminated or transformed so that development can take place – while left critics and the advocates of

postdevelopment may see them as signs of underdevelopment or of inef-
fectual resistance to development (since the development of global capitalism more or less inevitably constrains, undermines, and, eventually,
eliminates them). Here, a hierarchy is established between a vigorous,
effective capitalism and its passive and insubstantial noncapitalist other.

When noncapitalism is analyzed in terms of its articulation with capitalism, it is often understood to play a *complementary* role. This is the case,
for example, when rural activities are seen as providing the conditions of
existence of capitalist activity elsewhere. In the "articulation of modes of
production" approach, the relationship between capitalism and noncapitalism is conceived to be governed by the laws and needs of the capitalist
mode of production (see Wolpe 1980a and Chapter 6 of this volume). Rural
noncapitalism is cast in the role of providing underutilized savings and
labor for promoting capitalist industrialization, cheap means of production and wage goods, a reserve army of labor that serves to keep the value
of labor power lower than it otherwise might be, thereby creating the
conditions for an unequal exchange to take place between center and
periphery. In the literature on unequal exchange (e.g., Emmanuel 1972 and
Amin 1977), noncapitalism is relegated to the margins of the world of capitalist exchanges: Either noncapitalist forms of production disappear from
view or they serve merely to satisfy the conditions of existence of peripheral capitalism, such that the set of international commodity exchanges
leads to a net transfer of value from the hybrid (capitalist and noncapitalist) periphery to what is considered to be the fully capitalist center.
Noncapitalism only persists, therefore, in the local, heterogeneous sites in
and through which global capitalism is continually invigorated and reinvented.[6] Here, noncapitalism derives both its trajectory and its raison
d'être from serving the needs of capitalist development.

Finally, noncapitalism occupies a position *inside* capitalism to the extent
that it exists within a container called the capitalist world economy. While
there may be islands of noncapitalism – say, in grassroots producer cooperatives, local development efforts, alternative "intentional" economies,
and community initiatives – they have no independent, self-governing,
unfettered existence. They often are seen as remnants of another era (prior
to the rise of capitalism), unable to expand their reproduction, destined to
fill the small spaces that capitalism has not yet saturated with its own
economic practices and structures of meaning. Although not the same as
capitalism, the fragments of noncapitalism that persist are isolated,
perhaps experimental, elements of a landscape that is otherwise governed
by the laws of capitalist development.

It seems that capitalism has become such a powerful and centering
presence that it would take a superhuman effort to imagine, let alone
fashion and sustain, viable noncapitalist practices and institutions with
their own identities, energies, and trajectories. It is here that our more
modest intervention may have some value. We want to suggest an alterna-

tive conception of class that can help to render instances of capitalism smaller, more fragmented, and dispersed, and, thereby, liberate an economy of difference and divergence. Our aim is to produce a new economic knowledge of development that reshapes the discursive relationship between noncapitalist and capitalist economic practices. This project of using class to negotiate the paths beyond development is not unlike that of the postdevelopment critics. We, too, are interested in modifying political economies through semiotic resistance for the purpose of making other models visible. By producing the discursive conditions for a different relation to economic practices, we hope to foster new relations to the economy and to development more generally. A reinvented language of class can be an important part of this project.

Class processes and development stories

We define class, quite simply and minimally, in terms of the processes of producing, appropriating, and distributing surplus labor (Resnick and Wolff 1987b). The distinctiveness of different class processes emerges as they are particularized or concretized in a variety of social and discursive settings.[7] Some of the most familiar are the feudal, independent or ancient, communal, slave, and, of course, capitalist class processes. In each process, surplus labor is appropriated in a particular form (for example, as surplus-value or as feudal rents) and the distribution of appropriated surplus labor is conducted in particular ways (via contracted payments, gifts, intergenerational allocations, and so on).

To define class as a process is to shift the focus away from subjects and social groups – "class" as a noun – and toward certain practices and flows of labor in which subjects variously and multiply participate – "class" as an adjective. This approach unyokes property relations, power relations, and organizational capacities from the definition of class, allowing these determinants to interact interdependently with the processes by which the production, appropriation, and distribution of surplus labor takes place. So, for example, a communal class process in which surplus labor is collectively produced may also be one in which the distinction between necessary and surplus labor is communally agreed on and the destination of distributions of appropriated surplus labor collectively determined. But such "communism" might take place in very different contexts – of private or communally owned property, of equalized or uneven power relations, within highly politicized or distinctly apolitical organizations. In each situation the practice of a communal class process will be uniquely over-determined, as will the constitution of communal class subjects. This anti-essentialist perspective on class enables the envisioning of a diverse economic landscape in which noncapitalist class processes are liberated from the law of the capitalist "father" and economic subjects are always in the process of becoming.

A conception of class as a process differs markedly from the notion of class as a social grouping defined in terms of an amalgam of income-generating capacity, property, power, or organizational capacities. This latter categorical conception of class locates its members in terms of mutually exclusive positions in a stable structure, or in terms of a process of class formation whereby groups with common interests are seen to emerge in tandem with structural transitions. It is this conception of class that has largely been employed within discourses of development.

Given that class is, in this view, primarily bestowed by location in an economic structure, and this structure is, in turn, dominated by capitalism (or a capitalist mode of production), it is not surprising that, as a conceptual tool, the categorical notion of class has not been able to break away from capitalocentric visions. Thus, Third World societies undergoing transition are seen as producing a new proletariat or a new capitalist class or, most recently, a new "middle" class,[8] and these social mappings serve to reinforce the hegemony of an existing or emerging capitalist economic order.

We want to deploy our language of class in a project of undermining capitalocentrism and unmaking the global capitalist economy as a discursively hegemonic entity. In the remainder of this essay, we pursue a number of different strategies toward this end. One is to recognize class diversity and the specificity of economic practices that coexist in the Third World and to show how modernization interventions have, themselves, created a variety of noncapitalist (as well as capitalist) class processes, thereby adding to the diversity of the economic landscape rather than reducing it to homogeneity. This is a discursive strategy aimed at rereading the economy outside the hold of capitalocentrism.

The second strategy opens up the economy to new possibilities by theorizing a range of different and potential connections between class processes. It sketches an imagined political project that can perhaps articulate with the actions of the new social movements identified by post-development theory that are creating new subjectivities and forging new economic and social futures.

Strategy I: reading against capitalocentrism

The process of modernization and the development of global capitalism – including, to use Escobar's language, the "making of the Third World" – are represented as involving the creation of a hierarchically structured and predominantly capitalist landscape of developed and developing countries, with some nations designated more, and others less, developed. Our new mapping seeks to disrupt and reconfigure this ordered landscape by representing a terrain of latent diversity and disorder that can be described in class terms.

We start with all the premodern forms of economic and social organization that the project of modernization was supposed to have eliminated or transformed into capitalism – for example, feudal (e.g., plantation), independent, and communal forms of agricultural production. For many left critics of modernization, the demise of these forms of production is assumed to have occurred through the, more or less inexorable, "original accumulation of capital" or, for the postdevelopment theorists, the rise to dominance of global capital.[9] But, if we shift our focus from these teleological narratives, we might observe that the so-called destruction of these forms has often created the conditions for the emergence and reproduction of new noncapitalist forms of surplus-labor appropriation, perhaps alongside (but never subsumed by) both local and global instances of capitalism.

Michael Watts's fascinating study of contract agricultural labor in the Gambia focuses on changes in production relations prompted by the introduction of a state-sponsored rice irrigation project (Pred and Watts 1992). His study provides an excellent illustration of how a project of modernization destroyed one set of differentiated class processes, only to replace them with another. Household production in the local Mandinka society was traditionally based on the cultivation of both individual fields and collectively owned familial property and, under customary law, the rights of ownership and distribution of the crop produced on each type of property were different. The product of labor performed on collectively owned land was communally appropriated, but controlled and distributed by the senior male in the household, while the product of labor performed on individual land was appropriated individually. In the terms of our class analysis, we have here two different class processes with different conditions of existence: a communal class process in which the distributive moment is controlled by the patriarch (we could call it a patriarchal communal class process), and a self-appropriating class process in which each producer appropriates and distributes his or her own surplus.

Prior to the introduction of the irrigation project, rice production was women's work and was concentrated on swampland owned by women by individual right. With the introduction of the rice irrigation project and the movement of men into contract rice production for the global market, this complex of property relations and mix of household class processes was altered.[10] The sequestering of land to the project and associated rearrangement of property rights meant that women's access to their traditional land and to a self-appropriating class process was largely destroyed.

One response made by women who had been rendered landless was to join together with other similarly dispossessed women to sell their labor power. Drawing on traditional organizational practices and "customary social relations as a basis of recruitment" (Pred and Watts 1992, 96), women formed groups of similar age to work in gangs in the rice paddies. The labor teams (*kafo*) utilized reciprocal labor practices and negotiated a collective wage that was distributed equally among the members. In effect, the women swapped a self-appropriating class process for a capitalist class process in which they sold their labor power to the growers. As members of a team of "proletarian gang labor" (1992, 96), the women are exploited but powerful, in the sense that the growers are entirely dependent on them. We could see here one of the contradictory effects of state intervention into rice production as enabling the establishment of a women's capitalist class process in which their produced surplus was partially distributed back to them (in the form of a wage premium) because of their bargaining power.

The men, on the other hand, were operating in two class processes: as independent self-appropriating rice producers, and as capitalists extracting surplus-value from the women's *kafo*. Despite their independent and capitalist class positions, the men retained little surplus once the women's wage premium and state costs were met. This new articulation of class processes was overdetermined by a multiplicity of determinants and conditions of existence and had, as one of its effects, the exacerbation of struggles between men and women in Mandinka society.[11]

Reading for class outside of a capitalocentric discourse releases us from the imperative to homogenize the experience of men and women and see them as members of an emerging global proletariat (Pred and Watts 1992, 96).[12] The representation of class diversity in any one place or individual becomes possible only if we distinguish relations of power (whether exercised directly over the labor process or indirectly via financing and exchange) from relations of property, exploitation, and organizational capacity and, in so doing, open up the linkages between these different sets of relations to examination. Then we can recognize the range of labor practices and class processes (communal, self-appropriating, capitalist), the various class and nonclass identities, the different kinds of power struggles and their loci – between men and women in households and in their different class practices within communities, between producers and the state in commodity and finance markets – that make up the economic landscape.

Even if we focus on the emergence of capitalist class processes associated with successful projects of modernization, this need not mean that the class landscape becomes uniformly capitalist. When we broaden our view to consider social sites other than farms, factories, streets, and offices – the formal sites of modernization or the public economy – we find evidence, in households and community structures, of class changes that are not simply governed by, or reducible to, capitalism. Rather than reading households and communities simply as sites of capitalist reproduction, our anticapitalocentric reading makes visible the variety of noncapitalist class processes in the households of workers employed in capitalist industry (Gibson-Graham 1996).

Much attention has been paid to the participation of Third World women in capitalist wage employment and their *proletarianization* in export-processing zones or *maquiladora* border industries. Commentators point to the patriarchal nature of this kind of capitalist development, emphasizing the ways in which new spatial and gendered divisions of labor are dominated by the twin and codependent logics of capitalist exploitation and patriarchal oppression (e.g., Nash and Fernandez-Kelly 1983). There is, however, a growing number of studies that highlight how these changes are precipitating what we would read as new class relations in the household sector (Cravey 1997, Phongpaichit 1988, and Strauch 1984).

Women who, in the global factories, participate in capitalist forms of surplus-labor appropriation engage in many practices of resistance and transformation, not only in the sites of their formal sector employment (Ong 1987 and Porpora *et al.* 1989), but also in their households and communities. Thus, we find that these wage-laborers are often able to disrupt the existing exploitation practices of their parents, husbands, in-laws, or community elders, in some cases enacting the formation of independent or communal class processes at home or in the communities in which they live. Altha Cravey (1997) describes the reshaping of Mexican households and the increased contribution of men to domestic labor associated with the factories established most recently along the United States–Mexico border. In class terms, these households may be experiencing a transition, from a class process in which a man appropriates surplus labor from his female partner (in what we can call a domestic feudal class process), to a more communal class process in which surplus labor is jointly produced and appropriated. In the process, gender relations are being renegotiated in ways that have interesting effects on class politics at the factory. In this sense, the development of capitalism in some social sites – successful modernization, by most accounts – is accompanied by the development of new forms of noncapitalism in other social locations.

Reading the economic landscape outside of a capitalocentric discourse allows us to see sites of economic invention woven into the very fabric of a so-called newly emerging capitalist society. This reading also enables us to situate subjects in a variety of class subject positions. No longer are we tempted to position a young woman worker in an export-processing-zone factory only as a proletarian (with all the expectations of a workerist subjectivity that accompany this designation). She can now be seen to occupy a class position within a domestic class process, and perhaps another class position within a more extended or distant family-based class process. Her political subjectivity will be overdetermined by these multiple class positions, as well as a range of other social, cultural, and physical relations. The complex picture of economy and subjectivity that emerges from an anticapitalocentric reading opens the way even further for imagining different forms of noncapitalist politics.

Strategy 2: economic politics "after" capitalocentrism

A new class mapping of the economic and social landscape of modernization both disrupts and poses an alternative to existing capitalocentric
discourses of development. The economy is seen to be different from itself
– made up of multiple class processes and decentered economic subjects,
who negotiate markets, commodification, investment flows, and enterprises in a variety of nondeterministic ways. Outside of a colonizing capitalocentric discourse, the economic realm can be represented as a site, not
only of limits and constraints, but also of freedoms and openings, where
transformations and capture are not always into and by capitalism. This
vision of a new economic terrain suggests a range of imaginative possibilities for enacting noncapitalist class politics and bringing into being an
even more diversified economy.

In our class reading against capitalocentrism, we identified noncapitalist class processes and illustrated instances of their continual creation in
and alongside projects of modernization in the Third World. An anticapitalocentric reading can also be turned on capitalist class processes to illustrate their decentered and overdetermined nature. Destabilizing the
capitalist identity and breaking apart the association of markets, commodities, money, and the enterprise with capitalism creates openings for
noncapitalism to emerge. To conclude this essay, we explore one actual
and one imaginary intervention that are enabled when commodities,
markets, money, and the enterprise are liberated from capitalocentric
discourse.

Many of the projects of the Singapore-based nongovernmental organization ENGENDER are aimed at preserving and revaluing the traditional
craft skills and indigenous knowledges (especially those of women) of
endangered communities in Asia and the Pacific.[13] These communities are
still largely sustained by noncapitalist class processes in which surplus
labor is produced, appropriated, and distributed either individually or
collectively. One of ENGENDER'S projects involves establishing a Gender
and Development Resources Bank, a "multinational corporation of the
poor," in which a wealth of survival skills and environmental knowledges
are deposited and translated into market values that can generate earnings for women in rural and indigenous communities. Working with
community-based researchers in Bangladesh, Kathmandu, Thailand,
Malaysia, Singapore, and Indonesia, ENGENDER and associated NGOs
are helping to document knowledges and practices that are fast being
destroyed, replaced, or stolen. This documentation process represents an
intervention to protect a crucial condition for the continued existence of
noncapitalist livelihoods. It articulates with another important project that
involves building economic relationships between women's craft collec-
tives and transnational corporations by "capturing space in existing
markets for products and services derived from [women's] indigenous

skills and knowledges" (ENGENDER 1996, 19). With the help of ENGENDER, GAIA Crafts, for example, has established a market niche by tapping into the internal markets of a large tourist industry and computer corporations in the vicinity of producer communities and supplying locally made products such as soaps, printed cloth, and woven tote bags as substitutes for imported goods. The aim is to develop links between rural craft producers and global commercial markets that incorporate the poor "as partners in production" (ENGENDER 1995, 10) and that foster a different form of "socio-cultural interfacing" between local and multinational capitalist business operations and traditional communities.

By engaging with the global economy in new and innovative ways, ENGENDER has developed an active politics of protection and development of noncapitalist class processes and indigenous lifestyles. This intervention has introduced commodification and money flows into noncapitalist and previously noncommodified class processes. It has engineered an engagement with the global market and contact between transnational corporations and local indigenous communities. But it has turned its own apparatus of capture onto the capitalist corporations. The result has been an income flow into the local community that sustains noncapitalist class processes, protects traditional knowledge, and maintains indigenous technologies. The market is the conduit through which flows of money ensure the sustainability of local lifestyles and a viable noncapitalist economy alongside capitalist industrialization.[14]

The last intervention we want to review is one focused on the internal operations of the capitalist enterprise as a site of generative possibilities for noncapitalist class practices. Our antiessentialist class analysis highlights the importance of the distributive, as well as the exploitative, class process. The distributive class process involves the allocation of appropriated surplus labor (in whatever form) to a range of claimants who, in turn, provide the conditions of existence for continued class appropriation. Within the capitalist enterprise, surplus-value is distributed, for example, to a wide variety of destinations, both inside and outside the enterprise, including investment in capital expansion (accumulation), the payment of supervisory labor, accounting, merchanting, the servicing of debt, state taxes, bribes, and so on. Each constellation of such distributions is the result of competitive tensions and struggles, negotiations and agreements, that take place in and around the firm. Diverse economic and social practices are currently enabled by flows of surplus-value that percolate around and through capitalist enterprises. We are interested in exploring the possibilities of changing the quantitative and qualitative dimensions of those flows and exploring their potential for creating new class practices.

The recognition of stakeholders in capitalist enterprise has recently extended the range of subjects (beyond the traditional grouping of workers, management, and shareholders) ostensibly connected to and interested in corporate practice. Local communities, retrenched workers, traditional landowners, and even residents at some distance from capitalist industrial activities whose environment has been degraded have all asserted claims on corporate funds for compensation or environmental or cultural restitution. In different governmental and legal contexts, these claims have been recognized and distributions of surplus-value redirected accordingly. There is growing international pressure for accepted ethical and environmental standards that will ensure that what were once viewed as irregular or occasional distributive payments become part of the regular enterprise calculus. This suggests that distributions of surplus could potentially be tapped by those interested in establishing noncapitalist economic alternatives.

New alliances – among, for example, indigenous peoples, national and international human rights and green activists, labor organizers, and independent or collective producers using "appropriate" technologies – could emerge to put pressure on and bargain with the directors of the enterprise to divert some of the appropriated surplus-value into a fund to improve the local conditions under which capitalism operates or to support the development of noncapitalist class practices. Such strategies have been pursued in a number of sites. Local communities in the vicinity of large multinationals have made claims, based on arguments from natural right, on the surplus-value circulating within the enterprise and have exacted flows from capitalist firms into their own noncapitalist enterprises. Aborigines in Northern Australia, for example, initiated a project to create a cooperative, sustainable, and renewable resource extraction industry (fish farming) by diverting funds from a transnational mining company undertaking nonrenewable resource extraction on aboriginal land (Howitt 1994a and 1994b). Projects such as this illustrate the way in which diverse alliances (including with capitalist appropriators themselves) might change existing distributions and create new ones, thereby altering the capitalist environment. In such cases, the conditions traditionally associated with capitalism are disrupted and transformed: while relying on (and perhaps even strengthening) the capitalist appropriation of surplus labor, the surplus extracted in that process is directed to noncapitalist activities or their conditions of existence (Gibson-Graham and O'Neill 2001).

What these examples suggest is not only the range of possibilities for developing new class practices and new forms of surplus appropriation and distribution but also the role of class discourse in making such innovations possible. The ability to describe and envision class processes other than capitalist ones is a crucial condition of existence of alternative class possibilities.[15]

Conclusion

Postdevelopment theorists fundamentally question the need for development, arguing in favor of greater autonomy for local social and cultural models. They recognize that predevelopment models of economy persist, albeit in hybrid form, through their "transformative engagement with modernity" (Escobar 1995, 219) and advocate creating conditions conducive to local and regional experiments that do not necessarily conform to a single, overarching development scheme. We have argued that an anti-essentialist class analysis can aid in the project of building new economic futures after development.

A language of class can be used to constitute a landscape of economic difference within which an anticapitalist imaginary can flourish. Outside the (discursively constituted) "hegemonic class forces of capitalism" (Watts 1993, 268) projects of noncapitalist construction might articulate with the political energies of new social movements. Our task has been simply to make noncapitalist class processes and projects more visible and less "unrealistic," as one step toward invigorating an inventive anticapitalocentric economic politics. In this way, we may perhaps contribute to the emergence of a new panorama of community, in which communal relations of surplus appropriation and distribution are centrally involved in projects of economic and social transformation after development.

(original version published in 2001)

Acknowledgements

We want to acknowledge the helpful comments and suggestions made by the participants in the workshop on class analysis that took place at the University of Massachusetts, Amherst, in June 1996. We also want to thank Serap Kayatekin for her contributions to the conversations that preceded the writing of this chapter and Stephen Resnick and Richard Wolff for their thoughtful comments on earlier drafts. Finally, we want to acknowledge our debt to Arturo Escobar, for his work and for the generous way in which he has entered into dialogue with us around the topic of this essay.

Notes

1   In his excellent review of the discursive turn in development studies, Michael Watts (1993) identifies a coherent antidevelopment discourse associated with the work of Escobar (1992), Shiva (1991), Pieterse (1991), Manzo (1991), and Norgaard (1992).

2   Other contributions include Alvares (1994), Banuri (1990a, and 1990b), Beverley and Oviedo (1993), Crush (1995), Dallmayr (1992), Manzo (1991), Marchand and Parpart (1995), Nandy (1987), Rahnema (1997), Sachs (1992), and Slater (1992).

3   This positioning effects an interesting complication of what Althusser identified as economic essentialism:

According to the economistic or mechanistic hypothesis, the role of the essence/phenomena opposition is to explain the non-economic as a phenomenon of the economic, which is its essence. In this operation, the theoretical (and the "abstract") is surreptitiously substituted for the economy (since we have its theory in *Capital*) and the empirical or "concrete" for the non-economic, i.e., for politics, ideology, etc. The essence/phenomena opposition performs this role well enough so long as we regard the "phenomena" as the empirical, and the essence as the non-empirical, as the abstract, as the truth of the phenomena. The result is to set up an absurd relationship between the theoretical (the economic) and the empirical (the non-economic) by a change in partners which compares the knowledge of one object with the existence of another – which is to commit us to a fallacy.

(Althusser and Balibar 1975, 111)

When a realist epistemology is added to the essentialist thinking outlined by Althusser, we see the representation of the economy as both the abstract essence of all things noneconomic and as the true "real."

4 "Whenever women or femininity are conceived in terms of either an identity or sameness with men; or of their opposition or inversion of the masculine; or of a complementarity with men, their representation is phallocentric" (Grosz 1990, 150).

5 Bagchi (1982), for example, tends to see sharecropping and other nominally noncapitalist forms of agricultural production, not as forms of precapitalism (itself another capitalocentric formulation,) but rather of "retarded capitalism."

6 According to this vision, the nature of capitalism is "not to create an homogeneous economic system but rather to dominate and draw profit from the diversity and inequality that remain in permanence" (Berger 1980).

7 For more complete elaborations of the category of class and certain of its forms, see Resnick and Wolff (1987b) and Gibson-Graham (1996).

8 Meanwhile traditional class positions – such as feudal landlord or rural peasant – are seen as declining.

9 See de Janvry (1981) and Harvey (1982) for traditional and teleological interpretations of Marx's discussion of the primitive accumulation of capital.

10 Land for the project was sequestered from collective household property as well as from individual women, and, in addition, was newly cleared by men who argued, drawing on customary law, that this labor conferred ownership on the clearer of land, and that they were now the traditional owners.

11 Women not only withdrew from working on their individual land – which had been taken – but also withdrew their labor from collective household production in order to work in the *kafo*. This resulted in domestic violence and divorce (Pred and Watts 1992, 96).

12 Watts's interest in empirically illustrating the ways in which "capitalism may contribute to the reproduction of nonwage labor" (1992, 105), that is, produce a de facto working class, leads him to produce a capitalocentric analysis that fails, in our eyes, to highlight the political potentialities of an intensely varied terrain of production relations, property relations, oppositional struggles, and symbolic conflicts.

13 The work of ENGENDER is aimed at disrupting many of the dichotomies that structure traditional development discourse, both in its overarching philosophy and in projects carried out in its name. As their report notes,

Our aim is to contribute to a paradigmatic shift in development thinking, planning and practice, through the formation of new modes of sustainability and equity that would be viable and relevant in a modern world-system. In this context, ENGENDER is examining the experiences of different development choices, ideologies and practices, with the aim of evaluating their consequences for human development and environmental sustainability. This includes different combinations of (1) labour intensive and capital intensive production, (2) public and private sector participation, and (3) the degree of consistency between state ideologies on the one hand and on the other hand government and private sector practices.

(1995, 6)

14 ENGENDER's relations with transnational corporations can be seen as aimed at constituting a corporate philanthropic subjectivity in its attempts to capture corporate internal markets, in the name of not only a better product but also a local product whose sale will support an endangered livelihood.
15 This does not mean that we advocate all the class processes we foreground, or even the political projects that we envision to be possible.

12 Reading Harold: Class analysis, capital accumulation, and the role of the intellectual

I wrote this essay at the invitation of Ann-Marie Wolpe for the conference, "Engaging Silences and Unresolved Issues in the Political Economy of South Africa," organized by the Harold Wolpe Memorial Trust, Cape Town, South Africa, 22–23 September 2006. This is the first time it has been published. I have deliberately left intact the informal language of oral presentation.

When I first sat down to write this paper, I entertained more than my usual doubts about how I should approach the topic, and about whether or not I had anything to contribute to the discussion. I had accepted an invitation to prepare my thoughts for a conference organized by the Harold Wolpe Memorial Trust – and I had never met the man. On top of that, the conference theme is the political economy of South Africa – and I have never been to that country, much less do I consider myself any kind of expert on its political economy.

My only real connections to South Africa are relatively minor and indirect: involvement in the anti-apartheid movement (mostly in the United States but also as a member of the Portuguese delegation to the International Conference Against Apartheid, which took place in Lisbon in 1976), supervising the PhD dissertation of a very bright South African student at Notre Dame (Murray Leibbrandt is now a tenured professor of economics at the University of Cape Town), and my friendship with an inspiring and committed South African cricketer in exile (becoming one of Peter Walshe's colleagues has been one of the highlights of my time at Notre Dame). Indeed, most of my own work in applied or concrete political economy has not been about South or Southern Africa, but has mostly concerned Latin America.

As for Harold (if I may), the connection is a bit more direct: I was a member of the founding editorial board of *Rethinking Marxism* (RM) and, because of his standing and stature as a Marxist intellectual and activist whose contributions to the rethinking of Marxism we admired and sought to emulate, we invited Harold to join our initial international advisory board.[1] He graciously accepted and, because we continue to want to identify RM with his pioneering intellectual work, Harold's name continues to grace our masthead, in memoriam. Along the way, I have encountered many people who knew him, and I have chanced upon more than a few eloquent testimonies by his comrades and friends. And, of course, I have read (and reread) almost all of his published work. So, while we never met, I feel eerily close to him, and I am quite honored to have been invited to present a paper at a conference in his memory and honor.

From my perspective, this conference is the perfect way to extend Harold's work, by "engaging silences and unresolved issues." Because that's what his theorizing (not to mention his activism, which I know about only indirectly) was all about. And that's what the best tradition of Marxist theorizing, to which Harold made his own seminal contributions, is meant to do: identify and directly engage the issues about which others (especially those in power) want us to remain silent, or from which they want to deflect attention. We also need to admit the problems and issues that remain unresolved, both in theory and in the social formations within which we work. We need to conduct the abstract theorizing and concrete analyses that, in the end, show that silence reproduces the status quo (or worse) and reproducing the status quo – in theory, in reality – cannot but leave the important topics unresolved.

It was Harold's determined unwillingness to remain silent – in the face of open questions within Marxist theory, confronting and seeking to undo the brutal repressions meted out by South African apartheid and capitalism, imagining both a different Marxism and a different South Africa, and his unrelenting honesty in engaging the unresolved issues of Marxist theory and practice – issues that require us to rethink and not simply abandon the Marxist tradition, even when we draw from and, in turn, contribute to other critical traditions – that should serve as our template of a real intellectual. Those qualities, which separate the best intellectuals of the Marxist tradition and of our own time (and which we can only hope to bequeath to the coming generations) from the academic professionals, expert advisors, and media commentators who either remain silent in the face of, or offer false solutions to, the theoretical and social problems of our time. They seek to find their position within the status quo; our goal is to change it.

So, what is it that made Harold's work so powerful? What is it in that work that allows us, today, to take up the silenced and unresolved issues in political economy? Needless to say, I cannot evaluate the significance or validity of his claims about South Africa per se; I will leave that task to those more qualified than I, and I look forward to reading and hearing their commentaries and interpretations during the course of the conference. For my part, Harold's contributions to Marxism – to the Marxist critique of political economy, his approach to theoretical and social issues, the theoretical incisiveness and innovative methodology he deployed – made the Marxian tradition come alive, by breaking down the limitations that had been imposed on (and, unfortunately, continue to be erected around) Marxian theory from inside and outside that tradition and by using reformulated and reinvigorated concepts to carry out a series of original analyses of contemporary social reality.

As it turns out, those of us associated with RM (and its sponsoring organization, the Association for Economic and Social Analysis) have been pursuing a similar approach for the better part of the past 30 years. We have attempted – in the context of national, anticolonial, and revolutionary struggles across the globe, from Southern Africa to Latin America, as part of the profound questioning of "really existing socialism," encouraged by the rereading of Marxian theory carried out by Louis Althusser, Etienne Balibar, and others – to rethink some of the key concepts and methods of analysis within the Marxian tradition, to discover moments within that tradition that had been forgotten or overlooked and to reinvigorate that tradition by taking detours through other approaches to critical social theory (including poststructuralism and postmodernism).

Of course, Harold did not solve all the problems he tackled, although he made what can only be considered valiant efforts. And that's the legacy that has been handed down to us: not the conclusions necessarily, nor formulas that we can merely replicate or repeat, but a way of identifying and grappling with difficult issues and unresolved problems. In other words, he left to us a way of proceeding, of breaking through the theoretical logjams and impasses that have been produced within and by the Marxian tradition, of opening up Marxism to a different encounter – with itself and with social reality.

My aim in this brief paper is to report on our project of rethinking Marxism and to identify the parallels with and departures from Harold's work, explaining what I consider we have accomplished and identifying what I think remains to be done. In doing so, I want to focus on three areas that are central to Harold's work and our own: class formation, capital accumulation, and the problem of the intellectual. And, while I will not dare directly address issues of South African reality – of the real problems that need to be confronted and engaged in the current conjuncture – I do hope this commentary will contribute to a dialogue wherein those issues that have been met with silence can be given an open and honest hearing and real solutions can be formulated.

Reading Harold

The international Marxist and left intellectual communities, to the extent that they know of and cite Harold's work, focus most of their attention on his essays concerning the articulation of modes of production and the problem of cheap labor power in South Africa. I am no exception, since that's where I started many years ago in conducting my own analysis of the history of modes of production in Peru (from the Incas to the 1920s

[Ruccio 1976]) and, a couple of years later, in beginning my doctoral studies at the University of Massachusetts-Amherst, where a group of graduate students and faculty members (especially my eventual dissertation advisors, Stephen Resnick and Richard Wolff) were reading the works of Althusser, Barry Hindess and Paul Hirst, and others in what (at least from my perspective) came to be erroneously known as "structuralist Marxism." In preparation for writing this paper, I had the enormous privilege of rereading Harold's best-known essays and of rediscovering (and, in some cases, encountering for the first time) his other texts.

What struck me most, on this particular re/reading of Harold's work, was the combination of theoretical rigor and concrete analysis that characterized his writings. On one hand, he was inclined to identify an analytical problem that could ultimately be traced to the use of fuzzy or poorly defined concepts (such as the working class or exploitation) or an essentialist methodology (such as race or economic reductionism). The solution he then proposed was to carefully develop the appropriate Marxist concept (e.g., mode of production, articulation, and so on) in a manner that broke with the kinds of determinisms that have long bedeviled the Marxist tradition.[2] On the other hand, and because of the approach he adopted, theoretical clarity and rigor did not represent the final solution, but only the conceptual prelude to conducting a concrete analysis of a particular social situation or event. It was never a matter of deducing general laws from the concepts – as if social reality were governed by, or could be explained in terms of, always/already known "ultimately determining factors" or "iron laws" of necessity – but, rather, of using the concepts to produce new knowledges of a complex, contradictory, and changing social reality. His goal, as I see it, was to overcome theoretical barriers in order to move beyond "false" resolutions (the product of idealist theoretical schemes) so that he was better able to formulate "real" (i.e., materialist) solutions.[3]

In this movement from the abstract to the concrete – in other words, in this resolutely antiempiricist working from relatively abstract Marxist concepts to produce relatively concrete Marxist conceptions of social reality – Harold seems to have been always inclined to emphasize contingent relations and specific characteristics. Thus, instead of presuming or looking for a fixed causal relationship between race and class, he focused on the uneven, asymmetrical, contradictory, shifting, and unstable relationship between those two key elements of the South African social formation. Similarly, he saw white domination and capitalist development in terms of both a functional (i.e., mutually supportive) and contradictory relationship, forever looking for elements of diversity and discontinuity in a pattern of continuity – and, perhaps most controversially, paying attention to "openings" created within and by the apartheid state. He eschewed the idea that there were universal conditions of existence for capital accumulation and sought, instead, to examine the changing economic and political conditions that made the accumulation of capital possible. Following from this, Harold was at great pains to distinguish – and then examine – the specific relations that obtained between, different aspects of social reality: race and class, economics and politics, and so on. Thus, for example, he discovered that class struggles could – in certain periods, under specific circumstances – assume the form of struggles over race, and that political battles could not simply be deduced from economic conditions but needed to take into account the real, material specificity of political institutions, levels of organization, and political discourses.

And no matter how nuanced and sophisticated were the analyses Harold elaborated, the point was not just to conduct first-rate academic research (even though his met the highest standards, far exceeding what seems to be the surfeit of mindless research being conducted these days in the academy). He was keen to point out that theoretical positions had political effects; that choosing one set of concepts over another had enormous implications for the conceptions of social reality that were produced and, thus, the forms of political intervention that could be imagined and formulated. And, of course, the political strategies he was inclined to advocate, support, and put into practice were those that expressed oppositional political discourses and took the form, not of individual stances and actions, but of joint, organized activity.

The context of our work was, of course, different. We were not, like Harold, participants in the diverse movement confronting the ravages of South African apartheid capitalism. We had not been imprisoned nor were we living in exile. Instead, we were Marxists, living in the United States, many of us participants in the anticolonial, antiimperialist, and antiwar movements, schooled in both the Old Left and the New Left, searching for ways to keep Marxism alive, especially in and around the discipline of economics. On one hand, the specificity of Marxism had become lost or underplayed in much of the radical theorizing of the 1960s and 1970s – in favor of a critique of unequal power relations. On the other hand, what Marxist theorizing did exist had, in many cases, been reduced to an economic analysis of the stagnation and fragility of monopoly capitalism and the promise of revolution in the Third World – with little patience for elaborating the terms of Marxism's philosophical "break" from mainstream social science.

As it turns out, we were inspired to rethink key Marxian concepts and to elaborate what made Marxism different from bourgeois thought, inside and outside economics, by many of the same authors and texts that left their traces in Harold's writings. Althusser and Balibar, of course – and, through them, both a new encounter with the Marxist tradition (including Lenin, Antonio Gramsci, and Gyorg Lukács) and with new Marxist thinkers (such as Hindess and Hirst, Ernesto Laclau, Nicos Poulantzas, Charles Bettelheim, Pierre-Philipe Rey, Emanuel Terray, and Stuart Hall, to name just a few). In our case, this contact also extended into the work of some of Althusser's colleagues and students, especially Michel Foucault, Jean-François Lyotard, and Jacques Derrida. Therefore, while we have long understood our work in terms of an antiessentialist or nondeterminist Marxism, our approach has also been referred to as postmodern or poststructuralist Marxism.

One of the key concepts we borrowed from Althusser was overdetermination, which we used to criticize and move away from essentialist tendencies in traditional or classical Marxist methodology (particularly economism and theoretical humanism) and epistemology (both rationalism and empiricism). In terms of social analysis, the idea was that, instead of either presuming or looking for a causal hierarchy (wherein either the economy or some part of it, such as the relations or forces of production, or some set of universal human attributes, whether labor or desire, would be seen as the ultimate determinant of society and human activity), each practice, event, or institution under analysis would be understood – conceptually produced – as the outcome of an infinite multiplicity of complex, contradictory effects. The overlaps with the antiessentialism and nondeterminism of Harold's approach are considerable.

For us, one consequence of invoking this combination of "mutual constitutivity" and "relative autonomy" of economics, politics, and culture has been to forego the elaboration of general laws and to reinvigorate the concrete analysis of concrete situations. This has led us beyond the development of new concepts to a Marxist investigation of a wide range of social phenomena, from concepts of capitalism (Gibson-Graham 1996), commodity fetishism (Amariglio and Callari 1993), and capitalist competition (Ruccio and Amariglio 1998) to the Soviet Union (Resnick and Wolff 2002), China (Gabriel 2005), and India (Chakrabarti and Cullenberg 2003). My own research in this vein has focused on such diverse topics as Marxist conceptions of socialism and socialist planning (Chapter 3 of this volume and Ruccio 1992) through the role of the state, planning, and the worker–peasant alliance in revolutionary Nicaragua (Chapters 4, 5, and 7 of this volume) and the problems of stabilization and adjustment (Chapter 8 of this volume), foreign debt (Chapter 9 of this volume), and capitalist industrialization in Latin America (Chapter 10 of this volume) to the role of class in international political economy (Chapter 14 of this volume) and contemporary discourses of globalization and imperialism (Chapter 16 of this volume). This antiessentialist approach to Marxism has also meant changing the terms of the Marxian focus on class, from one of causal essence to discursive priority: instead of presuming or attempting to demonstrate that class was "in the end" the ultimate determinant of social life, we have come to explain the focus on class – the goal of producing a class knowledge of society – as one of the *differentia specifica* of Marxian discourses, the lens that distinguishes Marxism from other approaches to economic and social analysis.

Turning to the Marxian theory of knowledge, we have sought to distance ourselves from absolute and transtheoretical notions of truth in favor of relative, internal criteria (each theory has its own protocols of analysis and produces its own objects or, in Althusserian language, thought-concretes) and an emphasis on the contrasting effects or consequences of different discourses. Thus, for example, Marxism not only has objects that are different from those of mainstream (neoclassical and Keynesian) economics; it also leads to strategies and policies quite different from those put forward by mainstream economists. To the extent that we advocate a Marxian, class-analytical perspective and criticize the methods and conclusions of bourgeois thought, we end up with an epistemological position that some of us have come to refer to as "partisan relativism."

As Harold fully understood, not only do Marxist knowledges of history and contemporary social formations differ radically from those elaborated within liberal and other non-Marxian social theories; different Marxist knowledges – analyses produced by different definitions and uses of key Marxian concepts – also have contrasting implications for how we analyze social problems, what we put forward as solutions, and how we go about implementing or seeking to create the conditions for those solutions.

While RM has, from the beginning, attempted to break down disciplinary barriers, publishing scholarly articles across the range of social thought, as well as visual art, fiction, and poetry, the bulk of our efforts have been directed to issues and problems in the broadly defined area of economics or political economy.[4] Therefore, I wish to focus the remainder of my comments in this area, especially on two key issues – class formation and capital accumulation – before returning to the problem of the intellectual.

Classes and class formation

No one can come away from even a quick perusal of Harold's work without understanding that classes and class formation were central to his concerns. Those of us associated with RM share that perspective. The question is, why is class important and how are classes defined within Marxian theory?

My own reading suggests that classes and class formation played three key roles within Harold's research – in relation to structure, agenda, and agency. First, the class structure was central to Harold's conception of capitalism and of the "structural conditions" that characterized the South African social formation. Thus, the focus of Harold's analysis of South African capitalism was not, as in mainstream economics, free markets and private property, macroeconomic stability, and economic growth (although he touched on all three themes) or, even, as in heterodox economics, large corporations, poverty, or inequalities in the distribution of income and wealth (although, again, he had something to say about all three issues). No, Harold was clear that class exploitation, and the conditions and consequences of exploitation – especially the need for, and policies designed to provide, cheap labor power – were central to the existence and changing nature of South African capitalism.

Second, focusing on the class dimensions of South African development placed certain issues on the agenda of social change, particularly in the replacing of the apartheid regime. Thus, for example, it was not sufficient to dismantle the racial dimensions of apartheid, nor was it desirable to establish independent or semi-independent African zones or forms of self-government. As long as the capitalist extraction of surplus-value continued to exist, whether in the segregationist gold mines and agricultural enterprises or the factories and offices of the apartheid manufacturing sector, national liberation involved the elimination of both racial oppression and capitalist exploitation. My sense from Harold's writings (although I stand to be corrected by those who were acquainted with him and his political views) is that ending capitalist exploitation was both a goal in itself – because collective appropriation of the surplus was preferable to capitalist exploitation – and an important condition for eliminating racial inequality in South Africa. That is, he seems to have imagined not only a new, racially inclusive South Africa but, in contrast to other sectors of the antiapartheid movement, one substantially free from capitalist exploitation.

The third significance of class was bound up with the problem of political and social agency. If South African society was based, at least in part, on capitalist exploitation, and if class transformation was one of the key issues on the political agenda, were class formations such that they – classes, classes in formation, class fractions, class alliances – could or would effectively struggle to transform the social structure in order to end apartheid and exploitation? In addition, how were these class formations overlain with racial formations, and how did they combine – if indeed they do – to become agents of antiracial and anticapitalist struggle? Here, Harold sought to distinguish the abstract level, where classes (such as capital and labor) are conceived as "unitary and homogeneous," from the more concrete level where, because of both economic and noneconomic conditions, classes were not unified forces but, rather, "patchworks or segments which are differentiated and divided on a variety of bases and by varied processes." They only achieved class unity – if indeed they did – not as a natural or inevitable process, but through their practices, discourses, and organizations, as a "conjunctural phenomenon" (1988a, 50, 51).

Of course, the way Harold addressed these three themes – the manner in which he criticized the approaches of others and articulated his own position – depended crucially on how he interpreted the Marxian conception of class. Harold was clear that class should be defined, at the abstract level at least, in terms of relations of production, including the mode of exploitation or the relationship to the appropriation of surplus labor.[5] He thus rejected other possible (and, then as now, quite common) definitions of class, such as property relations, degrees of compulsion of labor, and income shares. He was particularly adamant that class was a structural position, defined within a mode of production, and not a question of ideological self-identification or relative access to or distance from political power. Still, this did not prevent him from developing a class analysis that was more complex than that of the traditional capital/labor dyad, leading to his identification of class fractions (such as productive and unproductive workers, large-scale and small-scale capital, and so on) and a new middle class, all defined "in the sphere of production" (1976, 220).

Harold put this class-analytical framework to use for two main purposes: to understand the changing configuration of the capitalist class and its interest in white domination, and to determine the possibilities of an interracial working-class alliance to challenge both white domination and capitalist exploitation. While he provided many important insights along the way, the two key results of Harold's class analysis were the novel periodization of South African capitalism (including, famously, the articulation with noncapitalist African modes of production) and the careful deconstruction of the then-prevalent notion of the white working class (especially its supposed position as exploiter of black workers). In addition, Harold continued to grapple (not always, in my humble opinion, with complete success) to address the problem of how to move from abstractly defined classes and class positions to more concretely specified classes as political actors and the forms that class struggle might take in the movement against apartheid.

Our own approach to class analysis emerged from concerns similar to those that inspired Harold, and we have pursued approaches that bear a distinct resemblance to the paths he followed. At the same time, those of us associated with RM have reached some conclusions which differed from those I have encountered in Harold's work. My hope is that a discussion of this combination of similarities and differences can help us to identify the silences and point in the direction of new resolutions to the remaining problems of South African political economy.

Like Harold, we have interpreted the Marxian definition of class in a relatively restricted manner – in our case, as the way in which surplus labor is performed (by the direct producers) and appropriated (by another group, or by the laborers themselves). We have added to that fundamental or appropriative class process another one: the subsumed or distributive class process, whereby surplus labor is transferred (a position which may or may not be occupied by the appropriators) and received (by still others, who thus share in a portion of the surplus labor performed by the direct producers without, however, necessarily being the appropriators).[6] The focus of such a definition is thus not on classes as economic or social groups but, rather, on class processes and class positions, a particular subset of the social processes and positions that can be said to make up society.

So, as in Harold's case, for us, the class structure turns out to be richer, and more complex, than the one conceived in traditional Marxism (let alone non-Marxian forms of economic and social thought). For example, the capitalist class structure includes processes whereby wage-laborers produce surplus-value (hence the term "productive labor"), which is appropriated by the functioning or industrial capitalists. This surplus-value is, in turn, distributed and received – within and by such entities as enterprise managers and supervisors (so-called unproductive labor), the state (in the form of taxes), financial capitalists (as interest payments), other capitalists (as competitive super-profits), and so on – in return for providing some of the economic, political, and cultural conditions of exis-tence of continued capitalist exploitation. In addition, any social formation (such as the United States or, for that matter, South Africa) can be expected to include a variety of such class structures: capitalist as well as ancient (where we find individuals appropriating and distributing their own surplus labor), feudal (wherein feudal lords appropriate and distribute the surplus labor performed by serfs), slave (in which slaveowners appro-priate and distribute slave surplus labor), and collective or communal (when the direct producers and perhaps others in the community collec-tively appropriate and distribute the surplus labor).

Based on this definition, one of the key questions for Marxists becomes: what is the class structure – what is the particular pattern or combination of appropriative and distributive class processes – that characterizes any particular social formation or institution or practice within that society? Whether at the level of a country or some national or international entity (from enterprises and households to states and multinational organiza-tions), it is a matter of concrete investigation to determine if one or more class processes are present and, if so, what form they assume. And, while the abstract definition of class is quite restricted, such an investigation necessarily involves an analysis of the most diverse social conditions of existence of those class processes, as well as of the forms of interaction that obtain among and between them. It also means examining the relation-ship between such a complex class structure and all those nonclass dimen-sions of political economy – such as markets and property, macroeconomic conditions, patterns and rates of economic growth, the size and market share of corporations, the levels of poverty, and the distribution of income and wealth – that are, in part, constituted by the prevailing class structure.

Focusing on class in this manner places class transformation on the existing agenda of economic and social transformation. That is, what Marxists bring to the political table, what Marxists place on the agenda for discussion, debate, and action, what they seek to locate within the political imaginary, is the possibility of transforming the prevailing class structure.

The idea is to go beyond mitigating the worst effects of exploitative class structures – for example, by calling for more public ownership or state regulation – to actually changing the ways in which surplus labor is appropriated and distributed and forming alternative class structures. Thus, a new articulation of class structures can involve siphoning off distributions of surplus-value to form new initiatives for the benefit of the community. And it can mean creating collective ways of appropriating the surplus within new community economies. Adding these issues to the agenda radically transforms the existing debate, by reinforcing the point that capitalism is not the only game in town; both in the sense that noncapitalist economic and social structures already exist, and by reinforcing the demand for additional forms of noncapitalism.

The third consequence of this particular approach to Marxian class analysis is that it redefines the terms of social, including class, agency. Instead of seeing classes as unified, unitary actors, in the place of building from a presumed fixity or givenness of class identities, we have begun to explore the possibility of formulating a class politics based on the idea that class identities are the outcome, not the precondition, of cultural and political processes. That is, we have begun to work on the idea that acting in common to create new, noncapitalist class structures – the idea of "being in common" rather than presuming or imposing a "common being" – cannot simply be read off the insults and injuries meted out within and by exploitative class structures; rather, they are (or, in the case of identities which we are interested in fostering, can be) the products of cultural formations, forms of political organization, processes of identity formation.[7] In other words, the task before us is to understand how diverse practices – producing theoretical knowledges of a class-structured society and elaborating forms of class justice, understanding how class is represented in the everyday world of music and movies, pursuing a politics of resubjectification, forming organizations to pursue collective goals – combine to produce (instead of merely symbolizing or expressing) identities that both resent the existing class structure and desire new class ways of organizing the economy and society.[8]

Capital accumulation

One of the obstacles to imagining and formulating such a politics of class is the idea that societies in which capitalist class processes exist are governed by the "laws of motion" of capitalism (Gibson-Graham *et al.* 2001). That is, when capitalist social formations are posed as unified social totalities, which can be explained in terms of one or another of their key elements or driving forces (often, but not always, an economic one), the existence of a diverse class landscape is met with silence and the possibility of noncapitalist class processes is deferred to a distant, barely discernible future. Political options are then reduced to generally accommodating the "needs" of individual capitalists and of the capitalist "system," and perhaps alleviating the worst effects of the activities of capitalists and of capitalism as a whole. Focusing on the possibility of strengthening and creating noncapitalism is, in turn, often seen as threatening "real" improvements – more jobs, higher wages, improved safety measures, environmental regulations, and so on – in pursuit of an admirable, but ultimately utopian, dream.

I can't follow Harold in speaking directly to the discussion in South Africa. But this "retreat from class" is certainly true in the United States, where many radical economists and economic activists view "the economy" – variously referred to as the market, postindustrialism, global capitalism, and so on – as a unified, centered totality that sets the limits on what can be imagined and created. If anything, this perspective has expanded in recent years, as the distribution of income and wealth has been made (through changes in capitalism and government policies) more unequal and (again, through a combination of structural changes and policies) the standard of living of the working class has slowly but persistently deteriorated. The project of eliminating exploitation and creating new appropriative and distributive class processes is replaced by initiatives to protect and improve existing state programs (such as social security and tax concessions for implementing environmentally friendly technologies) and to raise workers' living standards (by creating living-wage ordinances, reforming the pension system, and providing wider access to health care). The challenge for the Left, given the ongoing attacks on all manner of public programs, is how to combine support for the idea of state initiatives – through which care is extended to all citizens – with the possibility of class transformation.

Within the Marxian tradition, this tendency to make capitalism a unified and all-powerful entity is the result of seeing the accumulation of capital as the singular logic that governs individual capitalist enterprises, as well as the capitalist system as a whole. Studying the process of capital accumulation therefore becomes the key to unlocking the "logic" of the economic order – the manner in which capitalism is reproduced and the path it inexorably follows to expansion, both nationally and internationally. And everything else that exists within the social formation – political forces, cultural formations, and forms of economy other than capitalism – is rendered functionally dependent on the needs of accumulation.

The problem, as Bruce Norton has pointed out in a series of remarkable studies (1992, 1994, 1995, 2001), is that the various attempts by Marxists (and radical economists more generally) to "discern capitalism's destiny-determining inner contradictions" – by identifying the laws governing the accumulation of capital to determine the inner contradictions that led to capitalism's increasing dysfunctionality – have marginalized another dimension of the Marxian project: "to conceive the historically changing dimensions of class exploitation – and envision associated transformational possibilities" (2001, 24). That is, some Marxian economists have focused on one of a number of inherent contradiction within capitalism – under-consumption, stagnation, a falling rate of profit, and so on – and tied this to the inherent drive on the part of capitalists to accumulate capital. Class only exists in such approaches to the extent that it designates positions that entail a categorical imperative. Thus, workers produce and consume; capitalists, for their part, exploit and expand.

This is how the famous passage in Marx's *Capital* – "Accumulate, accu-mulate! That is Moses and the prophets!" (1977, 742) – is generally inter-preted; as a summary description of the driving force of capitalists, the product of an inner drive of being a capitalist and/or of competitive pres-sure from other capitalists. In either case, the point is that capitalists have a fixed and unwavering drive to expand, based on the use of surplus-value to accumulate additional (constant and variable) capital. There are, however, two difficulties with such an interpretation: one textual, the other theoretical. When Norton reads this passage in its full context, his conclusion is that Marx is not making this claim for himself, in terms of his understanding of capitalists and the capitalist mode of production; rather, he is parodying the classical political economists, who ascribed to capital-ists the "historical mission" of creating additional wealth (or, alterna-tively, of failing to fulfill their mission by consuming the surplus unproductively).

Theoretically, for Marxists to focus on capital accumulation and unpro-ductive consumption as the only two uses to which surplus-value can be put, means ignoring all the other distributions of surplus-value that capi-talists make in order to attempt to secure the conditions of existence of exploitation. As a result, they ignore both the complex pattern of capitalist appropriations and distributions of surplus-value, with the correspond-ingly complex – shifting, changing – capitalist class structure, and the effects on the wider society of capitalist control over distributions of the surplus. Transformations in the structure of capitalist enterprises and of a capitalist social formation as a whole depend, at least in part, on how and to whom capitalists distribute the surplus and in what manner those who receive a cut of the surplus spend their class revenues. In other words, one of the goals of the Marxian critique of political economy is to call into ques-tion the identity of capitalists as presumed within classical political economy (and, for that matter, within contemporary, both mainstream and heterodox, economics) and then, on its own terms, to account for the changing constellation of class processes, positions, and struggles associ-ated with the existence of capitalist class exploitation.

The accumulation of capital figures prominently within Harold's anal-yses of South African capitalism. And, while he never defines the term (perhaps surprising for such an otherwise meticulous and rigorous theo-rist), my sense (although, again, I stand to be corrected here) is that he used it, not in the restricted sense to which Norton refers, but with a more general meaning. That is, instead of referring to the accumulation of capital as a particular distribution of the surplus (and, therefore, as the essential condition of capitalist growth and expansion), Harold let it stand for the reproduction of the totality of economic and social conditions associated with capitalist exploitation. Thus, in his texts, the accumulation of capital refers to the changing way in which the continued existence of the extraction of surplus-value from South African workers was secured – by the activities of individual capitalists as well as the various entities (security, military, political, and so forth) of the South African state.

If this is, in fact, what the accumulation of capital means for Harold, then his analyses are relieved of some of the burdens imposed by the strict economistic logic of Marxian crisis theories. Yet, even in this more general sense, an understanding of the South African social formation rooted in capital accumulation does carry with it the problems of systemic order and driving force. That is, when the accumulation of capital is placed at the center of the story, all other phenomena – capitalist decisions, state policies, limits on worker demands, noncapitalist forms of economy and social life – tend to be reduced to, and explained in terms of, a drive, a mission – however complex and contradictory – to reproduce the conditions of existence of capitalist exploitation.

Still, in Harold's texts, such a tendency is combined with a concern to document the process of historical change, by identifying the changes and discontinuities in the manner whereby capitalism continued to exist and even to flourish in South Africa. If we follow this path, then the goal of Marxist interventions in political economy is precisely to destabilize the fixed identities and behaviors often attributed to capitalist classes – workers, capitalists, and so on – in order to understand and trace the effects of the changing distributions of surplus-value on capitalist enterprises and the social formation as a whole. When we conduct such an analysis for the current situation – in the United States, South Africa, or anywhere else in the world – then class analysis is released from being merely a support of given drives and dynamics, of either capitalism's inevitable distress or its systemic integrity, inevitability, and expansion, to become a way of documenting the injustices of capitalist exploitation, analyzing the causes of such injustices, and seeking openings for noncapitalist class transformations that will end those injustices.

Intellectuals

Just as Marxism can be articulated in different ways, and be put to different uses, so the problem of the intellectual can be posed in various ways. If class analysis is subordinated to economic laws of motion, when capitalist classes and class formations are made to be the supports of an overarching logic of capital accumulation – that is, when a Marxian politics of class becomes an identity politics – then the role of the Marxist intellectual is to conduct an analysis of the existing structure and to translate the conclusions of that analysis, via a given set of interests and identities, into a corresponding set of predictions and political strategies. If, however, one of the aims of Marxian class analysis is to challenge the existing terrain of political economy, to make it different from itself, to show how new structures and identities can be imagined and invented, then Marxist intellectuals have a different role: to intervene to develop new discursive openings, and new ways of seeing the social reality that exists and the social formations that can be brought into being.

It is not at all surprising that Harold was keenly aware of, and offered his views on, both issues: the political effects of different ways of interpreting and deploying basic Marxian concepts in social analysis, and what the position of critical/committed intellectuals should be. He showed, for example, that conflating race and class (such as in theories of internal colonialism), and not analyzing the "internal class structures" of racial or ethnic groups, might lead to a contradictory position according to which power is exercised by one entire group (whites) but where the ruling class is constituted by only part of that group (monopoly capitalists) or, alternatively, to the conclusion that a relationship of exploitation exists between modes of production (such that capitalism can be said to exploit noncapitalism). The political implication in both cases is that the real injustices associated with capitalist relations of class exploitation – and therefore the possible class formations and alliances to oppose the particular form assumed by South African capitalism – would be obscured or overlooked.

If different forms of class analysis had contrasting political implications, what should the role of intellectuals and intellectual work be? Harold wrote directly on this topic – and in his characteristic manner, not by addressing the issue abstractly but in the context of quite concrete situations. He outlined two alternative positions: on one hand, in a situation in which intellectuals oppose a government and its policies, they should protect their "autonomy" and resist any attempts on the part of the state to direct or curtail critical research. On the other hand, when intellectuals are allied to a movement of national liberation (whether it has already occupied the state or has as its goal the seizure of state power), the position is fundamentally different. Here, intellectuals need to avoid either proclaiming their absolute autonomy or serving the ideological function of conducting research to justify or corroborate already defined political decisions. Harold's view was that "theory and analysis" are – and, as I interpret him, should be – a site of contestation within national liberation movements. Thus, the priorities of the political organization should be adopted by allied or affiliated intellectuals but, and this is crucial, "not as conclusions but as starting points for investigators" (1985a, 75). Presumably, it is this "relative autonomy" of critical intellectuals that led Harold, later on, after the apartheid regime (but not the effects of that regime) had been dismantled, to support the creation of an Institute for

Social Theory, to create an intellectual space that was committed to both national liberation and open-ended critical inquiry.

Harold went on to distinguish between an "analysis of structural constraints" and the "description of the experience, consciousness and struggles of individuals" (1985a, 77, 76). The former, he argued, was the proper domain of intellectuals, while the latter would be taken care of by the political organizations themselves. Clearly, Harold had something quite specific in mind in encouraging intellectuals to eschew "research by means of questionnaires and interviews" (I presume that the results of such methods gave evidence, in the context of brutal state repression, of widespread assent to ideas that ran counter to what the liberation movement was saying about the state of popular awareness and consciousness; but I may be wrong). The danger, of course, is that, to the extent that Marxists are interested precisely in the nexus of structure and agency – in how structures are lived and practiced through social agencies and how such agencies are themselves structured – focusing only on structures tends to render them given and immutable, and reinforces the idea that agency can simply be read off of structural positions. In the case of the contemporary United States, the texts by nonacademics concerning the tensions and contradictions of the hegemony of certain forms of right-wing thought (I am thinking, in particular, of recent books like Thomas Frank's *What's the Matter with Kansas?* [2004]) have more to tell us about the current conjuncture than most of the research being conducted by professional academics, both mainstream and radical.

Part of the problem, as Harold understood, is the position of intellectuals vis-à-vis the ruling ideas and structures. However, the danger, in the United States at least, is less the direct intervention of the state (although that is occurring, on issues ranging from global warming and evolution to Middle East studies) than the "marketization" of higher education. That is, in the name of academic excellence, what is being investigated and published has little to do with what we consider to be critical intellectual work and more with what "sells." What I mean by that is that the academy is becoming less a protected place where critical ideas are generated than one in which professional recognition circulates in the form of "academic value" that can be measured and rewarded – and punishments meted out to those who refuse to participate, or don't measure up – in the increasingly formalized "academic market." The quality of work that is being disseminated has, by any measure, increased but its intellectual significance, at least from the vantage point of critical thought, has certainly deteriorated.

The other part of the problem pertains to patterns of thought. If we reduce our Marxism to the investigation of the underlying structures of capitalism – and here I'm referring to the work that is often nowadays recognized as Marxian political economy – if we confine ourselves to seeking closure in the present and elaborating a predictable future, instead of creating openings of new class possibilities now and in the future, in structures as well as in practices and desires, then we forsake our status as critical intellectuals. However, if we accept our task as the "ruthless criticism of the existing order," if our stance always necessarily runs counter to the status quo, since we cannot accept either enforced silences or unresolved problems, then we must turn our critical gaze on our existing modes of thought, as well as on the existing structures of social life. This is the major lesson we can all take away from reading Harold.

Acknowledgements

I want to thank Ann-Marie Wolpe and the Harold Wolpe Memorial Trust for inviting me to address the colloquium and for making my visit to Cape Town so enjoyable. I also want to thank Andrew Nash for his generous comments on my paper and the participants in the colloquium for teaching me both about Harold Wolpe's work and about contemporary issues in South Africa.

Notes

1   The other members of the original RM advisory board included Michêle Barrett, Rosalyn Baxandall, Johnnetta Cole, Carmen Diana Deere, Terry Eagleton, Stephen Jay Gould (1941–2002), Frederic Jameson, Ernesto Laclau, Dominique Lecourt, Rayna Rapp, Stephen Resnick, Sheila Rowbotham, Meredith Tax, Cornel West, and Richard Wolff. Since then, the following scholars have been invited to join the advisory board: Jack Amariglio, Etienne Balibar, Joseph Buttigieg, Stephen Cullenberg, Nancy Fraser, Julie Graham, Stuart Hall, Manning Marable, Gayatri C. Spivak, and myself.
2   Although certainly not just Marxism. Non-Marxian economic and social theory – such as neoclassical economics and liberal political theory – has been based on more than its share of deterministic concepts and methods of analysis. In fact, one of the hallmarks of "modernist" social science has been to presume and then search for the ultimately determining factor – some notion of the individual and/or structure – that serves to cause and therefore explain all other social phenomena. See, for example, the discussions in *Postmodern Moments in Modern Economics* (Ruccio and Amariglio 2003) and *Postmodernism, Economics, and Knowledge* (Cullenberg *et al*. 2001).
3   In the past decade, materialism has received renewed attention, especially after the publication of Althusser's later manuscripts. See, for example, the discussion of "aleatory materialism" in *Postmodern Materialism and the Future of Marxist Theory* (Ruccio and Callari 1996), and the special issue of RM, "Rereading Althusser" (Ruccio and Callari 1998).
4   In my view, this is not because political economy – or, more accurately, the critique of political economy – is, or should be, taken to be the core of Marxian theory but, for a rather arbitrary reason: many of us associated with RM completed doctoral studies in economics (or focused on political economy in such disciplines as geography, anthropology, and education) and now teach in departments of economics (and related disciplines) in the United States and around the world. Therefore, our intellectual interventions are within what is traditionally considered the terrain of economics; at the same time, we have

sought to challenge the conventional boundaries of economics and economic thought.

5   Harold frequently refers to the complex of relations and forces of production but it is not at all clear how the latter enters into his analysis of classes and class formation.

6   This is one of the notable achievements of Resnick and Wolff (1987b), who connected the class analysis of the value theory presented in Volumes 1 and 3 of *Capital* via the concepts of fundamental and subsumed class processes.

7   On just this last point, that of identity formation, permit me to refer readers to the remarkable symposium on "subjects of economy" in the April 2006 (Vol. 18, No. 2) issue of RM. There, many of the authors explore the productive role that psychoanalysis (especially Lacanian theory) can play, both in imagining spaces of ethical and political possibility and in bringing into being subjects that seek to affirm and participate in noncapitalist class practices.

8   Many concrete examples of class analysis of the sort I have summarized here are presented in the two edited volumes, *Re/presenting Class* (Gibson-Graham *et al.* 2001) and *Class and Its Others* (Gibson-Graham *et al.* 2000). Jonathan Diskin (2005a) critically reviews the essays gathered in these two books. Elsewhere, in his discussion of the Marxian analysis of the Soviet Union carried out by Resnick and Wolff, Diskin (2005b) expresses his concern about the problem of functionalism in class analysis and suggests that we need to pay more attention to the "relationship between class and various notions of collectivity and identity," especially the "kinds of collectivity and agency people were trying to achieve (or to prevent)" (2005b, 557).

Globalization

The third topic of my research in this general area has been international political economy, or what has come to be called "globalization." Since I first started writing, globalization has displaced development in many ways as the key area of debate between mainstream and heterodox approaches to political economy.

Mainstream economists – both academic (like Jagdish Bhagwati) and "everyday" (such as Thomas Friedman) – tend to celebrate globalization. Their view is that the freeing up of commodity and financial markets on an international level, just as within nations, leads to an efficient allocation of scarce resources. The lowering of barriers to the flow of goods and services, as well as investment capital and finance, around the world promotes economic growth (of individual national economies and of the world economy as a whole) and thus promises a solution to poverty and underdevelopment.

The heterodox view is, of course, quite different. It emphasizes the unequal structure of global capitalism – both in terms of unequal nations (such that some nations benefit while other nations lose) and unequal actors (with large multinational financial, service, and manufacturing enterprises gaining at the expense of other groups, such as wage-laborers and small farmers). According to heterodox economists, the globalization of capitalism thus undermines the possibility of overcoming the problems of poverty and underdevelopment. Therefore, it needs to be contained and regulated, either by reinforcing national controls and forms of government intervention or by creating a supranational global authority.

Once again, I was frustrated by the existing debate – by the essentialist terms of the debate (individual choice versus unequal power) as well by the absence of a class analysis of globalization (on both sides). And, while there was a longstanding Marxian tradition of analyzing the global dimensions of capitalism (beginning with the *Communist Manifesto* and continuing through Lenin's famous treatise on imperialism), it was not at all clear how the rethinking of Marxism could be extended to examine the conditions and consequences of contemporary globalization. That was my next project.

I began my work on this topic with regulation theory. As far as the Marxian critique of political economy goes, it appeared that, after Michel Aglietta's initial volume and then Alain Lipietz's work, regulation theory would open up Marxian analyses of contemporary capitalism in a manner similar to the way that Althusser had for Marxian theory more generally. I expected that they would chart a path away from laws of motion and teleological histories and toward a more socially constructed, historically contingent theorization. But, alas, when I read what regulation theorists had done in analyzing capitalism on a world scale, I saw that many of the same mistakes were repeated.

For those not familiar with regulation theory or the work of Lipietz, the idea is that capitalism is made up of a regime of accumulation and a mode of regulation. Successful accumulation requires a particular balance between production and consumption. The mode of regulation is that set of institutional norms, procedures, and habits that either persuade or coerce economic agents to conform to a given regime of accumulation. And, because the mode of regulation is constituted outside the regime of accumulation, there is nothing automatic about it. The regulation theorists used this scheme both to reinterpret the history of capitalism (as a series of such modes and regimes) and to devise a new account of economic crises. According to my reading, this effort to "decenter" the process of accumulation leads to two additional problems: it reintroduces a model-like necessity at a different level and it leaves two key components – the role of accumulation itself and the state – as untheorized gaps in the explanation.

Regulation theory started out as a theory of national regulation. Once consolidated, it expanded its approach by considering the international dimensions of capitalist development in two areas: the role of international relations between the advanced capitalist nations in the rise and subsequent demise of Fordism, and the existence of national modes of regulation in the countries of the periphery and their insertion into the world economy. The problem here is that a model that was originally formulated to understand the dynamics of national regulation within the advanced capitalist nations is not so easily "opened up" to capture the dynamics of the world economy. Thus, for example, regulation theorists propose two separate and parallel explanations for the crisis of Fordism: on one hand, a decline in the rate of growth of productivity and the consequent profit-squeeze within nations and, on the other hand, the contradiction between national regimes of accumulation and the absence of an international mode of regulation. And there has never been an attempt to integrate them.

When it comes to the Third World, regulation theorists reject the traditional Marxian theory of imperialism and use the idea of Fordism to explain the export of capital to the Third World (as profitable opportunities dried up in the center), as an export from the metropolis (such that a Fordist regime of accumulation was set up in some parts of the Third

World), and as the cause of the crisis (since global monetarism destroys the favorable conditions for Fordist accumulation in the Third World).

My own view is different from that of others, who criticized regulation theory for straying too far from traditional Marxian analyses. I think, in contrast, their break is only partial and incomplete. For example, Lipietz's view is that Fordist accumulation in the Third World came about as a result of its being exported from the North. The only internal element that matters in his account is the form of the state. Now, while I'm all in favor of "bringing the state back in," what is missing is an analysis of the conditions within each nation that resulted in the primary accumulation of capital; that is, all those conditions – economic, political, and cultural – that created the possibility of accumulating capital and allowed for the emergence of capitalist fundamental and subsumed class processes, where they didn't already exist. And, in the end, Lipietz's story comes very close to that of Amin and the focus on autocentric or extraverted forms of capitalism.

While I think regulation theory made great strides in criticizing both the liberal separation of accumulation and regulation and the traditional Marxian essentialism of accumulation, it never went far enough in its "critique of political economy" to carry out the class analysis of the internal and external conditions that led both to the emergence and growth of capitalism and to its successive crises.

That is one approach that held a great deal of promise but then came up short. Another tendency in radical analyses, going back to dependency theory and continuing through to the present, is the idea that international economic phenomena – foreign investment, external debt, and so on – involve foreign exploitation. Once again, my disquiet stemmed not from the fact that radical economists and activists were focusing on the international dimensions of capitalism but, in my view, they weren't sufficiently concerned with the class and other phenomena that took place domestically *within* Third World countries. Therefore, they were missing the conditions and consequences of capitalist exploitation both theoretically, so that they might be analyzed, and politically, so that they might be changed.

With Resnick and Wolff, I set out to make sense of "class beyond the nation state" for a special joint issue of the *Review of Radical Political Economics* and *Capital and Class*. We focused our attention on the role of class in radical analyses of global capitalism, especially in two groups: the early theorists of imperialism and then dependency theory, and the world systems and internationalization of capital approach. There are, of course, many differences between them but they shared two key problems:

1   a presumed unity of the economic space (what we call economism), whether national or international, which serves to reinforce the national–international dichotomies that govern radical thought about global capitalism; and

2   a focus on unequal power relations (of some nation-states over other nation-states) instead of class.

Theorists of both approaches do, of course, mention classes (how could they not, and still call themselves radical?) but not as the entry point or in terms of flows of surplus labor.

So, how does one reinsert class into radical analyses of global capitalism? Where does one begin? In our view, what is important is to explicitly theorize the temporal and spatial dimensions of class processes:

- When does exploitation occur? When labor power is productively consumed by capitalists, after labor power is exchanged for a wage and before surplus-value is realized in the sale of commodities.
- Where does exploitation occur? Here, it is necessary to distinguish between the local sites of exploitation (where labor power is productively consumed) and the larger social expanse within which exploitation exists (which may be and often is on local, national and international scales).

According to this logic, the capitalist fundamental class process is neither intrinsically national nor international. We need to analyze the sites where exploitation takes place and the spaces within which the conditions of existence of exploitation – economic, political and cultural – are secured.

Where can we go with this? One direction is to interrogate the idea of foreign exploitation, which has long been a key idea within radical thought (both academic and nonacademic). Mainstream economists do not, of course, see exploitation – since their world is one in which individuals enter into voluntary contracts within free markets.[1] And radical theorists and activists tend to see exploitation when wages are low or when unequal power exists. In what sense, then, from a specifically Marxian perspective, can international capitalist relations be considered exploitative?

My view is that we need to theorize the relationship between class and international value flows. Thus, value flows included in typical balance-of-payments accounts will often (but not always) be distributions of appropriated surplus-value. In a class-analytical accounting framework, our conclusion is that foreign exploitation does not take place. One country cannot extract surplus labor from another country. The international flows of value that characterize global capitalism comprise a complex, changing combination of subsumed class and nonclass payments.

To what extent, then, is capitalism global? One form of global capitalism is when the conditions of existence of the extraction of surplus-value in industrial sites located within one country are performed outside the borders of that country. These include exports of finished goods, imports of intermediate goods, the adjudication of legal disputes, and the production of capitalist values and norms. Another form is when sites of capitalist exploitation exist within different nation-states across the globe. These two different senses of global capitalism show that capitalism has been global from the very beginning (since, even though sites of capitalist exploitation were originally concentrated in one group of countries, colonialism and imperialism meant the securing of conditions of existence elsewhere in the world) and that global capitalism has changed over time (since, later, sites of capitalist exploitation emerged in other parts of the world). Recognizing the changing shape of global capitalism leads both to new ways of analyzing globalization and to new policies to transform and eliminate capitalist exploitation wherever it exists.

Later, sometime in the 1990s, globalization itself became the hot topic, the new development (or so many thought) that challenged existing knowledges and required new theorizations. That's when I set to work with another University of Massachusetts former graduate student, Serap Kayatekin, to make sense of what we perceived to be the problems associated with the new globalization discourses. Our main questions were relatively straightforward: what are the forms of subjectivity presumed and/or produced by the discourses of globalization? And, following on from that, what were the possible politics of class transformation deriving from these?

These questions emerged from our critical review of the literatures in political economy and cultural studies: in both cases, there was a presumption that global capital was omnipotent, that all spaces and subjectivities had become inscribed within and by the power of global capital, that global capitalism was in the process of (or had already succeeded in) annihilating all its noncapitalist others. What we found in the economistic logic with which many scholars were making sense of globalization were two subjectivities: what we call the "national Keynesian" and the "global imperative" subject positions. We detected the national Keynesian in calls for national development; for example, imposing restrictions on movements of capital across national boundaries in the face of global pressures. Today, that would be Lou Dobbs or the AFL-CIO. The global imperative stemmed from the conclusion that national identities had been effectively undermined and effaced by the globalization of capital – Thomas Friedman, if you will. What of all the other subjectivities and forms of political activity that are not dictated by the logic of global capitalism and that might serve as forms of opposition, resistance, and alternatives? We did find more interest in diverse, hybrid, localized subjectivities in the cultural studies literature, but then they, too, subsumed these subjectivities within the logic of global capitalism.

Our problem, then, was that everyone seemed to be reading a unique set of subjectivities and political possibilities off the globalizing logic of capital. As Kayatekin and I saw it, there was no attempt to make sense of the range of alternative forms of recognition – and, of course, misrecognition – that are, or can be, constituted within and alongside the processes of global expansion. This is what we called the "relative autonomy" of the social constitution of subjectivity, which was connected with the new ideas about space being produced by postmodern and Marxist geographers, such as Edward Soja and David Harvey, according to whom globalization was eliminating certain spatial barriers, changing other spaces, and creating still newer spaces. The result was a heterogeneous spatial landscape that we analyzed in terms of "place-bound identities," which people like Harvey (and, later, Hardt and Negri, when they refer to the multitude) consider to be reactionary.

This, in turn, led us to imagine and focus on specific localities of otherwise global operations – such as branch plants, diasporic communities and so forth – that can be understood as specific combinations of both local instantiation and global connection. We were interested – remember, this was the time when antisweatshop campaigns were just getting off the ground – in the possibilities occasioned by the interplay between imagined communities in one location (for example, where goods were being consumed) and other locations (for instance, where the goods were being produced). We imagined here an interplay that would change the awareness of the local and global dimensions of both communities. Add to these subjectivities from "within global capitalism" the existence of identities constituted with respect to noncapitalist forms of economy and society – in households, home-based production, production cooperatives and so on – and we have a range of class subjectivities and class-oriented political projects within, alongside, and outside global capitalism. In our view, these subjectivities can serve to challenge the poverty of choice imposed by the national Keynesian and global imperative limits of the debate over globalization.

As the literature on globalization grew, I began to see other disturbing tendencies. For example, many contemporary observers (both those who celebrate globalization and those who are more critical) "forget about" earlier periods of globalization and overemphasize the novelty of the current period. In addition, the focus on globalization has tended to push aside one of the key Marxian concepts – imperialism – precisely when it is most needed. It was precisely at that point that I was invited to give a plenary talk on globalization (which was later published in *Rethinking Marxism*). I took as my goal to negotiate the distance that separates globalization and imperialism, which involved rethinking both concepts. (And I was somewhat surprised by the reaction to my talk, which was mostly positive, because the presumption seemed to be that a postmodern Marxian class analysis was inconsistent with the idea of imperialism.)

I first set out to contextualize globalization by noting the similarities between the current period and the period that extended from the end of the nineteenth century to the beginning of the twentieth. At least quantitatively – in terms of indicators of foreign investment, international trade, financial flows, and movements of people – the two periods are quite similar. The challenge, as I see it, is to mark those similarities and, at the same time, to make sense of the qualitative differences.

Why then, if the two periods are so similar, do many consider the idea of imperialism appropriate for the first and not the second? That is one reason for reinvigorating the idea of imperialism. The other reason has to do with its effects: contrary to globalization, imperialism refers to a multi-dimensional set of practices (economic, political, and cultural) with no necessary unity or inevitability about them. I then set out to examine the economic dimensions of imperialism (what I call imperial economies, as opposed to another project I'm currently working on, imperial economics), focusing on such issues as subcontracting to foreign sweatshops, foreign direct investment, and international lending in order to examine the class structure of each.

In Chapter 16, I also rethink the concept of imperialism, moving it away from the essentialist dimensions of Lenin's approach (and, for that matter, that of Kautsky). I borrow from the work of Gilles Deleuze and Félix Guattari to theorize an imperial-machine: a machine that energizes and is energized by capitalism. Finally, I connect the imperialism-machine to the disciplinary-machine of economics, the structure of the discipline of economics – both discursive and institutional – that permits some ways of analyzing and reacting to globalization and pushes others to (or beyond) the margins.

The goal of the Marxian critique of political economy is precisely to disrupt that disciplinary-machine, to change the terms of debate, to create the space for a nonessentialist class analysis of social reality.

Note

1 My own view is not that mainstream economists cannot see exploitation; rather, they *choose* not to see exploitation. As the work of John Roemer (1988), and Samuel Bowles and Herbert Gintis (1988 and 1992) has convincingly shown, it is possible to use the concepts and models of neoclassical economics – exogenous preferences, individual choice, equilibrium, and so on – and still show that exploitation takes place within capitalism. The notion of exploitation they use may not be a specifically Marxian one, but the fact that they can show that, within the terms of neoclassical theory, exploitation can exist means that neoclassical economists have chosen not to examine, much less emphasize, the role that exploitation plays within capitalist economies.

13 Fordism on a world scale: International dimensions of regulation

All theories have their histories as well as their concepts. In the case of regulation theory, the concept of national capitalist regulation was the first moment in a theoretical strategy designed to produce an alternative account of the long-period development of capital accumulation in the advanced capitalist economies. The theory of national capitalist regulation was then internationalized, in an attempt to investigate two additional themes. First, regulation theory was extended to encompass the international connections among and between the different modes of national regulation of the advanced capitalist nations. In traditional economics terminology, this is the "north–north" model offered by the Regulation School. Second, regulation theorists have turned their attention to the Third World: a "north–south" model of regulation was formulated in order to analyze the characteristics of capital accumulation in the peripheral south and the connections between southern and northern processes of accumulation.

This historical sequence – Fordism, global Fordism, and, finally, peripheral Fordism (all of which are defined below) – would appear to complete the Marxian agenda for theorizing capitalist development. As we are constantly reminded, Marx never finished his original project; he died before writing, in particular, the proposed volumes on international trade and the world market.[1] The challenge of "finishing" Marx's critique of political economy has attracted the attention of many: Lenin's *Imperialism*, André Gunder Frank's dependency theory, Immanuel Wallerstein's world-systems analysis, and Samir Amin's *Accumulation on a World Scale*, to name just a few, can be understood as so many attempts to fill the gap left by Marx's original scheme (cf. Brewer 1980). The work of the Regulation School is one of the most recent and comprehensive efforts to complete the international dimension of the Marxian project.

The present essay focuses on selected aspects of the work of one regulation theorist, Alain Lipietz. In an important series of articles and a powerful recent book, Lipietz has both sharpened and extended the initial work of the Regulation School.[2] Using the theory's account of regulation in the advanced capitalist countries as a backdrop, he has investigated the various cases of Third World industrialization during the 1970s, in terms of the expansion of Fordism on a world scale. The new international division of labor that emerges from this account, along with the Regulation School's analysis of the crisis of accumulation in the advanced capitalist economies, is used to explain both the early success and later failure of peripheral Fordism.

The theoretical construct that guides this analysis is the model of accumulation and regulation originally proposed to explain the long-term trends of capital accumulation in the United States and other advanced capitalist economies. Capitalism, according to Lipietz and the other regulation theorists, is best understood in terms of a model that connects a regime of accumulation and a mode of regulation. Periods of successful capitalist development are the result of a correspondence between a regime of accumulation and its mode of regulation; capitalist crises, in contrast, are explained by a lack of correspondence between accumulation and regulation.

The aim of the following analysis is to assess the contribution of regulation theory, as interpreted and further elaborated by Lipietz, to the existing debate and to the formulation of a specifically Marxian theory of world capitalist development. Particular attention is paid to the concepts, especially the accumulation/regulation model, with which capitalism has been theorized. This critical examination consists of two interrelated parts: I locate some of the important contributions and internal tensions that emerge from the Regulation School's attempt to transpose a theory of national regulation, originally developed for the advanced capitalist nations, to the world economy. In various places, I also briefly juxtapose regulation to an alternative interpretation of Marxian theory. Overall, I attempt to uncover the limits imposed by the regulation model for the further elaboration of a Marxian class analysis of capitalism.

The theory of regulation: questions of methods[3]

The work of Lipietz is an internationalized version of a theory of regulation initially proposed to explain the long-period swings of capital accumulation in the advanced capitalist countries, especially during the postwar period. Therefore, it is necessary to assess the initial project of the Regulation School in some detail, before proceeding to an analysis of Lipietz's theory of global Fordism.

Gramsci's analysis of "Americanism and Fordism" (1971) is one of the key inspirations for the regulation theorists' social theory of capital accumulation. There, Gramsci (1971, 293) focuses on the "particular environment, a particular social structure (or at least a determined intention to create it) and a certain type of State" without which Americanization is not possible. The accumulation of capital is, in this sense, shaped in important ways by the larger social environment within which accumulation takes place. Following Gramsci, the regulation theorists reject interpretations of accumulation that view it as the consequence of a logic intrinsic to the nature of competition among individual capitals, the innate behavior of economic agents, or some other essential factor. Rather, they have focused on, and attempted to theorize, the structure of social relations that gives content and cohesion to a regime of accumulation. Thus, they argue, "the regulation of capitalism must be interpreted as a social creation" (Aglietta 1979, 19).

The Regulation School's focus on the social structure of accumulation forces it into a confrontation with the Marxian tradition of long-period theories of accumulation. In particular, regulation theory may be seen as an attempt to formulate an alternative to the monopoly capital tradition of Josef Steindl, Paul Baran and Paul Sweezy and, more recently, John Bellamy Foster.[4] Although nowhere announced as such by the regulation theorists themselves, the notion of "regulation" may be understood as an attempt to formulate a nonreductionist, social conception of the capital accumulation process.[5]

The "mode of regulation" is the concept that summarizes the social structure of accumulation. The accumulation of capital is conceived to be regulated, in the sense that a set of structural forms in the field of capitalist relations – collective bargaining, social security, financial groups and conglomerates, and so on – serves to mitigate the contradictions inherent in capitalist commodity production. In the case of the postwar United States and the remaining advanced capitalist nations, the regulation theorists argue that these structural norms were successful in reproducing what are conceived to be the conditions of Fordist accumulation from the early 1950s into the 1970s. Specifically, mechanization and mass consumption could serve as the "internal" elements of the Fordist regime of intensive accumulation only to the extent that a multifaceted "external" environment existed that reproduced them over time.

Even at this general level of presentation, there are certain features of regulation theory that distinguish it from other theories of accumulation. For the purpose of carrying out the proposed assessment of Lipietz's contribution below, I focus on two: the connections between the regime of accumulation and the mode of regulation – the relationship between the so-called internal elements and their external environment – and the "gaps" that are left in the theory concerning the role of accumulation and the state.

Accumulation and regulation

The theory of regulation has taken as one of its principal goals the explanation of the current economic crisis. Other explanations – presuming, of course, that such a crisis exists – abound. In making their own contribution

to this debate, the regulation theorists have made a clear attempt to negotiate a path between two contrasting interpretations of the current crisis:
on one hand, they refuse to analyze the crisis in terms of accidents (such as
the pair of oil "shocks") or policy mistakes (such as the Volker interest-rate
"shock"); on the other hand, their analysis is designed to avoid the
problem of analyzing the current crisis as the final blow to capitalism.
Boyer (1986a, 226–27), for example, has written that "one must speak in
terms of end-of-century capitalisms, not of the end of capitalism."

The Regulation School theorists have produced the concepts of regime
of accumulation and mode of regulation in order to carry out this alternative analysis of the current crisis. In turn, these concepts have been
extended backward in time, to account for the historical process of accumulation that preceded the current crisis. They also serve as the basic
elements for the Regulation School's attempt to organize their understanding of the form of capitalism that may emerge from the present crisis.
This is what makes the theory of regulation such a forceful project: it is
nothing less than a recasting of the entire history of capitalist development
in terms of the concepts of accumulation and regulation.

For the theory of regulation to work, however, capitalism must be
understood as a system whose dynamic is determined by a process of
capital accumulation which, in turn, can be appropriately regulated. The
regulation theorists have focused their attention on the premise that the
successful completion of the circuit of capitalist production – and thus
the level and pace of accumulation – requires a certain balance between
the evolution of the production of wage goods and means of production.

The "regime of accumulation" is intended to conceptualize the evolution of this relationship between consumer and producer goods sectors. In
turn, successive regimes of accumulation – extensive, intensive, and so on
– depict specific configurations of this relationship. Fordism, for example,
is the name attributed to the intensive regime of accumulation that has
served as the basis of the advanced capitalist economies from the Great
Depression until the present decade. It has been characterized by two
simultaneous developments: high rates of growth of productivity and a
rise in mass consumption.[6]

There is no guarantee, however, that, at any point in time, the balance
between production and consumption – the relationship between the
departments of wage and producer goods production – will be "correct."
The mode of regulation captures the "institutional norms, procedures and
habits which either coerce or persuade private agents to conform" to a
given regime of accumulation (Lipietz 1987, 33). The mode of regulation is
therefore crucial to the reproduction of accumulation: it can either reproduce the "correct" balance between consumption and production or, by
producing an "incorrect" relationship between the evolution of the two
sectors, undermine the existing regime of accumulation.

Contribution and tensions

Instead of entering into the debate about whether or not one or another regime of accumulation/mode of regulation adequately "mirrors" the "actual" evolution of the United States or some other economy in any particular period, I want to raise three issues concerning the status of the concepts in the Regulation School's account of capitalist development.

As noted above, regulation theory represents a break from previous monopoly capital attempts to theorize the process of capital accumulation by constructing a social environment within which accumulation takes place. The result of defining these "external" social conditions is that accumulation is no longer conceived to be a self-regulating process. This is an important contribution to a Marxian tradition in which, all too often, capitalist development is reduced to some essential feature or causal factor. According to regulation theory, the regime of accumulation is successfully reproduced, if at all, by a mode of regulation that is constituted outside of it. This is the significance of the assertion that none of the "structural forms" of regulation "can play its role in the mitigation of social contradictions without the simultaneous operation of all the others. But this simultaneous operation is in no way inherent in the logic of accumulation" (Aglietta 1979: 383)

The role of the various components of the mode of regulation is to act on the regime of accumulation in "decisive areas" such that, in their combined influence, the correct balance between sectors is initially forged and then maintained over time.

The fact that the mode of regulation is constituted outside of the regime of accumulation means that the successful reproduction of accumulation is a contingent effect, dependent on conditions relatively autonomous from the structuring influence of the process of accumulation itself. However, this effort to "decenter" the process of accumulation leads to two additional problems:

1   it reintroduces a model-like necessity at a different level, and
2   it leaves two key components – the role of accumulation and of the state – as relatively untheorized "gaps" in the Regulation School's account of capitalist development.

The accumulation/regulation model

While forsaking the limits imposed by simple models of accumulation of the sort developed by Steindl and others, regulation theorists develop their own form of model in the notion of the correspondence between regimes of accumulation and modes of regulation. This model of correspondence carries with it the same kinds of problems inherent in more traditional models of the correspondence between, for example, the relations and forces of production. Ultimately, this notion of correspondence becomes an economic law that undermines the potential for regulation theory to develop a fully social, decentered or nonessentialist, notion of capitalist development.

The notion of correspondence enters the Regulation School's account in its analysis of the successive periods of crisis and stability in capital accumulation. Periods of successful capital accumulation – for example, the mid- to late-nineteenth century and the two postwar decades – are accounted for by the correspondence between a regime of accumulation and its "correct" (i.e., corresponding) mode of regulation. On the contrary, the crisis that characterized the late-nineteenth century, the 1930s, and the present conjuncture are analyzed in terms of a lack of correspondence between accumulation and regulation:

> "Major crises" indicate that the mode of regulation is not adequate to the regime of accumulation either because the emergence of a new regime is being held back by outdated forms of regulation (as in the crisis of 1930) or because the potential of the regime of accumulation has been exhausted, given the prevailing mode of regulation (this is probably true of both the late nineteenth century and of the present crisis).
>
> (Lipietz 1987: 34)

Although the regulation theorists stop short of asserting that the regime of accumulation "calls forth" its corresponding mode of regulation, their conception of corresponding regimes of accumulation and modes of regulation introduces a notion of "succession" in which each, admittedly "relatively autonomous," level – accumulation and regulation – is either "ahead of" or "behind" the other. This notion of historical succession means that the history of capitalist development is constructed on the basis of a notion of functional prerequisites in which the activities of agents are said to conform – either through coercion or persuasion – to the necessities of accumulation.

The problem with this conception of accumulation/regulation as a model of correspondence and historical succession is that it introduces law-like regularities into a historical process that might otherwise be understood in terms of the contradictory movement over time of the entire ensemble of social processes that can be said to condition the existence of the capitalist fundamental class process, namely, the extraction of surplus-value. The fact that the accumulation/regulation model operates in a law-like manner is borne out in the Regulation School's analysis of the current crisis. The only way for the model of postwar Fordism to be undermined is for an exogenous change to occur in the conditions that had previously guaranteed its success. Fordism is conceived to be a "well-regulated" regime of accumulation in which production and consumption were kept in balance until there was a drop in the rate of growth of productivity, beginning in the mid-1960s. The fall in the rate of growth of productivity caused a fall in the rate of profit which, in turn, slowed the rate of accumulation. This explanation of the regime of accumulation undermining the mode of regulation differs from the account of the crisis of the 1930s, in which the terms are reversed and the existing mode of regulation is conceived to "hold back" the regime of accumulation. In both cases, however, the model fails in its operation because of an exogenous change in one of the corresponding elements.

The point of criticizing the conception of the relationship between accumulation and regulation as a model of succession is not to deny that the accumulation of capital is complexly affected by its institutional, social environment. To do so would be to lapse back into a theory of accumulation in which capital accumulation regulates itself, through its own purely internal mechanisms. Nor am I interested in dismissing the use of all such models of economic and social phenomena. Models of regularity can have important heuristic value in illustrating, under clearly specified and limiting assumptions, the movement over time of a contradictory set of social (including economic) processes (Ruccio 1988). However, the purpose of Marxian models is to abstract from, or freeze the movement of processes by assuming a hypothetical equilibrium, in order to focus attention on the ceaseless movement and change of those processes. This is how I interpret Marx's procedure in the two most famous examples: the reproduction schemes and the formation of the general rate of profit in Volumes 2 and 3 of *Capital*, respectively. The traditional use of models in, for example, neoclassical theory is exactly the opposite. There, models are constructed as "real" equilibria – that is, the focus is on the points where the model is "solved," while the movement between equilibrium points is merely assumed.

The tension between a conception of capitalist development in terms of the contradictory movement of many, diverse social processes versus the understanding of capitalist dynamics as a model of two corresponding elements is inherent in the Regulation School's analysis of the current economic crisis. On one hand, the notion that capitalism can be successfully regulated – at least three relatively long previous historical periods illustrate this – has the advantage of shifting the discussion from alternative predictions of the nature of the final demise of capitalism to an investigation of the emergence of the elements of a possible post-crisis/post-Fordist form of capitalist development.[7] A "major crisis" in capitalist development need not lead, in any necessary or inexorable fashion, to a post-capitalist "solution" to the crisis. On the contrary, as the regulation theorists have successfully argued, a new capitalist "order" may arise out of the current "disorder."

However, the model of accumulation/regulation tends to impose severe limits on the investigation of the nature of this new capitalist order.

The use of the model focuses attention on the possibility that a new regime of accumulation and its corresponding mode of regulation will arise. This leads to an investigation into the necessary pieces of the "puzzle" – the elements of a new regime of accumulation and the components of a mode of regulation that function to distribute social production in the "correct" balance. The remaining social processes of the social formation, those that fall outside the accumulation/regulation model – processes that provide conditions of existence of the capitalist class process other than those that allow accumulation to take place, and processes that condition the existence of modes of surplus labor appropriation other than the capitalist extraction of surplus-value – tend to receive little, if any, attention. The focus of regulation theory is the set of "institutional norms, procedures, and habits" that reproduce a given class structure rather than, as one alternative, the changing class (and nonclass) structure of the various institutions and sites of social activity in a capitalist social formation.

Two "gaps": accumulation and the state

Even if we limit ourselves to the historical development of capitalism, the accumulation/regulation model suffers from two key "gaps": the theoretical significance of accumulation and the role of the state. These are curious omissions, given the central role of both concepts in the Regulation School's theory of capitalist development. Taken in turn, but without developing them in detail, the problems may be sketched as follows.

The regulation theory of capitalism's history and current crisis is based on the central role of capital accumulation. However, little attention is directed at justifying why this particular aspect of capitalism is singled out for attention. It would seem that the regulation theorists merely presume the central role of the accumulation process in determining the existence and reproduction over time of the capitalist class process. If this central role is taken as given, then the remainder of the project – the determination of the extensive or intensive nature of accumulation and the regulation of the conditions for reproducing one or another form of accumulation – would be the appropriate research agenda. Without such a justification, and given the alternative ways of organizing a Marxian analysis of capitalist development, there would appear to be a crippling omission in regulation theory.

It would, of course, be possible to return to Marx and note the importance accorded to accumulation in the "original" text. However, the most famous passage in *Capital* – "Accumulate, accumulate! That is Moses and the prophets!" – is not claimed by Marx, but rather attributed to the classical economists (Marx 1977, 742). If the accumulation of capital was (and remains – see, for example, Pasinetti 1983) the great discovery of classical economics, then how or why should Marxists justify its centrality in a Marxian theory of capitalist development? From a Marxian perspective, the accumulation of capital cannot be considered the only – or even the key – mechanism whereby the conditions of existence of the capitalist class process are reproduced. The mass of surplus-value, once extracted, is distributed in various directions in order to secure some of the economic, political and cultural conditions for the continued extraction of surplus-value.[8] Marx developed his theory of supervisory managers of joint-stock companies, interest-bearing capital, merchants, and landlords on this basis. They were theorized as agents who provide some of the economic conditions for capitalist production to take place. This theory of "subsumed classes" has recently been extended to consider not only additional economic, but also cultural and political, conditions of existence (Resnick and Wolff 1987b, especially Chap. 3). The capitalist class process is also complexly affected – overdetermined, to use Althusser's term – by social processes that do not entail a distribution of surplus-value.

My intention in raising this question is not to dismiss the importance of the accumulation of capital. Even as non-Marxists have argued, "the process of accumulation of capital goods is essential to the working of the whole production process and therefore cannot but be a matter for the economic system as a whole" (Pasinetti 1983, 411); and, I would add, a matter for Marxists. The social effects of capital accumulation – on the extraction of surplus-value, the working class, and the capitalist social formation as a whole – are too important and far-reaching for the matter to be left in the hands of bourgeois economists. However, it is a separate matter for accumulation to be placed at the center of the Marxian analysis of capitalist development.

To explain briefly: it is possible to accord discursive centrality to the accumulation of capital without attributing to it a priority in some kind of causal hierarchy of the myriad economic and noneconomic conditions of existence of the capitalist extraction of surplus-value. Given the determinant role of the accumulation of capital in non-Marxian – nonclass – economic theories, a Marxist may choose to focus on accumulation in order to demonstrate the class conditions and effects of accumulation that are left out of other accounts. This discursive move – to focus on the accumulation of capital in a particular analysis in order to criticize other theories – should be clearly distinguished from a long-standing tendency within the Marxian tradition to attribute causal priority to the accumulation of capital, as if it were the key feature (or one of a small subset of key features) of capitalist development. This latter move serves to reproduce, within Marxism, the economism characteristic of bourgeois (classical and neoclassical) economic theories.

A second important gap in regulation theory concerns its analysis of the state. The state figures prominently in the work of the members of the Regulation School because, they claim, it is the site where the various structural forms of regulation are concentrated and reproduced over time. The state lends coherence to the mode of regulation and, hence, to the regime of accumulation. This theory of the "regulatory state" defines a structural role for the state which, while avoiding some of the more essentialist concepts of the state that have marked the Marxian tradition (reviewed by, for example, Jessop 1978), reduces the state to the specific needs of the prevailing regime of accumulation. As a result, regulation theory tends to neglect the changing sites of regulation, both within and between social formations – the extent to which the forms of regulation may be secured not only in the state, but also in households, trade unions, enterprises, schools, churches, and elsewhere, depending on the social formation in question.[9]

The regulatory role of the state derives from the needs of accumulation. As discussed above, the prevailing regime of accumulation is seen to require a coherent and orderly set of regulatory mechanisms that is not guaranteed by the process of accumulation itself. The role of the state is to provide this order by carrying out the functions which establish the correct balance between production and consumption.

> It is in the state, and there alone, that the cohesion of these structural forms can be assured, permanently jeopardized and as permanently reproduced by the fluctuating compromises of economic policy.
>
> (Aglietta 1979, 383)

The fact that the state is "brought into" the analysis to resolve the contradictions inherent in the movement of accumulation over time means that the state is an expression of an essential set of tensions and conflicts generated by the regime of accumulation. The resolution of these contradictions is displaced from the regime of accumulation itself to the level of the state. In this way, the role and structure of the state are determined by the needs of accumulation to be regulated. In other words, the state is structured by the accumulation/regulation model discussed above.

This essential role of the state closes some of the distance that otherwise separates regulation theory from the theory of monopoly capitalism. According to monopoly capital theory, the capitalist state absorbs the economic surplus generated by accumulation under monopoly capitalist conditions. State expenditures, in turn, generate a level of aggregate demand appropriate to the needs of accumulation. The regulation theorists distance themselves from this story in focusing on the balance between sectors of production, and therefore on the diverse state initiatives that maintain the necessary balance, rather than on the absolute level of state expenditures. However, this difference in the role of state activities masks a fundamental similarity between the two approaches: in both cases, the role of the state is functionally determined by the needs of the prevailing regime of accumulation.

A second result of this "essentialist" approach to the state is that the nation is considered the proper focus of the analysis of the accumulation/

regulation problem. Primacy is accorded to national regulation because the development of capitalism is understood "first and foremost" as the "outcome of internal class struggles which result in embryonic regimes of accumulation being consolidated by forms of regulation that are backed by the local state" (Lipietz 1987, 19). The tensions generated by this focus on the national state as the site of the "unity" of accumulation and regulation are inherited by the Regulation School's attempt to consider the international dimensions of capitalist development.

The internationalization of national regulation

Once regulation theory was consolidated as a theory of national regulation, the Regulation School expanded its approach by considering the international dimensions of capitalist development. The internationalization of regulation theory has encompassed two distinct but related themes: on one hand, regulation theorists have analyzed the economic relations among the advanced capitalist nations. The key issue in this investigation has been the role of international dimensions in the rise and subsequent demise of the postwar pattern of Fordist development. On the other hand, regulation theorists have attempted to theorize the nature of capitalist development in the Third World. The principal questions in this regard have concerned the existence of national modes of regulation in the peripheral countries and their insertion into the international economy.

The internationalization of regulation theory both parallels and represents an important break from other contemporary attempts to understand the international dimensions of the current crisis. At the level of economic relations among the advanced capitalist nations, the internationalization of national regulatory regimes can be said to mirror the opening up of traditional macroeconomic models with respect to external trade and capital flows. The past decade has witnessed the emergence of both "global monetarist" and Keynesian "open-economy" macromodels. In all three cases, theories originally generated at the level of the national economy have been modified to encompass international economic relations. And, in all three cases, the results have been similar: the internationalization of national economies has reduced the scope and effectivity of traditional national economic policies.

The fact that regulation theory is based on a model of the accumulation of capital sets it apart from its orthodox counterparts in understanding the long-term dynamic of capitalist development. Still, each one of the theories is beset with a fundamental tension as a result of the attempt to "open" a theory originally formulated, and therefore "closed," at the national level. In the case of regulation theory, this tension is exhibited at the level of its analysis of the contribution of international factors to the current crisis. It also raises a more general issue of the way in which concepts are generated during the course of developing more concrete specifications of capitalist regulation.

International economic regulation

National versus international crisis

The Regulation School's theory of international economic relations plays an important and, at the same time, indeterminate role in its account of the initial rise and eventual demise of the postwar economic order. On one hand, the evolution of the economic relations that connect the various advanced capitalist economies would appear to explain the simultaneous diffusion of both the expansion and subsequent dysfunction of the intensive regime of accumulation characteristic of the Golden Age. In this sense, the expansion of the Fordist regime, from the United States to the other advanced capitalist economies, would explain the parallel emergence of Fordist regimes of accumulation across the northern tier of the world economy. Similarly, the simultaneous crisis of the various Fordist regimes would be accounted for by changes in the postwar configuration of international economic relations, which undermined the original balance among national regimes of accumulation. On the other hand, the indeterminacy of the role of international economic relations derives from the Regulation School's attempt to explain both the success and eventual crisis of the Fordist regime on the basis of the productivity component of the national accumulation/regulation model. The internal conditions that generate, first, an increase and, then, a decrease in the rate of growth of productivity are invoked as the essential conditions explaining the rise and demise of the postwar Fordist regimes.

The tension between analyzing postwar capitalist development in terms of internal (national) and external (international) conditions runs throughout the work of the regulation theorists. The result is that they offer two parallel explanations for the crisis of Fordism. One explanation is now classical: the rate of growth of productivity and, ultimately, the rate of profit begin to decline in the mid-1960s. This profit-squeeze leads to a slowdown in the rate of accumulation which, by definition, is the basis of the current crisis. The international dimension is absent from this explanation because, given the national conditions of productivity growth within the accumulation/regulation model, the contradiction between the existing national mode of regulation and changes in the regime of accumulation are sufficient to cause a capitalist crisis. The only question that remains is why this slowdown should occur simultaneously across different national economies.

Curiously, international economic relations are not brought in to provide this explanation. Rather, they seem to represent a second, parallel analysis of the causes of the current crisis. It would be possible, for example, to argue that one country (say, the United States) first experienced the productivity problems associated with the Fordist crisis and then "exported" them to the other OECD countries. However, the Regulation School does not attempt such an explanation. Instead, the international explanation tends to run parallel to the national profit-squeeze analysis.

The international explanation is based on the contradiction between national modes of regulation and, given the international economic relations among the advanced capitalist economies, the absence of an appropriate mode of international regulation. Therefore, instead of the contradiction between the national modes of regulation and their respective regimes of accumulation, the second explanation is based on the contradiction between or "ultimate incompatibility of national modes of regulation" (Aglietta 1982, 7).

The substitute for the mode of international regulation is a system of hegemony. An initial coherence among the various national modes of regulation was based on the existence of a hegemonic power, whence the original regime of accumulation was spread unevenly across national boundaries. Based on this hegemonic system, an international division of labor was established, which made the various national regimes of accumulation complementary. A system of international economic regulation existed to the extent that there was a set of international institutions, under the aegis of the hegemonic power, which governed the balance of payments of the various countries. Eventually, however, there was an accumulation of tensions, based on uneven development across the various national regimes of accumulation, which undermined the original hegemonic power. These tensions were further aggravated by the emergence of new international monetary relations (such as the international private credit system) that were beyond the regulation of any nation-state.

> There is a crisis, then, because the modes of expression of international monetary constraints (exchange-rate distortions, short-term capital transfers) do not result in adjustments capable of absorbing the structural distortions.
>
> (Aglietta 1982, 26)

What is the relationship between these two accounts of the rise and demise of the postwar capitalist order? One explanation stresses the internal, profit-squeeze causes of the crisis; the other focuses on the inherent instability of the international interactions among the advanced capitalist economies. In both cases, a simple contradiction is invoked to explain the origins of the crisis: the first explanation is based on the contradiction, at each national level, between the regime of accumulation and the mode of regulation; the second approach looks to the contradiction between national modes of regulation to explain the origins of the crisis.

The impasse between the two competing explanations is generated by the status of the original model of accumulation and regulation. Because the model was "complete" in its initial formulation at the national level, the regulation theorist is forced to choose between the two explanations. An alternative would be to integrate the two accounts and investigate the connections between the internal and external – national and international – changes in the conditions of capitalist development. However, this would require a different theoretical procedure in which the "abstract" relationships of the original model were modified as the mode of regulation was made more "concrete" – for example, through the specification of the international conditions of capital accumulation. However, the priority accorded to national regulation is a fundamental obstacle to this approach.[10]

The nation-state

The starting point for the Regulation School account of international economic relations is the nation-state. This is what the regulation theorists call the "primacy of the national dimension" (Aglietta 1982, 6). The world economy is theorized, in turn, as a "system of interacting national social formations" (1982, 6). The priority accorded to national regulation is justified with reference to its correspondence to concrete history. In one case, the assertion is that "[e]conomic history has ratified the general validity of this theoretical procedure by showing that there is no long-term trend for international relations to be harmonized through the homogenization of national economies and the equalization of growth rates" (1982, 6).

In another case, the priority accorded to national regulation is supported by reference to the fact that the "entire economic miracle of the sixteenth and seventeenth centuries revolved around the transition from city-centers to national economies, the key to transition itself being the shift from Amsterdam to London."[11]

A key problem with asserting the historical, and then theoretical, primacy of national regulation is that the status of "nationness" – the nation-centeredness of accumulation and regulation – is never itself investigated. If this term is attached to accumulation and regulation from the start, then international economic relations cannot be understood except as the set of relations that link different national modes of regulation (see, also, Willoughby 1988).

The point is that nationality is only one among the infinite number of concrete characteristics that can be attached to the process of accumulation or regulation or, for that matter, the extraction of surplus-value. Other concrete characteristics include race, gender, geographical location, and so on. A Marxian theory of capitalism, as I understand it, begins by abstracting from these features of the concrete context within which class processes occur. This is the procedure captured by the term "abstract labor." The capitalist class process (or accumulation or regulation) is not intrinsically either national (as in regulation theory) or international (as in Wallerstein's world-systems analysis); it is not reduced, in the first instance, to any one of the myriad processes that participate in determining its concrete existence in a given setting. Only as the analysis proceeds – as it becomes more concrete – is it possible to examine the particular effects of the component processes of national and international relations (or, again, of gender, race, geography, etc.) on the concrete constitution of the class process, thereby changing the initial abstract concept. Whether processes that are considered national or international are brought into the analysis at a particular point depends, not on some intrinsically national or international character of the capitalist class process but, rather, on the interests of the analyst (for a variety of theoretical and political reasons at a given point in time) in examining the complex ways in which one or another nonclass process participates in constituting the class process. The general point is that, instead of being fixed in an initial abstract sense, the effects of "nationness" would be considered one of the changing features of the social landscape within which the processes of accumulation, regulation and the extraction of surplus-value take place.

Fordism on a world scale

Imperialism

The second moment in the internationalization of regulation theory occurs in the Regulation School's treatment of the Third World. This aspect of the project was originally announced in Aglietta (1979) as a critique of the classical Marxian concept of imperialism. It has since been elaborated as an alternative to the radical theories of international relations that became predominant during the 1960s and 1970s – namely, dependency and world-systems theories. In both cases, however, the break is only partial and incomplete.

The thrust of the original attack on Lenin's theory is that imperialism had to be defined in political terms, as a set of relations of asymmetric power among and between different nation-states. Lenin, however, grounded his notion of imperialism in the monopoly stage of capitalism, characterized by the dominance of finance capital. Although nowhere presented in this fashion, the regulation theorists' critique of Lenin's conception of imperialism would seem to derive from their prior critique of the theory of capitalism based on monopoly power. Imperialism was initially theorized as the monopoly stage of capitalism – as the direct expression of the power of the merger of finance and industrial capital. Because regulation theory explicitly rejected the periodization of capitalism based on the form of competition, favoring instead the different regimes of accumulation, the concept of imperialism based on monopoly power was similarly rejected. Regulation theory proposed an alternative concept based on the priority of the nation-state, discussed above. Thus, the relationship between economics and politics is reversed. Whereas Lenin understood the *political* carving up of the world to be a direct expression of the *economic* status of finance capital, regulation theory proposed a concept of imperialism wherein the *economic* reach of multinational corporations is based on the prior system of unequal *political* relations among nation-states.

Notwithstanding this reversal in the order of causality, regulation theory's break from Lenin's concept of imperialism is incomplete. First, classical imperialism has been accepted as a descriptive account of the international division of labor between center and periphery during the late-nineteenth and early-twentieth centuries (e.g., by Lipietz 1987, 58). Second, the reversal of the causal priority of the economic and political dimensions of imperialism leaves the essentialist nature of the original concept intact (see, also, Willoughby 1986).

The effect of the regulation concept of imperialism is to shift the focus of analysis of typical "north–south" relations from the internationalization of capital to the internationalization of national economies.[12] One of the advantages of this regulation approach is that, by separating the political relations among nation-states from the activities of multinational corporations (and other forms of the internationalization of capital), rather than collapsing them into a single set of relations, it becomes possible to investigate the complex, changing relationship between such relations. There will be conflicting claims on the policies carried out by different nation-states, as domestic and "internationalized" enterprises (not to mention other social actors) require different conditions for expansion and development. And, as different groups struggle over state initiatives, the resulting policies will have contradictory effects on the class processes that exist within a given national context, as well as within international relations.

This positive contribution is undermined, however, by the attempt to reduce imperialism to its merely political dimension. This political definition of imperialism oversimplifies the complex set of social processes that make up imperialism to the same extent as do economic determinist approaches. It reduces a complex social practice to one of its component processes. This is especially true given, as analyzed above, its undertheorized concept of the state. It also leaves out of consideration other aspects of imperialism. The cultural processes that, in part, make up imperialism tend to be ignored in favor of political and economic processes. This is a serious omission, especially for a theory that has otherwise attempted to analyze the social regulation of accumulation.

Global Fordism

The project that was only proposed in *The Theory of Capitalist Regulation* has actually been carried out by other members of the Regulation School, especially Lipietz. Building on the critique of imperialism, Lipietz has also challenged the more recent theories of dependency and world systems. While acknowledging the positive contribution made by the radical theorists over and against neoclassical theories of harmonious world development, he criticizes both dependency and world-systems theorists for failing to analyze "the concrete conditions of capitalist accumulation either in the center or in the periphery" and, hence, the changing nature of the world capitalist economy (Lipietz 1987, 2).

Lipietz's critique of existing radical theories of development is carried out with a series of sophisticated arguments against functionalism, teleology, and the general procedure of presuming a single process which binds together and determines the position of the different regions and nations within the world economy. Instead, he offers a form of analysis that begins with different national regimes of accumulation and modes of regulation and then looks at center–periphery relations in terms of the interaction among and between these sets of national processes.

Based on this alternative form of analysis, Lipietz recognizes that capitalism can develop, and has developed, in the Third World. This sets his analysis apart from the theories of both "blocked development" and "dependent development" according to which capitalism would successfully develop only in the metropolitan center of the world economy (see Chapter 6 in this volume). In this sense, regulation theory takes up, at least in an initial fashion, the challenge posed by the development of capitalism in the so-called newly industrializing economies of East Asia and Latin America (Chakravarty 1987).

The key concept for Lipietz's account of world capitalist development is Fordism. As we saw above, regulation theory has analyzed the postwar success of the development of Fordism in terms of the ability of the advanced capitalist nations to regulate production and consumption, such that the conditions for capital accumulation and economic growth were guaranteed *inside* the Fordist economies. This is the basis of the conclusion that peripheral development was not functionally related to that of the center, at least in recent decades. Therefore, although the traditional center–periphery division of labor may have been characteristic of the earlier state of extensive accumulation and competitive regulation, it ceased both to exist and to serve as an adequate explanation of Third World development when intensive accumulation and monopoly regulation became the central features of postwar capitalist development in the center.

The concept of Fordism also serves as the basis of the second major conclusion of regulation theory concerning Third World development. The analysis of the emergence and development of capitalism in the periphery utilizes the concept of Fordism in a threefold way. First, Third World capitalist development is explained as the product of the expansion of the geographical basis of central Fordism. As a result of the profit-squeeze crisis of central Fordism in the 1970s, enterprises were forced to expand their scale of production and to find cheap wage zones in the periphery. Second, the new regime of accumulation introduced into the periphery is itself analyzed in terms of Fordism. Either Third World countries adopted the technology of Fordism, in which case Lipietz characterizes their industrialization as "primitive Taylorization," or they "took off' on the basis of mechanization and a growing market for consumer durables, such that they achieve the status of "peripheral Fordism." In this way, based on the crisis in central Fordism and the emergence of peripheral (either partial or complete) Fordist regimes, Lipietz concludes that Fordism becomes a global phenomenon. Third, and finally, the monetarist attempt to "solve" the crisis of central Fordism destroys the favorable conditions under which peripheral Fordist regimes first appeared and throws them into crisis.

Lipietz's use of Fordism to explain the development of capitalism in the Third World has great merit with respect to many postwar radical analyses of peripheral development. He has effectively explained that, contra dependency theorists, capitalist development is possible within the Third World and that, contra Warren and other theoreticians of universal capitalism, the development of capitalism in the Third World is necessarily partial and uneven.

The problem posed by Lipietz's analysis is not, as suggested by others (e.g., Andreff 1984), that this regulation approach has strayed too far from traditional radical analyses of peripheral capitalist development, but that the break is itself only partial and incomplete. To take one example, Lipietz argues that peripheral industrialization is based on the expansion of Fordism from the center to the periphery. The only internal element that is of any consequence for his analysis is the form of the state within the peripheral nation. He argues that the political regime capable of regulating the emergence of peripheral Fordism has to achieve a certain relative autonomy with respect to foreign domination, the traditional ruling classes, and the popular masses. Thus, he concludes, "it usually requires a dictatorship to break the old balance and to use the state to create managerial personnel who can play the part of the ruling classes within a new regime of accumulation" (Lipietz 1987, 73).

This focus on the role of the state follows the lead pioneered by Skocpol and other theorists of "bringing the state back in" (for example, Evans *et al.* 1985). However, while performing the positive role of revaluing the relative autonomy of the state in shaping capitalist development, such analyses tend to "forget about" the other roles of the state in creating a "hothouse" for capitalism and (with or without state initiatives) the emergence of the other economic, political, and cultural conditions of existence of the capitalist class process. The story of this "primary accumulation of capital" cannot be reduced to the training of administrators; instead, it must encompass the variety of protracted struggles and historical events – from trade protection to land reform – that form the "pre-history of capital" in the Third World.

Another, equally serious problem is that Lipietz's analysis ends up being very close to the previous explanations of Third World capitalist development offered by Amin (e.g., 1977 and 1988) and Alain de Janvry (1985). Although the specific terms used by the authors are different, in all three cases capitalist development is analyzed in terms of only two basic patterns. For Amin, capitalism is either "autocentric" or "extraverted," based on whether or not the two main departments of social production are located in the country in question. Thus, peripheral capitalism is considered extraverted, and therefore incomplete, because the production of capital goods takes place in the advanced capitalist countries. De Janvry follows Amin's lead in distinguishing between socially "articulated" and "disarticulated" growth. Articulation is equivalent to wage-led development, while disarticulated development refers to export or luxury-led growth patterns. Thus, the articulation/disarticulation distinction also relies on a division of social production, in de Janvry's case, into exportables, luxury goods, and wage goods. The Regulation School makes a similar distinction between patterns or periods of capitalist development; between extensive and intensive accumulation and their corresponding modes of regulation. Autocentric and articulated growth correspond almost exactly to the regulation theory of intensive accumulation and monopoly accumulation; in other words, to Fordism. Similarly, extraverted development, disarticulation, and extensive accumulation/competitive regulation (in the periphery, primitive Taylorization) all characterize a situation in which growth is based on exports and luxury goods.

Differences remain among these three approaches. However, they are in fundamental agreement in defining development in terms of the appropriate distribution of social production across (two or three basic) sectors. This, as I showed above, is exactly how regulation theory characterizes the periods or forms of capitalist development in both the center and the periphery. Peripheral Fordism is distinguished from primitive Taylorization on the basis of whether or not "growth in the home market for manufactured goods plays a real part in the national regime of accumulation" (Lipietz 1987, 80); it is considered peripheral, rather than central, Fordism because skilled manufacturing production and engineering are located outside the countries concerned.

The analysis of peripheral capitalism in terms of the "incompleteness" (or the extraverted or disarticulated nature) of the regime of accumulation leads to a form of analysis in which the goal of the investigation is to determine why one or another element of a particular regime of accumulation does not emerge. There is a single model (Fordist accumulation/regulation, autocentric development, or social articulation) based on an essential element – the correct balance between production and consumption. In

Lipietz's view, peripheral Fordist regimes remain peripheral precisely because the proper balance between production and consumption never emerged in the so-called newly industrializing countries. This is, therefore, a one-sided view of peripheral capitalism.[13]

Conclusion

In the preceding discussion, I have presented what I see as both the positive contributions and the remaining tensions and weaknesses of regulation theory from the perspective of the need to elaborate an adequate – class-analytic and nonessentialist – Marxian theory of capitalist development.

The work of Lipietz and other members of the Regulation School can, I think, be credited with offering a number of significant challenges and alternatives to existing Marxian and other radical approaches to capitalist development. Among them are the following: the view that the accumulation of capital does not follow some "inner logic" but, rather, that there is a changing social (political and economic, including macroeconomic) environment within which accumulation takes place; the recognition that the accumulation of capital within the advanced capitalist nations has been affected by international relations and institutions and, therefore, that it is necessary to consider the role of those relations and institutions in the rise and eventual demise of the postwar (Fordist) regime of accumulation; and, finally, the idea that capitalism can, and did, emerge in various Third World countries during the 1970s and that it is important to analyze the concrete conditions within the world economy (both within and between countries) that made such developments possible.

At the same time, the work of the Regulation School is beset with important problems in terms of its potential contribution to reformulating and extending a Marxian approach to social analysis. Regulation theory, at the most general level, introduces a law of correspondence between accumulation and regulation and, ultimately, fails to theorize both the essential status that I attributed to capital accumulation and the role of the state. In terms of the analysis of international relations among the advanced capitalist nations, the work of the regulation theorists is undermined by the initial insistence on the national character of accumulation and regulation. Finally, the regulation approach to Third World development fails to break sufficiently from existing models of balance between production and consumption and thus fails to elaborate the concepts necessary to theorize the uneven, contradictory emergence of the capitalist class process in the periphery.

Notwithstanding its initial grounding in Marxism and Marxian value theory, it would appear, then, that regulation theory has fallen somewhat short of its early promise to develop and extend Marxian social theory. One question that remains is why, given these problems, the concept of

Fordism and regulation theory as a whole have come to serve as the basis for a wide variety of contemporary debates, for example, on "post-Fordism" in England (Rustin 1989) and, in the United States, on postmodernity (Harvey 1989). By way of concluding this essay, let me venture a preliminary answer to that question. My response also indicates the kind of work I think remains to be done.

The accumulation/regulation model that serves as the basis of the regulation theorists' notion of Fordism (and, of course, global Fordism and peripheral Fordism) solves a problem inherent in contemporary political economy – namely, how to conceptualize the relationship between economy and politics or, more precisely, accumulation and the state.[14] In liberal political economy, these two spheres are theorized as separate domains, each the object of study of different disciplines. Radical political economy, in contrast, has rightly called this separation into question and, historically, has sought to close the gap in a variety of different ways. Regulation theory is the most recent solution to this problem: the path between accumulation and the state is traced through the mode of regulation of the regime of accumulation. Economy and politics are linked; the problem of liberal political economy is thus solved.

What appears to be forgotten in the rush to adopt this solution is the "critique of political economy" under whose name Marxism was originally put forward. This critique involves a double move. It is, of course, important to contest and declare invalid the separation of economy and politics characteristic of liberal political economy. It is also necessary to go beyond that challenge, not simply by relating one domain to the other, but by calling into question and reconceptualizing the very terms on which that relationship is founded.

The concepts of class exploitation – the performance, appropriation, and distribution of surplus labor – are Marxism's way of rethinking the very definitions of economy and politics in liberal political economy. Thus, in the case of capitalism, it is necessary to trace through the various and changing ways in which every aspect of the economy and politics (both national and international) is affected – literally constituted – by the processes of extracting and distributing surplus-value and how, in turn, these class processes are modified and changed – even created and destroyed – by nonclass economic and political (not to mention cultural) processes. Following this path means opening up an entirely new set of theoretical questions concerning every aspect of the world political economy, from international trade to external debt and economic stabilization and adjustment policies.[15]

Not only does the centrality of class analysis pose a new set of theoretical issues. It also has important political implications for contemporary events, for example, in the Third World. The conclusion of the regulation approach to political economy is succinctly stated by Lipietz:

International solidarity with the peoples of the Third World must involve a struggle against everything which blocks their national growth – even in a Fordist-capitalist sense – or which steers it to barbaric forms of primitive Taylorization.

(1987, 193)

Marxian class analysis, as I understand it, is aimed not at the promotion of capitalist economic growth but, rather, at the elimination of capitalist exploitation. Just as succinctly, international solidarity, from a Marxian perspective, means creating the conditions, both here and abroad, within which struggles against such exploitation can take place.

One of the theoretical and political challenges facing radicals in this "end-of-century capitalism" is to carry out the kind of class analyses that will make it possible to incorporate the valuable insights and contributions of regulation theory into a Marxian critique of international political economy.

(original version published in 1989)

Notes

1   Marx proposed a critique of political economy consisting of six books – encompassing capital, landed property, wage-labor, the state, international trade, and the world market – in a letter to Ferdinand Lasalle, 22 February 1858; see Marx and Engels (1983, 270).
2   I focus here on Lipietz (1987). The series of papers leading up to *Mirages and Miracles* are listed by Lipietz on p. 198, fn. 9. For reasons of space, and because Lipietz incorporates many of their insights, I will not treat two other recent attempts to produce a regulation-inspired analysis of the Third World. The reader is referred to C. Ominami, "Chili: Echec du monétarisme périphérique," and R. Hausmann and G. Marquez, "Vénézuela: Du bon côte du choc pétrolier," both in Boyer (1986a).
3   This section is based largely on my reading of what still must be considered the central text of regulation theory, namely, Aglietta (1979). Boyer (1986b, Chap. 1) has written more extensively on the differences between regulation theory and both neoclassical and traditional Marxian theories. Jessop (1988) has discussed the differences among the various approaches to regulation theory in Western Europe and the United States. Clarke (1988) and de Vroey (1984) are other, recent introductions to regulation theory.
4   The monopoly capital tradition and recent alternatives, such as the work of Ernest Mandel and the social structures of accumulation theory presented by Samuel Bowles, David Gordon, and Thomas Weisskopf, are analyzed by Norton (1988a and 1988b). Norton's articles, as well as his earlier doctoral dissertation (1983), have influenced the present effort in important ways. Both the regulation and social structures of accumulation theorists have noted the affinity of their respective projects of reformulating the traditional Marxian notions of the capital accumulation process. Kotz (1988) has attempted to unravel some of the differences between the two approaches.
5   Aglietta's only specific criticism of Baran and Sweezy's theory of monopoly

capitalism concerns their Keynesian conception of state expenditures; see Aglietta (1979, 27–28). Aglietta does, however, frequently criticize neoclassical theory for its reductionist procedures. Boyer (1986b, 77) has criticized, in a more explicit fashion, the essentialism inherent in traditional Marxian approaches to capital accumulation.

6 Longer, more detailed lists of the elements of Fordism have been presented by others, including Jessop (1989, 263–64) and Rustin (1989, 56–57). Harvey (1989, 338–42) has extended this kind of listing of elements to describe what he calls "Fordist modernity."

7 In fact, it has become almost axiomatic for each and every regulation theorist to complete an article by "speculating" (in the best sense of that term) on the possible configurations of capitalism that may emerge out of the current situation. These observations provide a rich source for analyzing, and therefore intervening to change, the possible paths that different social formations may follow from the current crisis.

8 Aglietta (1979, 85–87) does, in fact, recognize the existence of distributions of surplus-value in addition to that portion involved in the accumulation of capital. However, casual priority is attributed to distributions of surplus-value to capital accumulation over all other such distributions by Aglietta as well as the other regulation theorists.

9 This was one of the key contributions of Althusser (1971, 127–86) in his discussion of "Ideology and Ideological State Apparatuses."

10 Willoughby (1989) presents additional criticisms of the role of international relations in regulation theory (and related) explanations of the crisis of Fordism.

11 Translation of Lipietz (1984, 58), modified from Lipietz (1987, 56). In the latter text, the corresponding passage refers to the "seventeenth and eighteenth" centuries.

12 This shift is noted and criticized by, among others, Andreff (1984).

13 See also Mandel's (1978, Chap. 1) extended discussion of the misuse of Marx's reproduction schemes to analyze capitalist development.

14 For a related discussion of the problem of political economy, see Balibar (1988).

15 See Chapters 8 and 9 of this volume for some initial steps in this direction.

14 Class beyond the nation-state

(with Stephen Resnick and Richard Wolff)

> Prophesy now involves a geographical rather than historical projection; it is space not time that hides consequences from us.
>
> Berger (1974, 40)

Vast changes continue to be wrought on the landscape of capitalism. According to many observers, the defining characteristic of the most recent phase of capitalist development is the emergence of a truly global form of capitalist economy. A wide range of debates and literature focuses on what is variously called the globalization or internationalization or multinationalization of economic processes in the contemporary world.[1] Radical economists, especially, have emphasized the extent to which the dynamic of capitalist development has spilled beyond the borders and, in turn, challenged the autonomy of individual nation-states.[2]

We, too, are impressed and challenged by ongoing changes in world economy and society. For example, the growth in international trade continues to outstrip the growth in world output (trade growth was more than double output growth in 1989). The so-called debt crisis of the 1980s still engulfs a large part of the Third World, together with Poland, Hungary, and other Eastern European countries. These developments have been accompanied by the steady growth of multinational corporations (in manufacturing, as well as in finance and services), by huge, rapid flows of money among different national stock and capital markets, and by the emergence of worldwide telecommunications networks. It would appear that we are living through another period of time–space compression (Harvey 1989) similar in scope (although radically different in content) to that which was experienced at the turn of this century (Kern 1983).

While these changes may seem obvious, how to analyze them from a global perspective is not at all self-evident: in particular, a Marxian class analysis appears to be problematic. If we are compelled by such changes to move beyond the nation-state, does that mean that we are also beyond class, as proclaimed in so many quarters (e.g., Laclau and Mouffe 1985)?

We don't think so. We argue that the tendency for class to be deemphasized (or forgotten altogether) in analyses of global capitalism results in the loss of a vital factor in the understanding of critical issues in the world today – from calls for protecting national markets or, alternatively, for "belt-tightening" in the face of international competition to debates about the contours of postmodernism.

The problem of where and how class fits into an analysis of global capitalism is not of recent origin. The relationship between class and the national and international dimensions of capitalism has long been a theoretical and political problem, not least for the radical tradition. Marx's own writings do not chart a clear path on this point. For example, some (e.g., Bowles 1988) have claimed that Marx's conception of capitalism is based on a model of a "closed economy." Marx, however, states quite clearly in the *Grundrisse* that "the tendency to create the world market is directly given in the concept of capital itself" (1973, 408). However, Marx (with Engels 1976, 494–95) concluded that, although the proletariat was stripped of "every trace of national character," the struggle between the proletariat and the bourgeoisie, "though not in substance, yet in form . . . is at first a national struggle." This is not, at least at first glance, a particularly well-defined legacy for contemporary analyses of global capitalism. Although the so-called need to expand internationally can be derived from the first point, the second point permits national class struggle to become the reflection and focus of this international need.

How, then, is class situated in this nexus of national and international dimensions of capitalist development? The radical tradition since Marx has evolved two main lines of thought concerning the role of class vis-à-vis the nation-state and the relations between nation-states. The first emerges in the writings of the early theorists of imperialism and of the so-called Dependency School – of Lenin (1933), Nikolai Bukharin (1972), and Rudolf Hilferding (1981); and of Paul Baran (1957), André Gunder Frank (1969), and Samir Amin (1975). A second approach, known under the rubrics of world-systems analysis and the internationalization of capital approach, is associated with the writings of, for the former, Immanuel Wallerstein (1979) and, for the latter, Christian Palloix (1975) and Rhys Jenkins (1987).

Concerned with the place of class in radical analyses of global capitalism, we can identify two major problems shared by these approaches: first, their economism, and, second, their focus on power relations instead of class. In focusing on these common problems, we do not dismiss the many fruitful contributions of both approaches; nor do we want to ignore the otherwise significant differences between them. To choose just one example of these differences, the two approaches follow diametrically opposite paths in analyzing the relationship between the nation-state and international relations. Those who follow the first approach begin with a theory of the economic laws of motion within nation-states and, on that basis, construct an analysis of the international dimensions of capitalism.[3] The advocates of the second approach, in contrast, begin with an understanding of capitalism at an international level, which is then used to explain the nature and role of individual (and groups of) nation-states.[4]

Notwithstanding such differences, these approaches present two main problems with respect to a *class* analysis of global capitalism. First, both approaches are grounded in a presumed and untheorized unity of the economic space (national in one case, international in the other) which serves as the starting point of analysis. This is a kind of "economism" according to which the capitalist economy is considered to be a self-regulated space, whose dynamic is given by its inherent laws of competition, accumulation of capital, or other, similarly essentialist, driving forces. The economy is thus conceived as a self-reproducing totality which is intrinsically either national or international, depending on the level at which the underlying economic dynamic is theorized to play itself out.[5] Economism, therefore, reinforces the strict national–international dichotomies that have long governed radical thought concerning the nature of social actors, including their identities and struggles within global capitalism.[6]

The second problem follows from the first: starting with a self-reproducing economic totality, both approaches conclude by deriving various kinds of power relations. Their analyses tend to focus on these power relations and, consequently, to deemphasize or neglect the specific role of class. In one case, the laws of motion within national economies generate (via the export of capital or the expansion of markets) power struggles among the advanced capitalist nation-states and the wielding of power by these nations over the less-advanced countries of the periphery. In the other case, a parallel logic has the world economy and international circuits of capital generating power relations among nation-states and exercising power over the allocation of labor. In both cases, the tendency is to focus on unequal power relations (and their effects) and to lose sight of the specific nature and role of capitalist (and noncapitalist) class processes, both within and between nation-states.

To be clear, we recognize that classes are mentioned in the two approaches; the issue is not whether class is included somewhere in the analysis – it usually is. Nor do we wish to deny the importance of many nonclass economic and political processes within the relations that exist between nation-states. Rather, a problem from our perspective arises when class is made secondary to those other processes and, therefore, is displaced from the center of analysis or is lost from sight altogether.

Moving beyond the nation-state has thus prompted at least some important Marxian thinkers to deemphasize the role of class or to downplay its significance. This is both surprising and not surprising. It is surprising because, if Marxian theory has anything to offer that is radically different from other, non-Marxian approaches to global capitalism, it is its unique concepts and approach to class. We have argued elsewhere (in detail we cannot replicate here) that, at least upon one interpretation, class is the focus or "entry point" for Marxian analyses of social reality (Chapter 13 of this volume, Resnick and Wolff 1987b). If that is the case, then it seems to us that a class analysis of international capitalism should be a principle focus and product of a uniquely Marxian theory of international capitalism. It is Marxism's special contribution. The tendency to lose sight of class when thinking beyond the nation-state is, at the same time, not surprising, given the implications of a consistent class analysis. As we demonstrate below, the use of the entry-point concept of class, defined in terms of surplus labor, rules out notions of foreign exploitation. It therefore problematizes any simple or mechanical extension of class to capitalist international relations.

Our aim is to recover the specificity of class and to produce a Marxian class analysis of global capitalism. Our first task is to address some of the important space (and time) dimensions of class processes and, therefore, to rethink the relationship between class and nation-states/international relations. We then examine international value flows from the perspective of particular concepts of class, defined in terms of surplus labor. Finally, we turn our attention to the spatial configuration of class within the history of capitalist development and to some of the more important theoretical and political implications of this approach.

This essay thus offers both a distinctive Marxist theory of global capitalism and several examples of the insights that theory enables. Together, these represent our contribution to the project of reinscribing class in the Marxian discourse on imperialism and, more generally, of meeting the need for a class mapping of global capitalism.

We begin by developing concepts that incorporate some of the important spatial and temporal dimensions of class. This procedure responds to the argument currently being advanced by many social theorists, including radical geographers (especially Harvey 1989 and Soja 1989), that the spatiality of social processes has been neglected in Marxist theories. Our purpose in this section is to develop a set of initial, abstract concepts that can be used to construct a more concrete class analysis of global capitalism, including the kinds of international flows of value that characterize capitalist commodity production.

The space and time of class

If Marxism distinguishes itself from non-Marxian approaches, at least in part by its focus on class, the specific content of its analyses is affected in important ways by the manner in which class is defined. Here, the discussion follows our own previous work (for example, Resnick and Wolff 1982 and Chapter 5 of this volume) and that of others (for example, Curtis 1988, Feiner 1988, Norton 1988a, and Saitta 1988) in interpreting and applying Marxian definitions of class in terms of the performance, appropriation, and distribution of surplus labor. This immediately distinguishes our approach from others, in which class represents differences in power, property, or income. Our concept of the fundamental class process (FCP) refers, not to inequalities between two groups of people with respect to their command over each other or assets or flows of income, but to a particular social process in and through which surplus labor is performed and appropriated. Thus, the specifically capitalist form of the FCP involves the performance/appropriation of surplus labor in the form of surplus-value.

The analytical problem of reinserting class within the context of global capitalism can be remedied by taking this notion of the capitalist FCP and explicitly theorizing its temporal and spatial dimensions.[7] Consider, first, the time of the capitalist FCP. According to Marxian value theory,[8] the creation of surplus-value occurs when surplus labor is extracted from labor power; that is when, after the purchase of labor power is completed, the capitalist consumes this labor power by setting it to work producing commodities. This is also the period of time (measured in hours of abstract labor) during which surplus-value is produced by laborers and appropriated by capitalists. This means that both aspects of the capitalist FCP occur simultaneously.

To turn next to the spatial nature of the capitalist FCP, it is helpful to make a distinction between the specific site of the FCP and the larger expanse within which it exists. Because the capitalist FCP is defined as the productive consumption of the commodity labor power, the site of that consumption is also the site where the production and appropriation of surplus-value take place. Following Marx's reference to the capitalist who appropriates surplus-value as the industrial capitalist, we call this place the "industrial site." It is the specific space where the production and appropriation of surplus-value (and thus the process of capitalist exploitation) take place. Such sites are constituted within, but have a spatiality distinct from, the geographic boundaries of individual nation-states.

In this precise sense, the capitalist FCP is neither national nor international. The process of capitalist exploitation is conceived as having particular temporal and spatial dimensions which are not reducible to either level of the geographical hierarchy of global capitalism. It is not that sites of the production and appropriation of surplus-value are intrinsically national or that they were at first national and then became international, or, finally, that they have always been international. All such approaches enforce a one-to-one class-to-geography mapping that negates the specific time–space configuration of the capitalist FCP.[9]

Recognizing the spatiality of the sites of capitalist exploitation does not mean denigrating the larger social expanse within which those sites exist. On the contrary, this expanse can, and should, be theorized as the space within which the diverse conditions of existence of the FCP are secured. Because we theorize the FCP only as it is constituted by the effects of myriad economic, political, and cultural processes – that is, as it is overdetermined by all those social processes – the space within which those processes exist represents the social expanse within which the FCP is constituted as a site of exploitation. For example, one of the social processes that can be said to condition the existence of the capitalist FCP is the economic process of exchanging the commodity labor power for money. The spatial location of that exchange process participates in defining the larger social expanse within which the FCP exists. A similar spatial analysis can be carried out with respect to other conditions of existence – for instance, the political process of legislating citizenship, the cultural process of language, and other economic processes, such as producing and lending money and exchanging other goods and services.

The general point is that the various locations of all of these processes together constitute the social – political and cultural as well as economic – expanse within which an industrial site, and therefore the capitalist FCP, exists. Some of these processes will occur within the same nation-state as the industrial site, while others are reproduced in areas outside of that nation-state. Neither the nation-state nor the international arena can be seen as the unified or primary space within which the conditions of existence of the capitalist FCP are secured. Both have their different relations to each industrial site of the capitalist FCP.

This necessarily brief consideration of the temporal and spatial dimensions of the capitalist FCP has far-reaching implications for a class analysis of the kinds of international flows of value that characterize global capitalism. Contemporary capitalism can be characterized, in part, by the number and type of value flows that occur between individuals and enterprises situated in different nation-states. These include international trade in goods and services, profit remittances, inter-governmental aid, foreign loans, external debt service payments, and the like.

One important issue concerns whether or not any of these international value flows represents the appropriation of surplus-value for, if it does, then the term foreign exploitation – in the sense of one geographic area exploiting another – has some validity. According to the logic of the preceding analysis, the production and appropriation of surplus-value occur simultaneously and at the same site. This means that there is neither a temporal nor a spatial separation in the two "moments" of capitalist exploitation. The only possible conclusion, then, is that the appropriation of surplus-value does not occur internationally (or, for that matter, nationally) and thus does not take the form of a flow of value between different nation-states.

In what sense, then, can the relations between nation-states be said to be exploitative? Passing reference to the idea of national exploitation can be found in the writings of both Marx and Engels (1976, 503) and Lenin (1975, 727). The idea that the nations of the center exploit peripheral or Third World nations came to occupy the center of debate among Marxists in the 1970s and 1980s (see, for example, Emmanuel 1972 and Roemer 1983). Such notions of foreign exploitation can be regarded as challenging some of the more idyllic conceptions of capitalism as put forward, for example, by neoclassical theorists of comparative advantage. However, focusing on the unequal international power relations that characterize capitalist society can, and often does, obscure the specific dimensions of the production/appropriation of surplus-value. It does so because it conflates class exploitation with international domination. The unequal wielding of national, typically state, power is either defined as, or becomes the essential condition of, foreign exploitation. One of the political implications often drawn from this conflation is a tendency, in effect, to privilege domestic exploitation over foreign exploitation, or, as Marx once noted, "It is better to be exploited by one's fellow-countrymen than by foreigners" (1976, 280).

Subsumed classes

We must therefore set aside many of the traditional attempts to theorize class beyond the nation-state insofar as they fail to keep logically distinct the Marxian notion of class as surplus labor appropriation and the flows of value among nations. The relationship between class and international value flows emerges, rather, by extending the class analysis initially formulated in Marx's theorization in Volume 3 of *Capital*. There, the issue is not exploitation (the production/appropriation of surplus-value) but the different issue of the distributions of surplus-value (to landlords, merchant capitalists, money capitalists and so forth) in order to secure some of the conditions of existence of capitalist exploitation. This process of distributing and receiving surplus-value has elsewhere (see Resnick and Wolff 1987b) been termed the subsumed class process (SCP).

To see the relevance of capitalist SCPs (distributions of already appropriated surplus-value) to international value flows, let us specify their temporal and spatial dimensions along the same lines as those followed above for the FCP (exploitation). Just as there is no separation in time between the production and appropriation of surplus-value, the distribution and receipt of surplus-value take place simultaneously. This is the case, for example, when the industrial capitalist distributes a portion of surplus-value to the merchant capitalist in order to secure one of the important conditions of existence of the capitalist FCP: a shortening of the time lost in the realization of surplus-value. The subsumed class payment is made at the moment when the merchant capitalist purchases the commodity from the industrial capitalist at less than its value before reselling it at its value.[10] Through this transaction, the merchant capitalist receives a share of the surplus-value appropriated at the site of exploitation.[11] The same temporal simultaneity is observed in the variety of other subsumed class distributions, to landlords, money capitalists, the state, and others. In each case, the industrial capitalist's distribution of surplus-value and its receipt by the subsumed class occur simultaneously.

However, the similarity between the FCP and the SCP ends when we consider their different spatial dimensions. While the production and appropriation of surplus-value occur at the same site, the distribution and receipt of surplus-value can, and often do, occur at different sites. This spatial dislocation can exist at any level of the geographical hierarchy, from different towns and cities through regions to nation-states. Thus, for example, a capitalist may appropriate surplus-value in an industrial site in one country and proceed to make a subsumed class distribution from that same site. However, the subsumed class (merchant or banker, etc.) may receive that payment in a site located in an entirely different country. This means that, although the capitalist FCP occurs at the same site – and thus within the boundaries of a single nation-state – the SCP can take place in two different sites – and thus in two different nation-states. Therefore, it is quite possible – indeed likely, at least in contemporary circumstances – for subsumed class payments to cross national boundaries.

This adds a new class dimension to our previous analysis: value flows included in balance-of-payments accounts, while not appropriations of surplus-value, will typically be subsumed class distributions of surplus-value. Of course, not all international value flows represent subsumed class payments: only those that are distributions of surplus-value from industrial capitalists to recipients in other countries do.[12] Examples of subsumed class international value flows are distributions of surplus-value by industrial capitalists in one country in the form of debt-service payments to overseas lenders, royalties and patent fees to parent companies located in other countries, taxes paid to foreign governments, and so on. In these cases, distributions of portions of the surplus-value appropriated in an industrial site located within one country are made to individuals located in another.

In this class-analytic accounting framework, then, the appropriation of surplus-value (and, generally, surplus labor) cannot occur between nation-states. One country cannot extract (in the Marxian sense of the term) surplus from another. However, once the surplus-value has been appropriated from the direct producers, it may move from one nation-state to another in the form of subsumed class payments.

Global capitalism and class

The international flows of value that characterize global capitalism comprise a complex, changing combination of subsumed class and nonclass payments. These flows are one index of the internationalization of capitalism. For example, debt-service payments by an industrial capitalist in one country to a money capitalist in another country, although not exploitation, still introduce an important international dimension to the growth and development of capitalist class structures. The fact that one of the conditions of existence of the capitalist FCP is provided in the form of foreign loans, means that the continued existence of the site of capitalist exploitation in one country is conditioned, at least in part, by the activities of money capitalists and the policies set by the monetary authorities of another country. The existence of such subsumed class international flows of value implies that the extraction of surplus-value in industrial sites located within one country are predicated, in particular ways, on the events and occurrences that take place among and within other countries.

We are led, then, to a specifically class conceptualization of global capitalism, in two senses. First, to the extent that cultural, political, and economic processes that condition the existence of the extraction of surplus-value in industrial sites located in one country are performed outside the borders of that country, we can conclude that the space of capitalism is multinational in character. Processes enacted in one part of the globe participate, in one way or another, in constituting (overdetermining) capitalist exploitation in a different part. Second, the space of capitalism can be said to be multinational to the extent that sites of capitalist exploitation exist within different nation-states across the globe. Whereas the first notion of multinationalization focuses on the extent to which the conditions of existence of the capitalist FCP located within one nation-state are secured by processes that occur partially or wholly within the borders of other nation-states, this second notion is defined by the global dispersion of sites where the extraction of surplus-value itself takes place.

These two different senses of multinationalization suggest a distinctive way of elaborating a class analysis of the changing space of capitalism on a world scale. The expansion of the space of class began with the emergence of the capitalist FCP in the "old" centers of capitalism – for example, in Western Europe and the United States – which, in turn, involved the creation of world markets and, in general, the securing of various conditions of the capitalist FCP around the globe. Scarcely a corner of the globe has not been drawn into this space–time nexus of the reproduction of capitalist class processes. In this sense, a self-contained West (that is, a national capitalism which only later became international) is a mere fiction. Imperialist projects determined, from the beginning, that non-Western societies would provide an ever-changing array of conditions of existence for the capitalist FCP in the West.

The international development of the space of capitalism also transformed noncapitalist social formations around the globe. In some cases, existing noncapitalist (e.g., slave, feudal, primitive communal and so on) FCPs were strengthened; elsewhere, new noncapitalist FCPs emerged. In other situations, the extension of capitalist space so disrupted existing societies as to enable – because of those societies' particularities – the establishment of new industrial sites of capitalist exploitation, most notably in Japan and, later, in the Third World, especially in the postwar period.

However, this global expansion of capitalist class processes and their conditions of existence has not meant the creation of a homogeneous capitalist space – then or now. Noncapitalist class processes have continued to exist – and, in many cases, thrive – among and within nation-states across the globe. In some cases, such noncapitalist class processes have emerged and continued to exist quite separate from the "needs of capital"; in other cases, capitalist class processes have created, and even strengthened, noncapitalist class processes. Two of many possible examples of the presence today of noncapitalist class processes are the large number of self-employed ("petty" or "ancient") producers throughout the world (Gabriel 1990) and the existence of feudal and communal class processes within the production activities inside households (Fraad *et al.* 1989). In this sense, the global space that others see as exclusively capitalist has been, and continues to be, constituted, in significant fashion, by noncapitalist class processes as well.

Consequences

These general points have far-reaching consequences for the kinds of theoretical analyses and political activities that are of particular interest to radical economists and others in the world today. Two such implications should be noted here. First, placing class at the center of radical theory creates the possibility of producing a specifically class-analytical knowledge of global capitalism. It means asking particular types of questions, such as: How have specific class processes contributed, along with all other social processes, to producing a particular event? What are the effects of such an event on the fundamental class processes within contemporary nation-states and the subsumed class processes between them? Following such a procedure does not mean reducing all events to a set of essential class causes. We reject that course as simply substituting a class determinism for the economism we criticized above. Rather, our notion of making class the entry point involves focusing analytically on the particular role of class – as both cause and effect – in the ever-changing landscape of global capitalism. Marxism's contribution is this focus on class, rather than any claim that class is more or less important than other factors overdetermining international relations.

The second implication concerns radical politics. Focusing on class means that the interpretation of the relative success or failure of the policies currently being advocated and practiced in the world today – by radicals and nonradicals alike – must take account of the class effects of those policies. This is especially important because the ongoing debates about such policies are usually conducted within the limits set by theoretical perspectives that downplay, or disregard altogether, the class consequences of alternative policies. One example is the contemporary debate over macroeconomic stabilization and adjustment.[13] Neoclassical and structuralist economic theories have determined the parameters of that debate. In Latin America, when the policies derived from one theory were said to have failed, economists and policymakers often turned to the policies derived from the other theory. However, the sequential alternation of neoclassical and structuralist policy phases coincided there with the systematic growth of sites of capitalist exploitation and the globalization of their conditions of existence. In short, from a Marxian class-analytical standpoint, Latin American policy packages were not failures in either of their phases. They were "successes" in the sense of widening and deepening capitalism in those societies.

Subscribers to each of those theories denounced phases of the other theory's policy dominance as failures because their criteria – output growth, income distribution, fiscal deficits, and so on – all abstracted from any class contents and consequences of the policies. That is precisely our point: abstracting from class made both sides, including the many radical economists on the left wing of the structuralists, see "failures" and indeed "successes" in nonclass terms. They thereby missed the class implications and consequences of the interaction of international economic changes and national economic policies. They were correspondingly unable to contribute a class dimension to radical movements to resist and transform those policies throughout Latin America.

Insofar as class transformations are included among the objectives of radical social change, class analyses of national and international economic developments are required. If Marxian concepts of social justice and democracy include the notion that people should collectively participate in and determine the production, appropriation, and distribution of the surplus labor they perform, then Marxian analyses must foreground the class dimensions of the societies they aim to change and, especially, as we have tried to sketch here, of the increasingly important international economic activities of those societies.

(original version published in 1990)

Acknowledgements

We want to thank David Fasenfest, Alan Patterson, and Simon Clarke for comments on an earlier version.

Notes

1   Fredric Jameson (1984), for example, refers to post-modernism as the cultural logic of the stage of late, multinational capitalism. Another prominent theorist of post-modernism, Jean-François Lyotard (1984, 5–6), also emphasizes the changing nature of the world economy, especially the growth of multinational corporations. From a different quarter, *Business Week* (1990) devoted a recent cover story to the emergence of the "stateless corporation."

2   Gordon (1988), however, has called into question both the degree to which recent changes in the world economy represent the inauguration of a new stage in capitalist development and the extent to which national institutions have been undermined.

3   Thus, although their conclusions are radically different, both "inter-imperialist rivalry" and the "development of underdevelopment" are explained in terms of a logic that presumes a national economy and analyzes international relations in terms of forces emanating from the nation-state. The imperialism theorists, for example, stress the formation of monopolies within the advanced capitalist nation-states and, on this basis, the emergence of international rivalries between national groupings of capital which, through capital export, create the conditions for capitalist development in less-advanced countries. Similarly, the dependency theorists analyze the extension of markets from one group of nations (the center or metropolis) to another group of nations (the hinterland or periphery) which, in turn, allow the first group to exercise control over, and to develop at the expense of, the second.

4   Both the "world system" and the "internationalization of the circuits of capital" are seen as the overarching international structures which give rise to different (central and peripheral) forms of national development. According to world-systems theorists, for example, capital is a supranational system in which different geographical areas or nation-states and different forms of "labor control" are the results of the place occupied by the areas concerned in a capitalist world system. The logic of the internationalization of capital thinkers is much the same: different forms and levels of national development are created by the different roles played by specific areas and nation-states within the set of international circuits of capital.

5   In this sense, the positing of an "open economy" model (as, for example, in Bowles 1988) does not represent a solution to the ambiguity in Marx's approach to theorizing the national and international dimensions of capitalist classes and class struggles; although international factors (such as the external terms of trade, capital flows, etc.) serve to open up the "closed economy" model, the presumed and untheorized unity of the economy as a self-reproducing totality is itself preserved.

6   See Amariglio and Callari (1989) who compare the pitfalls of economism with an alternative approach based on "overdetermination."

7   This issue was never directly tackled by Marx, although there are certain suggestive elements in his writings, such as the comments in the *Grundrisse* on the spatial and temporal aspects of commodity circulation; see, in particular, Marx (1973, 533–37).

8   Since much of the following argument uses basic Marxian value theory, perhaps a few words are in order concerning our use of this approach. Value theory remains, for us, a logical and viable theoretical construct, notwithstanding the various controversies within and outside the Marxian tradition – for example, over the so-called transformation problem and the redundancy or irrelevance of values vis-à-vis prices or labor inputs. Wolff, Callari, and Roberts (1984) have discussed the insights and even mathematical "solutions" that emerge when class is defined in terms of surplus labor and when overdetermination is substituted for the determinist approaches that otherwise dominate the literature.

9   Although the FCP is conceived as neither national nor international, the producers and appropriators of surplus-value can have multiple and different (overlapping and non-overlapping) characteristics, including nationality. For example, consider an industrial site within Brazil, in which the direct producers are Brazilian and the appropriators are of various foreign (US,

Japanese, etc.) nationalities. Just as the location of the industrial site within Brazilian national boundaries does not make the process of exploitation intrinsically or simplistically Brazilian (i.e., national), the participation of individuals of foreign nationality as the appropriators of surplus-value does not make that process similarly foreign or international. This example can, and should, be extended to include individuals who also have different gender, ethnic, racial, age, and other characteristics. Exploitation has many dimensions.

10 Although there is no theoretical necessity for assuming that commodities are purchased at less than their value and then sold at value, we follow Marx in using this simplifying assumption.

11 It remains for the merchant capitalist to sell the commodities at their value in order to realize his/her subsumed class payments in the form of money, just as the industrial capitalist must realize the commodity's value before making other subsumed class distributions of surplus-value in money form. However, the subsumed class distribution and receipt of surplus-value occur at the moment when ownership of the commodities is transferred from the industrial capitalist to the merchant capitalist.

12 All other international payments would then be considered nonclass value flows.

13 For further discussion of this debate, see Chapter 13 of this volume.

15 Global fragments: Subjectivity and class politics in discourses of globalization

(with Serap A. Kayatekin)

> It is easier to register the loss of traditional order of difference than to perceive the emergence of new ones.
>
> Clifford (1988, 15)

The view from above

In an essay apparently far removed from the concerns of political economy, Michel de Certeau (1984) distinguishes the voyeuristic desire to see the "panorama-city" – the view from the 100th floor of the World Trade Center, the representation created and shared by urban planners and cartographers – from the images produced by "walking in the city," by those who live "down below." Each is a viewpoint, a way of looking at and experiencing the city. From the top of the tower, the city is readable and transparent; it becomes a universal and anonymous subject, capable of being ordered and administered by those whose thrill comes from making the various parts and functions conform to its concept. "'The city,' like a proper name, thus provides a way of conceiving and constructing space on the basis of a finite number of stable, isolatable, and inter-connected properties" (de Certeau 1984, 94). Once this city is established, and its rules codified and unified in discourses of geographical and geometrical space, all of the other elements – the fragments and differentiations, movements and redistributions, that do not seemingly fit the order – can be either eliminated or subsumed within the functionalist administration.

But, for de Certeau, there is an alternative to the official discourses of urbanism:

> one can analyse the microbe-like, singular and plural spaces which an urbanistic system was supposed to administer or suppress, but which have outlived its decay; one can follow the swarming activity of these procedures that, far from being regulated or eliminated by panoptic administration, have reinforced themselves in a proliferating illegitimacy, developed and insinuated themselves into the networks of surveillance, and combined in accord with unreadable but stable

tactics to the point of constituting everyday regulations and surreptitious creativities that are merely concealed by the frantic mechanisms and discourses of the observational organization.

(de Certeau 1984, 96)

For this, it is necessary to begin at ground level, to follow the footsteps of passers-by, to examine the other names that the walkers encounter, the different stories and styles that disrupt the uniformity of the presumed and constructed order. Along the way, new subjectivities are discovered, and identities created, that allow for a range of signifying practices which serve to invent a plurality of spaces. In this way, the uniform mode of "the city," the modernist dream of the urban designers (which is also, of course, the nightmare of their opponents) can be recognized and displaced, thereby giving way to heterogeneous, and even contrary, elements of living within and transforming the existing landscape. The city is thereby shown to be different from itself.

Discourses of globalization

Perhaps we are not so far, after all, from the realm of political economy, especially the discourses of globalization that are our object in this essay. Like the successive generations of urban planners, the architects of the "new world order," whether located in the City, the meetings that concluded the Uruguay Round of negotiations for the General Agreement on Tariffs and Trade, or the global operations sections of the burgeoning number of multinational corporations, seek to exclude (or, alternatively, to reintroduce as the means for producing a more extensive and denser order) the detritus that threatens to frustrate their desire to plan and administer their city – the global marketplace. And, of course, mainstream economists (both neoclassical and Keynesian, each in their different way) have been only too willing to celebrate the efforts at "international economic integration" and to create the concept of the world economy to which these efforts can be seen to contribute.[1]

This view "from above" is also shared by a wide variety of heterodox observers of contemporary processes and events. Globalization has become a crucial theme as well as a key analytical concept, in a rapidly burgeoning literature which, while often designed to expose the nightmarish effects of the emergent (or, for some, already established) global order, appears to partake of the ecstasy of the totalizing vision. The range of disciplines that has been exposed to the tremendous hold of this concept includes politics, sociology, geography, cultural studies, and, of course, radical political economy. We believe that this wide appeal is, like the "fiction of knowledge" afforded by the concept-city, an invitation to critical scrutiny. Upon closer examination, what lends this concept of globalization its legitimacy can be understood and, if need be, subverted. The following should be understood, then, as the beginning of a theoretical journey without a fixed destination; the footsteps we take are meant to be part of a process of questioning this concept (or its various concept-formations) and of investigating its implications. Of utmost significance to us among these possible implications are the politics of globalization, the ways in which the discourses of globalization, especially those produced and debated by radical political economists and cultural analysts, create or, alternatively, obscure the possibility of intervening to shape contemporary economic and social events.

A crucial link in this quest is the issue of subjectivity, the positions, agencies, and forms of consciousness in and through which identities, decisions, choices, and interventions are produced and enacted. The ways in which different forms of subjectivity are invoked and elaborated by theoretical discourses are issues that have engendered rich and extensive debate in literary, psychoanalytic, and cultural circles but which, until recently, have remained distant (at least in terms of explicit treatment) from the concerns of economists, including radical political economists.[2] Here, we join this discussion with an eye towards investigating the relations among radical discourses of globalization, the implied notions of subjectivity, and the alternative forms of political intervention that are envisioned and created by such discourses. We argue that the existing discourses of globalization can be challenged from within as well as from the outside. This theoretical endeavor allows us not only to expand the range of the existing subjectivities and identities, but also to transform them, thus widening the space for new political possibilities.

A broad sweep of the recent literature on globalization reveals certain themes as the foci.[3] Among these we count the increase in the number of international (multinational and transnational) corporations (and the related phenomena of international flows of foreign direct investment and other forms of international investment cooperation such as licensing, offshore processing, and so-called strategic alliances), the internationalization of money and capital markets, the increasing volume of trade in manufactured and semi-manufactured goods between industrialized nations, the economic miracles of the "dragons of Asia," and the recent rise to international economic power of China.

Let us consider a couple of these in turn. The study of internationalized enterprises has long been a key theme in radical political economy, one that can be traced back to the late 1960s and early 1970s, especially in the pioneering work of the late Stephen Hymer (1972a, 1972b, 1976). While, in that period, the process of globalization via the multinational corporation was clearly viewed within the global division of labor between the central and peripheral nations, and thus in terms of an unequal bipolar distribution of power, the contemporary literature includes conceptions of globalization in which the structure of power relations between nation-states is rendered as a much more ambiguous phenomenon. In fact, the fall from grace of the concept of imperialism (consider that few on the Left were willing to consider such a classic example as the Gulf War in terms even vaguely related to those of imperialism) needs to be explained precisely by this perceived ambiguity: the inability to locate power within a single national unit that hegemonizes the world, or significant parts of it, has rendered any notion of imperialist expansion problematic. As Étienne Balibar has observed,

> if we think of a "crisis" of the world order, of which the collapse of the "socialist" semiperiphery could be the signal, is it not because, among other things, we are faced with the disturbing impression that most "peripheries remain desperately peripheral," while the "central" position of the traditional "centers" is not so secure?
>
> (1995, 408)

This ambiguity is also implicit in the literature on the "Asian miracles": the Korean path to industrialization has been a particularly unsettling one, setting off a heated debate on whether the conditions of industrialization were unique or if the experience could be repeated elsewhere. The terms of the debate were significant for, if one took the latter point of view, the whole conceptual scheme of the center and periphery had to be called into question. The major change that we detect in the globalization literature over the course of the past 30 years or so is tied up with this issue of power: whereas, early on, the emphasis was on the ways in which globalization created and reproduced the division of the world economy into two (or more) poles, with the center exercising control over the periphery (and, perhaps, semiperiphery), now the idea seems to be that the globalizing forces and institutions stand above and beyond all nations, thereby radically transforming, and perhaps even displacing, the pivotal status accorded to the relations between center and periphery. This is the concern that induces Mike Featherstone to refer to the creation of "global modernities":

> It is no longer possible to conceive global processes in terms of the dominance of a single center over the peripheries. Rather there are a number of competing centers which are bringing about shifts in the global balance of power between nation-states and blocs and forging new sets of interdependencies. This is not to suggest a condition of equality between participants but a process which is seeing more players admitted to the game who are demanding access to means of communication and the right to be heard. The expansion and speed of forms of communication means that it is more difficult for governments to police and control the volume of information and image flows that cross their frontiers.
>
> (1995, 12–13)

In the realm of politics, the dominant theme is the undermining of the sovereignty of nation-states. This issue is especially prominent in development studies. The 1980s, it is often argued, represented a turning point in the histories of most of the periphery, as these economies, at various speeds and with different combinations of internal and external strife, began implementing "neoliberal" stabilization and structural adjustment programs and export-oriented forms of industrialization, which were made conditional on aid by the two main multilateral financing bodies – the World Bank and the International Monetary Fund. Implemented in the aftermath of a long period of import-substitution industrialization, these programs have come to be seen as the main mechanism whereby the periphery's integration into the world division of labor has not only intensified but also changed form. A crucial dimension of this change, it is claimed, has been the loss of sovereign power by peripheral nation-states. A related scenario is said to apply to the central economies: where once Keynesian-inspired macroeconomic policies had been capable of generating and maintaining internal and external balances (perhaps this is itself a myth that radical political economists need to dispel), the globalization of production and finance has undermined the ability of economic policy-makers to manage national economic activity effectively, at least insofar as policies are attempted that do not fit into the international framework set by extranational (or transnational) global forces.[4]

The prevalent economic images that emerge from the literature on globalization coincide with this recasting of international relations: casino capitalism; the "rootlessness" of capital; the incessant drive, the inner essence of capital to accumulate on a world scale, thereby overcoming and transcending national boundaries; the denationalization of enterprises; "footloose" capital, moving with remarkable fluidity and ease between different locations, between Mexico City and Miami, for example, or between New York and London. (We note here that, within radical political economy, Hegelian readings of Marx, especially *Capital*, provide the background for these images.) The globalization of capital is seen to be all-encompassing, taking hold of and recasting, making its own, the different economic forms and relations that it encounters as it speeds around the globe. It is, in part, this set of images, this perception of a worldwide logic, a unifying vision, that lends the existing discourses of globalization their power. Everything is said to be subsumed within, and thus can be explained by, the network of globalized capitalist power.

These economic images have also found their counterparts in a set of cultural symbols, especially those which represent the global reach and consequent homogenization of the media and of consumption: *Dallas*, CNN, and the Live Aid concerts broadcast around the world; McDonald's located on the Champs Elysées, in Beijing, and in post-perestroika Moscow. Contemporary culture has thus become global, driven by the same force – global capital. It is, in fact, these cultural images that have given the decisive impetus to the discourses of globalization, rendering them, so to speak, "popular." Perhaps, then, it is not surprising to find some of the more significant contributions to the globalization analyses in the realm of culture. In fact, it is only in the cultural studies literature that the question of subjectivity in relation to globalization is tackled in any explicit fashion. It is thus imperative, for the purposes of our investigation, to look at this literature, albeit briefly.[5]

Globalization is conceptualized as an economically driven phenomenon, the cultural awareness of which is an equally important aspect.[6] It is this question of "awareness" that, in turn, brings in the further question of subjectivity. Roland Robertson (1992), to consider a representative perspective, argues that the essential character of globalization is the consciousness of the global; the understanding that we all participate in the global. The question of what precisely constitutes the "we" is a fundamental one, as the clues to the question of subjectivity need to be sought there. Depending on "who" we are, it is quite likely that the meaning that is attributed to "global" will change. The point that there is more than one way of interpreting the global is readily conceded by the cultural analysts. Jonathan Friedman (1994), for example, claims that Robertson's analysis of the global is "very much a question of competing interpretations." One would think, then, that the problem of globalization is, at least in part, discursive in nature. On this point, the literature on the culture of globalization leaves us with a conceptual tension. On one hand, it is acknowledged that globalization is a matter of different interpretations. On the other hand, these very interpretations are conceived to be created by the process of globalization which, it seems, is neutral – indifferent to our interpretations. We will return to this tension later, for it seems to us to be the core of the many strengths and weaknesses, theoretical and political, of existing discourses of globalization. The resolution of this tension is also the basis of the dynamics of identity formation and the relation thereof to power, which we tackle in a later section. However, one can infer from existing treatments that there are multiple identities and that these range from individual subjectivities to global, collective ones.

Friedman argues that the "global arena" is a precondition for globalization. The global arena, although not very clearly defined, is "a product of a definite set of dynamic properties including the formation of center/ periphery structures and their expansion, contraction, fragmentation and re-establishment throughout cycles of hegemon" (1994, 199). Here, through the concept of hegemony, yet another crucial dimension of the analysis is introduced – that of power. The global arena, the global space, is constituted not only by the profound transformations of the economic structures, but also by the changing relations of power. The very definitions of center and periphery, after all, entail, in part, such relations of power. The transformations of global systems – now substituted for the term "global arena" – imply differential changes in the "life conditions" in different sectors of the system which, in turn, condition the "identity spaces" from which emerge the culturally specific institutional and representational forms.

In other words, the historical processes of expansion or contraction of global systems, which involve a multitude of changes – among which are changing hegemonic structures – shape processes of representation and meaning attribution. So, there are differential attributions of meaning and different interpretations, but the existence of this multiplicity seems to be essentially a consequence of the differential "nature" of the global system(s).

Perhaps, then, at least in the case of Friedman's analysis, the above-mentioned tension vis-à-vis the problem of identity and globalization is resolved in favor of the latter: the positing of a multiplicity of identities (therefore, of multiple interpretations) that are "ultimately" shaped by the processes of globalization which, in the final analysis, are "immune" to our interpretations. Here, not only is there no space for the "creation" of global-ization by its interpreters, but the subjects, in whatever forms and which-ever number, appear as mere "recipients" of processes. We can argue, then, that subjects in this vision are subjects "in" globalization rather than (or, at least, more so than) subjects "of" globalization. Indeed, these subjects are "objects" of globalization insofar as processes are exerted upon them.[7] Friedman's distinction between "weak" and 'strong" forms of globaliza-tion supports this view. What is necessary for the weak form of globaliza-tion is the existence of a "global frame of reference," such as the Internet. The strong form of globalization, however, which is also the "homoge-nizing" form, involves the "creation" of subjects that interpret the world in the same way. The significance of this latter form lies in the fact that the "mechanisms of appropriation of the global have become global them-selves." These mechanisms of appropriating the global, the local cultural forms and representations may, and sometimes do, after all submit to the cold logic of the global. Does this mean then that the global is, finally, something over, above, certainly "around us," but not really, as was suggested earlier in the analysis, "part of us"? It is the realization of "some-thing bigger than us," as Friedman refers to in relation to Robertson's work, which we are all part of. If that which is bigger than all of us is global-ized capital, how precisely does it shape our identities? What, furthermore, are the avenues of political struggle to transform it? We query the argu-ments of the cultural analysts in detail later; suffice it to note at this point that, despite the significant differences between the political economy and the cultural analysis literatures, a unifying point seems to be a theoretical submission to the (conceptualization of the) omnipotence of global capital.

Political economy of globalization: the power of capital and subjectivity

We noted above that there is a certain ambiguity within the political economy literature on globalization concerning relations of power. This is significant, in that theoretical differences on the matter often result in divergent political options. Much of the debate here has turned on the distinction between a "worldwide" international economy and a "globalized" international economy.[8] We consider both of them as part of the more general phenomenon of globalization, each representing a particular set of conclusions concerning the processes whereby international economic and political integration has taken place (or is currently taking place). Whereas worldwide integration refers to the growing interconnections between national economies, thereby keeping nation-states as the principal units of analysis, the creation of a globalized economy is said to emerge if and when distinct national economies are subsumed and rearticulated into the international economic system by essentially international processes and transactions.

For those who argue that worldwide, but not globalized, integration is occurring, national economies are said to maintain a significant degree of autonomy, such that national governments, alone or in regional trading blocs (for example, the European Community, the North American Free Trade Agreement, Japan and Southeast Asia), still have the power to bargain with transnational capital and/or to engage in "national economic management." In this sense, the international economy is understood to be governed, however imperfectly, through the limited cooperation of the major nation-states and trading blocs. The strictly interpreted globalized view, in contrast, views power as ultimately belonging to an all-encompassing capital that transgresses and transcends national and regional barriers. Therefore, any notion of national policymaking except, perhaps, as it is functionally dictated by the logic of transnational capital, is rendered problematic. In terms of the politics of intervention and transformation, then, whereas the former view holds out for a considerable degree of national control and effective international coordination between nations and regional alliances, the latter argues that only supranational institutions and regimes – for example, a global macroeconomic policy – and coordination of activities (among those most vulnerable to globalizing forces; for example, trade unions) can match the global expansion of economic processes taking place within the world today.

Let us pose, once again, our main questions: What are the forms of subjectivity presumed and/or produced by the discourses of globalization? And, what are the possible politics of transformation deriving from these? If capital is seen to annihilate all of its "others," if its globalizing tendencies break through and recast all of its "barriers," then are we turned into its passive "victims"? If we are all marked, and our actions circumscribed by the uniformizing effects of globalization, do we retreat into cynicism, admiring and celebrating the United States for being at the frontier of capitalist culture (the position at which Baudrillard seems to have arrived) or can we imagine ourselves and others being able to formulate and carry out a radical internationalist politics? What are the effects of globalization on subjectivity, if this is a process of capital expansion that takes hold of and transforms its others? Transformation implies that the other at least offers resistance to unconditional conquest if not a set of alternative projects of making and doing. What, then, are the sources of this resistance and carrying out of alternative projects within the forms of subjectivity associated with globalization, and how effectively can they serve as the basis for anticapitalist (or noncapitalist) politics?

In the radical globalization literature, the general procedure is to derive subject positions from the effects of the globalization of capital. In this sense, subjectivity is closely tied to economic processes and institutions; it is conceived in a largely economistic fashion.[9] What we mean by this is, first, that the existing discourses of globalization tend to consider the political – and, we should add, cultural – interests and consciousnesses of actors as corresponding to their position as economic agents, from the positions they occupy in the "real" economic mechanisms associated with global capitalism. The tendency, then, is to downplay, or ignore altogether, the surplus of identities, the range of (multiple, contradictory) subject positions, that can be said to be produced in social realms within, alongside, and outside (although never entirely separate from) the economic sphere – and which, in turn, participate in constituting the "economy" as such. Furthermore, these economic mechanisms are often theorized in a "closed" fashion, such that the existence and reproduction of global capitalism are seen to be governed by its own purely economic logic. Here, the globalization of capitalism is conceived to be the more or less inevitable outcome of, for example, the expansion into the international arena of originally national units of capital, which take the form of multinational and transnational corporations, due to competitive pressures exerted by each enterprise on all others, or of the internationalization of the circuits of merchant, finance, and productive capital, determined by the "inner drive" on the part of capital as a whole to accumulate on a worldwide basis.

Within the political economy literature, two forms of subjectivity emerge from this economizing logic: one we can refer to as "national Keynesian," the other as "global imperative." The national Keynesian subject position stems from the idea that, while a globalizing logic exists on the part of capital, the agencies associated with national identity continue to exist. On one hand, such agencies have not been entirely subsumed by international capital movements; at least some actors are conceived still to have interests associated with the relative success or failure of national economic goals and policies. On the other hand, these agencies can be enacted to reassert national control over the economic space. References to a national Keynesian subjectivity can often be detected in calls to impose restrictions on the free movement of capital across national boundaries and in moves to oppose international trading agreements.

The other position, that of the global imperative, stems from the conclusion that national identities have been effectively undermined and subsumed by the globalization of capital; that it is important to "catch up" with capital's ability to elude and override national controls and to play off any remaining (because not yet rendered insignificant) national and regional differences. From this perspective, global capital has succeeded in creating a set of global economic mechanisms, for example, an "international wage relation," with and against which any actors that operate on a less-than-global basis are ill-equipped to bargain. Therefore, it becomes imperative for individuals and groups to shed their previous (false?) national identities and to recognize the (true?) global subjectivity which corresponds to the worldwide basis and reach of capital. This subjectivity is often announced in attempts to move trade unions from their traditional national organizational structures to adopt a more "internationalist" approach – for example, by engaging in international solidarity and other forms of global cooperation.[10]

As is immediately evident, the national Keynesian/global imperative duality rehearses the classic debate between reformism and revolution.[11] While many criticisms could be formulated with respect to this opposition, our main concern here is that the terms of the debate presume, and are governed by, subjectivities that are conceived to be "given" by the economic processes that represent the partial or complete globalization of capitalism. Thus, while we recognize that each of these subjectivities serves as the basis for particular, and often valuable, kinds of political activism, we also find that the subjectivities and forms of politics remain inscribed within the totalizing vision of globalization. They are "read off" and then, in turn, are directed at matching or resisting the process of economic globalization. What we think are elided in the desire to embrace this vision are the diverse forms of subjectivity and political activity, especially those related to noncapitalist forms of economic and social life, which are not dictated by the uniform, homogenizing economic logic attributed to the forces of globalization – not only the diversity that can be found within the globalizing trends of capitalism, but also that which lies alongside and outside it, escaping its totalizing effects.

Cultural analyses of globalization perhaps go further than the political economy literature, in that they acknowledge a diversity of subjectivities that can be found within the framework of globalization. Nevertheless, this diversity is dictated by the inner logic of globalization which, as a concept itself, does not receive the necessary theoretical scrutiny. It is this givenness, the tacit understanding that globalization is a concept around which there is consensus in terms of its existence and its necessary effects, that renders these analyses vulnerable to criticism. Let us examine this argument in more detail.

Cultural analyses of globalization: hegemony and subjectivity formation

Earlier we argued that, in the cultural analyses of globalization, the concept of power embedded within the concept of hegemony is crucial to the formation of subjectivity. Historical changes in the world systems are, in part, constituted by transformations of the hegemonic orders, which explain the rise and the demise of subjectivities. Friedman, more than others, in an interesting comparison of the history of the formation ("birth") of Greek and Hawaiian identities, explores this thesis.

Greek identity, Friedman claims, is not a construction that has been in continuous existence since ancient times. Although it would be wrong to state that there was no such identity until recently, it would be appropriate to claim that this history is marked by discontinuities rather than by continuity. The grounds for the modern Greek identity are to be found in the Ottoman era, where, as part of the (Eastern) Orthodoxy, it could define itself in opposition both to Western Latin Catholicism and to Islam. The ethnic division of labor within the empire that reflected the territorial divisions proved to be fertile grounds for the formation of the "Greeks." As the Western part of the empire became integrated into the expanding European world economy as a periphery, the modern Greek nation was born in opposition to the Empire's definition of it (the *Romii* in reference to the Byzantine era as an extension of the Eastern Roman empire). An equally important process here was Europe's new definition of itself where the latter found its "roots" in "ancient Greece." It is in this manner that Greece became an integral part of the "European" civilization, a cornerstone of the European modern identity. The rising hegemony of the ascendant European world economy and the disintegration of the Ottoman Empire were the two "global" processes without which it would be impossible to understand the evolution of the Greek identity (Friedman 1994, 118–23).

In the second case study presented, Friedman argues that contemporary Hawaiian identity was born in opposition to "Western society" and to other social forms that dominated the islands. During the nineteenth century, Hawaiian history – as written by the missionaries – was depicted in terms of a non-Christian, nonmodern life (i.e., in opposition to Christian and modern life). After the Second World War, from which the United States emerged as the new world hegemonic power, an exploding tourist industry supplanted the sugar plantations on the islands. It is during this period that the cliché images of the Hawaiians, much celebrated in Hollywood films of the period – as a hula-performing hedonistic people, living in paradise, who do not seem to have any preoccupations other than dancing and feasting – were born. The "indigenous" formulations of a modern Hawaiian identity came into being during the 1970s, when the position of the United States was being questioned. It is no coincidence that the birth of the modern Hawaiian identity and the undermining of US hegemony were two processes that worked in tandem. Contemporary Hawaiian identity asserts itself not only in opposition to the Western understanding of life (especially as it is manifested in the United States), but to that of Tahiti, for example – the identity of which, claim some contemporary Hawaiians, was imposed on the island by the Western historiographers. It is this period, which precedes contact with the West, that becomes the reference for the "roots" of the modern Hawaiians (Friedman 1994, 123–31).

In these histories of identity formation, subjectivities are born and reborn with the changing conditions of globalization. But this, in fact, would be the weaker claim of the cultural analysts of globalization. The stronger position that emerges from their analyses is that subjectivities are invented *as a consequence* of changing global circumstances. The history of identities is also the history of cycles of globalization and the subsequent transformations of the political captured repeatedly in the term "hegemony." If hegemony figures prominently in such analyses, it is worth pursuing further its connection with subjectivity. In fact, it is precisely in its connection with power that cultural analysts discuss the plurality (or lack thereof) of subjectivities.

Let us start with a quote from Friedman, whose position is echoed and pushed further by Featherstone:

> The political conditions of global processes are such that cultural heterogeneity is inversely related to political hegemony over time. And since history is the history of identity, the question of who "owns" or appropriates the past is a question of who is able to identify him- or herself and the other at a given time and place. If the fragmentation of a cultural world order implies the multiplication of cultural identities, the latter is expressed in the proliferation of histories. Multiple identities implies multiple histories.
>
> (1994, 142)[12]

Cultural analysts, as is explicitly stated above, do take the position that subjectivity and the conception of history are inextricably linked; that is to say, how "we" view history has a lot to do with who "we" are. So, for instance, a particular group's or alliance's perception of "the past" can be challenged by another which, in turn, will contribute directly to the undermining of the power of the former. Modern Greek identity was a challenge to the Ottoman hegemonic discourse; similarly, the contemporary Hawaiian identity can be explained as both an alternative and a challenge to the US and other discourses on Hawaii. If alternative subjectivities imply alternative readings and constructions of history (on which point we are in agreement with the cultural analysts of globalization), one wonders why the very concept of globalization is not susceptible to any such challenge. If there were an acknowledgment to that effect – that globalization, too, in part, is constituted discursively; that, it, too, is one among alternative readings of history – then there would be an element of self-reflexivity which is missing in globalization theories. Without that element, we seem to be left with the fundamental argument that subjectivities, although providing different versions of history, are determined by the omnipotent forces of globalization.

This lack of self-reflection seems to lead to yet another point of divergence: Friedman, although putting forward a powerful and convincing historical analysis of how Greek and Hawaiian identities were born, does not question the "singularity" of those identities. In other words, there appears to be consensus concerning the social constitution of being Greek or Hawaiian. It is here that postmodern theory would offer the challenge of conceiving the multiple, shifting, incomplete definitions of those identities; in other words, the meaning of being Greek or Hawaiian would be construed differently *at the same historical time*. What we are offering here is a supplement to Friedman's cultural analysis of the changing constitution of identities over time: that, depending on the *overdetermined* interpretation of those very historical circumstances, there one would expect the *differential* constitution of identities at any point in time.

The quotation above invites one more observation: that Friedman posits an inverse relation between hegemony and the "range" of subjectivities. The disruption of a hegemonic order implies the fragmentation of subjectivities; the corollary of this is that strong hegemony implies homogenized subjectivities (strong form of globalization?).[13]

The cultural analyses of globalization have a special place in the literature in exploring the connection between identity formation and globalization. In multilayered analyses – at times complemented by rich historical work – they contribute significantly to our understanding of how subjectivity, in fact, needs to be contextualized. Our disagreements certainly do not concern that desire to situate subjectivity; they emerge, rather, on how to conceptualize those "contexts."

The dimensions of space and class: new political possibilities

We can begin the process of widening the range of subjectivities and political practices – both actual and potential – by considering the cultural dimensions often associated with globalization. For this, we need to return to a previous period, the late-nineteenth and early-twentieth centuries, when an analogous process of capitalist expansion and global reduction is said to have occurred. According to Stephen Kern, "sweeping changes in technology and culture created distinctive new modes of thinking about and experiencing time and space" (1983, 1). These are the new modes of thinking that we now associate with the emergence of modernism.

What is remarkable, for our purposes, is not that these changes took place – then, as now, we should expect the social upheavals associated with the "shrinking of the globe" to disturb old ways of analyzing and depicting the dimensions of time and space and to lead to the creation of new ones – but that there is no one-to-one correspondence between them. Thus, for example, while the new forms of time (such as the introduction of standard time at the end of the nineteenth century) were an attempt to establish a certain uniformity in the way time was recorded and experienced, what stands out during this period is the proliferation of nonuniform, "private" modes of treating temporal movements and durations (such as in Henri Bergson's philosophy). Similarly, the positive treatment of "negative space" in Cubism can be contrasted to the "annihilation of space" created by the development of new modes of transportation. In fact, Kern notes that this period can be characterized in terms, not of establishing homogeneous and uniform modes of thinking and experience but, rather, of an "affirmation of a plurality of times and places" (1983, 8).

This conclusion should give us pause when considering the issue of the relationship between globalization and subjectivity. Instead of presuming that some "real" set of globalizing tendencies calls forth or determines a corresponding set of identities and consciousnesses, we should consider the range of alternative forms of recognition and, of course, misrecognition, that are or can be constituted within and alongside the processes of global expansion. It is precisely this "relative autonomy" of the social constitution of subjectivity that, as we show below, opens up new spaces for political intervention. On this point, certain key insights are offered by postmodern theory, which, should they be taken seriously, can assist this theoretical and political endeavor.

One such insight is given by the critique of representation, that the "real" can be adequately captured by a discourse. According to this argument, existing discourses of globalization can be challenged, not on traditional empiricist or rationalist grounds, but in terms of the conditions and consequences of marginalizing or excluding the forms (including subjectivities) of economic and social life that are produced in other discourses. It is not our goal, therefore, to argue that existing discourses of globalization are inadequate, either because they miss aspects of what is occurring "out there" (for example, the existence of economic and social "facts" that have not been or cannot be incorporated within the existing theories of globalization) or because they do not correspond to a rational order constituted within theory, be it the traditional Marxian "logic of capital" or another discourse. Rather, our point here is that globalization should not be rendered as a given, singular phenomenon, with its corresponding, necessary effects, but, instead, that different discourses of globalization have different implications for the constitution of the subjectivities through which alternative economic and social arrangements can be imagined and realized. Another crucial point to which we have already made reference is the idea that the relations among and between the different spheres of economic and social life can be sketched in nondeterministic ways. This allows us to argue both that subjectivities are constituted only partly by economic processes and that cultural identities are, in fact, constitutive *of* economic processes themselves. Finally, the postmodern concern for multiple, decentered subjects has important implications for imagining forms of subjectivity other than those associated with existing discourses of globalization and, therefore, of encouraging new forms of noncapitalist politics.

The focus on differentiation and fragmentation, which, as we have portrayed it here, is the hallmark of postmodern approaches to social theory, is also evident in some of the treatments of globalization that have been developed outside economics. We can find two such examples in the concepts of cultural hybridity and heterogeneous space. Each represents, for us, an attempt to break up the uniformity and homogeneity otherwise associated with – as the result or expression of – globalization, in order to recognize and create new kinds of responses.

As we have seen, globalization is often portrayed in terms of the uniformity and flatness of cultural expression, as images are disseminated through vast networks into every nook and cranny of the world. Jan Pieterse, however, defines globalization as essentially an "increase in the available modes of organization" (1993, 6): global, international, regional, national and so on. This plurality in the modes of organization is, for him, the "structural corollary to the contemporary phenomenon of multiple identities and decentering of the social subject" (1993, 7). Globalization, as a process, thus increases the sources of the self. So, now we live in a world where we can refer to Asian rap, Chinese tacos, and Shakespeare being performed in Kabuki style. Mestizo cultures have thus become a global phenomenon. As a result, we are now in the age of "boundary-crossing," whereby identities based on notions of traditional communities no longer do, or should, suffice. For Pieterse, this antiessentialist conception of subjectivity, according to which the identity of the self is given by multiple sources, has important political implications: "A politics of hybridity means navigating these zones of instability, without clinging to the notion of fixed units, whether they be nations, classes or ethnic groups, as the necessary or ultimate basis of politics" (1993, 13–14).[14]

It is important to note an unresolved issue here: hybridization, for Pieterse, takes place under unequal power relations, which places this approach firmly within the strand of globalization discourses for which the distribution of power is not all that ambiguous, such that the notion of hegemony can still have analytical import. What are the implications of his acknowledgement for the constitution of subjectivities and politics? According to Pieterse, the politics of hybridization give no clear answers to this vexing problem; but "it does release political reflection and collective action from the boundaries of nation, community, ethnicity, or class. Fixities have become fragments and fragments realign as the kaleidoscope of collective experience is in motion" (1993, 14). Still, the question remains: if hybridization takes place under conditions of inequality, then do we affirm our hybrid selves and construct our politics on the basis of that hybridity, or do we respond to it by imagining and attempting to construct a different identity? Furthermore, if it is the inner drive of capital which serves as the source of hybridization, then how effectively anticapitalist or noncapitalist would such a politics be?

While we applaud Pieterse's efforts to create a discourse of hybridity, the fact that it is derived from, and inscribed entirely within, the processes and mechanisms of globalization imposes severe limits on the range of possible subject positions. We also find problematic the way that he ascribes the "traditional" (for want of a better word) sources of self as "fixities."[15] If this conception were replaced by one of "processes," how would we redefine subjectivity? If, for example, we defined class or gender as overdetermined social processes rather than fixed and stable groupings, would not our conception of subjectivity be radically trans-formed? Stuart Hall, one of the leading theoreticians of postmodern cultural theory, suggests a similar point: rather than thinking of identity as an "already accomplished fact," we should perhaps think of it as "production," one that is never complete and always constituted within, and not outside, representation (Rutherford 1990, 222). Would these novel conceptions not translate to new and different conceptions and forms of political intervention? In what follows it is these issues that we pursue.

Globalization is also often used to refer to the spatial extension of economic, as well as cultural and political, processes and institutions. The result is that space is rendered either homogeneous and uniform or diverse; but this diversity is still conceived to be determined by the logic of globalization. However, ongoing attempts to rethink the spatiality of global capitalism create an effect similar to that of hybridization. We find, in the work of geographers such as Edward Soja (1989) and David Harvey (1989), building in turn on the insights of Henri Lefebvre (1974), a recogni-tion that, while the process of globalization eliminates certain spatial barriers, old spaces are not completely eliminated (even as they are trans-formed) and new spaces are created, thus forming a fragmented, discon-tinuous, layered spatial configuration of, and in, the world. Lefebvre, for example, argues that "exchange with its circulatory systems and networks may occupy space worldwide, but consumption occurs only in this or that particular place" (1974, 341). One of his important contributions to Marxism is precisely the idea that spatiality is bound up with the relation-ship between global exchange and the specific locations of consumption (and production) and that qualitatively different use-values, all too often ignored by political economists, are key to the fragmentation of space. Soja devotes even more attention to the by-now-familiar processes of global-ization – the internationalization of productive and finance capital, the weakening of local controls and state regulation over an increasingly "footloose capital" – and their "broad patterning," but he, too, points out its heterogeneity, that it "is highly differentiated and unevenly developed . . . taking a variety of specific forms, not all of which can be seen as "functional" for the logic of capital or inherently antagonistic to the demands of labor" (Soja 1989, 184). Even Harvey, who is given over more than the others to the power of globalization and its ability to "annihilate space through time," admits that the new spatiality which is being created is characterized by "fragmentation, insecurity, and ephemeral uneven development" (1989, 296). What we find in all three cases, then, is the idea that, while the forces of global capitalism are cast in terms that tend to exaggerate their unity, singularity, and totality, space itself is conceived to be fragmented and differentiated.[16]

Notwithstanding their limitations, their tendency to be inscribed within, and to be governed by, discourses of economic globalization similar to those proposed by radical political economists, the notions of hybridized culture and heterogeneous space serve to recast what is generally seen to be a uniform and homogeneous globality, thereby making global capitalism different from itself.

Our view is that these and related contributions can be put to use in fragmenting and differentiating the notions of globalization that have emerged in the existing discourses of political economy with an eye towards recognizing and creating new subjectivities and forms of political intervention.[17] The alternative, as we have seen, is to remain subject to the existing discourses in which the choice is between reasserting the national administration and control of the mechanisms and processes of global capitalism, thereby resisting capital's otherwise inevitable globalizing dynamic, or following that global dynamic and searching for transnational forms of coordination that match capital's "global reach." The problem, we think, is that both sets of subjectivities and forms of political intervention are limited to the view "from on high," that is, they say perhaps both too much and too little: too much, in that they accede to the vision of the global planners, the idea that all economic and social processes are (or should be or eventually will be) governed by the rational logic of transnational capital; too little, in that they tend to efface the forms of hybridity and fragmentation that can be found if we walk "at ground level."

One way of proceeding is to take seriously the "place-bound identities" that others (e.g., Harvey) take as signs of the "reactionary politics of an aestheticized spatiality" (1989, 305). What we have in mind is that existing discourses of globalization tend to marginalize or exclude all "local" initiatives and the subjectivities and practices that are constituted in such places. Of course, we want to avoid any simple opposition between local and global: we recognize, from our reference points, that there are certain global processes (international flows of commodities, finance, labor, and so on) that constitute any social site – but the existence of such global dimensions does not eliminate the places in and through which many identities and activities, both those associated with global processes and others, are organized and enacted. And we want to add that every global process is carried out only in and through specific and concrete places.[18] Therefore, we need to reconsider the multiple subjectivities that are – and can be – constituted in such places in order to avoid the political paralysis and/or frustration that often accompanies the discourses and images of globalization.

One of the effects of focusing on the specific localities where the various parts of otherwise global operations are located is to challenge the presumed invulnerability of those operations and to invoke their potential fragility. It means, for example, that the awarenesses and sensibilities located at one site can be used both to combine with existing claims on other sites and to participate in the creation of entirely new ones, in both locations. The kinds of sites we have in mind include the familiar branch plants of transnational corporations and the various nodes of financial networks (where flows of finance are received and from which repayments are made) as well as the extended communities (from the neighborhood to the regional and national level) within which the "points" of production, finance, distribution, consumption, and so on exist. These are the sites that can be discursively constituted as specific combinations of both local instantiation and global connection – without the necessity of according priority (before or after the fact) to either pole. What we are particularly interested in are the possibilities for the emergence of subjectivities and identities that are collective in both these senses: that enact a story about the effects (and, perhaps even more important, about the changes in the effects) of a process on one or another dimension of the "imagined community" as it exists in one location – say, the modes of local consumption of goods that are produced elsewhere – and the ways in which processes in another location – say, the way in which those goods are produced – occur (and, again, can be changed). In this sense, we can talk about the interplay between communal subjectivities in both locations, as each takes into account and, by doing so, changes the awareness of the local and global dimensions of their own as well as the other's existence.[19]

We should add that it is not necessary for the subjectivities and identities constituted in and around the local sites of global operations to be singular ones, such as we saw above in the discussion of Greek and Hawaiian identities. We expect, on the contrary, that the ways in which individuals and groups become aware of – by discursively constituting – the complex interplay between the local and global conditions and effects of any particular economic process serve to enact an entire range of possible consciousnesses, alliances, and forms of intervention. Indeed, it is precisely the partial, fragmented nature of such identities – both as they encompass only a subset of the identities of economic and social actors and as they focus on only some of the possible local and global dimensions of those identities – that, in our view, creates the possibility of imagining and participating in projects to change the current situation. In other words, even under what other discourses might constitute as the most hegemonic of regimes – whether of a particular nation-state or trading bloc or, alternatively, of a transnational economic process such as the movement of international finance – it is precisely the emergence and joining together of "incomplete" identities in different locations that serves to enable collective projects of transformation to take place.

If the discourses of global capitalism can be challenged in this way "from within," so to speak, by mobilizing and coordinating the subjectivities and practices of two different places to challenge the same global processes that serve to connect them, we can also move "outside," to recognize the diversity of noncapitalist class processes and identities that are both enabled by and exist in a manner relatively autonomous from the global processes normally associated with capitalism. We are thinking here of the ways in which the spaces where the global networks of capitalist marketing, finance, labor migration, and product sourcing are located are always already characterized by other – ancient, feudal, communal, and so on – class processes. These can be found in the households, shops, home-based production facilities, production cooperatives, social service agencies, and other sites and organizations that constitute the dense and variegated class spaces of local communities. Many of these forms of noncapitalist production, consumption, and provisioning are, in turn, enabled and supported by the revenues that can be said to flow out of the porous structures of global capitalism. For example, wages paid by capitalist multinational corporations – whether located in Third World "free trade" zones, the inner cities of advanced nations, or rural areas around the globe – can be, and often are, used to establish noncapitalist forms of householding, production, and retail facilities.[20] Sourcing contracts can be, and often are, made with noncapitalist (both individual and communal) producers.[21] Bargaining over distributions of the surplus-value can be, and often is (through trade-union funds, local taxes and grants to environmental and other projects), directed at creating new cultural and physical infrastructures. In all these cases, a fragmented class landscape both exists apart from and, just as often, is made possible in and through the effects of global capitalism. The reproduction and transformation of these conditions can, we think, be made the subject of the demands of multiple communities that are not simply inscribed within or limited to the processes and mechanisms of capitalist globalization.

The important point is that noncapitalist identities can be (and, in many cases, are already being) enacted on the basis of the existing economic and social landscape, in conjunction with the de facto class diversity which has emerged within, alongside, and outside global capitalism. It is precisely the existence of such class and, in addition, nonclass subjectivities which, we think, challenges existing economic and cultural discourses of globalization and creates the conditions for the emergence and flourishing of other discourses, identities, and projects of change.

To be clear, it is not that we consider them necessarily "progressive," or that we would choose to support, any and all such noncapitalist subjectivities and movements. However, we do think that new discourses of globalization, through which forms of class heterogeneity are produced and recognized both in the interstices and at the margins of "global capitalism," can serve the important purpose of opening up and producing alternatives to the poverty of identities and forms of contestation (often limited, as we have seen, to the choice between the "national Keynesian" and the "global imperative") that we consider to be one of the effects of existing political economies of globalization. Then, as that new wealth of existing and potential subjectivities and political practices is elaborated, it becomes possible in specific settings, at particular sites, to foster, to intervene in, to envision, and to encourage projects of noncapitalist class transformation.

The view from below

As we descend from the "tower" and begin to walk down the streets and past the sites of the hybridized culture and heterogeneous spaces of the "global city," a transformation takes place: we are forced to confront our desire to be alternatively dazzled and horrified by the panoramic view "from above" and to embrace a new set of visions which, however partial and provisional, afford us the opportunity to live in and alter the fragmented, differentiated, "porous" order that we encounter "down below."

(original version published in 1998)

Notes

1   See, for example, the discussion by Diskin and Koechlin (1994).
2   Feminist economists, including Diana Strassmann (1993a, 1993b), have been at the forefront of attempts to interrogate mainstream economics for the forms of subjectivity that it presumes and constructs (particular notions of rationality, self-interest, etc.) and the other forms of subjectivity that it marginalizes or excludes (other notions of rationality, caring and nurturing, etc.). Among nondeterminist Marxists, Jack Amariglio and Antonio Callari (1989) and J. K. Gibson-Graham (1996) have explored the issue of subjectivity in relation to discourses of political economy. A good introduction to different conceptions of subjectivity, especially in relation to the problem of "resistance," is provided by Paul Smith (1988).
3   The reader will excuse us if, in this version, we avoid attributing particular arguments and examples to specific texts. The existing literature on globalization is extensive and, we presume, relatively well-known. The texts we have consulted include the following: Castells (1994), Ranney (1993), Willoughby (1991), Arsen (1991), the special issue of the *Review of Radical Political Economics* titled 'Beyond the Nation State: Global Perspectives on Capitalism" (1990),

MacEwan and Tabb (1989), Kolko (1988), Gordon (1988), Jenkins (1987), Grou (1985), and Radice (1975).

4 The experience of France with a socialist economic policy in the early 1980s is often cited as an example. Carole Biewener (1988, 1990) has put forward an alternative analysis.

5 What follows derives from two such analyses put forward by Jonathan Friedman (1994) and Mike Featherstone (1995).

6 In some analyses it can be clearly deduced that the history of globalization is not identical with that of capitalism. This can be seen, for example, in Friedman's analysis. Here (as also in world-systems theories) the argument is that there have been global systems prior to capitalism. It seems that such an argument would be crucial to the analysis, yet the point seems to get lost in the course of analysis and the theory of globalization becomes identical with that of capitalist globalization.

7 The whole point here is, in many ways, reminiscent of the criticism leveled against versions of structuralism.

8 These terms are from Hirst and Thompson (1992, 1996).

9 The tendency on the part of classical Marxism to economize the political is critically discussed by Antonio Callari (1991).

10 See, for example, the various proposals put forward in the issue of *Labor Research Review* (1995) titled "Confronting global power."

11 The same issue returns below, concerning the difference between local and global identities. We should mention the recent attempts by George DeMartino and Stephen Cullenberg (1994a and 1995) to bridge the gap separating the national Keynesian and global imperative subjectivities. Their proposal to create a system of social tariffs utilizes a national mechanism but allows for a plurality of global identities (concerning such issues as human rights, environmental protection, workers' rights, etc.).

12 The concept of hegemony is not defined in these texts; we therefore have to read into the analysis on this point. This concept has found its most eloquent elaboration in Gramsci's *Prison Notebooks* (1971). Gramsci refers to hegemony as the process whereby the ruling classes, having established the repressive mechanisms of the state apparatus, create a universal language that transcends their corporate class interests. Hegemony is, in other words, the process of the creation of a discourse of legitimation. Any undermining of hegemony, then, is the process of the challenging of this "universal" discourse, which, among other things, is brought about by the emergence of "competing" discourses.

13 Featherstone, on this point, borrows from the work of Norbert Elias who claims that, in situations in which ruling groups are in control, they develop a strong "we-image" and can colonize the "outsider" group in its own manner of conduct (1995, 124). We note that it is from this conception of the relationship between hegemony and subjectivity that something akin to the postmodern "fragmented" identity emerges: the disruption of the world hegemonic order in the recent decades, especially in the aftermath of the momentous changes of the 1980s, has led to the "proliferation" of identities, a clear symptom of postmodernity. This reading of postmodernity is clearly linked with Jameson's (1991) powerful analysis.

14 Friedman, in a manner which differs from that of Pieterse, argues that there are not, and have never been, "pure" cultures; that cultures are, and have always been, Creole at all times.

15 The problem arises from the conception that, in the past, subjectivities were fixities but, under the new conditions of capitalism, during the postmodern era, subjectivities have become hybridized by submitting to the logic of capital.

16 In ways reminiscent of many other conceptions of "Capitalism"; for a critique, see Gibson-Graham (1996).

17 We are referring to the work of the school of "postmodern Marxists" associated with the journal *Rethinking Marxism* which, in diverse ways, has fragmented and differentiated many of the categories and conceptual entities that have been part of the Marxian tradition – including methodology and epistemology, the categories of value theory and notions of the enterprise, markets, class, and capitalism itself – and transformed them in such a way that they become different from themselves.

18 The myriad issues concerning the "spatiality" of social and political identities are discussed at length in Keith and Pile (1993).

19 In our view, something of this sort seems to have been enacted in the 1995 negotiations concerning the sourcing operations of The Gap. In that case, consumers, religious groups, students, worker rights advocates, and others in the United States, brought together by the National Labor Committee, were able to sign an agreement that demands compliance with existing "Sourcing Principles and Guidelines" in order to protect the rights of union activists in El Salvador to organize local workers. Thus, the evaluation of the qualities associated with the commodities marketed and consumed in one location led to a practice of transforming the way in which those commodities are produced elsewhere. For more information, see Pattee (1996).

20 Kumudhini Rosa (1994), for example, shows how women working in Sri Lankan free-trade zones, on their own initiative and in conjunction with other groups, have used their wages to establish such projects as communal housing, food cooperatives, centers for legal advice, newspapers, and women's centers which offer medical assistance, education, and training in alternative skills.

21 The Self-Employed Women's Association (SEWA) in India is a good example of creating an awareness of and organizing as laborers who, instead of working for wages in large-scale manufacturing enterprises, produce as individuals and small collectivities, many on contract for multinational enterprises. SEWA has not only achieved recognition as a trade union but has also sponsored a wide variety of noncapitalist service and production cooperatives. See Jhabvala (1994) and Kabeer (1994, 321–61) for additional details concerning both the successes and the ongoing difficulties faced by SEWA.

16 Globalization and imperialism

Nicaragua is being colonized again.

Roberto Manzanares, fired Nicaraguan union leader
Gonzalez (2000)

America's entire war on terror is an exercise in imperialism . . . What else can you call America's legion of soldiers, spooks and Special Forces straddling the globe?

Michael Ignatieff (2002)

A visitor from another world would surely be perplexed were he to overhear a so-called old critic calling the new critics dangerous. What, this visitor, would ask, are they dangers to? The state? The mind? Authority?

Edward Said (1983)

Let me state, up front, that I am worried both about the ubiquity of the term globalization in our current thinking and about the effects of the meanings of the term on that thinking. In general, the many and varied uses of the term suggest that there is something fundamentally new happening in the world, that a more or less complete reorganization of culture, politics, and economics is taking place. This is the case on both the Right and the Left, in both mainstream and alternative analyses.

Of course, there is a great deal of nonsense coming from the Right, in the mainstream views that receive the bulk of publicity in the mass media – from both longstanding and well-respected academic experts (such as Samuel P. Huntington [1996] and Paul Krugman [1996]) and from self-styled (but often officially sanctioned) pundits (like the *New York Times*'s Thomas Friedman [2000]). Both utopias and dystopias are imagined. They write and speak of the end of the nation-state, the civilizing power of free markets, the Lexus running over the olive tree, and the increase in world welfare and social harmony created by the lowering of trade and financial barriers and the expansion of world economic interdependence – or, alternatively, of the clash of civilizations and the intensification of regional conflicts.

Is there anything to learn here? Aside from the content (that is, whether or not one agrees with or finds suggestive one or another aspect of their analyses), it is a lesson in manufacturing consent, in establishing the discursive conditions of hegemony. We are confronted by an uncoordinated effort (uncoordinated, that is, at the global level, in the sense that no one/no body is dictating the various contributions to this neoliberal hegemony, although there are many decentralized coordinations taking place) that is in the process of naturalizing and depoliticizing the existence and consequences of globalization. What we have is a thought factory, an ideology-machine, that includes the research departments of the World Bank and International Monetary Fund (IMF) (yes, alongside the conditionality of policies – the hostage-taking, with the consent of borrowing-country political and economic elites, of economic policy – there is the production and distribution of knowledges about the conditions and consequences of globalization), the news reports and editorial pages of major newspapers and magazines, members of the economics profession, a wide variety of commentators (from TV talking heads to the authors of airport books), the Clinton and Bush administrations, and the wide range of North American Free Trade Agreement and World Trade Organization (WTO) supporters that daily assault our senses and preach to us from their protected perches.

A good example is the 1996 World Bank study, *El Salvador: Meeting the Challenge of Globalization*. There, it is announced that the main goal for El Salvador's policymakers is to enhance "global competitiveness" by rapidly aiming for two main goals:

> (i) promote domestic and foreign investment and incorporate the country into the global production chain by lowering the costs of operating in the country; and (ii) reduce the size of the State through accelerated privatization, while strengthening the public sector's role as facilitator of private sector development.
>
> (World Bank 1996, 1)

This is the "common sense" of international openness and privatization that is regularly manufactured and disseminated, not only by the World Bank, but throughout the globalization industry. This makes it not unlike the development industry critically analyzed by Arturo Escobar (1995) and the other so-called postdevelopment thinkers: a set of discourses, policy recommendations, and aid packages that runs from the highest level of World Trade Organization negotiators and administrators to nongovernmental organization project officers and extension personnel who, instead of social justice and the amelioration of poverty, now talk in terms of *microempresas* and entrepreneurial initiatives among Andean alpaca herders.

But, as the postdevelopment thinkers have been reminded by their critics, the development industry is not monolithic. Nor, for that matter, is the globalization industry. It is contested both inside and outside – by rank opportunists such as Jeffrey Sachs, who jumps on the anti-IMF band-wagon when it suits his wavering reputation after the economic and social disasters he helped to engineer in Bolivia, Poland, and Russia, and by concerned neoclassical economists such as Dani Rodrik (1997), of the Institute for International Economics, and Branko Milanovic (2002), of the World Bank, who are worried that the case for free trade and the benefits of globalization are being mishandled because advocates have not taken into account either "legitimate" concerns with the increasing elasticity of the demand for unskilled labor or the "malignant side" of globalization. It is also challenged by well-meaning, committed development advisors and practitioners, who work with all kinds of local groups – not only herders but artisanal cooperatives, women's groups, savings and credit associa-tions, trade unions, health clinics, treatment and prevention programs for sexually transmitted diseases, slum-dwellers, human rights observers and advocates, and so on. These people often work inside the globalization industry, attempting to open up the language to alternative visions of what specific sectors of society might look like, making do with the bits of philanthropy, federal assistance, or foreign aid, the networks and exper-tise of international nongovernmental organizations, and local move-ments and leadership that they can muster to improve the lot of people in both First World and Third World countries. And, of course, we have the example of the organizers of and participants in campus groups, commu-nity meetings, and large-scale demonstrations in Seattle, Melbourne, and other cities around the globe, who have attacked World Bank policies, the effects of IMF conditionality, the proliferation of Third World sweatshops, and the corporate dominance of what they consider to be the new forms of global economy.

It is this set of understandings of globalization, on the broadly defined Left, that concerns me most. As much as they have mobilized large numbers of people in demonstrations against the current forms of gover-nance of the world economy – and, therefore, they pose an important political contestation – I worry about the ways in which they/we have come to accept the existence of globalization, to invoke it to explain every-thing that is happening in the world, to slide over or forgo concepts and modes of analysis that have long defined the Marxian tradition, to fore-close other ways of seeing and acting in the world. The concept of global-ization has become a gift that is not offered freely (because that is impossible, the gift always annuls itself) but, instead, creates a debt that must be repaid, sooner or later.

Novelty of globalization?

Most uses of the term globalization assert (or, at least, imply) that some-thing fundamentally new characterizes the world today. This is akin to the oft-repeated argument that the commodification of culture (signaling the age of postmodernity) began in the 1960s – an argument that forgets about the many ways in which the buying and selling of both popular and high cultural artifacts were a defining moment of modernism and even earlier. Let me suggest, in parallel, that the forms of global economic integration that we are witnessing today are, at least quantitatively, not so different from those of the late-nineteenth and early-twentieth centuries – say, the period 1870 to 1913.

Let us examine, if only briefly, some of the salient facts of this earlier period:

- From the 1860s onward, export growth and rising foreign trade shares were stimulated by the widening and deepening of capitalist class relations, along with breakthroughs in long-distance transportation (such as steamships) and communications (especially the telegraph). Thus, for example, the growth of international trade averaged 3.5 percent per annum compared with output growth of 2.7 percent. Of course, there was plenty of national and regional variation, including the United States, which erected high trade barriers and carried out a process of import-substitution industrialization (a form of industrialization that it, and the entire globalization industry, denies to El Salvador and many other countries today).

- The international economy was characterized by large and relatively stable capital flows, based on the spread of the gold standard, convertible currencies, and the financial hegemony of Great Britain. During the 1870–1913 period, the growth of portfolio investment exceeded the growth of trade, foreign direct investment, and output. In fact, by 1913, the volume of international capital flows had reached 5 percent of the gross national product of the capital-exporting countries, thereby establishing integrated international capital markets.

- Production was also internationalized during this earlier period, as foreign direct investment increased, the stock of which reached (according to the calculations of Paul Bairoch and Richard Kozul-Wright [1998]) 9 percent of world output by 1913, a level that was not attained again until the late 1990s. Of course, much of this foreign investment was directed into raw materials, but a significant amount found its way into infrastructure (especially railways and utilities) and manufacturing (particularly in the United States and Russia).

- Finally, international migrations of people were a significant phenomenon in the late-nineteenth and early-twentieth centuries. In absolute terms, the number of immigrants admitted to the United States during the 1901–20 period exceeded that of the 20-year period beginning in 1981 and, in relative terms, as a percentage of the entire US population, the earlier numbers far outweigh anything we have witnessed in the second half of the twentieth century.

To sum up, the activities of international trade, finance, production, and migration were evolving rapidly (if unevenly) from 1870 to 1913 and the levels in all these areas today have generally not surpassed the earlier ones.[1]

Which is not to say that everything has remained the same. But we should be cautious about taking ours to be an absolutely novel time. For example, much ink has been spilt analyzing and proffering alternative solutions to the recent meltdowns in such countries as Indonesia and Argentina, as if financial crises associated with international flows of capital were something new. However, Charles Kindleberger (1996), among others, reminds us of the long history of "manias, panics, and crashes" that were characteristic of earlier periods of globalization.

Similarly, the development of biotechnology and new forms of telecommunication have not eliminated, in the North or the South, the existence of industry or manufacturing, whether steel or sneakers or silicon chips. Quite the contrary! What is being produced in various places has changed (for example, textile production, which has moved, within the United States, from the Northeast to the South, then abroad, to China and elsewhere). But that does not mean that capitalist production (of goods as well as services) has been eliminated from the United States and other advanced capitalist nations – or that labor has been made "immaterial." That is to confuse concrete labor with abstract labor, to conflate them. The labor that is performed in the "white factories" of the computer industry in Japan and the United States, no less than the labor performed in the steel factories of Brazil or South Korea, if and when it is organized in a capitalist fashion, involves a process of valorization – the extraction of labor from labor power – that begets surplus-value. Or so the capitalists – those who extract surplus-value as well as those who receive a cut of the appropriated and realized surplus-value – hope.

At the same time, we should not overstate the similarities between the two periods. There *are* new features within the most recent forms of globalization. For example, while both periods are characterized by a strong North-South orientation, the colonial structures of the late-nineteenth century meant that many regions of Latin America, Africa, and Asia were forced to have the freedom to specialize in raw materials exports and manufacturing imports. This led to a deindustrialization of the South, whose share in global manufacturing production fell from one-third to under one-tenth of the world total. Today, in contrast, the internationalization of economic activity has been accompanied by a *re*industrialization of the Third World and a decline in manufacturing activity in the North.

Other new features of the contemporary global economy, compared to the 1870–1913 period, include the following:

- A growth in the number and size of transnational corporations (TNCs) – the number of TNCs from the major industrial countries rose from

7,000 in 1970 to 24,000 in 1990, while the number of people employed by TNCs rose over 80 percent during the same period. And trade within the TNCs went up as a proportion of world trade, from 20 percent in the 1970s to more than one-third in the 1990s. Transnational corporations were not absent in the earlier period but their global reach certainly increased in the closing decades of the twentieth century.

- The internationalization of service-sector activities (such as the retail and wholesale distribution of goods, banking and finance, insurance, hotels and tourism, business services, health, and telecommunications) that, again, played a role in the late-nineteenth and early-twentieth centuries, but their growth has far outpaced that of manufacturing and raw materials of late.
- The speed of capital flows around the world and the role of short-term capital movements, as national financial markets have been deregulated and liberalized (under the aegis of the World Bank and IMF) and new financial instruments invented.

The list of new dimensions of current globalizing tendencies could go on. My point is that concentrating solely on either "what is new" or "what is old" can only lead to errors for Marxist thinkers and activists. We need to pay attention to the current conjuncture for points of rupture, new challenges and new possibilities, but we don't need to rush into the wholesale movement toward globalization.

Like those who take the Internet and other new modes of information sharing to be the defining characteristic of the current period, a culmination of the various stages in the development of capitalism, that which has turned commodities into signs, which commodifies the signs themselves. There is clearly something new here, which has enabled new forms of global marketing, as well as forms of communication that allowed the organizers of the conference in which I first presented remarks on this subject to contact participants and attendees around the world and the various antiglobalization groups in Seattle and Genoa to coordinate their efforts.

But, again, let's be careful about the extent to which such new forms of communication govern everything or mark all social relations in a fundamentally new manner. It is not that nothing is new here, but we should it allow it to be more local, partial, and incomplete. For example, some young people are learning new forms of exchange – significantly noncapitalist, nonmarket exchange – in downloading and trading music and video files. Such a new practice (and others like it) is important for us to track and make sense of, precisely because it represents an exception to, and a break from, the presumed global dominance of capitalist markets.

So, I want to suggest, with globalization. In quantitative terms, it has increased in the past 50 years, but still (on many scales) only reaching the levels of the earlier period. And there are new elements, such as "hot money" and large, market-dominating and cross-border producing TNCs, along with new forms of global opening and governance, embodied in the WTO, the World Bank, and IMF. But we exaggerate that which is new, different, and all-encompassing at our peril.

The globalization debates

All of which leaves us trapped in sterile debates – for example, between a truly global economy versus the continued relevance of nation-states, international organizing versus national-level politics, free trade versus regulated trade, and so on. The result is to limit our conceptions of the possible, nowhere better represented than in the determined efforts on the part of radical economists to assert the continued relevance of domestic macroeconomic policy, capital controls, the Tobin tax, and so on. In their hands, progressive economic policy is reduced to a modified Keynesian project of national and international economic regulation, domestic expansionary policy, and international stability; as if encouraging capitalist economic growth and productive capital accumulation – and discouraging speculative financial investment – did not also provide some of the conditions of existence of exploitation. How and when did left political economy become confined to the choice between different patterns of capitalist development – more or less regulated, more or less state intervention, more or fewer controls, so-called profit-led versus wage-led growth?

This, it seems, is an effect of focusing on and opposing "neoliberalism," a mode of regulation and a celebration (especially within neoclassical economics) of free markets, international trade, and well-defined private-property rights. But this is a battle that takes place *within* mainstream economics, not a battle that is ours – for or against free trade, freer or more regulated forms of international economic activity (whether production, distribution, or finance). For every defender of untrammeled free trade, there is someone sounding the alarm that the system is about to collapse of its own uncontrolled, unregulated weight. For every Paul Krugman, a Joseph Stiglitz (2002); for each Thomas Friedman, a George Soros – and, for that matter, for every Soros who issues a warning that the global economy faces imminent crisis (1998), and becomes required reading for many on the Left, a more recent one who recants much of his earlier dire prognostication (2000). We have to recognize that there has been a battle within liberal (or, if you prefer, neoliberal) economics from the very beginning, for Adam Smith, as well as his classical and neoclassical successors, a tension born out of the desire to promote the widening and deepening of free capitalist markets and, since that is always a fragile and precarious project, to regulate all potential disruptions, whether of the feudal state then or the protectionist state now. Theirs has been a project both to celebrate the existence of capitalist markets and to regulate their creation which, as Karl Polanyi well understood, required the intervention of the state, then as now.

One of the most creative attempts to rethink and to regulate the effects of international markets is George DeMartino's (2000) ethical critique of both global neoliberalism and the kinds of competitiveness-enhancing and "leveling-down" policies advocated by mainstream economists and policymakers in the United States and elsewhere. DeMartino then devises a "leveling-up" strategy to fundamentally change the global trading regime, based on what he calls a social-index tariff structure that, while it presupposes global markets, seeks to remove critical aspects of social life from international competition.

And to those liberal thinkers who wring their hands about making cross-cultural ethical judgments (such as Martha Nussbaum and Amartya Sen, who think that the only alternative is a neoclassical relativism of individual calculations, and then attempt to establish universal foundations for such judgments), Marxism has a unique challenge and contribution: the recognition that people are not just standing around, waiting for enlightenment, but struggling to change the conditions that determine their lives.[2] And the goal of Marxist thinkers and radical activists is precisely to identify with many (but, of course, not all) of those struggles, to debate their significance and to participate in them, within and across countries.

If the terms of the debates concerning globalization are not ours, even less so is the inclination to invoke the economy (or some element thereof, such as computer and communications technology) as a demiurge, propelling all other elements of society to some endpoint, whether utopia or dystopia. Too much has been accomplished, including in the pages of *Rethinking Marxism* and elsewhere, with the aim of recovering and reinventing the noneconomistic elements of Marxism, to return to such traditional formulations. The critique of political economy is, among other things, a critique of this economizing tendency, embodied, for example, in mainstream (especially neoclassical) economics. This is the approach of Gary Becker and many other mainstream economists: to reduce the economy to a central organizing principle, and then to economize all other spheres of social existence (the household, gifting, the treatment of the environment, and so on).

Too much work has been carried out, both to decenter society from the economy and to decenter (fragment and disperse) the economy itself, for us to return to the economism of traditional Marxism: theoretical and empirical work by Stephen Resnick and Richard Wolff (1987b), J. K. Gibson-Graham (1996), Jack Amariglio and Antonio Callari (1993), Stephen Cullenberg (1994), and many other contemporary Marxist thinkers in political economy. They have not eliminated the economy from our work (in favor of some other instance, such as culture or politics, thereby creating a false choice) but, instead, have sought to revise existing Marxian conceptions – for example, by tracing through the complex and changing patterns of appropriations and distributions of surplus labor, examining the forms of economy that cannot simply be reduced to capitalism (thereby reminding us of the existence, today and not in some far-distant future, of various forms of noncapitalism), the forms of subjectivity associated with commodity fetishism that are not determined (socially or historically) by the economy itself, the overdetermination of the rate of profit; and so on. And much more needs to be done. In any case, we should not let globalization be the way that economism sneaks back into our theorizations of the contemporary world.

The irony, of course, is that one finds Marxists and other critical thinkers in the humanities – who spend their time analyzing literary and cultural texts and discourses – increasingly invoking unified, singular, and totalizing conceptions of capitalist economy, as if texts and discourses do not matter when it comes to the economy, as if the economy were simply "out there," beyond all textual and discursive determination and interpretation. While, at the same time, those of us in and around the discipline of economics (the best example of the fact that the Left has not captured the academy – would that it had!) have worked long and hard to undermine and provide alternatives to such modernist conceptions of the economy, precisely by examining the effects of the models and metaphors of economy (on discourse and politics, as well as on the economy itself) that have operated, not only within mainstream economics, but also in various heterodox traditions, including Marxism.

Finally, the focus on globalization (and, with it, neoliberalism and other such terms) has displaced other concepts or ways of making sense of the world. I am thinking, in particular, of the notion of imperialism.

Imperialism

Historically, let us remember that imperialism, as the term is often used, refers both to what Edward Said (1993) calls the age of high or classical imperialism and to the configuration of conditions that Lenin (1975) referred to as the highest stage of capitalism – exactly the time period (the carving up of the world by the European powers in the nineteenth century and the conditions leading up to the First World War) that can be characterized by a process of internationalization or globalization which, at least quantitatively, is very similar to our own. So, if we want to argue that the concept of imperialism held at least some validity for that time (and many of us do), what fundamentally has changed, to all but eliminate its use today? Not that the exact definitions need apply as theoreticians deployed it or as it emerged (as Said has so eloquently shown us) in the writings of novelists and others at the time.[3] Nor will the documents today necessarily mirror those collected by Barbara Harlow and Mia Carter (1999) in their recently published "documentary sourcebook" on imperialism and orientalism.

Today, such "formal empires" no longer (or, better, hardly) exist – precisely because the thinkers and movements of anti-imperialism and national liberation (from Mariátegui and Gandhi to Fanon and Che, from Peru and India to Algeria and Cuba) were successful, because imperialism was opposed both by broad alliances of subaltern, colonized peoples and by equally broad alliances within the imperial nations themselves. Not that the results were always what we (or they) had hoped. But since when, as Marxists, have we ever expected purity or finality in the real, concrete processes of history-in-the-making?

But, for all that, we are witnesses to events and activities that can only be understood in terms of some notion of imperialism – and that can only be opposed by sustained, broad, antiimperialist intellectual and political work. How else are we to understand the wars in the Gulf, Kosovo, and, after 9/11, in Afghanistan and countless other countries where US troops, advisors, and intelligence operatives are located? Are such massive military interventions so far away from the invasions of Grenada and Panama or the support for the Contras in Nicaragua and Honduras? Or the efforts to establish NAFTA and the WTO? The activities of the World Bank and the IMF?

No, these do not involve a political or economic carving up of the world, the imperialism that Jan Pieterse describes as "territorial, state driven, centrally orchestrated and marked by a clear division between colonizer and colonized" (2000, 132). Not exactly. It is not individual parts of the world, but the world as a whole, a project to recolonize the entire world, to remake it, with the zeal of a humanizing mission, precisely reminiscent of the "Civilization, Christianity, and Commerce" theme that, according to the legendary David Livingstone, was the basis of the European colonization of Africa. Today, for the imperial presidencies of Reagan, Bush I, Clinton, and Bush II, the mission can be summed up as "Democracy, Anticommunism, and Free Trade."

And, just like the classic imperialisms, the new one involves subject peoples who are producing their own vigorous cultures and economies of opposition and resistance.[4]

Wherein, then, resides the resistance to invoking imperialism to characterize and oppose at least some significant events and activities, frameworks and projects, in the world today? Let me venture at least a couple of reasons for such resistance, and respond (if only briefly) to each in turn.

One reason may be the "messiness" of recent military interventions – for example, the Gulf War. George Bush versus Saddam Hussein? One of the most discouraging personal episodes of that war was watching my liberal and even left-wing colleagues become supporters of the US-led "smart-bomb" alliance to drive Iraq out of Kuwait and, they hoped, into the grave. I watched my colleagues, at Notre Dame and elsewhere, become the liberal supporters of imperialism, the very professors I opposed when I was a high school and college student. But when did imperialism ever come dressed in the clearcut white and black cowboy hats of a John Huston or Clint Eastwood movie? It was never a question of choosing between the two, but of opposing the war based on an understanding of the history that gave rise to both – the invasion of Kuwait and the effort of the United States to obliterate Hussein, the failed negotiations, the massacre on the highway, and so on – in the first place. The fact that the victims of colonialism and imperialist aggression (or even many who have resisted them over the years) are never so innocent should not prevent us from understanding the institutions, practices, and projects that constitute what I would like to call imperialism.

A second reason may be the association of globalization with the universalization of capitalism – the idea in the minds of some, at least, that "every human practice, every social relationship, and the natural environment are subject to the same requirements of profit-maximization, capital accumulation, the constant self-expansion of capital" (Wood 1999, 8) – while imperialism has traditionally been associated with the relationship between capitalism and noncapitalism, the colonization of one by the other. However, it is a mistake to assume that, because capitalism has become global (was there ever a time when it was not?), all forms of noncapitalism have been eliminated, or that they can simply be ignored. It is the effect of our concepts of capitalism, as J. K. Gibson-Graham (1996) has so eloquently shown, that the wide variety of noncapitalist class processes that can be said to exist in the world are read out of the economic and social landscape.

So, the historical similarities between then and now constitute one reason to support the idea of invoking imperialism – alongside or in place of globalization or neoliberalism – to understand what is taking place in the world today.

Another reason to deploy the concept of imperialism has to do with its effects, its performativity, if you will. Imperialism, unlike globalization or other such terms, is a multidimensional set of practices (economic, political, and cultural) with no necessary unity or inevitability about them. They may, and often do, work together, but with no singular purpose or organizing entity. And, just as they are set in motion, they can be resisted, deflected, and even stopped. Globalization, in contrast, has a depressing inevitability about it. And that is because it is configured as an unfolding of an economic (and, often, below that, a technological) logic. Globalization is gigantic and apocalyptic. Imperialism, as I am using the term, is partial and incomplete, a project that is both powerful and fragile, less a description of an entire stage of capitalist or world development than a project *in* that world; an attempt to make and remake that world.[5]

I think it shares these features with another venerable Marxist concept: exploitation. Exploitation – the extraction of surplus labor from the direct producers by those who don't perform the labor – is a doing, a ripping-off (or, to use Marx's even more colorful phrase, a sucking of blood from the laborers), an activity that fits uneasily within bourgeois norms and sensibilities. There is nothing inevitable about exploitation, either in general or in its specific forms – capitalist, feudal, slave, individual, and so on. There is no single exploiter, no national or world bourgeoisie, and no single exploited, no national or international working class. Exploitation – in its capitalist form, the extraction of labor from labor power, the self-expansion of value – is a process, one among many within the social totality. Class, in this rendition, refers not to groups of people but to a process in which people participate, in which they are positioned as performers or appropriators of surplus labor. Qua exploiters, the boards of directors of capitalist enterprises appropriate the surplus-value produced by the laborers within those enterprises. This surplus is, in turn, distributed to merchants, bankers, the state, other capitalists, stockholders, and so on who, as occupants of so-called subsumed class positions, provide some of the economic, political, and cultural conditions under which that exploitation continues to take place. Such distributions – whether to the state in the form of taxes or to private shareholders as dividends, to finance capital as interest payments or to citizen "shareholders" to organize daycare centers or community outreach programs – profoundly shape the social and natural environment within which we live. What we call capitalism, then, is that constellation of conditions and effects that are associated (not abstractly or inevitably but concretely and contingently – in other words, socially and historically) with the extraction of surplus labor in the form of surplus-value.

Imperialism, in turn, is the set of conditions that shape, and are shaped by, the existence of this exploitation. Yes, capitalist imperialism – not because capitalists always get what they want nor because forms of colonial expansion and domination did not predate the emergence and development of capitalism nor, finally, because imperialism can be reduced to or explained entirely in terms of the economy (capitalist or otherwise), but because the particular forms of imperialism I am referring to (from the British annexation of India to the US military barrage on Iraqi forces and the new "war on terrorism") cannot be divorced from those (complex, changing) conditions and effects of capitalism to which I have just referred. And that is as true in the metropolitan centers as in the Southern periphery. Moreover, these conditions and effects can be felt throughout society, in culture, politics, and economics.

Imperial economies

But let me stay with the economics for the limited purposes of this chapter (leaving the remainder, not because they are any less important, to those with more expertise than I). As I see it, we need to understand both the economic dimensions of contemporary imperialism and the role of economic discourse in constituting and reproducing imperialism. That is, no less than the novels, movies, and other cultural artifacts analyzed by literary and cultural critics, economic discourse plays an important role within the imperial frame of contemporary capitalism.

I won't attempt to describe, in this brief essay, the myriad international economic activities that we witness today. Let me, instead, focus on one particular set: the flows of value associated with the class dimensions of capitalism. And, since I cannot cover the entire landscape, let me focus on the value flows and class dimensions of three activities that have been prominent in recent discussions:

1   subcontracting to foreign sweatshops,
2   foreign direct investment and
3   international lending.

The current imperial project (from the activities of individual multinational corporations to those of multilateral governmental organizations) includes a series of measures designed to make all three of these activities easier to carry out. But these examples also give us a sense of the complex class dynamics and forms of antiimperialist politics that can be and are being carried out.[6]

Briefly, in Marxian class terms, the subcontracted sweatshop production of Nike and other transnational manufacturers does not represent foreign exploitation (as is often believed) but, rather, an exchange relationship in which Nike and other such companies purchase commodities (goods or services, from sneakers, other forms of apparel, and computer software to grocery-coupon counting and data entry) from foreign suppliers. The fact that the purchaser is a capitalist enterprise does not, in and of itself, tell us the class character of the production that takes place at the other end. And, even if the supplier is a capitalist sweatshop (as many, although not all of them, are), we do not have any form of foreign exploitation taking place. An important part of the inducement to exploit (and to improve – or, from the perspective of the laborers, worsen – the conditions of exploitation) comes from the attempt to get and maintain the subcontract, but the capitalists of the domestic (in this case, US) buyer do not extract the surplus labor of the laborers within the foreign shop.

This makes transnational subcontracting different from the kinds of foreign direct investment in and through which foreign exploitation *does* take place – not nation by nation but by the capitalists located in one country who extract the surplus-value from laborers working in another country. While the performance and appropriation of surplus-value occur at the same time (during what Marxists call the process of valorization or the self-expansion of capital), they take place in different nations. In such cases, the capitalist appropriators of surplus-value may be, and often are, located in cities and countries remote from where the process of production (and, thus, the extraction of labor from labor power) is taking place.[7]

What *is* true is that the "imperial-machine" creates the conditions for both relationships to exist precisely by defining private property rights and opening up markets, reducing tariffs and other so-called barriers to trade, and encouraging the flows of goods and services (whether produced by subsidiaries, in which case we are dealing with intrafirm trade, or by subcontractors) to take place between countries.

But, what are the implications of this class distinction between market-mediated subcontracting and foreign direct investment? On one level, it makes no difference, at least insofar as consumers, workers' rights activists, religious groups, and others have joined together to hold the host companies responsible for the conditions (of pay, safety, working conditions, and so on) that obtain within their "affiliated" foreign plants, whether subcontractor or subsidiary. This is a significant achievement, as conditions of exploitation are put on the agenda, not only for those who produce the goods, but also for those who consume them. This is an important antiimperialist moment in contemporary politics. But, on another level, there are at least two important consequences that stem from making this distinction. First, as I mentioned above, the subcontracting enterprise need not be a capitalist one. One of the characteristics of markets is precisely the idea that commodities need not be capitalist commodities. Or, to put it differently, the existence of a particular class process cannot be read off or deduced from the existence of exchange-values and market relations. Noncapitalist producers can, and do, sell subcontracted goods and services to capitalist – including the largest transnational – corporations. Second, if and when the subcontractors are capitalist enterprises, then determining how and when exploitation takes place will depend on the nature of the enterprises. When they are local manufacturers, or even multinational subcontractors (which run many sweatshops for Nike and other such multinational buyers), then we have local (or regional) capitalists extracting surplus-value from "their" laborers, not the transnational "partner."

What this analysis helps us to do is to challenge the economic – in the case of particular interest to us here, the class – homogeneity imposed by most uses of the term globalization – the idea, for example, that capitalism has become singular and universal. We can begin, instead, to see a heterogeneous class landscape, filled with both different forms of capitalism and various types of noncapitalism, in the midst of the global reach of certain capitalist enterprises, private capital flows, and free international markets for goods and services. And yet, we can still identify the imperialist project and devise an antiimperialist political practice.

A similar conclusion derives from a class analysis of international lending. Again, we do not have the case of international exploitation because, when the interest on loans is paid to foreign banks, no surplus-value is being extracted. Rather, in the instances when the loans are being used to support capitalist exploitation, the banks receive a cut of the surplus-value extracted from foreign laborers. However, that is not the only possibility. As we have seen in Latin America and elsewhere, loan funds can, and often do, take the form of capital flight, in many cases to the same countries in which the loans originated – not only to purchase luxury condominiums in Miami but also to purchase shares of US corporations. In such cases, the effect of the loans is to provide the conditions of existence of exploiting workers there and elsewhere in the world, for which the peripheral stock-owners receive an aliquot share of the extracted surplus-value.[8] The world is seemingly turned upside down, as capital flows from the periphery and semiperiphery of the world economy into the metropolitan center, thereby strengthening the conditions of exploitation within the center.

This encourages me, at least, to borrow from Gilles Deleuze and Félix Guattari and to think of imperialism as a machine – as opposed to either a particular stage of capitalism (Lenin's preference) or merely a political choice (the approach of Lenin's nemesis, Karl Kautsky). Precisely the options that are repeated today. In contrast, the machinelike quality of imperialism gives a sense of the ways in which it has various parts that (often, but not always) work together, a set of energies, available identities and categories that propel individuals and groups, institutions and structures, to enact designs and to "civilize" those who attempt to resist its apparent lessons, to make them succumb to the naturalized logic. Not a stage of capitalism but rather a machine that energizes and is energized by capitalism at various points in its history.[9] Not a mere political choice available to ruling governments and regimes, although it does include various options: military bombardment or invasion, economic carrots and sticks, cultural hegemony and worldwide news reach . . .

. . . and the knowledges produced by economists, especially (but not only) in the United States. Economic analysis, as it has descended from Adam Smith, and as it is practiced today in the US academy, think tanks, and government agencies, cannot be maintained apart from the imperial-machine that attempts to discipline "us" as well as "them." It is the support and strategy of empire, along with the weak opposition to the effects of empire, that have to be laid at the doorstep of the so-called queen of the social sciences; the one most under the thrall of physics-envy. In other words, the disciplinary-machine dovetails and works with the imperial-machine. Without conducting a detailed history of economic thought, what I am referring to are the elaborate theoretical models and empirical estimations of the Hecksher-Ohlin-Samuelson theory of comparative advantage and the mutual benefits of free, international trade. Then, the seven Nobel laureates stand shoulder to shoulder to stamp their scientific imprimatur on NAFTA, while lesser lights attempt to convince us of the evils of economic regulation and of the welfare-enhancing effects of, first, the General Agreement on Tariffs and Trade (GATT), and, now, the WTO. Or the development economists who arrive at the conclusion, then repeated as if a holy mantra, that the hothouse for industry in the Third World, import-substitution industrialization, did not and could not work – while forgetting about the levels of industrialization that were achieved and the macroeconomic turbulence of the 1970s and 1980s that threw into crisis national economies that were not quick enough and did not have the foreign exchange reserves (and, in the recent case of Argentina, the right connections in Washington) to ride out the storm.[10] Or, finally, the macroeconomists who debate the relative merits of neoclassical and structuralist stabilization and adjustment policies that need to be adopted by third world countries – countries that are presented, as Suzanne Bergeron (2001 and 2005) has shown, in exactly the gendered and racialized terms that were applied to the subaltern groups of classical imperialism: out of control (instead of rationally directed), driven by passions (instead of interests), lazy, profligate – in need of the expert advice of objective, disinterested academic and institutional (World Bank and IMF) economists.[11]

This is precisely the position of academic economists with respect to all heterodox and nonacademic – in their terms, ersatz, or, as Jack Amariglio and I have referred to them, "everyday" – economic knowledges and practices.[12] It is an imperial position, a disciplinary-machine, that is turned on noneconomists as it (in perfect Foucauldean fashion) serves to discipline economists themselves. Thus, the disciplinary-machine of economics works to safeguard the core of neoclassical economics from other approaches, whether produced outside the discipline (among scholars in other disciplines, from anthropology to political science, as well as economic activists who live and work outside the academy) or inside (including among orthodox economists who, by virtue of disciplinary procedures and protocols, are forced to curtail what they say and how they say it).[13]

That's the mainstream. And then there is the weak opposition within the discipline, which testifies to the ravages committed in the name of the imperial-machine – the growing income gap between rich and poor nations (excluding, of course, India and China) and the increasing inequality of the world distribution of wealth, the swelling of the parking lot for the poor in the cities, the fragility of national macroeconomic accounts and policies in the face of volatile international capital flows, and so on – but then limits the political options available by arguing in favor of more regulation of trade and finance, faster growth rates through expansionary macroeconomic policies, and devising the appropriate enterprise strategies to achieve success within the global economy.

Our Marxian project is radically different. We need to theorize the imperial-machine – reminding ourselves of the complex, changing determinations and effects of capitalism's worldwide expansion. And, alongside our resolute opposition to imperialism, we also need to formulate and enact our own desires – for new, noncapitalist class arrangements and forms of globalization.

(original version published in 2003)

Acknowledgements

This essay is a revised and expanded version of a talk prepared for the "Global (Dis)Orders" plenary session at the Marxism 2000 conference, sponsored by *Rethinking Marxism*, University of Massachusetts-Amherst, 22 September 2000. I want to thank the conference organizers for their gracious invitation to participate in the session, Dwight Billings and Karen Tice for their kind hospitality during the summer of 2000, and Stephen Resnick, Janet Hotch, Joseph Buttigieg, Jack Amariglio, Carlos Nelson Coutinho, Jonathan Diskin, Will Milberg, and especially the two RM reviewers, Yahya Madra and Ceren Özselçuk, for their helpful comments and suggestions on earlier drafts.

Notes

1　See O'Rourke and Williamson (1999) for a comprehensive analysis of the ways in which both the forms of globalization that characterized the late-nineteenth and early-twentieth centuries, and the debates and "backlashes" that accompanied them, prefigure those of the post-Second World War period. Other insightful comparisons of the two periods include Baldwin and Martin (1999), Bairoch and Kozul-Wright (1998), and Hirst and Thompson (1996).

2　See Sandbrook (2000) for a critique of Sen's "pragmatic brand of neoliberalism."

3　See Boehmer (1998) for a good selection of texts from the colonial literature of the 1870–1918 period.

4　See the examples collected in Wignaraja (1993) and Gills (2000).

5　So as not to be misunderstood, I am not claiming that globalization, as a concept, is necessarily totalizing or essentialist. Indeed, various commentators – including Gibson-Graham (1996/97, 2003), Ruccio and Kayatekin (Chapter 15 of this volume), and Dirlik (2000) – have worked hard to deconstruct and transform existing theorizations of globalization, rendering them less unified and complete. My claim is, rather, that most concrete uses of the term, on both the Right and the Left, exhibit the "depressing inevitability" I refer to in the text. I think a similar problem arises with the concept of empire. As much as I admire many aspects of the project undertaken by Michael Hardt and Antonio Negri (2000), their approach relies too much on the idea that there is a single order to the world, which can be characterized as the full realization of the capitalist world market. Still, there are many overlaps between my notion of the imperial-machine and their notion of empire.

6　See Resnick and Wolff (2001) for other examples of the spatial dispersion of the production and appropriation of surplus labor in the context of older and newer forms of globalization.

7　This is a revision of the argument presented in Chapter 14 of this volume.

8　See Chapter 9 of this volume for a class analysis of external debt.

9 What is distinctive about the term "machine," as it used by Deleuze and Guattari (1983, 1987), is that it has no subject, in two senses: (a) there is no intention or intelligence (whether human or systemic, such as capitalism) that stands behind it and directs its operation, and (b) it is created by other machines, in an infinite regress, not by a subject (again, whether individuals or a system). Machines simply operate on flows and other machines, cutting and connecting them, thereby forming other machines. Thus, imperialism, conceived as a machine, is not a thing but a process, an act of producing that has no goal or telos. Like Deleuze and Guattari's desiring-machines, the imperialism-machine (and, as I discuss below, the disciplinary-machine) can never be "satisfied" or bring its tasks to completion.

10 Kalyan Sanyal (1993) has argued that the "new" mainstream development economics, based on the recognition that there are institutional conditions of and barriers to participation in markets, represents "an attempt to integrate community and commodity" (1993, 128) in order to reproduce (in new and changing ways) the hegemony of capital. Of course, we also have to be open to the possibility that the development-machine may, via its microenterprise and other programs, end up creating and promoting noncapitalist (including communal) class structures. This would be a Marxian class success, notwithstanding the terms under which such noncapitalist class processes were instigated.

11 Michael Bernstein, in his analysis of the evolution of US economics during and after World War II, concluded that "far from being a product of dispassionate inquiry, some of the major advances in modern economic theory . . . were the result of a symbiosis, a mutual interaction with the wartime concerns of government and the national security agenda of the Cold War years" (1999, 111).

12 We develop this argument in much greater detail in Ruccio and Amariglio (2003). A good example of the disciplinary-machine's treatment of the "ersatz" economic analyses produced outside the machine is the response by the Academic Consortium on International Trade (ACIT) to the campus-based campaigns to secure a living-wage for sweatshop workers abroad. Jagdish Bhagwati and his colleagues applaud the ethical concerns of antisweatshop activists but then treat their economic theory – which contravenes the free-trade dictates of neoclassical theory – as, at best, a clumsy parody of economic science. ACIT's "Anti-Sweatshop Letter" and other relevant materials can be found at the following website: www.spp.umich.edu/rsie/acit.

13 To say that the disciplinary-machine works does not imply that it is always successful. Indeed, I would argue that, precisely because it has worked in a particular fashion in the postwar period, producing a neoliberal economic orthodoxy with respect to globalization, it has created a vacuum that has been filled by theories and analyses that often run counter to the orthodoxy among economists, both inside and outside the academy. Thus, the disciplinary-machine not only presupposes but serves to bring into existence its "other."

References

Aglietta, M. 1979. *A Theory of Capitalist Regulation: The US Experience*, trans. D. Fembach, London: New Left Books.

——. 1982. "World capitalism in the eighties," *New Left Review*, no. 136 (November–Deccember), pp. 5–41.

Alavi, H. 1975. "India and the colonial mode of production," in *Socialist Register*, London: Merlin Press, pp. 160–97.

Althusser, L. 1970. *For Marx*, New York: Vintage.

——. 1971. *Lenin and Philosophy and Other Weapons*, trans. B. Brewster, London: New Left Books.

——. 1976. *Essays in Self-criticism*, trans. Grahame Lock, London: New Left Books.

Althusser, L. and E. Balibar. 1975. *Reading Capital*, London: New Left Books.

Alvares, C. 1994. *Science, Development and Violence*, Delhi: Oxford University Press.

Amariglio, J. 1988. "The body, economic discourse, and power: An economist's introduction to Foucault," *History of Political Economy*, 20 (4): 583–613.

——. 1990. "Economics as a postmodern discourse," in *Economics as Discourse: An Analysis of the Language of Economists*, W. Samuels, Boston: Kluwer Academic Publishers, pp. 15–46.

Amariglio, J. and A. Callari. 1989. "Marxian value theory and the problem of the subject: The role of commodity fetishism," *Rethinking Marxism*, 2 (Fall), pp.31–60.

——. 1993. "Marxian value theory and the problem of the subject: The role of commodity fetishism," in *Fetishism as Cultural Discourse*, E. Apter and W. Pietz, Ithaca, NY: Cornell University Press, pp. 186–216.

Ames, E. A. 1971. "Discussion," *American Economic Review*, 61 (May): 436–37.

Amin, S. 1966. *L'Economie du Maghreb*, 2 vols, Paris: Editions de Minuit.

——. 1967. *Le Développment du capitalisme en Côte d'Ivoire*, Paris: Editions de Minuit.

——. 1971. *L'Afrique de l'Ouest bloquée*, Paris: Editions de Minuit.

——. 1973. *Neo-Colonialism in West Africa*, trans. F. McDonagh, New York: Monthly Review Press.

——. 1974. "Accumulation and development: A theoretical model," *Review of African Political Economy*, no. 1, 9–26.

——. 1975. *Accumulation on a World Scale*, 2 vols, New York: Monthly Review Press.

——. 1976. *Unequal Development: An Essay on the Social Formations of Peripheral Capitalism*, trans. B. Pearce, New York: Monthly Review Press.

——. 1977. *Imperialism and Unequal Development*, New York: Monthly Review Press.

——. 1982. "Crisis, nationalism, and socialism," in *Dynamics of Global Crisis*, S. Amin, G. Arrighi, A. G. Frank, and I. Wallerstein, New York: Monthly Review Press.

——. 1983. "Expansion or crisis of capitalism?" *Third World Quarterly*, 5 (April): 361–85.

——. 1988. "Accumulation on a world scale: Thirty years later," *Rethinking Marxism*, 1 (Summer): 54–75.

Amsden, A. 1989. *Asia's Next Giant: South Korea and Late Industrialization*, New York: Oxford University Press.

Andreff, W. 1984. "The international centralization of capital and the re-ordering of world capitalism," *Capital and Class*, 22: 58–79.

Arida, P. 1986. "Macroeconomic issues for Latin America," *Journal of Development Economics*, 22 (June): 171–208.

Arndt, H. W. 1985. "The origins of structuralism," *World Development*, 13 (2): 151–59.

——. 1987. *Economic Development: The History of an Idea*, Chicago: University of Chicago Press.

Arrighi, G. 1970. "Labour supplies in historical perspective: A study of the proletarianization of the African peasantry in Rhodesia," *Journal of Development Studies*, 3: 197–234.

Arsen, D. D. 1991 "International and domestic forces in the postwar golden age," *Review of Radical Political Economics*, 23 (1 and 2): 1–11.

Atali, J. 1978. "Towards socialist planning," in *Beyond Capitalist Planning*, ed. S. Holland, New York: St. Martin's Press.

Bacha, E. L. 1986. "External shocks and growth prospects: The case of Brazil, 1973–89," *World Development*, 14 (August): 919–36.

Bacha, E. L. and Díaz-Alejandro, C. F. 1982. "International financial intermediation: A long and tropical view," *Essays in International Finance*, no. 127 (May), International Finance Section, Department of Economics, Princeton University.

Bachelard, G. 1949. *Le Nouvel Esprit Scientifique*, 5th edn, Paris: Presses Universitaires de France.

Badiou, A. 1970. *Le Concept de modèle*, Paris: F. Maspero.

Baer, W. 1987. "The Resurgence of inflation in Brazil, 1974–86," *World Development* 15 (August): 1007–34.

Baer, W., D. Biller and C. T. McDonald. 1989. "Austerity under different political regimes: The case of Brazil," in *Paying the Costs of Austerity in Latin America*, H. Handelman and W. Baer, Boulder, CO: Westview Press, pp. 19–42.

Bagchi, A. K. 1982. *The Political Economy of Underdevelopment*, Cambridge: Cambridge University Press.

Bairoch, P. and R. Kozul-Wright. 1998. "Globalization myths: Some historical reflections on integration, industrialization, and growth in the world economy," in *Transnational Corporations and the Global Economy*, R. Kozul-Wright and R. Rowthorn eds, New York: St. Martin's Press, pp. 37–68.

Balassa, B. 1982. "Structural adjustment policies in developing economies," *World Development*, 10 (January): 23–38.

——. 1988. "The lessons of East Asian development: An overview," *Economic Development and Cultural Change*, 36 (supplement): 272–90.

Baldwin, R. E. 1992. "Are economists' traditional trade policy views still valid?" *Journal of Economic Literature*, 30 (June): 804–29.

Baldwin, R. E. and P. Martin. 1999. *"Two Waves of Globalisation: Superficial Similarities, Fundamental Differences,"* NBER Working Paper 6904, Cambridge, MA: National Bureau of Economic Research.

Balibar, E. 1988. "The concept of class politics in Marx," *Rethinking Marxism*, 1 (Summer): 18–51.

——. 1995. "Has 'the world' changed?" in *Marxism in the Postmodern Age*, A. Callari *et al.*, New York: Guilford Press, pp. 405–14.

Banaji, J. 1972. "For a theory of colonial modes of production," *Economic and Political Weekly* (Bombay), 7 (December).

Banuri, T. 1990a. "Development and the politics of knowledge: A critical interpretation of the social role of modernization," in *Dominating Knowledge: Development, Culture, and Resistance*, F. Appfel-Marglin and S. Marglin, Oxford: Clarendon Press, pp. 29–73.

——. 1990b. "Modernization and its discontents: A cultural perspective on the theories of development," in *Dominating Knowledge: Development, Culture, and Resistance*, F. Appfel-Marglin and S. Marglin eds, Oxford: Clarendon Press.

Baran, P. 1957. *The Political Economy of Growth*, New York: Monthly Review Press.

Baranov, E. F., V. I. Danilov-Danil'ian, and M. G. Zabel'skii. 1981. "On a system of models for optimal long-term planning," *Matekon*, 17 (Summer): 3–10.

Barden, D. S. 1975. "Optimal planning: A radical critique," *Review of Radical Political Economics*, 7 (Winter): 33–47.

Bardhan, P. 1984. *Land, Labor and Rural Poverty: Essays in Development Economics*, New York: Columbia University Press.

——. 1986. "Marxist ideas in development economics: An evaluation," in *Analytical Marxism*, J. Roemer ed., Cambridge: Cambridge University and Paris: Edition de la Maison des Sciences de l'Honime, pp. 64–77.

Barkin, D. 1981. "Internationalization of capital: An alternative approach," *Latin American Perspectives*, 8 (Summer and Fall).

Barone, C. 1983. "Dependency, Marxist theory and salvaging the idea of capitalism in South Korea," *Review of Radical Political Economics*, 15 (Spring): 43–67.

——. 1984. "Reply to Martin Hart-Landsberg," *Review of Radical Political Economics*, 16 (Summer–Fall): 195–97.

Basu, K. 1990. *Agrarian Structure and Economic Underdevelopment*, New York: Harwood Publishers.

Bauer, P. T. 1984. *Reality and Rhetoric: Studies in the Economics of Development*, Cambridge, MA: Harvard University Press.

Becker, D. G., J. Frieden, S. P. Schartz, and R. L. Sklar. 1987. *Postimperialism: International Capitalism and Development in the Late Twentieth Century*, Boulder, CO: Lynne Rienner Publishers.

Beckerman, P. 1987. "Inflation and dollar accounts in Peru's banking system," *World Development*, 15 (August): 1087–106.

Beenstock, M. 1980. *A Neoclassical Analysis of Macro-economic Policy*, Cambridge: Cambridge University Press.

Bell, D. E. and M. R. Reich eds. 1988. *Health, Nutrition, and Economic Crises: Approaches to Policy in the Third World*, Dover, MA: Auburn House Publishing Company.

Berger, J. 1974. *The Look of Things*, New York: Viking Press.

Berger, S. 1980. "Discontinuity in the politics of industrial society," in *Dualism and Discontinuity in Industrial Societies*, S. Berger and M. Piore eds, Cambridge: Cambridge University Press, 129–41.

Bergeron, S. 2001. "Political economy discourses of globalization and feminist politics," *Signs*, 26 (4): 983–1006.

——. 2005. *Fragments of Development: Nation, Gender, and the Space of Modernity*, Ann Arbor, MI: University of Michigan Press.

Bernstein, M. A. 1999. "Economic knowledge, professional authority, and the state: The case of American economics during and after World War II," in R. F. Garnett ed., *What Do Economists Know? New Economics of Knowledge*, London: Routledge, pp. 103–122.

Best, M. 1990. *The New Competition: Institutions of Industrial Restructuring*, Cambridge: Harvard University Press.

Bettelheim, C. 1976. *Class Struggles in the USSR. First Period: 1917–1923*, trans. B. Perce, New York: Monthly Review Press.

Beverley, J. and J. Oviedo eds. 1993. "The postmodernism debate in Latin America," special issue of *Boundary 2*, 20 (Fall).

Bhagwati, J. N. and T. N. Srinivasan. 1983. *Lectures on International Trade*, Cambridge, MA: MIT Press.

Biewener, C. 1988. "Keynesian economics and socialist politics," *Review of Radical Political Economics*, 20 (2 and 3): 149–55.

——. 1990. "Loss of a socialist vision in France," *Rethinking Marxism*, 3 (3 and 4): 12–26.

Black, G. 1981. *Triumph of the People: The Sandinista Revolution in Nicaragua*, London: Zed Books.

Blejer, M. I. and N. Liviatan. 1987. "Fighting hyperinflation: Stabilization strategies in Argentina and Israel. 1985–86," *IMF Staff Papers*, 34 (September): 409–38.

Bliss, C. J. and N. H. Stern. 1982. *Palanpur: The Economy of an Indian Village*, Oxford: Oxford University Press.

Boehmer, E., ed. 1998. *Empire Writing: An Anthology of Colonial Literature, 1870–1918*, New York: Oxford University Press.

Bowles, S. 1988. "Profits and wages in an open economy," in *Three Worlds of Labor Economics*, G. Mangum and P. Philips eds, Armonk, NY: M. E. Sharpe, pp. 64–81.

Bowles, S. and H. Gintis. 1988. "Contested exchange: Political economy and modern economic theory," *American Economic Review*, 78 (May): 145–50.

——. 1990. "Contested exchange: New microfoundations of the political economy of capitalism," *Politics and Society*, 18 (2): 165–222.

——. 1992. "Power and wealth in a competitive capitalist economy," *Philosophy and Public Affairs*, 21 (Fall): 324–53.

——. 1993. "The revenge of homo economicus: Post-Walrasian economics and the revival of political economy," *Journal of Economic Perspectives*, 7 (Winter): 83–102.

Boyer, R., ed. 1986a. *Capitalismes fin de siècle*, Paris: Presses Universitaires de France.

——. 1986b. "La Théorie de la regulation: Une analyse critique," Paris: Editions La Découverte.

Bradby, B. 1980. "The destruction of natural economy," in *The Articulation of Modes of Production: Essays from Economy and Society*, H. Wolpe ed., London: Routledge & Kegan Paul, pp. 93–127.

Brenner, R. 1977. "The origins of capitalist development: A critique of neo-Smithian Marxism," *New Left Review*, no. 104 (July–August).

Bresser Pereira. L. 1987. "Inertial inflation and the Cruzado Plan," *World Development*, 15 (August): 1035–44.

Brewer, A. 1980. *Marxist Theories of Imperialism: A Critical Survey*, London: Routledge & Kegan Paul.

Bruno, M. 1979. "Stabilization and stagflation in a semi-industrialized economy," in *International Economic Policy: Theory and Evidence*, R. Dornbusch and J. A. Frenkel eds, Baltimore, MD: Johns Hopkins University Press.

Bruno, M., G. di Tella, R. Dornbusch, and S. Fischer eds. 1988. *Inflation Stabilization: The Experience of Israel, Argentina, Brazil, Bolivia, and Mexico*, Cambridge, MA: MIT Press.

Bryan, R. 1987. "The State and the internationalisation of capital: An approach to analysis," *Journal of Contemporary Asia*, 17 (3): 253–75.

Buffie, E. F. 1984. "Financial repression, the new structuralists, and stabilization policy in semi-industrialised economies," *Journal of Development Economics*, 14 (April): 305–22.

Bukharin, N. 1972. *Imperialism and the World Economy*, London: Merlin.

Bulmer-Thomas, V. 1987. "The balance-of-payments crisis and adjustment programmes in Central America," in *Latin American Debt and the Adjustment Crisis*, R. Thorp and L. Whitehead eds, Pittsburgh: University of Pittsburgh Press.

Burawoy, M. 2004. "From liberation to reconstruction: theory and practice in the life of Harold Wolpe," Harold Wolpe Memorial Lecture. Available at www.wolpetrust.org.za/lectures/ML2004Burawoy_pdf.pdf (accessed May 2010).

Business Week. 1990. "The Stateless Corporation," 14 May.

Cabieses, H. 1986. *Economía Nicaragüense, 1979–1986: Marco global para su análisis*, Managua: Departamento de Economia Agricola/UNAN.

Cabrales, R. 1987. "El Abastecimiento en ocho años de revolución," mimeo, Managua.

Callari, A. 1991. "Economic subjects and the shape of politics," *Review of Radical Political Economics*, 23 (1 and 2): 201–07.

Canitrot, A. 1980. "Discipline as the central economic objective of economic policy: An Essay on the economic programme of the Argentine government since 1976," *World Development*, 8 (11): 913–28.

——. 1981. "Teoría y práctica del liberalismo: Política antiinflacionária y apertura económica en la Argentina, 1976–81," *Desarrollo Económico*, 21: 131–90.

Cardoso, C. F. S. 1974. "Severo Martínez Pelaez y el carácter del régimen colonial," in Carlos Sempat Assadourian *et al.*, *Modes de Production en America Latina*, C. S. Assadourian ed., Cordoba, Argentina: Ediciones Pasado y Presente.

Cardoso, F. H. 1977. "The consumption of dependency theory in the United States," *Latin American Research Review*, 12 (3): 7–24.

Cardoso, F. H. and E. Faletto. 1979. *Dependency and Development in Latin America*, trans. M. M. Urquidi, Berkeley, CA: University of California Press.

Carr, E. H. and R. W. Davies 1969. *Foundations of a Planned Economy, 1926–1929*, London: Macmillan.

Castells, M. 1994. "European cities, the informational society, and the global economy," *New Left Review*, no. 204 (March–April): 18–32.

Cavaillès, J. 1962. *Philosophic mathématique*, Paris: Hermann.

Center on Budget and Policy Priorities. 1997. "Poverty rate fails to decline as income growth in 1996 favors the affluent." Available at www.cbpp.org/povday97.htm (accessed 6 June 1999).

de Certeau, M. 1984. "Walking in the city," in *The Practice of Everyday Life*, trans. S. Rendall, Berkeley, CA: University of California Press, pp. 91–110.

Chakrabarti, A. and S. Cullenberg. 2003. *Transition and Development in India*, New York: Routledge.

Chakravarty. S. 1987. "Marxist economics and contemporary developing economies," *Cambridge Journal of Economics*, 11 (March): 3–22.

Chang, H.-J. and R. Rowthorn. 1995. "Introduction," in *The Role of the State in Economic Change*, H.-J. Chang and R. Rowthorn eds, Oxford: Clarendon Press, pp. 1–27.

Chenery, H. B. and A. M. Strout. 1966. "Foreign assistance and economic development," *American Economic Review*, 56 (September): 679–733.

Clarke, S. 1988. "Overaccumulation, class struggle and the regulation approach," *Capital and Class*, no. 36 (Winter), 59–92.

Clifford, J. 1988. *The Predicament of Culture: Twentieth-Century Ethnography, Literature, and Art*, Cambridge, MA: Harvard University Press.

Cline, W. R. 1982. "Can the East Asian model of development be generalized?" *World Development*, 10 (2): 81–90.

——. 1983. *International Debt and the Stability of the World Economy*, Washington, DC: Institute for International Economics.

Comisión Económica para América Latina. 1979. *Nicaragua: Repercusiones económicas de los acontecimientos políticos recientes*, Santiago, Chile.

——. 1985. *Notas para el estudio económico de América Latina y el Caribe, 1984: Nicaragua*, México: CEPAL.

Cooper, R. N. 1971. "An assessment of currency devaluation in developing countries," in *Government and Economic Development*, G. Ranis ed., New Haven, CT: Yale University Press, pp. 472–513.

Coraggio, J. L. and G. Irvin. 1985 "Revolution and democracy in Nicaragua," *Latin American Perspectives*, 12 (Spring): 23–37.

Corbo, V. and J. de Melo. 1985. "Liberalization with stabilization in the Southern Cone of Latin America: Overview and summary," *World Development*, 13 (9): 5–15.

Cornia, G. A., R. Jolly and F. Stewart eds. 1988. *Adjustment with a Human Face*, 2 vols. Oxford: Oxford University Press.

Cravey, A. 1997. "The politics of reproduction: Households in the Mexican industrial transition," *Economic Geography*, 73 (2): 166–86.

Crush, J., ed. 1995. *Power of Development*, New York: Routledge.

Cullenberg, S. 1994. *The Marxian Debate Over the Tendency of the Rate of Profit to Fall: A Methodological Reconstruction and New Directions*, London: Pluto.

Cullenberg, S., J. Amariglio and D. F. Ruccio eds. 2001. *Postmodernism, Economics, and Knowledge*, New York: Routledge.

Cumby, R. and R. Levich. 1987. "On the definition and magnitude of recent capital flight," in *Capital Flight and Third World Debt*, D. R. Lessard and J. Williamson eds, Washington, DC: Institute for International Economics, pp. 27–67.

Curtis, F. 1988. "Race and class in South Africa: Socialist politics in the current conjuncture," *Rethinking Marxism*, 1 (Spring): 108–34.

Cypher, J. M. 1979. "The Internationalization of capital and the transformation of social formations: A critique of the Monthly Review school," *Review of Radical Political Economics*, 11 (1979): 33–49.

Dallmayr, F. 1992. "Modernization and postmodernization: Whither India?" *Alternatives*, 17: 421–52.

Davis, P. J. and R. Hersh. 1980. *The Mathematical Experience*, intro. Gian-Carlo Rota, Boston: Birkhauser.

Deere, C. D. 1986. "The Peasantry in political economy: Trends of the 1980s," paper presented at session, "Peasant Studies: Obstacles to Theoretical Advances," Latin American Studies Association Meetings, 23–25 October, Boston, MA.

Deere, C. D., P. Marchetti, and N. Reinhardt. 1985. "The peasantry and the development of Sandinista agrarian policy, 1979–84," *Latin American Research Review*, 20 (1985): 75–109.

Deleuze, F. and F. Guattari. 1983. *Anti-Oedipus: Capitalism and Schizophrenia*, trans. R. Hurley *et al.*, Minneapolis: University of Minnesota Press.

——. 1987. *A Thousand Plateaus: Capitalism and Schizophrenia*, trans. B. Massumi. Minneapolis: University of Minnesota Press.

Delgado, C. R. 1985. *Sobre las medidas de ajuste y la crisis económica de Nicaragua, Ediciones Nicaragua Hoy*, Managua: Centro de Investigación y Asesoria Socio-Económica.

DeMartino, G. 1996. "Industrial policies versus competitiveness strategies: In pursuit of prosperity in the global economy," *International Papers in Political Economy*, 3 (2).

——. 2000. *Global Economy, Global Justice: Theoretical and Policy Alternatives to Neoliberalism*, New York: Routledge.

DeMartino, G. and S. Cullenberg. 1994a. "Beyond the competitiveness debate," *Social Text*, 41 (Winter): 11–39.

——. 1994b. "The social index tariff structure: An internationalist response to economic integration," *Review of Radical Political Economics*, 26 (3): 76–85.

——. 1995. "Economic integration in an uneven world: An internationalist perspective," *International Review of Applied Economics*, 9 (1): 1–21.

Demery, L. and T. Addison. 1987. "Stabilization policy and income distribution in developing countries," *World Development*, 15 (12): 1483–98.

Department of Sociology, Central American University (Managua). 1986. "Managua's economic crisis – how do the poor survive?" *Envío*, 5 (December): 36–56.

DeWitt, R. P. and J. F. Petras. 1979. "Political economy of international debt: The dynamics of financial capital," in *Debt and the Less Developed Countries*, J. D. Aronson ed., Boulder, CO: Westview Press, pp. 191–215.

Díaz-Alejandro, C. F. 1981. "Southern Cone stabilization plans," in *Economic Stabilization in Developing Countries*, W. R. Cline and S. Weintraub eds, 119–41. Washington, DC: Brookings Institution, pp. 191–215.

Dirlik, A. 2000. "Globalization as the end and the beginning of history: The contradictory implications of a new paradigm," *Rethinking Marxism*, 12 (4): 4–22.

Diskin, J. 2005a. "Focusing and expanding class analysis," *Rethinking Marxism*, 17 (1): 1–8.

——. 2005b. "From communism to capitalism: Rethinking the boundaries of class analysis," *Rethinking Marxism*, 17 (4): 552–58.

Diskin, J. and T. Koechlin. 1994. "Liberal political economy and global capitalism," *Review of Radical Political Economics*, 26 (3): 86–94.

Dobb, M. 1947. *Studies in the Development of Capitalism*, New York: International Publishers.

Dorfman, R., P. A. Samuelson, and R. M. Solow. 1958. *Linear Programming and Economic Analysis*, New York: McGraw-Hill.

Dornbusch, R. 1980. *Open Economy Macroeconomics*, New York: Basic Books.

——. 1982. "Stabilization policies in developing countries: What have we learned?" *World Development*, 10 (September): 701–08.

——. 1988. "Overvaluation and trade balances," in *The Open Economy: Tools for Policymakers in Developing Countries*, R. Dornbusch and F. L. C. H. Helmers eds, New York: Oxford University Press for the World Bank, pp. 80–107.

Economic Commission for Latin America (ECLA). 1982. *Economic Survey of Latin America and the Caribbean, 1981*, Santiago, Chile: United Nations.

——. 1983. *Economic Survey of Latin America, 1981*, Santiago, Chile: ECLA.

——. 1984. "The crisis in Central America: Its origins, scope and consequences," *CEPAL Review*, no. 22 (April): 53–80.

Economic Commission for Latin America and the Caribbean (ECLAC). 1984. *Economic Survey of Latin America and the Caribbean, 1983*, Vol. 1. Santiago: United Nations.

——. 1986a. *América Latina y el Caribe: Balance de pagos 1950–1984*, Santiago: United Nations.

——. 1986b. *Economic Survey of Latin America and the Caribbean, 1984*, Santiago: United Nations.

——. 1987a. *Economic Survey of Latin America and the Caribbean, 1985*, Santiago, United Nations.

——. 1987b. *Estudio económico de América Latina y el Caribe, 1986: Nicaragua*, Santiago: United Nations.

——. 1989. *Preliminary Overview of the Economy of Latin America and the Caribbean 1989*, Santiago: United Nations.

Ellman, M. 1973. *Planning Problems in the USSR: The Contribution of Mathematical Economics to Their Solution, 1960–1971*, New York: Cambridge University Press.

——. 1979. *Socialist Planning*, 2nd edn, New York: Cambridge University Press.

——. 1983. "Changing views on central economic planning: 1958–83," *ACES Bulletin* 25 (Spring): 11–34.

Emmanuel, A. 1972. *Unequal Exchange. A Study of the Imperialism of Trade*, trans. B. Pearce, New York: Monthly Review Press.

ENGENDER. 1995. "Report on work activities, 8 December 1992–31 March 1995," unpublished manuscript, ENGENDER, Centre for Environment, Gender and Development, Singapore.

——. 1996. "The gender and development resource bank: A concept paper for an innovative approach to poverty alleviation," unpublished manuscript, ENGENDER, Centre for Environment, Gender and Development, Singapore.

Enriquez, L. J. and R. J. Spalding. 1987. "Banking systems and revolutionary change: The politics of agricultural credit in Nicaragua," in *The Political Economy of Revolutionary Nicaragua*, R. J. Spalding ed., Boston: Allen & Unwin, pp. 105–25.

Epstein, E. C. 1987. "Recent stabilization programs in Argentina, 1973–86," *World Development*, 15 (8): 991–1015.

Escobar, A. 1984. "Discourse and power in development: Michel Foucault and the relevance of his work to the Third World," *Alternatives*, 10 (3): 377–400.

——. 1992. "Reflections on 'development': Grassroots approaches and alternative politics in the Third World," *Futures*, 24 (5): 411–36.

——. 1995. *Encountering Development: The Making and Unmaking of the Third World*, Princeton, NJ: Princeton University Press.

Escobar, A. and S. E. Alvarez eds. 1992. *The Making of Social Movements in Latin America*, Boulder, CO: Westview Press.

Evans, D. 1984. "A critical assessment of some neo-Marxian trade theories," *Journal of Development Studies*, 20 (January): 202–26.

Evans, P. 1985. "After democracy: Recent studies of class, state, and industrialization," *Latin American Research Review*, 20 (2): 149–60.

——. 1987. "Class, state, and dependence in East Asia: Lessons for Latin Americanists," in *The Political Economy of the New Asian Industrialism*, F. C. Deyo ed., Ithaca, NY: Cornell University Press, pp. 203–26.

Evans, P., D. Rueschemeyer, and T. Skocpol eds. 1985. *Bringing the State Back In*, Cambridge: Cambridge University Press.

Fagen, R. R., C. D. Deere, and J. L Coraggio. 1986. "Introduction," in *Transition and Development: Problems of Third World Socialism*, New York: Monthly Review Press.

Featherstone, M. 1995. *Undoing Culture: Globalization, Postmodern and Identity*, London: Sage.

Feinberg, R. E. and R. Ffrench-Davis eds. 1988. *Development and External Debt in Latin America: Bases for a New Consensus*, Notre Dame, IN: University of Notre Dame Press.

Feiner, S. 1982. "Factors, bankers and masters: Class relations in the antebellum south," *Journal of Economic History*, 42 (March): 61–67.

——. 1988. "Slavery, classes, and accumulation in the antebellum south," *Rethinking Marxism*, 1 (Summer): 116–41.

Ffrench-Davis, R., ed. 1983. *Relaciones financieras externas y su efecto en la economía latinoamericana*, Mexico: Fondo de Cultura Económica.

Ffrench-Davis, R. and de Gregorio, J. 1985. "La renegociación de la deuda externa de Chile: Antecedentes y comentarios," *Colección estudios CIEPLAN*, no. 17 (September): 9–32.

Fishlow, A. 1981. "Comment," in *Economic Stabilization in Developing Countries*, W. R. Cline and S. Weintraub eds, Washington, DC: Brookings Institution, pp. 229–32.

FitzGerald, E. V. K. 1982a. "The economics of the revolution," in *Nicaragua in Revolution*, T. W. Walker ed., New York: Praeger, pp. 203–21.

——. 1982b. "Planned accumulation and income distribution in the small peripheral economy," mimeo.

——. 1985a. "La economía national en 1985: La transición como coyuntura," paper presented at the 1985 Annual Congress of Nicaraguan Social Scientists, Managua, August.

——. 1985b. "The problem of balance in the peripheral socialist economy," *World Development*, 13, 5–14.

——. 1985c. "Planned accumulation and income distribution in the small peripheral economy," in *Towards an Alternative for Central America and the Caribbean*, G. Irvin and X. Gorostiaga eds, London: George Allen & Unwin, pp. 95–110.

——. 1985d "Stabilization and economic justice: The case of Nicaragua," in *Debt and Development in Latin America*, K. S. Kim and D. F. Ruccio eds, Notre Dame, IN: University of Notre Dame Press.

——. 1987. "An evaluation of the economic costs to Nicaragua of U.S. agression: 1980–84," in *The Political Economy of Revolutionary Nicaragua*, R. J. Spalding ed., Boston: Allen & Unwin, pp. 195–213.

Foster-Carter, A. 1978. "The modes of production controversy," *New Left Review*, no. 107 (January–February): 47–77.

Foxley, A. 1983. *Latin American Experiments in Neoconservative Economics*, Berkeley, CA: University of California Press.

——. 1987. "Latin American development after the debt crisis," *Journal of Development Economics*, 27 (October): 201–25.

Fraad, H., S. Resnick, and R. Wolff. 1989. "For every knight in shining armor, there's a castle waiting to be cleaned: A Marxist-Feminist analysis of the household," *Rethinking Marxism*, 2 (Winter): 10–69.

——. 1994. *Bringing It All Back Home: Class, Gender, and Power in the American Household*, Boulder, CO: Pluto.

Frank, A. G. 1967. *Capitalism and Underdevelopment in Latin America: Historical Studies of Chile and Brazil*, New York: Monthly Review Press.

——. 1969. *Latin America: Underdevelopment or Revolution*, New York: Monthly Review Press.

——. 1972. *Lumpenbourgeoisie: Lumpendevelopment: Dependence, Class, and Politics in Latin America*, New York: Monthly Review Press.

——. 1978. *World Accumulation 1492–1978*, New York: Monthly Review Press.

——. 1979. *Dependent Accumulation and Underdevelopment*, New York: Monthly Review Press.

——. 1984. *Critique and Anti-Critique: Essays on Dependence and Reformism*, New York: Praeger.

Frank, T. 2004. *What's the Matter with Kansas? How Conservatives Won the Heart of America*, New York: Henry Holt and Company.

Frenkel, R. 1987. "Heterodox theory and policy: The plan austral in Argentina," *Journal of Development Economics*, 27 (October): 307–38.

Friedman, J. 1994. *Cultural Identity and Global Process*, London: Sage.

Friedman, T. L. 2000. *The Lexus and the Olive Tree*, New York: Anchor Books.

Frobel, F., J. Heinrichs, and O. Kreye. 1981. *The New International Division of Labour: Structural Unemployment in Industrialised Countries and Industrialisation in Developing Countries*, Cambridge: Cambridge University Press.

Gabriel, S. 1990. "Ancients: A Marxian theory of self-exploitation," *Rethinking Marxism*, 3 (Spring): 85–106.

——. 2005. *Chinese Capitalism and the Modernist Vision*, New York: Routledge.

Georgescu-Roegen, N. 1971. *The Entropy Law and the Economic Process*, Cambridge, MA: Harvard University Press.

Gerwel, J. 2002. "Jakes Gerwel's Lecture," Harold Wolpe Memorial Lecture. Available at www.wolpetrust.org.za/lectures/ML2002Gerwel.pdf (accessed 6 June 2006).

Gibson-Graham, J.-K. 1996. *The End of Capitalism (As We Knew It): A Feminist Critique of Political Economy*, Cambridge, MA: Blackwell.

——. 1996/97. "Querying globalization," *Rethinking Marxism*, 9 (1): 1–27.

——. 2003. "An ethics of the local," *Rethinking Marxism*, 15 (1): 49–74.

Gibson-Graham, J.-K. and P. O'Neill. 2001. "Exploring a new class politics of the enterprise," in *Re/presenting Class: Essays in Postmodern Marxism*, J.-K. Gibson-Graham *et al.* eds, Durham: Duke University Press, 56–80.

Gibson-Graham, J.-K., S. Resnick, and R. Wolff. 2000. *Class and Its Others*, Minneapolis: University of Minnesota Press.

——. 2001. "Toward a poststructuralist political economy," in *Re/presenting Class: Essays in Postmodern Marxism*, Durham: Duke University Press, pp. 1–22.

Gills, B. K., ed. 2000. *Globalization and the Politics of Resistance*, Basingstoke: Macmillan.

Glucksmann, M. 1974. *Structuralist Analysis in Contemporary Social Thought*, London: Routledge and Kegan Paul.

Gonzalez, D. 2000. "Nicaragua's trade zone: Battleground for unions," *New York Times*, 16 September, A3.

Gordon, D. M. 1988. "The global economy: New edifice or crumbling foundations?" *New Left Review*, no. 168 (March–April): 24–64.

Gourevitch, P. A. 1978. "The international system and regime formation: A critical review of Anderson and Wallerstein," *Comparative Politics*, 10 (April): 419–38.

Gramsci, A. 1971. *Selections from t,he Prison Notebooks*, ed. and trans. Q. Hoare and G. N. Smith, New York International Publishers.

Griffin, K. and J. Gurley. 1985. "Radical analyses of imperialism, the third world, and the transition to socialism: A survey article," *Journal of Economic Literature*, 23 (September): 1089–143.

Griffith-Jones, S. 1981. *The Role of Finance in the Transition to Socialism*, London: Frances Pinter.

Grosz, E. 1990. "Philosophy," in *Feminist Knowledge: Critique and Construct*, S. Gunew, ed., New York: Routledge, 147–74.

Grou, P. 1985. *The Financial Structure of Multinational Capitalism*, Dover, NH: Berg.

Gunnarsson, C. 1985. "Development theory and third world industrialisation: A comparison of patterns of industrialisation in 19th Century Europe and the Third World," *Journal of Contemporary Asia*, 15 (2): 183–206.

Hardt, M. and A. Negri. 2000. *Empire*, Cambridge, MA: Harvard University Press.

Harlow, B. and M. Carter eds. 1999. *Imperialism and Orientalism: A Documentary Sourcebook*, Malden, MA: Blackwell.

Harris, R. L. 1986. *Economic Development and Revolutionary Transformation in Nicaragua*, Latin American Issues No. 3.

Harris, R. L. and C. M. Vilas. 1985. *Nicaragua: A Revolution under Siege*, London: Zed Press.

Hart-Landsberg, M. 1984. "Capitalism and third world economic development: A Critical look at the South Korean 'miracle'," *Review of Radical Political Economics*, 16 (Summer–Fall): 181–93.

Harvey, D. 1982. *The Limits to Capital*, Chicago: University of Chicago Press.

——. 1989. *The Condition of Postmodernity: An Enquiry into the Origins of Cultural Change*, Cambridge, MA: Basil Blackwell.

Hawley, J. 1979. "The internationalization of capital: Banks, eurocurrency, and the instability of the world monetary system," *Review of Radical Political Economics*, 11 (Winter): 78–90.

Helleiner, G. K. 1986. "Balance-of-payments experience and growth prospects of developing countries: A synthesis," *World Development*, 14: 877–908.

Herrick, B. and C. P. Kindleberger. 1983. *Economic Development*, 4th edn, New York: McGraw-Hill.

Heymann, D. 1986. "La inflación argentina de los ochenta y el plan austral," *Pensamiento Iberoamericano*, 9 (January–June): 89–128.

Hilferding, R. 1981. *Finance Capital: A Study of the Latest Phase of Capitalist Development*, T. Bottomore ed., Boston: Routledge & Kegan Paul.

Hindess, B. 1971. "Materialist mathematics," *Theoretical Practice*, 3–4 (Autumn): 82–103.

Hindess, B. and P. Hirst. 1975. *Pre-Capitalist Modes of Production*, London and Boston: Routledge & Kegan Paul.

——. 1977. *Modes of Production and Social Formation: An Auto-Critique of "Pre-Capitalist Modes of Production,"* Atlantic Highlands, NJ: Humanities Press.

Hirst, P. and G. Thompson. 1992. "The problem of 'globalization': International economic relations, national economic management and the formation of trading blocs," *Economy and Society*, 21 (4): 357–96.

——. 1996. *Globalization in Question: The International Economy and the Possibilities of Governance*, Cambridge: Polity Press.

Hopkins, T. K. and I. Wallerstein *et al.* 1982. *World-Systems Analysis: Theory and Methodology*, Beverly Hills: Sage Publications.

Horvat, B. 1982. *The Political Economy of Socialism: A Marxist Social Theory*, Armonk, NY: M.E. Sharpe.

Howitt, R. 1994a. "Aborigines, bauxite and gold: Land, resources and identity in a rapidly changing context," unpublished paper, Department of Human Geography, Macquarie University, Sydney.

——. 1994b "SIA, sustainability and the narratives of resource regions: Aboriginal interventions in impact stories," unpublished paper, Department of Human Geography, Macquarie University, Sydney.

Huntington, S. P. 1996. *The Clash Of Civilizations and the Remaking of World Order*, New York: Simon and Schuster.

Hymer, S. 1972a. "The internationalization of capital," *Journal of Economic Issues*, 6 (1): 91–111.

——. 1972b "The multinational corporation and the law of uneven development," in *Economics and World Order from the 1970s to the 1990s*, J. Bhagwati ed., New York: Collier-Macmillan, pp. 113–40.

——. 1976. *The International Operations of National Firms: A Study of Direct Foreign Investment*, Cambridge, MA: MIT Press.

Ignatieff, M. 2002. "Nation-building lite," *New York Times Magazine*, 28 July, pp. 26–31, 54, 57, 59.

Inter-American Development Bank. 1983. *Informe económico: Nicaragua*, Washington, DC: IDB.

International Labour Office. 1995. *World Labour Report 1995*, Geneva: International Labour Organization.

——. 1997. *World Labour Report 1997–98*, Geneva: International Labour Organization.

International Monetary Fund. 1977. *The Monetary Approach to the Balance of Payments*, Washington, DC: IMF.

——. 1987. "Nicaragua: Recent economic developments," mimeo, 1 June.

——. 1988. *International Financial Statistics Yearbook, 1988*, Washington, DC: IMF.

——. 1990. *World Economic Outlook*, Washington, DC: International Monetary Fund.

——. 1993. "Revised weights for the world economic outlook," in *World Economic Outlook*, Washington, DC: International Monetary Fund.

Irvin, G. 1983. "Establishing the state as the centre of accumulation," *Cambridge Journal of Economics*, 7, 125–39.

Islam, S. 1984. "Devaluation, stabilization policies and the developing countries: A macroeconomic analysis," *Journal of Development Economics*, 14 (January–February): 37–60.

James, S. 1984. *The Content of Social Explanation*, London: Cambridge University Press.

Jameson, F. 1984. "Postmodernism, or the cultural logic of late capitalism," *New Left Review*, no. 146 (July–August): 53–92.

——. 1987. "Tomás Borge on the Nicaraguan Revolution," *New Left Review*, no. 164 (July–August).

——. 1991. *Postmodernism or, the Cultural Logic of Late Capitalism*, Durham: Duke University Press.

Jameson, K. P. 1986. "Latin American structuralism: A methodological perspective," *World Development*, 14 (February): 223–32.

de Janvry, A. 1981. *The Agrarian Question and Reformism in Latin America*, Baltimore, MD: Johns Hopkins University Press.

——. 1985. "Social disarticulation in Latin American history," in *Debt and Development in Latin America*, D. F. Ruccio and K. S. Kim eds, Notre Dame, IN: University of Notre Dame Press, pp. 32–73.

de Janvry, A. and F. Kramer. 1979. "The limits of unequal exchange," *Review of Radical Political Economics*, 11 (Winter): 3–15.

de Janvry, A. and E. Sadoulet. 1983. "Social articulation as a condition for equitable growth," *Journal of Development Economics*, 13, 275–303.

Jenkins, R. 1984. "Divisions over the international division of labour," *Capital and Class*, no. 22 (Spring): 28–57.

——. 1987. *Transnational Corporations and Uneven Development: The Internationalisation of Capital and the Third World*, New York: Methuen.

Jensen, R. 1982. "The transition from primitive communism: The Wolof social formation of West Africa," *Journal of Economic History*, 42 (March): 69–76.

Jessop, B. 1978. *The Capitalist State: Marxist Theories and Methods*, London: Basil Blackwell.

——. 1988. "Regulation theories in retrospect and prospect," paper presented at the International Conference on Regulation Theory, Barcelona, Spain, June.

——. 1989. "Conservative regimes and the transition to post-Fordism: The cases of Great Britain and West Germany," in *Capitalist Development and Crisis Theory: Accumulation, Regulation and Spatial Restructuring*, M. Gottdiener and N. Komninos eds, New York St. Martin's Press, pp. 261–99.

Jhabvala, R. 1994. "Self-Employed Women's Association: Organizing women by struggle and development," in *Dignity and Daily Bread: New Forms of Economic Organising among Poor Women in the Third World and the First*, S. Rowbotham and S. Mitter eds, New York: Routledge, pp. 114–38.

Kabeer, N. 1994. *Reversed Realities: Gender Hierarchies in Development Thought*, New York: Verso.

Kantorovich, L. V. 1960. "Mathematical methods of organizing and planning production," *Management Science*, 6 (July): 366–422.

——. 1965. *The Best Use of Economic Resources*, trans. P. F. Knightsfield, Cambridge, MA: Harvard University Press.

——. 1976. *Essays in Optimal Planning*, ed. and intro. L. Smolinski, White Plains, NY: International Arts & Sciences Press.

Keith, M. and S. Pile, eds. 1993. *Place and the Politics of Identity*, New York: Routledge.

Kern, S. 1983. *The Culture of Time and Space, 1880–1918*, Cambridge, MA: Harvard University Press.

Khan, M. S. and M. D. Knight. 1981. "Stabilization programs in developing countries: A formal framework," *IMF Staff Papers* 28 (March): 1–53.

——. 1982. "Some theoretical and empirical issues relating to economic stabilization in developing countries," *World Development*, 10 (September): 709–30.

Kim, K. S. 1985. "Industrial policy and industrialization in South Korea: 1961–82: Lessons on industrial policies for other developing countries," Kellogg Institute Working Paper 39, Notre Dame, IN: Kellogg Institute.

Kindleberger, C. P. 1996. *Manias, Panics, and Crashes: A History of Financial Crises*, 3rd edn, New York: John Wiley and Sons.

Kissinger Commission. 1984. *Report of the National Bipartisan Commission on Central America*, Washington, DC: US Government Printing Office.

Kline, M. 1980. *Mathematics: The Loss of Certainty*, London and New York: Oxford University Press.

Kolko, J. 1988. *Restructuring the World Economy*, New York: Pantheon Books.

Kornai, J. 1970. "A general descriptive model of planning processes," *Economics of Planning*, 10: 1–19.

——. 1975. *Mathematical Planning of Structural Decisions*, Amsterdam: North-Holland Publishing.

Kornbluh, P. 1987. *Nicaragua, the Price of Intervention: Reagan's War Against the Sandinistas*, Washington, DC: Institute for Policy Studies.

Kotz, D. M. 1988. "A comparative analysis of the theory of regulation and the social structure of accumulation theory," paper presented at the International Conference on Regulation Theory, Barcelona, Spain, June.

Krugman, P. R. 1996. *Pop Internationalism*, Cambridge, MA: MIT Press.

——. 1987. "Is free trade passé?" *Journal of Economic Perspectives*, 1 (Fall): 131–44.

——. 1992. "The rich, the right, and the facts," *The American Prospect*, no. 11 (Fall), 19–31.

Krugman, P. R. and L. Taylor 1978. "Contractionary effects of devaluation," *Journal of International Economics*, 8 (August): 445–56.

Kuttner, R. 1996. "Peddling Krugman," *The American Prospect*, no. 28 (September–October): 78–86. Available at http://epn.org/prospect/28/28kutt.html (accessed May 2010).

Labor Research Review. 1995. "Confronting global power," 23.

Laclau, E. 1971. "Feudalism and capitalism in Latin America," *New Left Review*, no. 67 (May–June): 19–38.

Laclau, E. and C. Mouffe. 1985. *Hegemony and Socialist Strategy: Towards a Radical Democratic Politics*, New York: Verso.

Lall, S. 1975. "Is 'dependence' a useful concept in analysing underdevelopment?" *World Development*, 3 (November and December): 799–810.

Landsberg, M. 1979. "Export-led industrialization in the Third World: Manufacturing imperialism," *Review of Radical Political Economics*, 11 (Winter): 50–63.

Latour, B. and S. Woolgar. 1979. *Laboratory Life: The Social Construction of Scientific Facts*, intro. J. Salk, Beverly Hills, CA: Sage Publications.

Lazonick, W. and W. Mass eds. 1995. *Organizational Capability and Competitive Advantage: Debates, Dynamics, and Policy*, Brookfield, VT: Edward Elgar.

Lazonick, W., R. Dore and H.W. de Jong. 1997. *The Corporate Triangle: The Structure and Performance of Corporate Systems in a Global Economy*, Oxford: Blackwell.

Lecourt, D. 1972. *Marxism and Epistemology*, trans. B. Brewster, London: New Left Books.

——. 1977. *Proletarian Science? The Case of Lysenko*, trans. B. Brewster, intro. L. Althusser, London: New Left Books.

Lefebvre, H. 1974. *The Production of Space*, trans. D. Nicholson-Smith. Cambridge, MA: Blackwell.

Lenin, V. I. 1933 (1917). *Imperialism: The Highest Stage of Capitalism*, New York: International.

——. 1975. "Imperialism, the highest stage of capitalism," in *Selected Works*, 1, Moscow: Progress Publishers, pp. 634–731.

Lewis, W. A. 1984. "The state of development theory," *American Economic Review*, 74 (March): 1–10.

Lipietz, A. 1984. "De la nouvelle division internationale du travail à la crise du fordisme périphérique," *Espaces et societés*, no. 44: 51–78.

——. 1987. *Mirages and Miracles: The Crises of Global Fordism*, trans. D. Macey, London: Verso.

Lubell, H. 1991. *The Informal Sector in the 1980s and 1990s*, Paris: Development Centre of the Organisation for Economic Co-operation and Development.

Luxemburg, R. 1951 (1913). *The Accumulation of Capital*, London: Routledge & Kegan Paul.

Lyotard, J.-F. 1984. *The Postmodern Condition: A Report on Knowledge*, trans. G. Bennington and B. Massumi, Minneapolis: University of Minnesota Press.

MacEwan, A. 1985. "The current crisis in Latin America," *Monthly Review*, 36 (February): 1–18.

——. 1987. "Imperial decline and international disorder: An illustration from the debt crisis," in *The Imperiled Economy, Book I: Macroeconomics from a Left Perspective*, R. Cherry *et al.* eds, New York: Union for Radical Political Economics, pp. 205–14.

MacEwan, A. and W. Tabb eds. 1989. *Instability and Change in the World Economy*, New York: Monthly Review Press.

Mandel, E. 1978. *Late Capitalism*, trans. J. De Bres, London: Verso.

——. 1986. "In Defense of Socialist Planning," *New Left Review*, 159 (September–October): 5–37.

Mangieri, T., M. McCourt, N. Ruiz-Junco and J. West. 2004. "Rethinking politics, scholarship, and economics: An interview with David F. Ruccio," *Disclosure*, no. 13, 39–64.

Manzetti, L. and M. Dell'Aquila. 1988. "Economic stabilization in Argentina: The Austral Plan," *Journal of Latin American Studies*, 20 (May): 1–26.

Manzo, K. 1991. "Modernist discourse and the crisis of development theory," *Studies in Comparative International Development*, 26 (Summer): 3–36.

Marchand, M. H. and J. L. Parpart eds. 1995. *Feminism/Postmodernism/Development*, New York: Routledge.

Marchetti, P. E. 1986. "War, popular participation, and transition to socialism: The case of Nicaragua," in *Transition and Development: Problems of Third World Socialism*, R. R. Fagen, C. D. Deere, and J. L Coraggio eds, New York: Monthly Review Press, pp. 303–30.

Marx, K. 1967. *Capital*, Vols 1–3, New York: International Publishers.

——. 1970. *A Contribution to the Critique of Political Economy*, New York: International Publishers.

——. 1973. *Grundrisse*, trans. M. Nicolaus, New York: Vintage Books.

——. 1976. "The protectionists, the free traders and the working class," in *Collected Works*, Vol. 6, New York: International Publishers, pp. 279–81.

——. 1977. *Capital*, Vol. 1, Intro. E. Mandel, trans. B. Fowkes, New York: Vintage Books.

——. 1981. *Capital*, Vol. 3, trans. D. Fernbach, London: Vintage Books.

Marx K. and F. Engels. 1959. *Basic Writings on Politics and Philosophy*, L. S. Feuer, ed., Garden City, NY: Doubleday.

——. 1976. "Manifesto of the Communist Party," in *Collected Works*, Vol. 6, New York: International Publishers, pp. 477–519.

——. 1983. *Collected Works*, Vol. 40, New York: International Publishers.

Medley, J. 1981. "Economic growth and development: A critique of Samir Amin's conception of capital accumulation and development," unpublished PhD dissertation, University of Massachusetts-Amherst (May).

Melotti, U. 1974. *Marx y el Tercer Mundo*, Buenos Aires: Amorrortu.

Milanovic, B. 2002. "The two faces of globalization: Against globalization as we know it," *World Development*, 41 (4): 667–83.

Ministry of Planning (MIPLAN). 1980a. *Programa de reactivación económica en benefício del pueblo*, Managua: Secretaría Nacional de Propaganda y Educación Política, F.S.L.N.

——. 1980b. "Resúmen y conclusiones de 1980: El primer año de economía Sandinista," internal report.

——. 1981a. *Programa económico de austeridad y eficiencia 81*, Managua: MIPLAN.

——. 1981b. "Conclusiones y recomendaciones del II seminario de planificación en Nicaragua," internal report.

——. 1982. "Nicaragua: Programa Económico," internal report.

——. 1984. "Programa Económico, 1984," internal report.

——. 1985. "Plan Económico 1985," internal report.

Modiano, E. M. 1988. "The Cruzado first attempt: The Brazilian stabilization program of February 1986," in *Inflation Stabilization: The Experience of Israel, Argentina, Brazil, Bolivia and Mexico*, M. Bruno *et al.* eds, Cambridge, MA: MIT Press, pp. 215–58.

Mudretsov, A. F. and E. G. Shargunov. 1976. "The economic valuation of labor resources and payment for their use," *Matekon*, 13: 30–36.

Nandy, A. 1987. "Cultural frames for social transformation: A credo," *Alternatives*, 12: 113–17.

Nash, J. and M. P. Fernandez-Kelly eds. 1983. *Women, Men and the International Division of Labor*, Albany: State University of New York Press.

National Reconstruction Government of Nicaragua (JGRN). 1983. "Economic policy guidelines 1983–88," internal report.

Nemchinov, V. S. ed. 1965. *The Use of Mathematics in Economics*, Cambridge, MA: MIT Press.

Nicaraguan Institute of Statistics and Censuses (INEC). 1986. "Nicaragua en cifras," mimeo.

Nolan, P. 1983. "De-collectivisation of agriculture in China, 1979–82: A long-term perspective," *Cambridge Journal of Economics*, 7: 381–403.

Norgaard, R. 1992. *Development Reportrayed*, London: Routledge.

Norton, B. 1983. "The accumulation of capital and market structure: A critique of the theory of monopoly capitalism," PhD dissertation, University of Massachusetts-Amherst.

——. 1988a. "Epochs and essences: essentialist reasoning in Marxian long-period accumulation theories," *Cambridge Journal of Economics*, 12 (June).

——. 1988b. "The power axis: Bowles, Gordon, and Weisskopf's theory of postwar U.S. accumulation," *Rethinking Marxism*, 1 (Fall): 6–43.

——. 1992. "Radical theories of accumulation and crisis: Developments and discussions," in *Radical Economics*, B. B. Roberts and S. F. Feiner eds, Boston: Kluwer-Nijhoff, pp. 155–93.

——. 1994. "Moses and the Prophets! Radical economics and the search for a foundation (in Marx's analysis of accumulation in volume one of *Capital*)," *Review of Radical Political Economics*, 26 (3): 111–18.

——. 1995. "The theory of monopoly capitalism and classical economics," *History of Political Economy*, 27 (4): 737–53.

——. 2001. "Reading Marx for class," in *Re/presenting Class: Essays in Postmodern Marxism*, J. K. Gibson-Graham *et al.* eds, Durham: Duke University Press, pp. 23–55.

Nove, A. 1968. "Planners' preference, priorities and reforms," in *New Currents in Soviet-Type Economies*, G. R. Feiwel ed., Scranton, PA: International Textbook Company, pp. 28–95.

——. 1983 *The Economics of Feasible Socialism*, London: Allen & Unwin.

Oman, C. P. and G. Wignaraja. 1991. *The Postwar Evolution of Development Thinking*, New York: St. Martin's Press.

Ong, A. 1987. "Disassembling gender in the electronics age," *Feminist Studies*, 13: 609–26.

O'Rourke, K. H. and J. G. Williamson. 1999. *Globalization and History: The Evolution of a Nineteenth-century Atlantic Economy*, Cambridge, MA: MIT Press.

Ortega, M. 1985. "Workers' participation in the management of the agro-enterprises of the APP," *Latin American Perspectives*, 12 (Spring): 69–81.

Palloix, C. 1975. "The internationalization of capital and the circuit of social capital," in *International Firms and Modern Imperialism*, H. Radice ed., New York: Penguin.

Palma, G. 1978. "Dependency: A formal theory of underdevelopment or a methodology for the analysis of concrete situations of underdevelopment?" *World Development*, 6 (July–August): 881–924.

Pasinetti, L. L. 1983. "The accumulation of capital," *Cambridge Journal of Economics*, 7: 405–11.

Pastor, Jr., M. 1987a. "The effects of IMF programs in the Third World: Debate and evidence from Latin America," *World Development*, 15 (February): 249–62.

——. 1987b. *The International Monetary Fund and Latin America*, Boulder, CO: Westview Press, 1987.

Pattee, J. 1996. "'Gapatistas' win a victory," *Labor Research Review*, 24 (Summer): 77–85.

Payer, C. 1974. *The Debt Trap: The International Monetary Fund and the Third World*, New York: Monthly Review Press.

——. 1982. *The World Bank: A Critical Analysis*, New York: Monthly Review Press.

Petrazzini, B. A. 1996. "The labor sector: A post-privatization assessment," in *Bigger Economies, Smaller Governments: Privatization in Latin America*, W. Glade ed., Boulder, CO: Westview Press, pp. 347–68.

Pettit, P. 1975. *The Concept of Structuralism: A Critical Analysis*, Berkeley, CA: University of California Press.

Phongpaichit, P. 1988. "Two roads to the factory: Industrialisation strategies and women's employment," in *Structures of Patriarchy: the State, the Community and the Household*, B. Agarwal ed., London: Zed Press, pp. 150–63.

Pieterse, J. N. 1991. "Dilemmas of development discourse: The crisis of developmentalism and comparative method," *Development and Change*, 22: 5–29.

——. 1993. "Globalization as hybridization," Institute of Social Studies Working Paper 152, June.

——. 2000. "Globalization north and south: Representations of uneven development and the interactions of modernities," *Theory, Culture and Society*, 17 (1): 129–37.

Pirenne, H. 1937. *Economic and Social History of Medieval Europe*, New York: Harcourt, Brace and World.

Pissarides, C. A. 1989. "Unemployment and macroeconomics," *Economica*, 56 (February): 1–14.

Pizarro, R. 1987. "The new economic policy: A necessary readjustment," in *The Political Economy of Revolutionary Nicaragua*, R. J. Spalding ed., Boston: Allen & Unwin, pp. 217–32.

Polack, J. J. 1957. "Monetary analysis of income formation and payments problems," *IMF Staff Papers*, 6 (November): 1–50.

Porpora, D., M. H. Lim and U. Prommas. 1989 "The role of women in the international division of labour: The case of Thailand," *Development and Change*, 20: 269–94.

Porter, R. C. and S. I. Ranney. 1982. "An eclectic model of recent LDC macroeconomic policy analyses," *World Development*, 10 (September): 751–65.

Pred, A. and M. Watts. 1992. *Reworking Modernity: Capitalisms and Symbolic Discontent*, New Brunswick, NJ: Rutgers University Press.

Quijano Obregón, A. 1980. "The marginal pole of the economy and the marginalised labour force," in *The Articulation of Modes of Production: Essays from Economy and Society*, H. Wolpe ed., London: Routledge & Kegan Paul.

Radice, H. ed. 1975. *International Firms and Modern Imperialism*, New York: Penguin.

Ranney, D. C. 1993. "NAFTA and the new transnational corporate agenda," *Review of Radical Political Economics*, 25 (4): 1–13.

Raymond, P. 1978. *L'Histoire et les sciences, suivi de cinq questions sur l'histoire des mathématiques*, Paris: F. Maspero.

Resnick, S. and R. Wolff. 1982. "Classes in Marxian theory," *Review of Radical Political Economics*, 13 (Winter): 1–18.

——. 1983a. "Marxist epistemology: The critique of economic determinism," *Social Text*, 6 (Spring): 37–72.

——. 1983b. "A Marxist theory of the state," in Larry L. Wade ed., *Political Economy: Recent Views*, Boston: Kluwer-Nijhoff.

——. 1983c. "A Marxian reconceptualization of income distribution," Association for Economic and Social Analysis Discussion Paper No. 15, University of Massachusetts-Amherst, November.

——. 1987a. *Economics: Marxian Versus Neoclassical*, Baltimore, MD: Johns Hopkins University Press.

——. 1987b. *Knowledge and Class: A Marxian Critique of Political Economy*, Chicago: University of Chicago Press.

——. 1992. "Radical economics: A tradition of theoretical differences," in *Radical Economics*, S. Feiner and B. Roberts ed., Boston: Kluwer-Nijhoff.

——. 2001. "Empire and class analysis," *Rethinking Marxism*, 13 (3/4): 61–69.

——. 2002. *Class Theory and History: Capitalism and Communism in the USSR*, New York: Routledge.

Resnick, S., J. Sinisi and R. Wolff. 1985. "Class analysis of international economic relations," in *An International Political Economy*, W. L. Hollist and F. L. Tullis eds, Boulder, CO: Westview Press, pp. 87–123.

Review of Radical Political Economics. 1990. Special issue on "Beyond the nation state: global perspectives on capitalism," 22 (1).

Rey, P.-P. 1971. *Colonialisme, neo-colonialisme, et transition au capitalisme*, Paris: Maspero, 1971.

——. 1973. *Les Alliances de Classes*, Paris: Maspero.

——. 1975. "The lineage mode of production," *Critique of Anthropology*, no. 3 (Spring), 27–79.

Richards, A. 1986. "Development and Modes of Production in Marxian Economics: A Critical Evaluation," *Fundamentals of Pure and Applied Economics*, 12, New York: Harwood Academic Publishers.

Richards, L. 1977. "The context of foreign aid: Modern imperialism," *Review of Radical Political Economics*, 9 (Winter): 43–75.

Roberts, B. 1981. "Value categories and Marxian method: A different view of value-price transformation," unpublished PhD dissertation, University of Massachusetts-Amherst (September).

——. 1987. "Marx after Steedman: Separating Marxism from 'surplus theory'," *Capital and Class*, no. 32 (Fall): 84–103.

Robertson, R. 1992. *Globalization: Social Theory and Global Culture*, London: Sage.

Rodrik, D. 1997. *Has globalization gone too far?*, Washington, DC: Institute for International Economics.

Roemer, J. 1983. "Unequal exchange, labor migration, and international capital flows: A theoretical synthesis," in *Marxism, Central Planning, and the Soviet Economy: Economic Essays in Honor of Alexander Erlich*, P. Desai ed., Cambridge, MA: MIT Press.

——. 1988. *Free to Lose: An Introduction to Marxist Economic Philosophy*, Cambridge, MA: Harvard University Press.

Rorty, R. 1979. *Philosophy and the Mirror of Nature*, Princeton, NJ: Princeton University Press.

Rosa, K. 1994. "The conditions and organizational activities of women in free trade zones: Malaysia, Philippines, and Sri Lanka, 1970–90," in *Dignity and Daily Bread: New Forms of Economic Organising among Poor Women in the Third World and the First*, S. Rowbotham and S. Mitter eds, New York: Routledge, pp. 73–99.

Rostow, W. W. 1960. *The Stages of Economic Growth*, Cambridge: Cambridge University Press.

Ruccio, D. F. 1976. "The Marxian theory of historical development: An analysis of modes of production in the historical process of Peruvian underdevelopment," Honors thesis, Department of Economics, Bowdoin College, unpublished typescript.

——. 1984a. "Optimal planning theory and theories of socialist planning," PhD dissertation, University of Massachusetts-Amherst.

——. 1984b. untitled review essay, *History of Political Economy*, 16 (Spring): 144–48.

——. 1987. "The state, planning and transition in Nicaragua," *Development and Change*, 18 (January): 5–27.

——. 1988. "The merchant of venice, or Marxism in the mathematical mode," *Rethinking Marxism*, 1 (Winter): 36–68.

——. 1992. "Failure of socialism, future of socialists?" *Rethinking Marxism*, 5 (Summer): 7–22.

——. 1993. "The hidden successes of failed economic policies," *NACLA's Report on the Americas*, 26 (February): 38–43, 45–46.

Ruccio, D. F. and J. Amariglio. 1998. "The (dis)orderly process of capitalist competition," in *Marxian Economics: A Centenary Appraisal*, Vol. 1, R. Bellofiore ed., London: MacMillan, pp. 94–108.

——. 2003. *Postmodern Moments in Modern Economics*, Princeton, NJ: Princeton University Press.

Ruccio, D. F. and A. Callari eds. 1996. *Postmodern Materialism and the Future of Marxist Theory: Essays in the Althusserian Tradition*, Middletown, CT: Wesleyan University Press.

——. 1998. "Rereading Althusser," special issue of *Rethinking Marxism*, 10 (Fall).

Ruccio, D. F. and K. S. Kim eds. 1986. *Debt and Development in Latin America*, Notre Dame, IN: University of Notre Dame Press.

Ruccio, D. F and L. H. Simon. 1986a. "Methodological aspects of a marxian approach to development: An analysis of the modes of production school," *World Development*, 14 (February): 211–22.

——. 1986b. "A methodological analysis of dependency theory: Explanation in André Gunder Frank," *World Development*, 14 (February): 195–209.

Ruccio, D. F. and R. D. Wolff. 1989. "Outside equilibrium," mimeo, University of Notre Dame, IN.

Rustin, M. 1989. "The politics of post-Fordism: Or, the trouble with 'new times'," *New Left Review*, no. 175 (May–June): 54–77.

Rutherford, J. ed. 1990. *Identity: Community, Culture, Difference*, London: Lawrence & Wishart.

Sachs, W., ed. 1992. *The Development Dictionary: A Guide to Knowledge as Power*, London: Zed Books.

Said, E. W. 1983. *The World, the Text, and the Critic*, Cambridge, MA: Harvard University Press.

——. 1993. *Culture and Imperialism*, New York: Vintage Books.

Saitta, D. J. 1988. "Marxism, prehistory, and primitive communism," *Rethinking Marxism*, 1 (Winter): 145–68.

Samuels, W. 1979. "Aspects of soviet economic planning: Power and the optimal use of planning techniques: A review article," *Review of Social Economy*, 37 (October): 231–39.

Sandbrook, R. 2000. "Globalization and the limits of neoliberal doctrine," *Third World Quarterly*, 21 (6): 1071–80.

dos Santos, T. 1970. "The structure of dependence," *American Economic Review*, Papers and Proceedings, 40 (May): 231–36.

Sanyal, K. P. 1993. "Capital, primitive accumulation, and the third world: From annihilation to appropriation," *Rethinking Marxism*, 6 (3): 117–30.

Saul, J. S. 1986. "The role of ideology in the transition to socialism," in *Transition and Development: Problems of Third World Socialism*, R. R. Fagen, C. D. Deere and J. L Coraggio eds, New York: Monthly Review Press, pp. 212–30.

Schiffer, J. 1981. "The changing postwar pattern of development or the accumulated wisdom of Samir Amin," *World Development*, 9: 515–37.

Schultz, T. W. 1964. *Transforming Traditional Agriculture*, New Haven, CT: Yale University Press.

Secretariat of Planning and the Budget (SPP). 1985a. "Bosquejo del plan económico 1986," internal report.

——. 1985b. "Evaluación y perspectivas económicas 1985," internal report.

——. 1986. "Nicaragua: Plan economico nacional, 1987," mimeo (December).

Sender, J. and S. Smith. 1986. *The Development of Capitalism in Africa*, New York: Methuen.

Sevilla, M. A., R. Stahler-Sholk and G. Timossi Dolinsky. 1987. "Deuda, estabilización y ajuste: La transformación en Nicaragua, 1979–86," mimeo, Coordinadora Regional de Investigaciones Económicas y Sociales (August).

Shiva, V. 1991. *The Violence of the Green Revolution*, London: Zed Press.

Singer. P. 1989. "Democracy and inflation, in the light of the Brazilian experience," in *Lost Promises: Debt, Austerity, and Development in Latin America*, W. L. Canak ed., Boulder, CO: Westview Press, pp. 31–46.

Singh, A. 1986. "The great continental divide: Asian and Latin American Countries in the world economic crisis," *Labour and Society*, 11 (September): 415–32.

——. 1995. "The state and industrialization in India: Successes and failures and the lessons for the future," in *The Role of the State in Economic Change*, H.-J. Chang and R. Rowthorn eds, Oxford: Clarendon Press, pp. 170–86.

Skocpol, T. 1977. "Wallerstein's world capitalism: A theoretical and historical criticism," *American Journal of Sociology*, 82 (March): 1075–89.

Slater, D. 1992. "Theories of development and politics of the post-modern: Exploring a border zone," *Development and Change*, 23 (3): 283–319.

Smith, P. 1988. *Discerning the Subject*, Minneapolis: University of Minnesota Press.

Smith, S. 1980. "The ideas of Samir Amin: Theory or tautology," *Journal of Development Studies*, 17 (October).

——. 1982. "Class analysis versus world systems: Critique of Samir Amin's typology of Underdevelopment," *Journal of Contemporary Asia*, 12: 7–18.

Soja, E. W. 1989. *Postmodern Geographies: The Reassertion of Space in Critical Social Theory*, New York: Verso.

Soper, K. 1986. *Humanism and Anti-humanism*, London: Hutchinson.

Soros, G. 1998. *The Crisis of Global Capitalism: Open Society Endangered*, New York: Public Affairs.

——. 2000. *Open Society: Reforming Global Capitalism*, New York: Public Affairs.

Stahler-Sholk, R. 1985. "Pago en especies," mimeo, Coordinadora Regional de Investigaciones Económicas y Sociales (July).

——. 1987. "Foreign debt and economic stabilization policies in revolutionary Nicaragua," in *The Political Economy of Revolutionary Nicaragua*, R. J. Spalding ed., Boston: Allen and Unwin.

Stalin, J. V. 1952. *Works*, Vol. 1 (1901–07), Moscow: Foreign Languages Publishing House.

Stallings, B. 1986. "External finance and the transition to socialism in small peripheral societies," in *Transition and Development: Problems of Third World Socialism*, R. R. Fagen, C. D. Deere, and J. L. Coraggio eds, New York: Monthly Review Press, pp. 54–78.

Stiglitz, J. E. 2002. *Globalization and its Discontents*, New York: W. W. Norton.

Stiglitz, J. E. and L. Squire. 1998. "International development: Is it possible?" *Foreign Policy* (Spring): 138–51.

Strassmann, D. 1993a. "Not a free market: The rhetoric of disciplinary authority in economics," in *Beyond Economic Man*, M. A. Ferber and J. A. Nelson eds, Chicago: University of Chicago Press, pp. 54–68.

——. 1993b. "The stories of economics and the power of the storyteller," *History of Political Economy*, 25 (1): 147–65.

Strauch, J. 1984. "Women in rural–urban circulation networks: Implications for social structural change," in *Women in the Cities of Asia: Migration and Urban Adaptation*, J. Fawcett, S. Khoo and P. Smith eds, Boulder, CO: Westview Press, pp. 60–77.

Streeten, P. 1987. "Structural adjustment: A survey of the issues and options," *World Development*, 15 (12): 1469–82.

Swann, M. J. 1975. "On the theory of optimal planning in the Soviet Union," *Australian Economic Papers*, 14 (June): 41–56.

Sweezy, P. 1976. "A critique," in *The Transition from Feudalism to Capitalism*, intro. R. Hilton, London: New Left Books.

Szentes, T. 1985. *Theories of World Capitalist Economy: A Critical Survey of Conventional, Reformist and Radical Views*, Budapest Akademai Kiado.

Taylor, J. G. 1979. *From Modernization to Modes of Production: A Critique of the Sociologies of Development and Underdevelopment*, London: Macmillan Press.

Taylor, L. 1981. "IS/LM in the tropics: Diagrammatics of the new structuralist macro critique," in *Economic Stabilization in Developing Countries*, W. Cline and S. Weintraub eds, Washington, DC: Brookings Institution, pp. 465–503.

——. 1983. *Structuralist Macroeconomics: Applicable Models for the Third World*, New York: Basic Books.

——. 1987. "Varieties of stabilization experience," mimeo, Massachusetts Institute of Technology, April.

——. 1988a. "Macro effects of myriad shocks: Developing countries in the world economy," in *Health, Nutrition, and Economic Crises: Approaches to Policy in the Third World*, D. E. Bell and M. R. Reich eds, Dover, MA: Auburn House Publishing, pp. 17–37.

——. 1988b. *Varieties of Stabilization Experience: Towards a Sensible Macroeconomics in the Third World*, Oxford: Clarendon Press.

——. 1989. *Stabilization and Growth in Developing Countries, A Structuralist Approach*. New York: Harwood Academic Publishers.

Thomas, C. 1974. *Socialism and Transformation: The Economics of the Transition to Socialism*, New York: Monthly Review Press.

——. 1984. *The Rise of the Authoritarian State in Peripheral Societies*, New York: Monthly Review Press.

Thorp, R. 1979. "The Stabilization crisis in Peru 1975–78," in *Inflation and Stabilisation in Latin America*, R. Thorp and L. Whitehead eds, New York: Holmes and Meier, pp. 110–43.

Tirado López, V. 1985 *La prirnera gran conquista: La toma del poder político*, Managua: Trabajadores series, Central Sandinista de Trabajadores.

Tribe, K. 1978. *Land, Labour, and Economic Discourse*, New York: Routledge.

Tyler, W. G. 1986. "Stabilization, external adjustment, and recession in Brazil: Perspectives in the mid-1980s," *Studies in Comparative International Development*, 21 (2): 5–33.

Ugarteche, O. 1988. "Peru: The foreign debt and heterodox adjustment policy under Alain García," in *Managing world debt*, S. Griffith-Jones ed., New York: St. Martin's, pp. 170–92.

United for a Fair Economy and Institute for Policy Studies. 1998. "Executive excess '98: CEO gains from massive downsizing." Available at www.stw.org/html/exec_excess_98.html (accessed May 2010).

United Nations Development Programme. 1997. *Human Development Report 1997*, New York: Oxford University Press.

Utting, P. 1987. "Domestic supply and food shortages," in *The Political Economy of Revolutionary Nicaragua*, R. J. Spalding ed., Boston: Allen & Unwin.

Van Wijnbergen, S. 1986. "Exchange rate management and stabilization policies in developing countries," *Journal of Development Economics*, 23 (October): 227–47.

Vilas, C. M. 1984. *Perfíles de la Revolución Sandinista*, Havana: Casa de las Américas.

——. 1986. *The Sandinista Revolution: National Liberation and Social Transformation in Central America*, trans. J. Butler, New York: Monthly Review Press.

De Vroey, M. 1984. "A regulation approach interpretation of contemporary crisis," *Capital and Class*, 23: 45–66.

Wade, R. 1995. "Resolving the state-market dilemma in East Asia," in *The Role of the State in Economic Change*, H. J. Chang and R. Rowthorn eds, Oxford: Clarendon Press, pp. 114–36.

Walker, T. W. ed. 1985. *Nicaragua: The First Five Years*, New York: Praeger.

Wallerstein, I. 1974. *The Modern World System: Capitalist Agriculture and the Origins of the European World: Economy in the Sixteenth Century*, New York: Academic Press.

——. 1979. *The Capitalist World Economy*, Cambridge: Cambridge University Press.

——. 1980. *The Modern World-System I: Mercantilism and the Consolidation of the European World-Economy, 1600–1750*, New York: Academic Press.

Warren, B. 1973. "Imperialism and capitalist industrialization," *New Left Review*, no. 81 (September–October): 3–44.

——. 1980. *Imperialism: Pioneer of Capitalism*, London: New Left Books.

Watts, M. J. 1993. "Development 1: power, knowledge, discursive practice," *Progress in Human Geography*, 17 (2): 257–72

Weeks, J. 1986. "The mixed economy in Nicaragua: The economic battlefield," in *The Political Economy of Revolutionary Nicaragua*, R. J. Spalding ed., Boston: Allen and Unwin, pp. 43–60.

Weeks, J. and E. Dore. 1979. "International exchange and the causes of backwardness," *Latin American Perspectives*, 6 (Spring): 71–77.

Weinberg, D.N. 1996. *A Brief Look at Postwar U.S. Income Inequality*, Washington, DC: Bureau of the Census, U.S. Department of Commerce.

Weiss, R. 1982. "Primitive accumulation in the United States: The interaction between capitalist and noncapitalist class relations in seventeenth-century Massachusetts," *Journal of Economic History*, 42 (March): 77–82.

Wells, J. R. 1979. "Brazil and the post-1973 crisis in the international economy," in *Inflation and Stabilisation in Latin America*, R. Thorp and L. Whitehead eds, New York: Holmes and Meier, pp. 227–63.

Wheelock Román, J. 1979. *Imperialismo y dictadura: Crisis de una formación social*, 3rd edn, México: Siglo Veintiuno.

——. 1983. *El gran desafío*, Managua: Nueva Nicaragua.

White, O. C. and A. Bhatia. 1998. *Privatization in Africa*, Washington, DC: World Bank.

Wignaraja, P. ed. 1993. *New Social Movements in the South: Empowering the People*, New Jersey: Zed Books.

Willoughby, J. 1986. "Capitalist imperialism, crisis and the state," *Fundamentals of Pure and Applied Economics*, 7, New York: Harwood.

——. 1988. "The continued presence of U.S. hegemony: A friendly critique of Marxian common sense," paper presented at the International Conference on Regulation Theory, Barcelona, Spain, June.

——. 1989. "Is global capitalism in crisis? A critique of postwar crisis theories," *Rethinking Marxism*, 2 (Summer): 83–102.

——. 1991. "Nationalism and globalism: Beyond the neo-Leninist tradition," *Rethinking Marxism*, 4 (2): 134–42.

Wogart, J. P. 1983. "Combining price stabilization with trade and financial liberalization policies: The Argentine experience, 1976–81," *Journal of Interamerican Studies and World Affairs*, 25 (November): 445–76.

Wolff, E. N. 1995. "How the pie is sliced: America's growing concentration of wealth," *The American Prospect*, no. 22 (Summer), 58–64.

——. 1996. *Top Heavy: The Increasing Inequality of Wealth in America and What Can Be Done About It*, New York: New Press

Wolff, R. D. 1978. "Marxian crisis theory: Structure and implications," *Review of Radical Political Economics*, 10 (Spring).

Wolff, R. D., A. Callari and B. Roberts. 1984. "A Marxian alternative to the traditional 'transformation problem'," *Review of Radical Political Economics*, 16 (Summer–Fall): 115–35.

Wolff, R. D., B. Roberts, and A. Callari. 1982. "Marx's (not Ricardo's) 'transformation problem': A radical reconceptualization," *History of Political Economy*, 14 (Winter): 564–82.

Wolpe, H. 1975. "The theory of internal colonialism: The South African case," in *Beyond the Sociology of Development*, I. Oxhaal *et al.* eds, Boston, MA: Routledge & Kegan Paul.

——. 1976. "The 'white working class' in South Africa," *Economy and Society*, 5 (May): 197–240.

——. 1978. "A comment on 'the poverty of neo-Marxism'," *Journal of Southern African Studies*, 4 (April): 240–56.

——. ed. 1980a. *The Articulation of Modes of Production: Essays from Economy and Society*, H. Wolpe ed., London: Routledge & Kegan Paul.

——. 1980b. "Capitalism and cheap labour-power in South Africa: From segregation to apartheid," in *The Articulation of Modes of Production*, Boston: Routledge & Kegan Paul, pp. 289–320.

——. 1980c. "Towards an analysis of the South African state," *International Journal of the Sociology of Law*, 8 (4): 399–421.

——. 1985a. "The liberation struggle and research," *Review of African Political Economy*, no. 32 (April): 72–78.

——. 1985b. "Political strategies and the law in South Africa: Analytical considerations," *Journal of Southern African Studies*, 12 (1): 12–24.

——. 1988a. *Race, Class & the Apartheid State*, Paris: Unesco Press.

——. 1988b. "Review of *Apartheid's Rebels: Inside South Africa's Hidden War*," *Journal of Southern African Studies*, 15 (1): 133–34.

——. 1995. "The debate on university transformation in South Africa: The case of the University of the Western Cape," *Comparative Education*, 31 (2): 275–92.

Wood, E. M. 1999. "Unhappy families: Global capitalism in a world of nation-states," *Monthly Review*, 51 (July–August): 1–12.

World Bank. 1980. *World Tables*, 2nd edn, Baltimore, MD: Johns Hopkins University Press.

——. 1981. *Nicaragua: The Challenge of Reconstruction*, Washington, DC: IBRD.

——. 1988. *World Development Report*, 1988, Washington, DC: World Bank.

——. 1990. *World Development Report 1990*, New York: Oxford University Press.

——. 1996. *El Salvador: Meeting the Challenge of Globalization*, Washington, DC: World Bank.

——. 1997. *World Development Report 1997*, New York: Oxford University Press.

Wright, E. O. 1985. *Classes*, London: Verso.

Zalkin, M. 1987. "Food policy and class transformation in revolutionary Nicaragua, 1979–86," *World Development*, 15 (July): 961–84.

Zauberman, A. 1976. *Mathematical Theory in Soviet Planning: Concepts, Methods, Techniques*, London and New York: Oxford University Press.

Index

Note: "n." after a page reference indicates the number of a note on that page.